AMENITY LANDSCAPE MANAGEMENT
A RESOURCES HANDBOOK

AMENITY LANDSCAPE MANAGEMENT
A RESOURCES HANDBOOK

Edited by RALPH COBHAM

Compilers
Nick Burton
Rodney Helliwell
Tony Kendle
Suki Pryce
Margery Slatter

Illustrator
Henry Steed

Cobham Resource Consultants
Oxford, Manchester, Edinburgh

London New York
E. & F.N. SPON

First published in 1990 by
E. & F.N. Spon Ltd
11 New Fetter Lane, London EC4P 4EE

Published in the USA by
Van Nostrand Reinhold
115 Fifth Avenue, New York, NY 10003

Typeset in 10/12pt Times by Best-set Typesetter Ltd.

Printed in Great Britain by
Richard Clay (The Chaucer Press) Ltd,
Bungay, Suffolk

ISBN 0 419 11570 6
       0 442 31153 2 (US)

British Library Cataloguing in Publication Data

Amenity landscape management: a resources
handbook.
    1. Great Britain. Recreation land.
Management
    I. Cobham, Ralph
    333.78′0941

    ISBN 0-419-11570-6

Library of Congress Cataloging in Publication Data available

CONTENTS

ACKNOWLEDGEMENTS

My first thanks are due to the five people who, during various phases in the development of this book have helped to compile the information and guidelines contained in Parts Two, Three, Four, Five and Six. They are Nick Burton, Rodney Helliwell and Tony Kendle, along with two former members of Cobham Resource Consultants, Suki Pryce and Margery Slatter. However, whilst their assistance has been invaluable, responsibility for any errors of fact, interpretation and omission rests solely with the editor.

In the initial drafting stages I was particularly fortunate in receiving considerable guidance and information from the members of a steering committee, consisting of: J. Bauer, Recreation Department, Sheffield City Council; C.J. Forestier-Walker, formerly of the Property Services Agency; J.C. Parker, Estates and Valuation Department, Kent County Council; J.W. Patrick, National Exhibition Centre (at the time); P.R. Thoday, Department of Horticulture, University of Bath; T.W.J. Wright, Department of Horticulture, Wye College. Their help and encouragement largely in the late 1970s and early 1980s was, and is, greatly appreciated. Particular thanks are due to Charles Forestier-Walker, who introduced the idea for the book to the publishers.

I am especially grateful for the significant contributions to specific sections and chapters which were received from: J. Baker, The Electricity Council (Chapter 24); G.C. Barrow, The Centre for Environmental Interpretation, Manchester Polytechnic, formerly of Cobham Resource Consultants (Chapter 8); J. Csaky, Fitch and Co., formerly Milton Keynes Development Corporation (Chapter 22); J.C. Kelcey, Ecological Consultant, formerly Milton Keynes Development Corporation (Chapter 21); P.R. Thoday and J.D. Hitchmough, University of Bath (Chapter 19); and J.R. Matthews, Cobham Resource Consultants, formerly Norfolk County Council.

Numerous sources have been used in the preparation of this handbook. Appropriate reference is made to these in each of the Tables and Figures. The opportunity to include the information is gratefully acknowledged.

There is also a long list of organizations and individuals who have supplied information. Sincere thanks to each of them is recorded here.

C. Addison   Bath City Council
C. Allsebrook   Guthrie Allsebrook and
                             Company Ltd

J. Bauer	Sheffield City Council
P. Bird	Landscape Institute
H. Boylan	Warrington and Runcorn Development Corporation
R. Bunce	ITE
A.G. Crouch	University of Exeter
Cameron Irrigation	A Division of Wright Rain Limited
J. Davison	Weed Research Organization
J. Dean	GC & HTJ
P.L.K. Dury	Nottinghamshire County Council
R. Ellis	Bath City Council
I. Fenn	Bromley Borough Council
Dr T. Hall	University of Oxford
S.D. Hitt	Bath City Council
J. Houston	Sefton Coast
C. Lane	Bromley Borough Council
R. Manning	Greenwich Borough Council
J.M. Marsh	California
R. Newman	GC & HTJ
G. Patterson	Gordon Patterson & Partners, Stevenage
G. Paul	May & Baker
J.C. Parker	Kent County Council
S. Prescott	University of East Anglia
P. Reynard	BALI
D. Rice	Wiltshire County Council
N. Ritchie	CM Ltd
C. Rose	Milton Keynes Development Corporation
J. Shildrick	Sports Turf Research Institute
Skelmersdale Development Corporation	
G. Soltys	Bath City Council
Telford Development Corporation	
The Keep Britain Tidy Group	
P. Thoday	University of Bath
R. Tregay	Warrington and Runcorn Development Corporation
R. Turner	Bourton-on-the-Water
S. Walker	TRRU
D. Waterhouse	Plymouth City Council
A. Winning	Sheffield City Council
T.W.J. Wright	Wye College, University of London

Special acknowledgement is due to two personal friends. First to Henry Steed, who prepared the illustrations and in some cases caricatures of the Amenity Manager at work (and play). These capture the essence of the book with a lightness inevitably missing from the text and tabulations. I am sure that many readers along with me will appreciate his poignant contribution: secondly, to Chris Gethin, a chartered planner and freelance environmental journalist, who assisted with editing a second draft.

Particular thanks are due to Professor David Bellamy for making time in his busy programme to write the Foreword.

Many present and former colleagues in CRC are due thanks: Paul Bramhill, Ian Burton, Richard Burton, Rebecca Field, Marcus Potts and Eve Risbridger have also helped. This has been greatly appreciated. I am particularly grateful to my Partners – Russel Matthews, Andrew McNab, Russ Canning and Jonathan Wager. Without their tolerance and patience, this book would never have been completed.

Most importantly, I thank Phillip Read, Managing Director of E. & F.N. Spon Ltd for his readiness to believe that one day a book would be ready for publication. I am also most grateful to Madeleine Metcalfe, Alison Jesnick, Peter Martin and their colleagues who have handled the presentation and publication of the material with great efficiency and sensitivity.

There are many other people who have assisted the completion of this handbook over ten years. It is not possible to thank them all individually. I therefore do so collectively.

Last, and yet foremost, in this credits list are Alison Buckley, the Administrator of CRC, and her colleagues, and Christine Sharrock in particular. They have contributed hours, days and weeks of fast finger work and invaluable assistance.

The editor

PREFACE

Amenities, which give pleasure to large numbers of people in primarily urban societies, are usually the products of careful planning and management. Amenity land and landscapes are no exceptions.

The successful establishment and continuing provision of public open space in cities and towns require the services of efficient amenity management and maintenance professions, as well as inspired designers. Where such services are provided by closely knit professional teams, the amenities can be particularly pleasing, as in the case of several new towns and renewed inner cities. The same requirement exists in urban fringe and rural areas, indeed everywhere. Possibly nowhere does this apply more than in those parts of the countryside designated for recreational use. There, informal recreation is usually but one of many different uses. These include farming; forestry; water catchment and storage; military defence; the conservation of wildlife, scenic, historic and cultural features; field sports; education, etc. The integration of such activities, in whatever combinations, calls for management skills of a high order. The amenity professions, like all others, require certain tools with which to do their jobs. Statements about this, contributed by the Editor, featured in the first edition of *Landscape Design with Plants* (Clouston, 1977);

> To fulfil the essential management annd maintenance functions there must be access to adequate technical performance data and costing information, the sources of which are at present unfortunately diffuse. A Landscape Manager is currently not as well served as either his professional design or agricultural counterparts by a central pool of information. He has no equivalent to the design handbooks, e.g. 'Spons' or to the annual reports of the Provincial Agricultural Economic Centres upon which to draw.

This was followed by a comment that:

> Within central and local government and other organizations, there exists a substantial amount of unpublished technical and financial data, which if and when published would undoubtedly be of benefit to the profession. There would be much to commend the coordination of all the known landscape management data in the form of an annual reference manual or information digest.

That was written in 1977 and has since remained unchallenged. Unfortunately at the time of publication, little interest was displayed in filling the information gap. This was due, in part, to both the enormity of the task and the many pit-falls involved. Indeed, any possible candidates for such an assignment could be forgiven for fearing that they would be accused of joining a long and infamous procession; namely, of those who have walked where only fools do not fear to tread!

It was over ten years ago that the publisher investigated the possibilities for preparing such a handbook. The enquiries led directly to Charles Forestier-Walker, then shortly to retire as Head of estate maintenance operations for the Property Services Agency. He, together with a few members of the newly formed Management branch within the Landscape Institute, pointed the publisher in a particular direction; almost certainly with some trepidation!

Unfortunately, but inevitably, the gestation period involved in 'giving birth' to this handbook has been long. Many sources have had to be identified and explored, many people have had to be consulted, and all in the context of a busy consultancy life. However, this lengthy process has exposed the endeavours of both the chief compilers and the editor to a wide range of practical situations.

This book is intended largely as a reference source for practising Amenity Managers. The primary audiences therefore are envisaged as being Leisure, Amenity and Landscape Managers (Parks and Recreation Managers, Sports Facility Managers, Horticulturalists, Foresters and Arboricultralists); the Managers of private estates and properties, including country and leisure parks, which are open to the public; Maintenance Officers; Landscape Architects; Architects, Engineers and Quantity Surveyors and Contractors. It is hoped that members of several professional institutes and associations will find the handbook helpful as a reference source; in particular, members of the Royal Town Planning Institute, the Royal Institute of British Architects and the Royal Institution of Chartered Surveyors (RICS). The Landscape Institute, The Institute of Leisure and Amenity Management (ILAM), The Institute of Biology, The Institute of Horticulture, The Institute of Chartered Foresters, The Arboricultural Association, The British Institute of Agricultural Consultants, The Institute of Civil Engineers, The British Ecological Society and The British Society for Soil Science. The list of potential users also includes university and college lecturers, together with their students.

Several books are available on the management of farms, estates, forests, playing fields and gardens. However, none exists which brings together comprehensively the relevant information on amenity land resource requirements in a form which is readily usable by the Amenity Manager. It is hoped that this book will fill a notable gap in the current literature. The aim is to provide some of the main 'building blocks' for those interested in preparing and implementing plans, concerning both the provision and management of public amenities and leisure facilities.

The data relates specifically to the main individual components of most amenity landscapes: grass, woody plants, other plants, water, hard surfaces, structures and services. The book intentionally stops short of covering the main types of amenities and landscapes, which range from national parks and heritage coasts through to urban parks and private properties which are open to the public. Such amenities vary so greatly in terms of size, location, objectives and so on, that meaningful resource data cannot be assembled for use on a national scale.

A conscious attempt has been made to avoid falling into the trap of separating the management of 'urban', 'intensively used' or 'high maintenance' areas from 'rural', 'lightly used' or 'low maintenance' areas. Such categorizations have seemed inappropriate, because it is increasingly difficult to separate 'urban' from 'rural' amenity management methods, except in the most extreme cases. Indeed, some management methods commonly used in urban areas may on occasion be used in rural settings. The converse, of course, applies to an even greater extent.

If the book helps readers to avoid preconceived or standardized solutions to management tasks and problems, it will achieve one of the Editor's main aims. There are few ready-made answers to most of the questions and problems, which are likely to confront an Amenity Manager. By providing clearly labelled tables and figures, explanatory supporting text and an adequate index, it is hoped that readers will be able to find the necessary information. Frequently, the answer to a particular management planning or budgeting task lies in synthesizing information from many different sources. Thus readers may need to refer to several sections of the book before reaching a conclusion or decision. In particular, the presentation of the extensive reference lists is intended to help readers in their search for information.

No attempt has been made to describe in any great length the actual procedures involved in amenity maintenance. The draft British Standard Recommendations for Grounds Maintenance, and indeed the several other relevant British Standards, cover this aspect in some detail. Furthermore, many very good monographs already exist, covering specific aspects of agricultural, forestry, horticultural and ecological management and maintenance.

Most of the estimates given in the tables have been rounded, in order to avoid any false sense of accuracy. With the large number of variables involved, it would be misleading to try to provide precise resource requirement estimates.

This book has been prepared using information taken almost entirely from sources relating to the British Isles. Management approaches, practices and climatic conditions in other parts of Europe may all differ to some extent. However, it is likely that there will be some similarity in, for example, the number of man-hours required to carry out a particular task in different parts of the temperate world.

As this is the first edition of a book, which to a large extent covers new ground, there are inevitably some omissions, and there may be a number of errors. If readers feel strongly about these, it is hoped that they will send their constructive comments to the publishers, in order that subsequent editions may be improved. Appropriately the book ends by repeating this invitation to all members of the amenity profession.

Ralph Cobham
The Mead, Wantage.

Paradise Street, Oxford.

Avalon House, Abingdon.

The Kalahari.
1979–1989

Reference   Clouston, J.B. (Ed.) (1977) *Landscape Design with Plants*, 1st edn, Heinemann.

FOREWORD

Before the advent of people on the world scene, every square metre of the planet was serviced by a self-sustaining living system, very simple at the poles, ultra complex in the wet tropics. Together these had performed all the vital functions which maintained the changing pace of life on Earth for over 3.6 billion years.

I like to call these functions Ecosystem Services INC, International Non-profit-taking Concerns, for they recycled all their non-renewable resources and derived the vast majority of their power from the Sun.

Since the advent of people, and especially agricultural and industrial people, on the scene, Ecosystem Services INC have been rapidly and catastrophically replaced by Ecosystem Services PLC, Public Liability Corporation, and what a liability they have become.

The cost of purifying water, treating waste, recycling non-renewables, purifying air, stabilizing soil, preventing erosion, regulating the greenhouse effect, healing holes in the outer atmosphere and conserving genetic resources escalates all the time, as does the spectre of ecosystem collapse.

In recent times a significant and rapidly increasing fraction of this landscape management practise has related to so-called amenityscapes, and it has been from this sector that environmental concern has been turned into green action of a very positive sort: softer management with green gain as a growing part of the more economic management practise.

Here at last is a handbook written by a practitioner for the practitioner, a handbook of how it is done. And it is more than that, you have in your hands a *vade mecum* of green landscape practise from how to mow a meadow and keep it full of flowers to an economic audit for the living equivalent of astroturf complete with, I quote Alien Parking.

The latter may never be filled with little green people but I know that if you follow the good advice contained in these pages people's lives will become greener. The cost of amenity landcare will be reduced as our native flora and fauna complete with ecosystem-friendly creepy crawlies, and the original working components of Ecosystem Services INC make a welcome comeback into our lives and landscapes.

A good guide to the present, a green print for the future. Analyses of the facts contained; the cost of your labours will go down, the benefit to the community must go up.

Over to you.

David Bellamy
D.B. Associates Environmental Consultants
Mountjoy
Durham City

GLOSSARY OF ACRONYMS

ARC	Agricultural Research Council
AWA	Anglian Water Authority
BALI	British Association of Landscape Industries
BCPC	British Crop Protection Council
BSI	British Standards Institute
CEGB	Central Electricity Generating Board
CIRIA	Construction Industry Research and Information Association
CLOA	Chief Leisure Officers Association
CRC	Cobham Resource Consultants
CURS	Centre for Urban and Regional Studies
DoE	Department of the Environment
GC & HTJ	Gardeners Chronicle and Horticultural Trade Journal
HEA	Horticultural Education Association
HMSO	Her Majesty's Stationery Office
HTA	Horticultural Trades Association
ILA	Institute of Landscape Architects
ILAM	Institute of Leisure and Amenity Management
IRR	Internal Rate of Return
ITE	Institute of Terrestrial Ecology
JCLI	Joint Council for Landscape Industries
MH	Maleic Hydrazide
NCC	Nature Conservancy Council
NCR	Nature Conservation Review
NERC	Natural Environment Research Council
NTC	National Turf Council
NPFA	National Playing Fields Association
RIBA	Royal Institute of British Architects
RICS	Royal Institution of Chartered Surveyors
RSNC	Royal Society for Nature Conservation
RTPI	Royal Town Planning Institute
SMV	Standard Minute Value
TRRU	Tourism and Recreation Research Unit
UNDP	United National Development Programme
USEPA	United States Environmental Protection Agency

Part One

The Scope of Amenity Landscape Management

This part describes the background to the book and the issues responsible for its preparation.

In Chapter 1 the scope and objectives of the book are explained. It is also devoted to exploring the various dimensions of the primary task, namely of improving the 'cost-effectiveness' achieved by managers in caring for amenity land.

The second chapter provides readers with guidelines on how the handbook can be used to best effect, as well as explaining the main sources of the data presented.

In essence the third chapter provides an introduction to Parts Two, Three, Four and Five, which concentrate upon providing the Resource Guidelines for the main components or features of amenity land. The chapter describes the all-important factors or variables which play a part in determining the resource requirements of any amenity site. The principal factors are climate, topography, ground conditions and, more particularly, the effects which they have upon the overall management task. Their impacts, although felt on all amenity sites, are likely to differ significantly, both within and between different regions, counties, parishes and even individual properties. It is these factors, together with market forces, which in large measure are responsible for the variety and spice of an Amenity Manager's job. In some senses they are the site-specific factors, yet they are largely outside the immediate control of Amenity Managers. Because of this and their strong influence upon the amenity potential of all sites, they are referred to as the 'External Factors' influencing the resource requirements.

1

ORIGINS, ISSUES, CONCEPTS
AND DIMENSIONS

1.1
Introduction

HISTORIC TRADITIONS

Up to the 19th century the management of Britain's landscapes was under-taken mainly by landowners and farmers, whose primary concern was with food or timber production. The management of large tracts of land for amenity or pleasure was confined almost exclusively to hunting and a variety of field sports. On a smaller scale, in cottage gardens and in the grounds of large houses, a tradition of landscape maintenance was estab-lished on the basis of agricultural and horticultural methods. This tradition has been extended, during the last two hundred years or so, to the main-tenance of public parks, playing fields, roadways and the grounds of public buildings and factories.

Until relatively recent times, the division of landscape management and maintenance activities into two distinct categories was clear cut: essen-tially large-scale or rural management activities on the one hand and do-mestic or urban on the other. Three different classes of 'managed' land were discernible:

1. The extensive areas of agricultural and forest lands, managed primarily for production and commercial purposes.
2. The formal and intensively maintained public parks and gardens in urban areas and their rural counterparts: the privately-owned land-scape parks and pleasure grounds.
3. The extensive areas of common land and seemingly waste areas, such as heaths, sand dunes, mountain tops and scrub woodland where 'management by neglect', conscious or otherwise, was the hall-mark.

EVOLUTIONARY FORCES

The origins of the present-day landscape management profession, and in particular the changes experienced during the past 200 years, were amplified in one of the many enlightening papers presented (Neve, 1987) at the Landscape Management Discussion Forum, held at the University of Manchester:

All landscapes have seen considerable change in the last two hundred years, but perhaps these pleasure oriented land uses have experienced the greatest revolution. Since the eighteenth century the gardener's role, in particular, has expanded to include, by the nineteenth century, the municipal parks manager as well as the private estate worker. In the twentieth century this expansion has been compounded by an increase in the variety of garden or park landscapes, particularly in the industrial and commercial sectors.

In recent years several factors, both individually and in combination, have been responsible for major changes in both the roles of the Amenity Manager and the ways in which they are carried out. These factors include:

- The increased mechanization and intensity of agricultural management;
- The increased mobility and leisure time of an enlarged population. These have increased the recreational demands on the British landscape. As a result the Amenity Manager is faced with satisfying a bigger and more demanding clientèle;
- The increased areas of land, which are neither agricultural nor horticultural in character. These include the areas of land reserved alongside motorways; the landscape infrastructures of new towns and housing estates; the land designated as country parks and recreation areas; and the land around factories, schools, sewage works and public buildings;
- The increase in real wages of the lowest-paid workers. This has made it impossible for any but the wealthiest of individuals or public bodies to employ the numbers of gardeners which formerly enabled grounds to be maintained to very high standards;
- The new machines, chemicals and varieties of plants which are available for use in creating and managing landscapes.

Collectively the larger population, the rises in living standards, the greater personal mobility and the changes in technology have created a greater realization of the need to improve public amenities. Today not only have the distinctions between urban and rural land become blurred, but there are many more forms of land use in general and of amenity land in particular. Thus amenity management activities have been extended to include such facilities as regional parks, leisure centres, country parks, theme parks, linear walkways, adventure play areas...This, in turn, has led to recognition of the need to find both new and cost-effective methods for their management. One of the factors responsible for this is the importance accorded to conserving both wild plants and animals, together with their habitats. As a result there is now a greater requirement for the positive management of areas of land and water as nature reserves. The situation experienced by the Amenity Manager is, therefore, one of rapid change, in which traditional attitudes and practices often become quickly out of date. Instead frequent appraisals of both strategies and techniques are required.

Whilst a basic knowledge of plants, soil, machinery and labour will always be the manager's stock-in-trade, an increasing preoccupation is the search for more cost-effective ways of using these basic 'tools'. As Helen Neve has pointed out (Neve, 1987):

> In the twentieth century, a similar role change is occurring for other land managers, such as farmers, foresters, game keepers etc. Increasing demand for recreation, for nature and landscape conservation, and changing economic patterns have increasingly forced farmers and foresters to consider management for amenity; (perhaps it could be called 'leisure, pleasure and treasure' management). There has also been an increase in the variety of amenity or conservation linked rural landscapes – the rise of country parks, National Parks, Areas of Outstanding Natural Beauty, long distance footpaths, Environmentally Sensitive Areas and so forth.

Today all land can and should be regarded as 'amenity land', because all land impinges on the visual senses of people, for better or worse. However, whilst this may be correct, it is considered helpful to classify (Thoday, 1987) land and landscape resources, from an amenity standpoint, into three categories:

1. Sites with full public access;
2. Sites with restricted access;
3. Sites which are privately owned.

AMENITY LAND AND VALUES

Each year an increasing area of Britain is devoted to providing public pleasures of one sort of another. Frequently such pleasures are referred to as the amenity uses of land. Amenity land comes in all types, sizes and shapes. There are areas used exclusively for leisure and recreation purposes: sports fields, urban parks and pleasure gardens. There are other areas where the amenity activities represent only part of the user interests in the site, such as the grounds of hospitals, science parks and other public institutions. In addition there are large tracts of land where the amenity interests are either absent or subservient to the satisfaction of commercial or service interests, such as those associated with the functions of farming, forestry, manufacturing industry, transport and so on. Frequently in the case of such areas, the amenities are restricted to visual appreciation or limited access via public rights of way. Indeed, the list of the different types of land areas which play a subsidiary amenity role is extremely long.

The greater area of amenity land, which is available to fulfil primary, partial or subsidiary amenity roles, is a reflection of growing public interest in the number and extent of amenities, uses and values.

Amenity land is usually valued for one or more of the following purposes:

● It delights both the eye and aesthetic senses;
● It satisfies historic and cultural interests;

- It contains a range of wildlife habitats, features and species;
- It provides the space and facilities for one or more forms of active or passive leisure and recreational pursuits; and, most importantly,
- It contributes to the wealth, employment and health of communities.

1.2
Management issues, challenges and goals

TRENDS

The resources both required and actually used to manage amenity land and landscapes are growing by the year. Although not yet well recognized, the public money involved, both as capital and as revenue expenditure, is increasing in real terms all the time. This stems not only from the growing amount of amenity land, but also as a result of demand factors. As living standards improve and awareness of the available amenities increases, through, for example, garden festivals, Britain in Bloom competitions, etc., so public expectations tend to grow. Likewise, for many amenity areas, the public often expects the standards of maintenance achieved to be higher than was formerly the case, regardless of whether they are communally or privately owned.

Against this background it is inevitable that attention should focus increasingly upon some key questions: Are the customers – the active and passive users of amenity land – obtaining value for money? Are the right resources used to manage and maintain the land? Are these resources applied using the most appropriate methods? Are the results cost-effective? Can the nation afford to go on increasing its areas of amenity land?

Indeed, the level of interest and concern amongst public administrators has reached the point where, at last, in 1988, after two earlier attempts, legislation has been introduced (The Local Government Act 1988) covering the improvement of amenity management activities.

Even if this does not lead to the general privatization of amenity land management tasks, it is expected to increase the competitiveness and thus efficiency of those responsible for providing the services. All of this interest has placed the spot-light firmly upon both management skills and the results achieved. In an increasingly competitive 'climate', the manager can afford to leave nothing to chance. The successful management of amenity land is a challenging job. It includes many tasks, such as imaginative and effective resource planning and budgeting; the wise choice of maintenance methods; appropriate supervision and careful monitoring.

Yet there is cause for concern, based on evidence provided by professional researchers, practitioners and Government agencies, about the ineffectiveness of the funds expended on both providing and maintaining many public amenities. Some of the principal areas of ineffective expenditure and causes for concern are said to be as follows:

- *Urban parks and recreation grounds*
  'inappropriately designed and maintained green deserts'.

'Victorian facilities are still maintained even though the Victorian tastes have long since gone.'

This was amplified in an official consultation paper (Sports Council, 1981):

'Private philanthropy and public planning have left most of Britain's towns with a fine mixed legacy of parks, recreation grounds and play areas, but they are very mixed in attractiveness, usage and cost. With some notable exceptions the function and management of these facilities have attracted growing political and professional uncertainty as to whether the service provided is either what the community as a whole wants or what is appropriate in the late 20th Century, given that they account for a large proportion of public sector expenditure on leisure'.

- *Reclamation sites*
  'poor relationship between the capital outlays and ongoing maintenance costs'.
- *New town landscapes* (even in the case of the highly successful Mark III new towns)
  'poor handover provisions'.
- *Heritage landscapes* (e.g. City of Bath; Richmondshire)
  'treescapes in decline/overmature and in some cases suffering from neglect'.

Cures for the basic malady and its various manifestations have been suggested and in some cases implemented, often, unfortunately, on a piecemeal basis. These include:

- Introduction of revenue earning/capital releasing activities;
- Devolution of responsibilities to the private/voluntary sectors;
- Provision of mandatory conditions associated with Government expenditure/grant aid (i.e. preparation of management plans);
- Adoption of both a better resource planning approach and new technology/management systems (e.g. the nature in cities/ecological landscapes approach);
- Addition of new attractions/facilities (e.g. Milton Keynes 'Bowl', Theme Parks such as Alton Towers, Corby, etc.);
- Establishment of a national leisure and amenity study/demonstration centre.

Whilst at least some of these have merit, there appears to be no overall guiding light or national overview. Moreover, many of the facts required by either a single co-ordinating organization or interest groups for decision taking on the effective use of resources are not known. Rather than performing as a national co-ordinator, the Department of the Environment (DoE) regards expenditure on public open space, sports and recreation facilities as a matter requiring decision primarily by Local Authorities. To date the Local Authority Associations have not, however, performed the essential co-ordinating role.

As a result, at least until the advent of the Audit Commission, little attention had been paid nationally to achieving the following results from the resources allocated to public open space, sports and recreation facilities:

- 'Value for money' on behalf of taxpayers, local residents and users of the facilities;
- 'Cost-effectiveness' in both the short and longer term;
- Maintenance of the national image as 'a green and pleasant' land for tourists;
- Provision of additional cost-effective employment.

Whilst it is recognized that, despite certain administrative difficulties, the introduction of competitive tendering for public direct works organizations will result in some open space improvements, it cannot be regarded as a panacea.

It seems clear that corrective action needs to be taken on a broad front, in order that significant improvements are achieved.

OBJECTIVES AND SCOPE

The Amenity Manager is expected in the first instance to achieve a cost-effective result and thereafter to improve cost-effectiveness. This book has been compiled with the aim of assisting Amenity Managers to achieve such results. It takes the form of a handbook or reference source, from which Amenity Managers can obtain guidelines in performing their many duties, especially those entailing aspects of resource planning, covering both physical and financial dimensions.

The resources available to Amenity Managers in looking after amenity land are frequently known as 'the 5 "m"'s': manpower, machinery, materials, methods and management aids. Along with money and management skills, they represent the total resources package. To some afflicted with 'mnemonic madness' they are known collectively as 'the magnificent 7 "m"'s'!

In preparing this book attention has concentrated primarily on three of these resources. These are the manpower requirements allied to the methods, which are considered the most appropriate for the particular tasks involved, and the management skills in deploying them. Since some of these inevitably entail the use of machinery, the book also provides insights into machinery requirements. Whilst the use of appropriate materials is identified, the specific resource requirements are not covered. However, this is not regarded as a major deficiency for several reasons. First, material inputs tend to represent a small proportion of the total annual resource requirements; secondly, they vary significantly from site to site; and thirdly, the manufacturing and supply trades provide extensive guidelines on the quantities of the particular seeds, fertilizers, chemicals, etc., required for different tasks. Labour accounts on average for between 66% and 75% of the total resources required to manage amenity land. It is for this reason that the guidelines focus on this particular resource. Labour also happens to be the physical resource, in which both managers and landowners tend either directly or indirectly to show greatest interest. This manifests itself in searches to reduce and even minimize manpower requirements through, for example, greater use of mechanical and chemical aids.

However, this book can no more than partly assist an Amenity Manager who is concerned with recreation and leisure management in the fullest sense. Such a manager is likely to have responsibility for most, if not all, of the tasks displayed in Table 1.1. In summary, these are:

- People management: the management of visitors seeking leisure and recreation, so that they receive satisfaction in all respects from their visit(s);
- Recreation facilities management: the management of the facilities so that they are effective physically, commercially and aesthetically;
- Environmental management: the management both of the external and internal landscapes and of the hard and soft components, so that they fulfil the functions intended by the planners/designers and required by the visitors. This includes management of the staff required to maintain the resources, so that they perform cost-effectively and at the same time achieve job satisfaction;
- Utilities management: the management of the essential infrastructural services – health, safety, buildings, drainage – so that they are cost-effective.

These four types of management are all essential components of successful Amenity Management. They can all be categorized under the general heading of Public Facilities Management as distinct from Internal Resource Management, as described in Table 1.1.

This book covers primarily those tasks associated with environmental or landscape management. At the same time it also relates to the management of both recreational facilities and utilities, as well as touching upon the management of both utilities and administrative services. Each of the five types of management featured in Table 1.1 tends to be the responsibility of a particular type of Amenity Manager. However, there are many generalists, capable of covering all of the main functions listed.

Environmental management tends to be the responsibility of Landscape Managers and Leisure/Parks Managers. Thus the book is likely to be of particular relevance to those two types of Amenity Manager. Their roles are further amplified in Figure 1.1. This Figure is also intended to enable readers to appreciate the contents of the handbook in a wider context. The list of Further Reading at the end of the chapter provides further insights into many of the decisions of amenity management featured in Table 1.1 and Figure 1.1, especially concerning Recreation Facilities and People Management.

All Amenity Managers, like managers in general, share two overriding interests, namely those of first assessing and then achieving the desired performance. This, needless to say, is where the problems arise.

Table 1.1   Amenity management functions, tasks and responsibilities

Type of management/function	Broad management/maintenance tasks	Specific items of responsibility
A. Public facilities management		
1. People management	A.1.1 The welcoming and guiding of visitors	– Admissions, guide books, leaflets
	A.1.2 The provision of visitor information	– Films, AV, information boards
	A.1.3 The organization of educational and cultural programmes etc	– Establishment of clubs and community development activities
	A.1.4 The provision of publicity, promotional and public relations services	Advertising, media briefing . . .
	A.1.5 The safety and care of visitors and facilities	– security functions – safety functions – first aid – emergencies: fire and ambulance
2. Recreation facilities management	A.2.1 The operation and supervision of recreational facilities for enjoyment by visitors	– amusement/recreational structures and play equipment – sports facilities (indoor and outdoor) – catering arrangements – internal transport facilities: monorail, etc. – bookings for use of facilities – letting of sporting equipment – shops and sale of consumer items – educational facilities ⟨ children / adults – care of animals/birds

Table 1.1 (cont'd)

Type of management/function	Broad management/maintenance tasks	Specific items of responsibility
3. Environmental management	A.3.1 The immediate care and longer-term maintenance of the District Park landscape	– plants and soft landscape areas – hard surfaces and walkways – water features
4. Utilities management	A.4.1 The provision and upkeep of essential services	– water – electrictity – telephone – drainage – sewage – litter and refuse collection – public toilets
	A.4.2 The maintenance of all buildings and structures	
B. Internal resource management		
1. Administrative services management	B.1.1 The provision of administrative services	– control of physical stock – payroll payments – routine bookkeeping and financial control – annual accounting/audit – contracts and franchises
	B.1.2 The management and training of staff	– supervisory staff – technical staff and operatives – administrative staff
	B.1.3 The management and monitoring of 'success'	– annual budgeting and control of physical and financial resource use – checking the levels of visitor use, complaints, requests, etc. – liaison with designers about shortcomings and updating of original designs

1.3
Costs, values and
performance concepts

The measurement of costs and values are central to the role of management. Measurement of such variables has long preoccupied economists and accountants, let alone philosophers. More recently the attentions of environmental economists have added weight to this interest (Price, 1978; Pearce, 1986; Pearce and Markandya, 1987; Perrings *et al.*, 1988). Such interest seems destined to continue in perpetuity, since quantification of values and costs is elusive (Cobham, 1983).

VALUES

Conventional wisdom suggests that the value of a commodity is measured by the price which people are prepared to pay for it, even if, like an amenity, it contains elements which are intangible. This, it is claimed, is a reflection of the strength of the demand for the commodity. However, as has been pointed out (Perrings *et al.*, 1988), 'recent work in environmental economics has made it clear that the sources of value are very much wider than traditionally thought, particularly for natural resources, and especially so for resources that have ecological and aesthetic features'. As they and other researchers (Clawson, 1959; Helliwell, 1969; Price, 1978) have noted, there are several aspects of value. Three are of particular significance:

1. The direct use value (DUV), which can be derived from the commodity or amenity, in terms of food, hunting, wildlife conservation, tourism, etc.
2. The option value (OV), which is defined as 'a further use value expressed by people who would like the resource (or amenity) to be conserved even though they make no actual use of it. Such people express a positive valuation, on the basis that they would like to retain the option of using the resource'. This is noted as being 'a real source of value, because it will translate into a willingness to pay to conserve the resource'.
3. The existence value (EV) of a resource or amenity. This relates to the value which people derive from knowing of both the existence and continued existence of the amenity, although they themselves do not visit it, do not even intend to visit it and thus do not use it in a physical sense. The fact that the resource or amenity exists for others to use and enjoy is sufficient for it to be valued by some 'non-users'.

The total economic value (TEV) of a resource or amenity can be said (Perrings *et al.*, 1988) to be, at least, the sum of the three values defined above, i.e.:

$$TEV = DUV + OV + EV$$

At least appreciation, and preferably measurement, of these three distinct types of value should be the concern of all Amenity Managers. This applies particularly in the case of those whose responsibilities involve both conservation and sustainable development of amenities or natural resources. Such values, if professionally assessed, can help in harnessing public, commercial and political support for appropriate conservation and development activities at local, district, national, regional and even international level (Cobham, 1988). Even professional value assessments are not fool-proof, as evidenced by the interminable debate concerning the appropriate rates for discounting the stream of continuing values or benefits which future generations will enjoy if the amenity under consideration is conserved. Furthermore, measurement of total economic value should not be regarded as anything but a partial indicator of the contribution made by an amenity and those responsible for managing it. This can safely be asserted, since the 'option' and 'existence' values do not cover all the intangible values which need to be considered. Another of the thought-provoking papers (Pryce, 1987) presented to the Landscape Management Forum, drew attention to the psychological and spiritual values often associated with landscape work. This applies particularly in the case of Far Eastern cultures. Greater cognisance of such values is required when evaluating success, even if the values can only be assessed through the results of, for example, public opinion surveys.

COSTS

Corresponding thought has been given to assessing the 'true' or social costs, involved in using natural resources or amenities. Likewise there are three components, in the case of the total costs, i.e.:

Total Social Costs = Direct Costs + External Costs + User Costs
(TSC)   (DC)   (EC)   (UC)

where the components are described as follows:

- The direct or tangible costs (DC) are those associated with using and managing amenities, such as land or water, from year to year. They include both variable and overhead or fixed costs.
- The 'external' costs of what are regarded as the indirect or 'knock-on' environmental effects resulting from the use of the amenity. These include, for example, the costs of environmental damage caused by pollution; the loss or diminution of both habitats and wildlife species; the reduction in amenity values not reflected by conventional valuation formulae. Such costs may, at least in part, be intangible and thus defy simple measurement.
- The 'user' costs associated with exploitation of the resource or amenity. Such costs are incurred if the current benefits and values conferred by the resource are denied to future generations through the actions of present-day users (and the Amenity Manager).

  'User' and 'external' costs are sometimes collectively referred to as the hidden costs.

As when assessing the three dimensions of total economic value, Amenity Managers should address themselves to all three components of total social costs. Even then, they may not have the complete picture, since 'opportunity costs', and many other cost dimensions – inescapable, unavoidable, fixed, common, joint and overhead; supplementary; escapable, postponable and variable; prime; public and private; historic or 'true'; real, unit, subsidized, net, shadow and imputed costs (Cobham, 1983), also have to be borne in mind. Reference is made to 'opportunity costs' in the section which follows.

COST-EFFECTIVENESS

The extent to which amenity landscapes are successful can only be known if in the first instance 'success' is defined. Thus one of an Amenity Manager's initial tasks must be to identify the management goals or objectives. This, as far as public amenities are concerned, usually involves defining at least a general, and on occasion a specific, relationship between the total economic value of certain desired or predicted benefits on one hand and the total social cost of resource inputs on the other.

Estimations of cost : benefit ratios and cost-effectiveness are undertaken to determine whether or not an acceptable match either has been or will be achieved between the financial resources available for amenity management, on the one hand, and consumers' declared requirements on the other. In short, such estimates are intended to provide a measure of the 'value for money' achieved. They indicate the extent to which customers and investors expect or actually receive satisfaction. Success in these terms is represented by achieving an array of benefits or outputs (the effectiveness dimensions) which exceed costs or inputs. The principle makes sense and sounds easy. However, as is well known, practice is frequently different. The main reason is that, as indicated earlier, the measurement of effectiveness is often extremely difficult, if not elusive. Subjectivity tends to be a stumbling block and personal, even professional, value judgements do not lend themselves readily to summation.

Various attempts have been made to overcome the problem, rarely with entire success from a quantitative standpoint (Cobham, 1983, Pearce, 1986). Although cost estimation presents less difficulty, there can be pitfalls, as noted earlier, in determining the three components of total social costs. In addition the opportunity costs need to be estimated as an important part of the overall appraisal. These represent the incomes forgone as a result of managing land in a particular way, when compared with the most lucrative alternative.

As with assessing the benefits of an amenity, the process of discounting an array of future expenditures ranging over several years can present problems. Legitimately, managers need to know the 'rolled-up' present day financial cost involved in using and managing an amenity over the remainder of its life. Yet the choice of the appropriate discount rate is not always straightforward, especially since the substantial benefits of new amenities often do not accrue for many years. The cultural and historic values of amenities, by their very nature, are usually slow to develop. However, as the contributions of tourism to the GNPs of most European countries suggest, caution is required in discounting the values and costs associated with such amenities.

Yet all of the various problems associated with measuring 'outputs' and 'inputs' do not appear to have deterred those responsible for managing public amenities from achieving cost-effective results in the eyes of consumers during past millenia. As Amenity Managers generally know, consumers are not slow in expressing consensus, sectional or minority views, either directly or with the help of the appropriate media. Public administrators, when presented with a combination of quantitative and qualitative information, are well accustomed to making value judgements. However, that should not be used as an excuse for recoiling from the need to pursue the challenges of quantifying the indirect benefits and costs to the limits of practicability. Rather it suggests that the problems of measurement need not, indeed should not, be allowed to constrain decision-making and implementation processes.

It is because accurate quantification of effectiveness is so difficult that Managers have to make special efforts to draw up at least an inventory of the needs and wishes of their clients. Such inventories are likely to consist of both qualitative and quantitative statements. Tables 1.2 and 1.3 provide insights into some of the 'effectiveness' and cost dimensions, which Amenity Managers consider when formulating their annual objectives and management plans. One point cannot be over-stressed, namely that the level of success achieved for an amenity project or landscape scheme is usually a function of the initial thought, which has been applied to establishing the objectives.

1.4 Management dimensions

SKILLS AND SCOPE

Thus far this chapter has reviewed the wide-ranging role and responsibilities of Amenity Managers in general. Attention now focuses more specifically on the activities of the Environmental or Landscape Manager. Whilst these are already well documented (Cobham, 1977, 1989; Wright and Parker, 1979; Wright, T.W.J., 1982; Harvey and Rettig, 1985; the Landscape Management Discussion Forum, 1987), the profession is developing fast and its overall role deserves to be better understood. As the illustrations suggest, the pressures and pitfalls, which a Landscape Manager can expect to face, call for a multiplicity of skills: not least a sense of humour and a cool head!

An official definition of the profession and its role was provided by the Landscape Institute in 1983. This does, unfortunately, give only a limited picture of what is detailed:

Landscape Management is the profession of Landscape Managers who

Table 1.2 Formulating effectiveness objectives for amenity land/landscapes

---

'Effectiveness' Dimensions/Benefits to be Achieved or Improved
Satisfying users/visitors in terms of the quality of the features provided and pursuits accommodated:

- aesthetic and visual features
- archaeological, historic and cultural features
- features of ecological, horticultural and scientific interest
- wildlife/nature conservation features
- active recreation and leisure pursuits
- passive recreation and leisure pursuits, educational pursuits

All the above in terms of the numbers of people that can be satisfied at the times and at prices or costs which are acceptable; and with the minimum of accidents, complaints, breakages, vandalism incidents, etc.

Conserving and sustaining the amenities, so that they are capable of providing satisfaction in the longer term.

Generating the levels of target revenues or incomes required to service loan changes, to break even, to yield a particular IRR or to achieve the specified financial goals.

Developing new facilities in phase with demand.

Maintaining the facilities to levels and standards which are both acceptable and realistic.

Providing job satisfaction for the managers, staff and Unions involved.

'use their detailed understanding of plants and the natural environment to advise on the long-term care and development of the changing landscape. This involves them in the financial and physical organization of manpower, machinery and materials'. Landscape Management also involves consideration of 'statutory measures such as planning lease and grant aid schemes in order to preserve and enhance the quality of the landscape'. The practitioners of the profession 'usually have a degree in horticulture, forestry or agriculture with further training in land management or other related disciplines'.

Greater insights on this subject were provided by those who participated in the Landscape Management Discussion Forum. The latter highlighted both the diverse and dynamic roles of the profession and its practitioners. In particular the following characteristics were emphasized:

- The focus of the profession is amenity land which more often than not has recently involved significant landscape change, such land and landscape being required to service the needs of diverse interest groups.

Table 1.3 Assessing the financial dimensions which influence the effectiveness of amenity land/landscape

---

Financial Considerations/Objectives

Adopting affordable management methods, maintenance standards, levels and frequencies of maintenance

Using the appropriate manpower levels and skills in relation to expenditures on machinery, materials, and monitoring visitors

Employing the most efficient management system/s based on direct, contract and voluntary labour

Achieving the necessary levels of publicity for the amenity

Achieving the cash flow targets

Procuring and working to the necessary capital expenditure budget

Achieving an acceptable relationship between the levels of capital and revenue expenditure

---

- The core expertise required is essentially practical in nature and includes a knowledge of horticulture; an understanding of recreation provision, its marketing and use; a good acquaintance with landscape design and ecology; an ability to prepare specifications, maintenance schedules and contract documentation; the skill to programme and control the use of funds, manpower and materials; a familiarity, like any other manager, with cost accounting and work study (Boylan, 1986).
- The need for the profession to combine with many others, particularly designers, in order to set and maintain high standards thereby achieving the long-term results desired by designers and clients alike. However, whilst the combination of design and management skills is vital, there is a variety of ways in which this can be achieved.
- The ultimate success achieved by a manager is often dependent upon both securing and sustaining community involvement.
- The dynamic nature of the biological, aesthetic, cultural, commercial and other processes with which the profession is involved.
- The profession involves many other dimensions, namely: an appreciation of historic values; the management of people in a variety of situations, involving both clients and staff; business management orientated to achieving 'optimum' rather than 'maximum' returns; a long time horizon and often considerable uncertainty; the need for well developed communication skills, both in relation to professional colleagues and to society in general; policy formulation and review at local or national levels; the formulation of performance goals and criteria for assessing the policy, planning and programming; results achieved, in relation to both the amenities and their clientèle.

- The requirement for managers frequently to undertake the role of co-ordinator and to present an integrated view of the profession to all interested parties.
- The ambidextrous nature of managers' basic tasks, which are orientated both to conserving the amenity resources and to serving the needs of those who seek to use and enjoy the resources.

Thus in terms of professional disciplines, the successful practitioner is likely to be a hybrid with, it is to be hoped, first generation vigour.

The Discussion Forum emphasized one particularly important fact, namely that not all amenity areas are managed by Amenity or Landscape Managers, just as not all external environments and landscapes are designed by professionally qualified, experienced Landscape Architects. It was confirmed that many of the new twentieth-century landscapes are managed by people 'in a legal or administrative sense, but who are increasingly divorced from the land itself'. Such managers are usually aware of the need to maintain the land in a rather static sense, but who may well, through no fault of their own, be ignorant of the need to manage land in a biological sense. Increasingly urban based, at home as well as at work, such managers are no longer aware of the dynamics of land which make its maintenance and management imperative. Land changes, not just on a daily or seasonal basis but annually and in perpetuity, and must be managed if its dynamics are not to turn it into something else again. This continual development is, it seems, seldom understood today (Neve, 1987).

This confirms the need for the profession not only to become more fully engaged in managing amenity land, but also to extend its influence much more widely, both through educational and public relations activities. Such education, it is suggested, continually needs to be provided by Amenity Managers to their designer colleagues, in order that management requirements and issues are adequately incorporated from the start of a project. Many designers have yet to appreciate that their greatest ally in confronting the challenge of time should invariably be the Landscape or Amenity Manager. It is such a Manager who is responsible for nurturing and husbanding a design through its various phases of initial establishment, adolescence, maturity and regeneration or replacement. In summary, Helen Neve states that the twentieth century has resulted in a two-fold situation where either: landscapes are increasingly required to accommodate land uses, for which their traditional managers have no training or particular expertise (and are thus heavily dependent upon the influence or advice of other organizations); or landscapes are formally designed, in which case, once the design work is completed and executed, the Manager tends to be a committee, a local authority, housing trust, etc., often with no land management expertise available at all.

She rightly concludes that in both cases there is an obvious need for a modern Landscape Manager, inextricably linked to amenity land uses and very much a product of the twentieth century.

I'M SORRY, BUT ITS ANOTHER GRANT APPLICATION FORM.

AN UP-DATED DEFINITION

Both in conclusion to the chapter and in an attempt to summarize the various strands, readers are offered a revised, formal definition of the landscape management profession and the main roles which its members should be expected to fulfil:

'Landscape Management' is a hybrid profession calling for the effective application of knowledge and skills obtained from training in the sciences and arts of both 'landscape' and 'management' related subjects. The profession is called upon to undertake the multiplicity of activities involved in conserving, planning and perpetuating areas of land and their associated features to achieve a variety of commercial and cultural ends. There are three main interested parties, to which the profession relates:

1. The needs of other professional advisers, notably: landscape architects, architects, planners, surveyors;
2. The landowners, both public and private;
3. The users of the landscape.

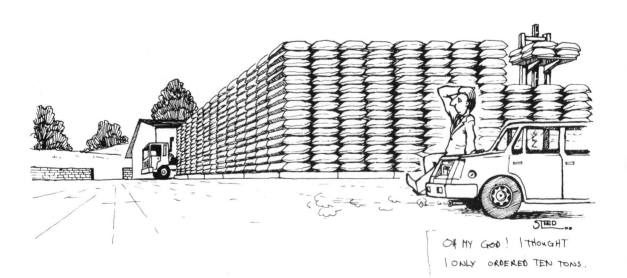

In addition, and most importantly, the profession has a responsibility to the landscape itself and both for conserving and enhancing its vegetation cover.

The profession first and foremost is founded upon a fundamental understanding of two subjects:

1. The functions which land and its associated resources comprising the landscape are required to fulfil, including the procurement of food, timber, fish, fur, minerals, etc.; the pursuit of leisure; the development of property for commercial and/or aesthetic gain; the conservation of visual, wildlife, historic and cultural features.
2. The ways in which these functions and resources themselves are changing.

Because longevity is a characteristic of many of the basic resources, the 'fourth dimension' is an aspect of management which demands both careful and continual attention by the profession.

The profession requires many different types of managers to fulfil the wide range of tasks involved in managing both large and small-scale landscapes. These include:

*   The formulation of policy, legislation and broad-scale planning;
*   The execution of design roles in rural situations;
*   All manner of practical tasks associated with the establishment and maintenance of landscapes through management of contractors, direct labour and/or volunteers;
*   The provision of popular leisure and recreation facilities, through the management of both visitors and the features themselves;
*   Procurement and employment of the resources required for effective single or multi-purpose use of a landscape.

In undertaking these tasks a clear distinction needs to be made between the large and small-scale landscapes.

In short, the profession is an important and essential service sector component of the national economy. (Cobham, 1987)

Two very important and closely related professional skills, upon which the successful Amenity Manager needs to draw regularly, are those of the Landscape Architect (design) and the Landscape Scientist (botanist, zoologist, ecologist, ornithologist, entomologist, hydrologist and soil scientist). The professions of Landscape Management, Landscape Science and Landscape Design are reflected in the three branch structure of the Landscape Institute. The Institute, which is a constituent member of the International Federation of Landscape Architects, is the core of the landscape profession in Britain. In performing this role, there is close

liaison with a number of related institutions and associations; in particular, with the British Association of Landscape Industries (BALI), the Institute of Leisure and Amenity Management (ILAM), the RICS, the RIBA and the RTPI.

References

Boylan, H. (1987) *Contribution to Landscape*, Management Discussion Forum, University of Manchester, 21 Feb.

Clawson, M. (1959) Methods for Measuring the Demand for Outdoor Recreation. Resources for the Future Inc: Washington.

Cobham, R.O. (1977, second edition 1989) *Landscape Management: the Fourth Design Dimension. Landscape Design with Plants*, (ed. J.B. Clouston) Heinemann.

Cobham, R.O. (1983) The economics of vegetation management. In *Management of Vegetation*. (ed. J.M. Way) British Crop Protection Council Monograph No. 26. Proceedings of a Symposium on the Management of Natural and Semi-Natural Vegetation.

Cobham, R.O. (1987) Contribution to Landscape Management Discussion Forum, University of Manchester, 21 Feb.

Cobham, R.O. (1988) Private sector development: Some Environmental considerations. In The National Conference on Strategies For Private Sector Development, Francistown, 4–6 July. U.N.D.P.

Harvey, S. and Rettig, S. (1985) *Fifty Years of Landscape Design*. Landscape Press,

Helliwell, D.R. (1969) Valuation of wildlife resources. *Regional Studies* **3**, 41–47.

Landscape Management Discussion Forum (1987) Conference at the University of Marchester (21 Feb).

Lovejoy, D. (ed.) (1988) *Spon's Landscape and External Works Price*

WHICH DO YOU PREFER, JACK; HIGH LEVEL OR LOW LEVEL MAINTENANCE?

Book. E. and F.N. Spon, London.

Neve, H. (1987) *Landscape Management: Its Practice and Future Development*, Landscape Management Discussion Forum, University of Manchester, 21 Feb.

Pearce, D.W. (1986) *Cost Benefit Analysis*, Macmillan, London.

Pearce, D.W. and Markandya A. (1987) Marginal opportunity cost as a planning concept in natural resource management, *Annals of Regional Science*.

Perrings, C., Opschoor, H., Arntzen, J., Gilbert, A. *et al.* (1988) *Economics for Sustainable Development*. I.U.C.N.

Price, C. (1978) *Landscape Economics*. Macmillan, London.

Pryce, S. (1987) *Some Psychological and Spiritual Aspects of Landscape Work*, Landscape Management Discussion Forum, University of Manchester, 21 Feb.

Sports Council (1981) *The Function and Managing of Town Parks*, Con-

CONTRACTORS, DIRECT LABOUR? OF COURSE NOT! ALL VOLUNTARY LABOUR.

sultation Paper.

Thoday, P.R. (1987) Contribution to Landscape Management Discussion Forum, University of Manchester, 21 Feb.

Wright, T.W.J. (1982) *Large Gardens and Parks: Maintenance, Management and Design.* Granada, St Albans.

Wright, T.W.J. and Parker, J.C. (1979) Landscape management, In: Weddle, A.E. (ed.) *Techniques of Landscape Architecture*, Heinemann, London.

Further reading   Addison, C.H. and Thoday, P.R. (eds) (1982) *Proceedings: Cost-effective Amenity Landscape Management.* Bath: Horticulture Education Association.

Bynner, J. and Stribley, K.M. (eds) (1978) *Social Research: Principles and Procedures.* Longman and Open University Press, Milton Keynes.

Cave, T.G. (1983) Management of vegetation in or near water. In: *Proceedings: Management of Natural and Semi-Natural Vegetation.* (ed. J.M. Way). British Crop Protection Council: Croydon.

Cobham, R.O. (1980) Integration of special interests: Conflict and compromise. In *Proceedings: Management Plans in the Countryside*, 33–46.

WHAT WITH SICKNESS, WET TIME AND SO ON
HE'S ONLY CUT ONE VERGE ALL SUMMER.

(eds C. Margules and M. B. Usher). Recreation Ecology Research Group, Report No. 5.

Corder, M. and Brookes, R. (1981) *Natural Economy: an Ecological Approach to Planting and Management Techniques in Urban Areas.* West Yorkshire: Kirklees Metropolitan Council.

Dangerfield, B.J. (ed.) (1981) *Recreation: Water and Land. Water Practice Manual.* The Institute of Water Engineers and Scientists, London (Chapter 5: The Management of Recreation Facilities).

Duffey, E., Morris, M.G., Sheail, J., Ward, L.K. *et al.* (1974) *Grassland Ecology and Wildlife Management.* Chapman and Hall, London.

Dunball, A.P. (1983) Management of herbaceous vegetation on the sides of roads and motorways. In *Proceedings: Management of Natural and Semi-Natural Vegetation.* (ed. J.M. Way), British Crop Protection Council, Croydon.

Gilmour, W.N.G. (1982) The management of green space on a low budget. In: *Cost Effective Amenity Land Management* (eds C.H. Adison and P.R. Thoday), University of Bath, Bath.

Gratton, C. and Taylor, P. (1985) *Sport and Recreation: An Economic Analysis.* E. and F.N. Spon, London.

Green, B.H. (1981) *Countryside Conservation*. George Allen and Unwin, London.

Gregory, R. (1976) The voluntary amenity movement. In *Future Landscapes* (ed. M. MacEwen), Chatto and Windus, London, pp. 199–217.

Lieber, S.R. and Fesenmaier, D.R. (1983) *Recreation Planning and Management*. E. and F.N. Spon Ltd, London (Chapter 1 : The Social Benefits of Outdoor Recreation).

Lowday, J.E. and Wells, T.C.E. (1977) *The Management of Grassland and Heathland in Country Parks*. Countryside Commission, CCP 105, Cheltenham.

MacEwen, A. and MacEwen, M. (1982) *National Parks: Conservation or Cosmetics*. George Allen and Unwin, London.

Miles, C.W. and Seabrooke, J. (1977) *Recreation Management*. E. and F.N. Spon Ltd, London.

Moss, G. (1981) *Britain's Wasting Areas: Land Use in a Changing Society*. Architectural Press, London.

Newby, H. (1980) *Green and Pleasant Land?* Penguin, Harmondsworth.

Nix, J. (1988) *Farm Management Pocketbook*, 18th edn. Farm Business Unit, School of Rural Economics, Wye College, University of London.

Parker, R.R. (1986) *Land New Ways To Profit: A Handbook of Alternative Enterprises*, Country Landowners' Association, London.

Peterken, G.F. (1981) Woodland Conservation and Management. Chapman and Hall, London.

Phillips, A.A.C and Roberts, M. (1973) The recreation and amenity value of the country-side. *Journal of Agricultural Economics*, **24**, 85–103.

Price, C. (1978) *Landscape Economics*. Macmillan Press, London.

Reid, I.G. (1963) The nomenclature of costs. *Farm Economist*, **10**, 125–9.

Royal Society for Nature Conservation (1981) *Towards 2000: A Place for Wildlife in a Landuse Strategy. A Consultation Paper*. RSNC, Nettleham, Lincs.

Sturrock, F. and Cathie, J. (1980) *Farm Modernization and the Countryside*. Occasional Paper No. 12, Department of Land Economy. Cambridge University Press, Cambridge.

Torkildson, G. (1986) *Leisure and Recreation Management*, E. and F.N. Spon, London.

Van Doren, C.S., Priddle, G.B. and Lewis, J.E. (1979) *Land and Leisure*, 2nd edn, Methuen and Co. Ltd., London.

Warren, A. and Harrison, C.M. (1978) Ecological information and the allocation of resources to recreation: experience in the South London green belt. In *Proceedings: Ecological Impact of Countryside Recreation-Priorities for Research*, (ed. J.P. Shildrick), Recreation Ecology Research Group, Report No. 3, pp. 17–28.

Weddle, A.E. (1979) *Landscape Techniques of Landscape Architecture*, Heinemann, London.

Whitby, M.C., Robins, D.L.J., Tansey, A.W. and Willis, K.G. (1974) *Rural Resource Development*. Methuen and Co, London.

Wright, S.E. and Buckley, G.P. (eds) (1979) *Proceedings: Ecology and*

Design in Amenity Land Management. Wye College and Recreation Ecology Research Group. Wye College, University of London.

Wright, T.W.J. (1979) Design and management of semi-natural areas in historic gardens and parks in Great Britain. In *Proceedings: Ecology and Design in Amenity Land Management* (eds S.E. Wright and G.P. Buckley), Wye College and Recreation Ecology Research Group. Wye College. University of London, pp. 216–24.

2

APPROACH, REFERENCE SOURCES AND GUIDELINES

2.1
Introduction

This chapter starts by describing the approach adopted in preparing this book, in terms of methodology and concepts. It also indicates both its intended roles and, most importantly, its limitations. This is undertaken in relation to the handbook, both as a separate entity and as one of a number of related handbooks. Next, the data sources used to compile the tables and figures are explained. This leads naturally to the final section, which attempts to provide readers with some guidelines concerning the use of the book.

2.2
Approach

LANDSCAPE COMPONENTS

This book covers all of the main features or components comprising the chief types of amenity landscape. Thus it reviews the principal operations and resources involved in managing all different forms of plant material, water bodies, hard and synthetic surfaces, structures including play equipment, seating, fencing, and finally services such as litter collection and lighting. Although great differences exist in the types of amenity land and landscape and in the uses made of them, they all tend to be composed of the same elements or features. For the purposes of this handbook, these components have been grouped into four broad categories

1. Amenity grasses and related ground covers;
2. Woody plants: amenity woodlands, trees and shrubs;
3. Other plants: climbers and herbaceous;
4. Other surfaces, structures and services: water, hard/synthetic surfaces and recreation structures.

Whilst such broad classifications are helpful, sub-groupings are required, especially concerning the vegetation component of amenity landscapes. The main vegetation elements covered in this handbook are listed below. Each of these is capable of accommodating and sustaining different levels of use, according to the overall design and management provisions.

AMENITY LANDSCAPE ELEMENTS

1. All forms of grassland: sports turf; lawns and fine turf; low wear and low maintenance areas; reclamation sites; wild flower areas; semi-natural habitats including heathland, moorland, chalk downs and sand dunes.
2. Woody plantings: trees and shrubs, featuring in woodlands, copses, spinneys, shelter belts, avenues, amenity plantings, hedges; individual and specimen plants; climbing and wall plants; roses.
3. Herbaceous plantings: borders; beds; climbing and wall plants; individual and specimen plants.
4. Container-grown plantings: woody and herbaceous plants.
5. Ground cover plantings: woody and herbaceous plants.

The main vegetation elements listed are by no means mutually exclusive or 'water-tight'. There are considerable overlaps between the different elements. For instance, the chapter devoted to climbing and wall plants inevitably makes reference to both woody and herbaceous species. The same applies in the case of both ground cover and container-grown plantings. Thus inevitably readers may find the need to refer to several chapters, in seeking the required information. The index is intended to help in this respect.

PHYSICAL RESOURCE ESTIMATES: VIRTUES

The main physical resource requirements of most landscapes can be compiled and assessed using information contained in the tables which appear in each of Parts 2, 3, 4 and 5. In effect the resource guidelines represent a series of basic 'building blocks' or 'assessment units', for use in management planning, work programming, budgeting and monitoring exercises.

In the interests of trying to ensure that the resource estimates provided do not quickly become out-of-date, the figures are mainly expressed in physical units. It is intended that readers should use the standard minute values and other time input figures, presented in the tables, for preparing their own financial estimates. In doing so, it is expected that readers will select the unit costs for manpower and machinery, which are appropriate for the specific operations, locality, etc., involved and which reflect current wage rates, overheads, technology, etc. By presenting the resource requirements in the form of physical figures and thereby insulating them from the effects of inflation, it is intended that they should remain relevant for as long as the maintenance methods described and the underlying technologies are in use.

The adoption of a standardized estimating procedure, based initially on physical units, should enable the figures prepared by different management agencies to be assessed and used without being distorted, as has happened in the past due to differences in cost accounting conventions adopted, for example, in allocating overheads. Comparisons based solely on financial estimates can be notoriously misleading and indeed meaningless. General expertise suggests that cost yardsticks are treated with considerable suspicion. In contrast, the provision of physical data, from which financial estimates – for particular combinations of landscape components and sets of operations – can be initially synthesized and then calculated, is generally acknowledged to be helpful.

THE FOURTH DIMENSION

Whenever appropriate, a distinction is made between the management operations and resources required during the phases in the life cycle of the particular landscape component. The duration of these phases differs according to the physiological and genetic characteristics of the particular landscape component, the landscape type of which it forms a part, the 'external factors', the nature and levels of use, management; in short a whole array of factors.

PRINCIPAL PHASES OF THE LANDSCAPE MANAGEMENT CYCLE

The main plant growth-cum-management phases are generally distinguishable for each of the components, especially those whose life-time spans several years. They are as follows:

- The period of pre-establishment operations, including planning, design and site preparation prior to planting;
- The establishment phase, which covers the period from planting through to the time when, apart from occasional, special tasks, only routine maintenance is required. The duration of this phase differs greatly, ranging from between 3 to 5 years in the case of trees to a few days or weeks for annual bedding plants;
- The period of 'adolescence', during which the plantings, although successfully established, still require occasional attention, in addition to routine maintenance operations;
- The period of 'maturity' when the vegetation only requires routine maintenance and periodic rejuvenation. In some cases, as with self-sustaining/regenerating (primary) woodlands, the latter may be negligible;
- The 'senile' or 'geriatric phase' when the vegetation is recognizably senile and when special care is required to extend its aesthetic life and possibly its physical life as well. This is the period when, in the case of some trees and shrubs, rejuvenation through special pruning, surgery and coppicing operations is required;
- The period or time of death, followed by either re-establishment or replacement. The latter period, of course, includes the possibility of introducing one or more entirely new components.

In most cases, there are no easily definable demarcations between the different phases. Generally they merge into each other. Since readers of this book are likely in the main to be involved with the management of features in the 'post-establishment' phases, the tables, figures and supporting guideline text focus first upon the operations involved in these phases. As a general procedure throughout the handbook, both pre-establishment and establishment operations are covered in the sections devoted to re-establishment tasks. Figures 2.1 and 2.2 provide diagrammatic representa-

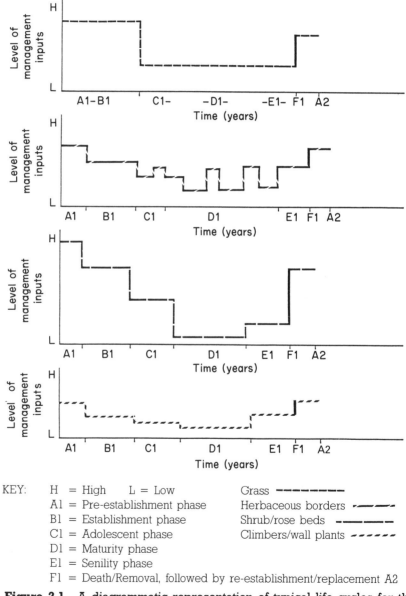

KEY: H = High   L = Low   Grass ----------
       A1 = Pre-establishment phase   Herbaceous borders ·——·—·
       B1 = Establishment phase   Shrub/rose beds ·—————
       C1 = Adolescent phase   Climbers/wall plants ------
       D1 = Maturity phase
       E1 = Senility phase
       F1 = Death/Removal, followed by re-establishment/replacement A2

Figure 2.1 A diagrammatic representation of typical life cycles for the management of different landscape components.

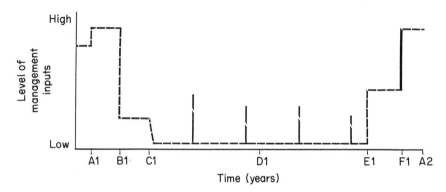

Key:
------- Level of management inputs required
~~— Signifies coppicing, where this management practice applies
A1   Pre-establishment phase
B1   Establishment phase
C1   Adolescent phase ⎱ Post-establishment phase
D1   Maturity phase   ⎰
E1   Senility phase (which may be extended by special rejuvenation)
F1   Death/felling followed by re-establishment/replacement A2

NB: Not drawn to scale

Figure 2.2 A diagrammatic representation of a typical life cycle or continuum for the management of amenity woodland trees and mass shrub plantings.

tions of typically generalized life cycles for the management of the five main landscape components. They are included at this stage as a means of emphasizing, for the benefit of readers, that an attempt has been made to structure the contents of the handbook according to the phase of the management cycle. The phases of the cycle, described above for individual landscape components, apply equally when considering one or more landscape types and even individual plant species.

Just as each individual component or feature of a landscape has its own management life cycle, so too does the complete landscape, comprising all of the components. The job of the Amenity Manager is not only to ensure that each of the components is appropriately managed and maintained throughout its life cycle, but that sensible relationships are maintained between the life cycles of the different components. Quite apart from the functional and aesthetic reasons for phasing management life cycles, it is in the interests of 'cost-effectiveness' to ensure that the regeneration and replacement operations are phased so as to avoid excessive demands on the 5 Ms at any one time. This calls for careful long-term planning, which is undoubtedly one of the most important responsibilities of the Amenity Manager. Management cycles for parkland and other landscape types, which are heavily dependent upon the continuing presence of a mature tree cover, are well documented (Cobham, 1977/1989; Carter, Cobham and Lloyd, 1979; Cobham, 1985).

Other authors have also found the concept of cycles helpful in presenting management guidelines. Handley and Bulmer, (1986) have referred to two generalized cycles covering landscape development and landscape management. Readers are likely to find the twin publications, drafted under contract for the D.O.E. by Dr John Handley and his colleague, particularly helpful. They are based on the operations of The Groundwork Trust and thus relate strongly to management associated with the restoration of damaged and neglected landscapes occurring in and around St. Helens and Knowsley, Merseyside. Despite this locational bias, the two publications are extremely useful and in many ways are complementary to this Handbook.

The challenges facing the Amenity Manager in relation to these various life cycles are numerous. In the case of the life cycle of:

1. An individual landscape component: the management task usually entails ensuring that the physical, aesthetic and other functions of the component are continued, by means of at least periodic (e.g. rotational), if not perpetual, regeneration;
2. A particular landscape type: the challenge involves adopting the most cost-effective method of perpetuating the landscape in accordance with the long-term objectives of both the designer and the client (private or institutional owner users, etc.).

The task of ensuring that all the physical, aesthetic and other functions of a complete landscape are at least capable of continuing either in perpetuity or in accordance with revised design guidelines, does not necessarily rule out the possibility of making conscious changes. It should, however, prevent the inevitable hiatus which occurs functionally, visually and commercially in landscapes that have suffered, either in part or entirely from neglect at some stage during the life cycle. Such a hiatus is particularly noticeable in the case of many of Britain's historic parklands and pleasure grounds, where unfortunately either little replanting or regenerative and rotational management was carried out over a score or more years.

It will be appreciated that the fourth dimension needs to feature centrally in the planning and work programming thoughts of Amenity Managers.

FUNCTIONS, OPERATIONS AND CHOICES

The different landscape components are usually required to fulfil several functions: physical, social, aesthetic, recreational, conservational, commercial and economic. A wide range of management and maintenance operations is available to the Amenity Manager in seeking to ensure that the required mix of functions is achieved. Such operations include all of those listed in Table 2.1. A primary task of the Amenity Manager is to identify the choices which need to be exercised before carrying out the

Table 2.1 A selection of the key choices which an Amenity Manager is required to make

The choices concerning the most cost-effective use of resources, individually and collectively	The main management-maintenance operations to be undertaken for each of the landscape components and types	The chief functions to be fulfilled
What types, levels and combination of:	Fertilizing	Physical
	Spraying	Economic/
Manpower inputs?	Growth regulation	financial
	Weed control	
Machinery inputs?		Social
	Mulching	
Materials inputs?		Aesthetic
	Irrigating	
		Recreational
	Pruning	
Methods (technological inputs?	Clearing	Conservational
	Brushing	.
Management aid inputs?	Thinning	.
	Coppicing	.
	Laying	.
	Layering	.
Management skills?		.
	Felling	.
		.
Monetary inputs?	Planting (incl. under and inter)	.
		.
To achieve the desired Management and maintenance levels:*	Sowing	.
	.	.
	.	.
1. High	.	.
2. Intermediate	.	.
3. Low	.	.
.	.	.

* Examples of the different maintenance levels in the case of grass areas are:

very high level	:	1–2 cuts per week during growing season.
standard level	:	1 cut per fortnight during growing season.
intermediate level	:	1 cut per month during growing season.
low level	:	1 to 2 cuts per year.

In the case of maintaining privet hedges, for example, the levels are differentiated as follows:

high level	:	4 cuts per year, May to September.
standard level	:	2 cuts per year, June to September.

operations. The choices which need to be made are also wide ranging and cover such important questions as:

- What *levels* of maintenance are required?
- Do the *types* and *levels* of use, together with the nature of the resource (the landscape components) dictate that the maintenance levels should be:
  (i)   high (i.e. well manicured)
  (ii)   low (i.e. minimal inputs of the '7 Ms')
  (iii) intermediate?
- What *standards* of management and maintenance should be adopted for the particular maintenance level chosen? Are there places, such as in wilderness areas, where the standards can be relaxed and need not, as in most public amenity areas, automatically be high?
- What are the *methods* or *techniques* available for undertaking the various operations, in terms of the different types of manpower, machinery and materials? Which combination of resources, i.e. method, is likely to produce the most cost-effective results in the long, as well as the short, term?
- When is it appropriate to mechanize and when to use manual labour? What is the best *size* of machine to buy and what *numbers* should be purchased in relation to the frequency of use, lifetime, depreciation, running (including maintenance) costs?
- What additional facilities are required such as depots, covered and secure storage *facilities*, rest rooms, holding nurseries, etc.?
- What is the most appropriate *implementation method*; would the tasks be most effectively performed by direct works labour, by contractors, by voluntary labour or by various combinations?
- Which of the following *routes to improving cost-effectiveness* are likely to produce the best results:
  (i)   replacing one operation with another, the SMV for which is lower;
  (ii)   reducing the frequencies with which operations are undertaken during the year/growing season;
  (iii) extending the lifetime or cycle of one or more landscape components;
  (iv)   modifying the original design;
  (v)   substituting a substantially different maintenance technique or implementation method;
  (vi)   changing the timing of the operations, especially between the growing and dormant seasons?

Even more fundamental choices need to be made at the initial planning and design stages. These concern the types and proportions of the various landscape components which should feature in the overall scheme. Many different criteria, covering functional, aesthetic and financial dimensions, are likely to be involved. It is important that Amenity Managers should participate first in determining the selection criteria and then in the selection process itself. In these two respects, Amenity Managers are well qualified to make two essential contributions:

1. To identify the short and longer-term maintenance resource (both capital and annual revenue expenditure) implications of the different landscape planning and design options;
2. To analyse and advise on the most cost-effective combinations of landscape components, with respect to the relationship between initial capital outlays and the subsequent arrays of annual expenditures over the remainder of the landscape cycles.

In short, Amenity Managers have major roles to play in ensuring that both the short and longer-term cost planning exercises yield the desired results, ensuring that cost-effectiveness is optimized.

The book does not purport to promote any particular management-cum-design approach, such as those colloquially referred to as 'the ecological/low productivity/nature-in-cities approach', the 'formal, high design–high manicure approach', 'the standard short-back-and-sides approach' and 'the gardenesque approach'. On the contrary, the merits of supporting a diversity of design and thus management approaches, reflecting the growing range of recreational needs, are recognized. Management systems are clearly required which enable each distinctive design (whatever the style) to be maintained and sustained in the most cost-effective manner. The Further Reading list serves to elaborate this point.

2.3
Reference sources

The tables in this Handbook have been compiled from a wide range of sources, covering the different regions: North West, North East, Midlands, South West and South East. This has been done in recognition of the wide diversity of landscape conditions existing in Britain, due principally to climatic factors but also a number of other regional differences.

DEFINITIONS

Table 2.2 provides a glossary for the abbreviations and acronyms which appear in the source columns of the tables throughout Parts 2, 3, 4 and 5. Another glossary, describing the principal items of machinery included in the tables, is featured in Table 2.3.

The term 'Amenity Manager' features frequently throughout the remainer of the book. It is used in two contexts:

1. In a generic sense to cover the four different types or dimensions of management, outlined in Chapter 1;
2. In referring to those managers, who are primarily concerned about the sustainable use and development (including conservation) of external environments or landscapes, for both recreation (active and passive) and related purposes.

Despite the male bias in the illustrations, for which the Editor assumes

Table 2.2   A glossary of reference source
abbreviations and acronyms

CCH	Country Conservation Handbook
CRC	Cobham Resource Consultants
D	Devon County Council
E	Essex County Council
FC	Forestry Commission
FMH	Farm Management Handbook
H	Hillingdon Borough Council Parks Department
JE	J. Epstein
K	Kent County Council
L	Lanark District Council
LBB	London Borough of Bromley
M	Manchester Parks Department
RB	R. Bisgrove, University of Reading
Sa	Shropshire County Council
SCS	Sefton Coast Scheme
Sh	Sheffield City Parks Department
T	Telford Development Corporation
TH	Dr T. Hall, Oxford University Parks
VC	Volunteer Corps
W	Warrington Development Corporation
Wi	Wiltshire County Council

no responsibility, the term 'Landscape Manager's is used in the text entirely
without gender.

STANDARD MINUTE VALUES

Standard minute values (SMVs) have been used throughout this book to
show the cost of operations in terms of man-hours. It is generally recognized that SMVs for similar operations can vary greatly between different
organizations. This variability may arise from differences in:

- The detailed nature of the job being carried out: pruning water shoots
  off a young standard tree may be significantly different from pruning
  off feathers, for example;
- The tools, techniques and method of work organization employed;
- The inclusion or exclusion of activities such as transport of materials on
  site.

In addition, the SMVs can vary in the amount and type of allowances and
other auxiliary activities which they include. For example, some of the
SMVs used contain a percentage to cover transport to, from and between,
sites, and loading and unloading. Others do not. Thus, in using the tables,
all readers should be aware of the dangers of comparing the SMV figures.
They are presented as guides only, not as definitive measurement. The

Table 2.3   Glossary of machinery and mechanical aids

Grass cutting and scrub flailing machinery

Allen scythe	:	a pedestrian power unit with front mounted reciprocal cutting knife blade.
Atco-24″	:	a self-propelled pedestrian cylinder mower with optional ride-on towed seat. 6 bladed steel cylinder and heavy duty rollers to give traditional striped lawn finish.
Atco-27″	:	as for Atco 24″, but including optional electric or recoil start and swinging light-weight grassbox to facilitate emptying. The cutting cyclinder can be disengaged to allow easy movement between cutting areas.
Bomford 468	:	a 4.6 m reach tractor mounted hydraulic flail.
Flymo	:	a large range of rotary/petrol and electric powered mowers.
Fuji Brushcutter	:	a hand held (with shoulder harness) lance mounted rotary saw with petrol engine.
Hayter Condor	:	a range of rotary and cylinder verge mowers with 30″ cut. Self-propelled with 5 forward gears and 2 gear driver cutting heads; 3 bladed cylinder mower with cut-out lever and roller; optimal trailed seat.
Hayter Osprey	:	a 24″ self-propelled rotary mower with belt driven cutter head and 4 swinging cutter blades, inset wheels, easy height adjustment and optional wheeled trailer seat.
Jungle Buster	:	a general term for heavy duty, rotary scrub cutters/rotary saw cutters.
Junior Triple	:	a small ride-on cylinder mower with two additional 'gangs', e.g. Ransomes Motor 180.
Mountfield	:	a range of rotary mowers with various widths of cut; self-propelled, using either side wheels or roller; optional grass boxes available.
Munro Bantum	:	a range of mowers for golf courses and sports pitches.
Turner Flail	:	a large range of flail and turbo-flail machines including a 30″ hydrostatic pedestrian model and 3 mechanical and pedestrian models with cutting widths of 22″ and 30″; also tractor mounted flails with cutting widths of 40″ and 46$^+$″.
Wheelhorse	:	garden tractors and ride-on rotary mowers with optional garden tool packages and grass collection boxes.

Grass aerating and rolling machinery

Horwood Powerake	:	self-propelled scarifier for de-thatching sports and lawn surfaces.
Pattison Spiker	:	a 22″ wide self-propelled spiker, with 72 tines (hollow, solid and root pruning), 320,000 holes per hour: 75 square yards, up to 4″ penetration; pneumatic wheels.
Sisis Aerator	:	a 30″ wide aerator, fitted with single-ended pointed tines for up to 5″ (13 cm) penetration.

Table 2.3 (cont'd)

Sisis Auto-turfman Spiker	:	a heavy duty powered aerator for year round use on turf, with a choice of tines; 74 cm wide; minimum surface disturbance.
Sisis Rotorake	:	a machine which handles like a mower with thatch removal blade reel, wire scarifying reel, thatch control reel and brush reel; optional collector; working width 18″ (46 cm).
Sisis Turfman Spiker	:	a spiker slitter for hand use or with Allen scythe power unit; interchangeable with a range of attachments; aerators, brushes, rakes and roller for smaller areas.
Vibroll Roller	:	a vibrating roller.

Weed control machinery

Granular Herbicide Applicator	:	a chest-mounted applicator; a 6.5 litre chest-worn tank with gravity feed to a spot gun, fitted with inter-changeable solid stream and full cone spray nozzles.
Victair Mist Blower	:	a tractor mounted sprayer; 3 models providing double or single sided symmetrical spraying in tree rows up to 10 metres wide. Pre-set directional control is possible with optional nozzle fittings.
Weedeater	:	a range of petrol or electric driven nylon cord trimmers. Larger models have inter-changeable brush and saw blades.

Fertilizer spreading machinery

Cyclone Spreader	:	a pedestrian fertilizer spinner with hopper feed; dry fertilizer spinner with a spread band width of 2–3 metres; mounted on two wheels with push handle; smooth tyred models are available.
Lute Top Dressing Spreader	:	a hand tool with handle mounted grid for spreading and working in top dressings, preparing seed beds (tilth) and levelling track surfaces: 24″ (61 cm) wide.
Sisis Coultas Spreader	:	a precision spreader with rotary brush and reduction gears for low volume application; clutch level control for cut off, applies wide range of dry, damp and 'clinging' materials. 36″ (92 cm) wide.
Tractor Vicon Spreader	:	a tractor p.t.o. mounted conical hopper, feeding to a rotating flicker/spinner for application of granular/dry mixed dressings.

Ground preparation machinery

Gravely Tractors	:	a lawn/garden tractor with a range of optional equipment for both rear and forward mounting.
Howard Gem Rotavator	:	a petrol or diesel engined pedestrian cultivator with 20″ and 24″ working widths; 3 forward speeds and reverse; multi-adjustable handlebars.
Pirminter Cultivator	:	a tractor drawn, 'harrow' type cultivator.

Drainage construction machinery/materials

Case Task force 300 or 700	:	a track mounted trencher. The 300 model is the smallest available on the market; similar to a mini-tractor.

cont'd

Table 2.3 (cont'd)

Case Trimline 200 Economy Trencher	:	a 12 h.p. self-propelled pedestrian model; petrol engine, hydrostatic drive.
J.C.B.	:	a range of specialized earth moving equipment, based on a tractor unit with hydraulically operated arm attachment.
Lampflex	:	a flexible coiled plastic drainage pipe; light weight; precision perforated; immune to soil-borne chemicals; has a controlled degree of linear flexibility.

only way for a manager to obtain more accurate figures is to gather specific work measurement data for the particular work force, operations and techniques used for the landscape components and sites concerned. Readers are encouraged to do this, since measured work values, with all their drawbacks, are still an invaluable management tool. Without them it is not possible to assess work loads and manpower requirements.

ALLOWANCES AND ADJUSTMENTS

It cannot be emphasized too strongly that care needs to be exercised in using the manpower data contained in the tables. Standard minute values on their own will not provide the complete picture on labour requirements. Adjustments are required to the figures, in order to take account of a whole series of additional elements, usually known as allowances. These cover such items as:

- Lost time due to weather
- Breakdowns
- Machinery maintenance
- Travel time between sites
- Personal duties and rest periods
- Keeping records
- Contingencies and emergencies
- Receiving instructions and discussing operations with supervisors
- Clearing up after completing operations

Conventions for dealing with allowances can differ significantly between Local Authorities; for example, Sheffield City Parks Department (Bauer, 1978) and the Estates Department of Kent County Council (Parker, 1980). No purpose is served by attempting to weigh the relative merits of the two approaches. It is enough merely to draw to the attention of readers, the necessity first of making adjustments, and secondly, of making sure that the convention, which is adopted, adequately caters for the circumstances, associated with both the particular operation and particular landscape component.

You Don't HAPPEN TO HAVE
TRANQUILLISERS, Do You?

2.4
Guidelines   GENERAL CONTEXT

The physical information contained in Parts 2, 3, 4 and 5, especially in the tables and figures, is intended to be helpful to those who are planning either to establish an amenity maintenance project or want to change and possibly expand their existing maintenance provisions. It will also serve as a starting point for readers interested in obtaining rough estimates of both labour and total costs. Since labour inputs account for between approximately 66% and 75% of the total direct expenditures incurred annually in managing an amenity landscape, the manpower figures provided can serve as a useful basis for estimating total costs. When wishing to up-date such broad estimates, the various cost indices published by the Central Statistics Office are likely to be helpful in making adjustments on account of inflation.

Many authorities use their standard minute values not only as a planning aid, by also as a productivity measure. The latter is often far from successful. Each of the measured times is in fact only a snapshot of how long the tasks take under a certain set of conditions. Obviously aspects such as 'hand weeding' depend on the type of soil, the weeds present, etc.

Standard minute values, in order to be of any value as a basis for determining productivity and thus bonus payments, need to reflect the specific conditions of each site.

However, under many productivity bonus schemes the workers are told exactly how long a certain job should take them, in order to achieve the bonus. There is a tendency, in the event that the real time proves to be much greater, for them either to skimp the work or become resentful that they are being cheated of their rightful earnings.

Of course, there are occasions where the SMV estimate is too low and the workers easily reach the target. It is only human nature that they will either keep quiet about this deliberately, or not even notice it as they make small adjustments to their work rate and the standards attained.

For the sake of fairness, ease of calculation and good labour relations many authorities are moving to a scheme where productivity levels are worked out on a group basis, or individually over a month, rather than for a specific task. In this way the easy and the difficult jobs tend to even out.

From earlier sections of this chapter, readers will have come to appreciate that the information contained in the tables needs to be handled with care. The SMVs are primarily intended to serve as indicative estimates for use by Amenity Managers who do not have their own work measurement data upon which to draw in preparing plans and in assessing performances.

The tables and figures presented in Parts 2 to 5, the core of the handbook, are supplemented by some general text. This serves to explain the context in which the data is likely to prove useful. It does not, however, provide detailed descriptions and reviews of the maintenance methods themselves. Instead, extensive reference and further reading lists are provided. Intentionally, these form a major component of the handbook, so as to assist readers wishing to investigate specific subjects in greater depth. Readers are likewise advised to use the index freely as a means of cross-referencing between different parts and sections of the book. Use of the index is essential in enabling readers to obtain full value from this handbook. The value of the handbook will also be enhanced by using it in conjunction with both the well established, related handbooks/professional guides, published by Spon and lesser known ones (Richards, Moorehead and Laing Ltd., 1987), which feature in the reference and further reading lists at the end of this chapter. At the same time it is assumed that readers will keep abreast of professional advances, particularly concerning techniques, through such journals and newsletters as *Turf Management*, *Horticulture Weekly*, *The Forestry*, *Landscape Industries*, *Landscaping* and *Landscape Design*. One companion handbook of particular importance is, of course, *Spon's Landscape and External Works Price Book* which provides capital cost guidelines in particular. However, as has been indicated earlier in Part One, the distinction between capital and ongoing revenue expenditures is often an artificial and misleading one. Instead decision-makers need to be made much more aware of the cost continuum before pursuing any major landscape projects, especially those which are likely to involve expensive maintenance outlays. Thus the relationship between design and management decisions should be made stronger through use of the two handbooks together.

The message to designers is a strong one; namely there are substantial benefits to be gained from turning to their resource management colleagues for help in both estimating and portraying the likely financial and other long-term implications of alternative design-cum-management options. The interactions between design and management decisions, whether intentionally as a result of close professional co-operation or by default, manifest themselves throughout the lifetime of a landscape. Consequently it makes eminently good sense for all interested parties to try to simulate the likely maintenance scenarios and their financial implications at the initial planning and design stages, long before the ink on the drawing board is dry. Thus, not surprisingly, this management handbook also contains some design guidelines which are known from experience to be particularly helpful to Amenity Managers in achieving cost-effective results.

Hitherto, most references to the resource requirements of a particular landscape have either been vague or have been computed on a dissimilar basis, thus making comparisons with figures for other landscapes virtually impossible. Such generalizations that have been put forward tend to be misleading. For instance, a league table showing those types of landscape which are cheapest, more and most expensive to maintain, will frequently show grass – rough grass – at the top of the league table as being the cheapest. However, in 1974 at the time of the first fuel crisis there was a hurried scramble on the part of many Parks Directors in recognition of the fact that as fuel costs escalated so grass was not necessarily the cheapest or the most effective landscape component. In reality it is impossible to generalize on such matters owing to differences in climate and a whole host of factors: size of area, shape of area, technique, time of year, type of use and so on. Thus this book steers away from the provision of national or even regional generalizations. Instead it seeks to provide a set of guidelines which will enable people to identify that particular set of landscape ingredients and management methods which for them will provide the most cost-effective result.

In short, this is not a book of absolutes but rather of pointers. Circumstances and conditions are so different across the face of even this small island that it is impossible to be precise about the resource requirements and thus the costs involved in adopting one particular maintenance and management technique as distinct from another. This book merely seeks to make people aware of the orders of magnitude. Its purpose is to enable people to establish systems of management and maintenance which are superior to those in existence today.

LIMITATIONS AND DISCLAIMERS

Whilst the need for disclaimers in preparing a handbook of this nature will be appreciated, equally the presentation of a long list is unpalatable.

However, there are a number of limitations, some inevitable and some intentional, of which the reader should be made aware at this stage.

First editions of a handbook are unlikely to be comprehensive in their coverage of topics. This one is no exception, in relation both to the landscape components and to the methods used to maintain them. For instance, the book stops short of providing data on the management and maintenance of the purpose-built structures, associated with recreational and landscape amenities, such as maintenance offices and machinery depots, sports stadiums and centres. No Chapter is specifically devoted to the management of recreational facilities and of people in particular, since other authors have already covered the topics at length. The same applies to office procedures, management of overheads and indeed to management as both an art and a business discipline.

The handbook focuses on manpower much more than any of the other resource inputs for the reasons already given. Furthermore, machinery and materials resource inputs – particularly concerning innovations – are regularly reviewed in a wide range of professional publications.

It will be appreciated that landscapes and recreational amenities, which depend on living systems, do not lend themselves to water-tight classification. Thus a workable, rather than a perfect, treatment of the landscape components has been sought. Some overlaps between parts are thus inevitable. However, since the aim has been to minimize duplication, it is essential that readers should make good use of the index for cross-referencing.

No apology is made for the fact that the lists of references are intended to be regarded as being of equal importance to the text. Despite care, some references may have been somewhat arbitrarily placed, especially in Part 3. Thus readers are urged to browse extensively through the reference sections.

It cannot be over-emphasized that, whilst the data presented in the book have been used successfully by the authorities concerned, the Tables at best provide general guidelines and imprecise building blocks. The book provides pointers rather than ready-made answers or automatic solutions. If the information presented serves as no more than a stimulus to encourage readers to collect their own data through locally conducted work measurement and related exercises, then it will have served a useful purpose.

Finally, it is important that attention should be drawn to the need to avoid placing too much reliance on management planning and controls in providing successful amenities. They form only part of a manager's armoury. Never should they be allowed to substitute for the essential combinations of skills and services: horticultural, ecological, recreation design and human. Unfortunately, at times such substitutions have seemed dangerously close.

WORK PLANNING, PROGRAMMING AND COST ESTIMATING

As a means of providing readers at the outset with an indication of the ways in which the data presented in Parts 2–5 can be applied, three worked examples are included at this stage. These are covered in Tables 2.4–2.6.

The examples link well with those presented in Part 6 as a means of demonstrating how the data can usefully be applied in a range of situations.

Table 2.4   The calculation of work loads – an example

a) Formula

Operation	Operation rate SMV	Operation timing	Operation frequency	Total quantity of work to be done	Manpower/ machining inputs required: hours per year
	(a) minutes per (b) units	Dates	(c)	(d) total number of units	$\dfrac{(a) \times (c)}{60} \times \dfrac{(d)}{(b)}$

b) Worked example

Operation	Operation rate SMV	Operation timing	Operation frequency	Total quantity of work to be done	Manpower/ machining inputs required: hours per year
Mow grass with 30″ rotary mower	6.2 min per 100 m^2	Every 2 weeks from April–October	14 per year	14 520 m^2	$\dfrac{6.2 \times 14}{60} \times \dfrac{14\,520}{100}$ $= 210$
Prune shrubs	38 min per 10 no	Winter	2 per year	391 m^2 @ 1 shrub per metre $= 391$ no	$\dfrac{38 \times 2}{60} \times \dfrac{391}{10}$ $= 50$

Table 2.5   The upkeep of grounds: times and costs – a worked example

1. *Calculation of man hours required*: for one or more landscape tasks
   1.1 Use Work Study times or make estimates of the times required for each task including:
      (a) routine contingencies such as clearing obstruction or adjustment of machines
      (b) rest allowances depending on the nature of the work (usually 15–20%).
   1.2 Add time for the preparation and disposal (P & D) of the machinery and tools, i.e. getting them ready for work and putting them away again and including any cleaning at the end of the job.
   1.3 Add time for walking about on site (usually based on the area of the site).
   1.4 Add time for travelling to the site.
   1.5 Add time for unloading and reloading the van.
   1.6 If work study times are used make allowance for expected rate of working (performance).

   Example   Assume two men in a mobile team but only one mowing machine.

Mow 2000 m^2 with 750 mm mows	60 mins
Add preparation & disposal time (P & D)	10
Clip 150 m of border edges	30
Add P & D	6

   cont'd

Table 2.5 (cont'd)

Handweed 150 m^2 of ground cover	75
Add P & D (2 men)	12
Site allowance (2 men walking on site)	2
Time for loading van, etc. (2 men)	10
Travelling time 5 miles @ 4 mins for 2 men	40
Sub total	245 mins
Allowance for 90% working performance $\dfrac{245 \times 100}{90}$	272 mins (Total time allowance)

2. *Calculation of manning levels*: the manpower requirements for routine maintenance throughout the season

   2.2 Decide on the peak work period for the year and then total the time required for all the work involved in a week (using the method in 1 above). If there are 'one -off' jobs like hedge cutting find the average times over 4 to 8 weeks.

   2.2 Add on time for travelling between sites, if it has not been included in 2.1. Assume one visit to each site and two or three men travelling.

   2.3 Add contingencies for:

Wet time and breakdowns	say 12%
Staff sickness	say 4%
Non-routine work	say 4%
Total	20%

   Assume that very little leave is taken during the peak period and all but the most urgent non-routine work is deferred until after the peak period.

   2.4 Add daily allowances for each man for each whole or part of a man day (i.e. starting and finishing each day at depot).

   2.5 Calculate manpower equivalent (divide total hours by normal working hours).

   Note: regular overtime will reduce staffing levels but leaves less in reserve for emergency situations. Four hours per week should probably be regarded as a maximum for regular overtime working.

   Example

Average peak workload (including site allowances)	84 hours/week
Travelling between sites 45 miles × 2 men × 4 mins	6 hours
Sub-total	90
20% contingency for wet weather, etc.	18 hours
Sub-total (= 13+ man-days)	108
Daily allowance	
14 man-days @ 20 min	say 3 hours
Total	111 hours/week

   Therefore manpower requirement $= \dfrac{111}{40} =$ say 3 men

   (2 travelling and one base man)

   but the team could cope with another 6 or 7 hours of work each week.

Table 2.5 (cont'd)

3. *Calculation of costs per hour*

The easiest method is to total all the costs of running the organization and divide the figure by the total number of effective working hours. This will give an all-in cost for a wide range of operations, but may be slightly unrealistic when comparing the actual costs of, say, hand mowing with gang mowing. It is however possible to calculate separate rates for, say, all pedestrian operations, tractor work and lorry work.

For simplicity the costs should include the average cost of transport, fuel and small machinery; commonly used materials should also be included, unless they are a considerable cost, e.g. plants or large-scale fertilizer dressings.

Example   An organization employing 100 staff

Costs (£)

Wages including National Insurance Superannuation	410,000
Salaries of Supervisors incl NI and Superann.	40,000
Machinery and transport including fuel, depreciation and repairs	130,000
Depots and offices including notional rents, rates and repairs	16,000
Protective clothing materials, etc.	16,000
Administration, management and training	28,000
Total	640,000

Annual work hours

Hours employed = 100 men for 52 weeks @ 40 hours =	208,000
+ overtime of 100 × 4 × 20 weeks =	8,000
Therefore total hours employed =	216,000

Less non-effective hours

Leave & Public holidays
100 × say, 25 × 8 = 20,000

Sick leave
say, 4% of 208,000 = 8,320

Sub-total	28,320
Therefore hours at work =	187,680

Wet time & breakdowns
say, 12% of 187,680 = 22,521

Depot & Machine servicing
say, 6% of 187,680 = 11,260

Sub-total	33,781
Total effective working hours are	153,899

$$\text{Cost per effective hour of work} = \frac{640,000}{153,899} = 4.15$$

Source: This table is based on information contained in a paper given to the editor in 1981 by John Parker. Estates and Valuation Department, Kent County Council.

Table 2.6   Resource planning – a worked example

Calculating the resources needed to maintain different types of landscape e.g. a housing area containing grass, shrub areas and hedges

1. *Calculate total Summer and Winter work loads*
   Use the method shown in Table 2.4 to work out the total SMVs required for each operation per season.

2. *Direct time required: Summer work load*   Standard Minutes
   (a) *Grass mowing*   *SMs/cycle or/year*
      (i)   *Double Wheel Multipower*
            Mow 99 447 sq.m at 3.8 SMs per 100 sq.m   =   3779
      (ii) *Flymo*
            Mow 562 sq.m at 25.1 SMs per 100 sq.m   =   141
      (iii) *27″ Ransome 'Spinner'*
            Mow 4732 sq.m at 5.2 SMs per 100 sq.m   =   246
            Add 13% travelling between patches   =   542

            Total SMs mowing   4708 SMs/cycle

   (b) *Hedge clipping*
      (i)   Clip 5814 sq.m of privet and hawthorn
            hedges at 2.9 per sq.m   =   16 862
      (ii) Clip 126.5 sq.m of poplar hedge at
            2.0 per sq. m   =   253
      (iii) Clip 532 sq.m of beech hedge at 1.7 per sq.m   =   905

            Total SMs hedges   =   18 020

            + twice per year privet and thorn   =   34 882 SMs/cycle

   (c) *Other operations*
      (i)   Border shearing, using long handled shears,
            including clearing up, 18 513 lin. metr. 4.6 SMs
            per 10 lin. m.   =   8516
      (ii) Hoe ground – shrubberies edge 2814 sq.m
            at 7.6 per 10 lin.m.   =   2139

            Total SMs other operations/cycle   10 655 SMs/cycle

3. *Direct time required: Winter work load*
   All done once per year: SMs/Year
      (i)   Prune and/or shape shrubs 1350 shrubs at 4.0 SMs
             per shrub   =   5400
      (ii)   Fork over and weed ground – rose beds, shrubberies,
             etc. 7446 sq.m at 33.9 SMs per 10   =   25 241
      (iii) Spray ground for grass control along edges of grass plots,
             8113 lin.m at 14.2 per 100 lin.m   =   1152
      (iv)   Spray ground for weed control – shale areas; 2415 sq.m
             at 20 SMs per 100 lin.m   =   483
      (v)   Spray round obstacles, 629 at 5.5 SMs per 10 obst   =   346

Table 2.6 (cont'd)

(vi)	Weed channels along wall sides, etc. 1010 lin.m at 11.5 SMs per 10 lin.m	=	1162
(vii)	Prune roses – bush and standard 5820 roses at 13 SMs per 10	=	7566
(viii)	Apply fertilizer to garden areas 1960 sq.m at 14.3 SMs per 10	=	2803
(ix)	Trim edges of paths, etc. with half moon or spade 10 981 lin.m at 10.2 SMs per 10 lin.m	=	11 201
	Total work load, Winter maintenance	=	55 354

The total seasonal SMVs show the amount of time which needs to be spent directly on the maintenance operations themselves. However, extra time also needs to be allowed for auxiliary work, lost time, etc.

4. *Auxiliary/allowance time required*
   In this example operations which entail machine maintenance are worked out separately from those which use only hand tools.
   (a) *Grass mowing*

Work time available per 8 hr day		=	480 Mins/Day

	% of Total Work Time available	Min/day
Less:		
Travel out from and back to cabin (twice per day, three times on Thursday)	9.4	45
Machine maintenance	6.25	30
Daily Allowance	4.1	20
Lost Time, weather and breakdown, etc. — allow 10%	10.0	48
Unmeasured work — assistance with other jobs etc. — 10%	10.0	48
	39.8	191

Net Time Available for Mowing per day	=	289 Mins/day

   (b) *Other operations*
   The time available for this work is as for (a) above except that no machine maintenance time has been allowed.

Therefore Net Time Available for other work	=	319 Mins/Day

5. *Manpower required*
   The formula used for calculating the manpower required is:

$$\text{Time required per cycle in man days} = \frac{\text{Total SMs work}}{\text{Time available}}$$

cont'd

Table 2.6 (cont'd)

(a) *Summer*
  (i) Mowing: 4708 SMs = 16.3 man days/cycle
      1.63, say *2 men* per 10 day cycle
  (ii) Hedge clipping: $\dfrac{34\,882 \text{ SMs}}{319 \text{ min}}$ = 109 man days/year
      1.36 men throughout the cutting season
  (iii) Other operations: $\dfrac{10\,655 \text{ SMs}}{319 \text{ min}}$ = 33.4 man days/cycle
      1.67, say 2 men per 20 day cycle

  Therefore total number of men needed for summer maintenance work = 5
(b) *Winter*
  Time required per season = $\dfrac{55\,354 \text{ SMs}}{319 \text{ min}}$ = 173 man days
                          = 7 weeks work for gang of 5 men

Source: This table is based on information contained in a paper given to the Editor in 1980 by John Bauer, Sheffield Metropolitan District Recreation Department.

References

Bauer, J. (1978) *Landscape Open Space Maintenance: Management Techniques*, Sheffield Metropolitan District Recreation Department.

Carter, C., Cobham, R.O. and Lloyd, R.J. (1979) The way ahead. In *After the Elm* (eds. J.B. Clouston and D. Stansfield) Heinemann, London.

Cobham, R.O. (1977/1989) Landscape management: the fourth design dimension. In: *Landscape Design with Plants*, (ed. J.B. Clouston), 1st and 2nd Editions, Heinemann, London.

Cobham, R.O. (1985) Blenheim: the art and management of landscape restoration, *Arboricultural Journal* **9**, (2), 81–100.

Groundwork Trust (1986) *Making the Most of Greenspace, Volume II: Output Guides For Landscape Management*, (Draft), Department of the Environment.

Handley, J.F. and Bulmer, P.G. (1986) *Making the Most of Greenspace* (Draft) *Volume 1*, Department of the Environment.

Parker, J.C. (1980) *Upkeep of Grounds: Times and Costs*. Estates and Valuation Department, Kent County Council.

Richards, Moorehead and Laing Ltd. (1987) *The Use of Vegetation in Civil Engineering*, CIRIA Research Project No. 379.

Further reading

Baines C. (1987) The future management of vegetation in the urban environment. In: *The Scientific Management of Vegetation in the Urban Environment* (eds. P.R. Thoday and D.W. Robinson) Acta Horticulturae 195.

Baines, J.C. and Smart, J. (1984) *A Guide to Habitat Creation*. Ecology Handbook No. 2. GLC London.

Beazley, E. (1969) Designed for Recreation: A practical handbook, Faber & Faber, London.

CEGB (1967) 'Economy in Landscape Maintenance' Symposium Summary.

CEGB (1972) *Landscape Code of Practice. Vol. 1.*

Cobham, R.O. (1983) The economics of vegetation management. In *Management of Vegetation* (ed. Way J.M.), British Crop Production Council, Monograph No 26.

Conover, H.S. (1958) *Grounds Maintenance Handbook*, McGraw-Hill, London.

Colvin, B., (1968) Landscape maintenance of large industrial sites, *ILA Journal* **84**, November.

Dale, C. (1980) A design tool for soft landscaping. *Landscape Design* **131**, 37–8

Department of the Environment (1973) *Schedule of Rates for the Preparation and Maintenance of Land.* H.M.S.O.

Emery, M. (1986) *Promoting Nature in Cities and Towns. A Practical Guide*, Croom Helm, Beckenham.

Evans, J. (1984) *Silviculture of Broadleaved Woodland*, Forestry Commission Research and Development Paper 62

Fairbrother, N. (1970) *New Lives New Landscapes*, Architectural Press, London

Fairbrother, N. (1974) *The Nature of Landscape Design*, Architectural Press, London, Chapter 7.

Gilmour, W.N.G. (1982) The management of greenspace on a low budget, *Cost-Effective Amenity Land Management* (eds. C.H. Adison and P.R. Thoday) University of Bath, Bath.

Hebblethwaite, R.L. (1967) *Landscape Maintenance*, CEGB.

Holden, R. (1987) Investing in maintenance. *Landscape Design* **168**, 46–52.

Hookway, R.J.S. (1967) *The Management of Britain's Rural Land.* Countryside Commission.

ILA (1963) *Landscape Maintenance.* Report of Symposium, June.

Insley, H. and Buckley, G. (1980) Some aspects of weed control for amenity trees on man made sites. *Proceedings of Weed Control in Forestry Conference.* Wye College, University of London, pp. 189–200.

Institute of Recreation Management (1975) *The Recreation Management Yearbook*, E. & F.N. Spon Ltd, London.

Laurie, I.C. (ed.) (1974) *Nature in Cities.* University of Manchester, Landscape Research Group Symposium.

Marren, P.R. (1975) *Ecology and Recreation, A Review of European Literature*, University College, London.

McHarg, I.C. (1956) Can we afford open space? A survey of landscaping costs, *Architects' Journal*, 8 and 15 March, pp. 261–74

Nix, J. (1988) *Farm Management Pocketbook*, 18th edn, Farm Business Unit, Department of Agricultural Economics, Wye College, University of London.

Parker, J.C. (1985) Just keep on mowing for 300 years. In *Fifty Years of Landscape Design*, (eds S. Harvey and S. Rettig) The Landscape Press, London.

Peterken, G.F. (1981) *Woodland Conservation and Management*, Chapman and Hall, London.

Roberts, H.A. (ed.) (1982) *Weed Control Handbook: Principles*, 7th edn, Blackwell Scientific Publications, Oxford.

Sellwood, M. (1986) Looking outside. *Horticulture Week*, January 10th.

Speight, M.C.D. (1973) Outdoor recreation and its ecological effects. *Discussion Papers in Conservation*, University College of London.

Thoday, P.R. (ed.) (1980) *Weed Control in Amenity Plantings*, Conference Proceedings, University of Bath.

Warnock, T. (1967) A surveyor looks at landscape maintenance. *The Surveyor*, September.

Weddle, A.E. and Pickard, J. (1971) Landscape management: site conservation at Heriot-Watt University. *ILA Journal*, **94**, May.

Wright, S.E. (1979) Rural conservation II. *Landscape Design* **124**, 27–30.

Wright. T.W.J., and Parker, J.C. (1979) Maintenance and conservation. In. *Landscape Techniques*, (A.E. Weddle), Heinemann, London.

Wright, T.W.J. (1982) *Large Gardens and Parks: Maintenance, Management and Design*, Granada, St. Albans.

Wright, T. (1975) Landscapes: The State of Welfare. *Gardeners' Chronicle*, **178**, (24), 26–8

Wye College (1972) *Kent, Aspects of Landscape Ecology and Maintenance.*

3 SITE VARIABLES

3.1 Introduction

Many factors influence the resources which are required by an Amenity Manager to achieve a cost-effective landscape. This applies especially in the case of what might be termed 'Site Variablies', such as climate, topography, ground conditions and market forces, which are at least to some extent beyond the control of a manager. In that respect they can be regarded as constraints. Without doubt they differ significantly from area to area and from region to region. It is principally for this reason that nationai resource guidelines cannot be expressed as single or simple standard figures, for individual tasks or landscape components. Such are the vagaries of weather and ground conditions that the resources required to maintain a particular landscape feature, for example a unit area of grass, woodland, shrubs, roses or bedding plants, are likely to vary significantly between different locations. Such differences are well recognized by the authors of other resource planning and management handbooks. For example, in the case of agricultural data, the Farm Management Handbook (Nix, 1987) which purports to furnish national yardsticks for each of the main farm enterprises, is supplemented by a series of regional handbooks, prepared by the Provincial Agricultural Economics Service on behalf of the Ministry of Agriculture, Fisheries and Food.

Consequently, space is given in this introductory section to the three site variables which are considered to be of prime importance in the case of amenity landscapes: climate, topography and ground conditions. By covering these factors at the outset it is hoped that the task of using the resource data, which follows in the later sections of the book, will be made easier for readers.

3.2 Climatic factors affecting management

The British climate is notoriously changeable and also surprisingly variable from region to region. Overall, It becomes colder and drier towards the north and east, and colder, windier and wetter with increasing altitude.

Climate affects the costs and benefits of amenity management in many ways. Some of the most important influences are summarized diagrammatically in Figure 3.1.

Maps showing the average potential moisture deficit, the durations of

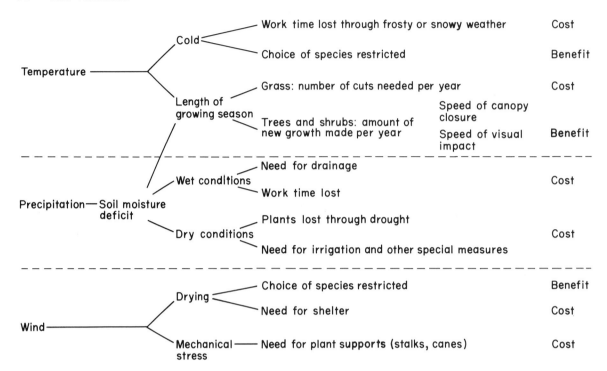

Figure 3.1 Effects of climate on landscape: costs and benefit.

the growing season and the frequency of irrigation needed in England and Wales are shown in Figures 3.2, 3.3, 3.4.

GROWING SEASON

In general, the most important climatic influence on management costs is probably the effect of the growing season upon grass mowing operations. This is because mowing is the most costly of all the maintenance operations in the majority of landscape management organizations. Gang mown grass in Plymouth, for example, may need at least 30 cuts per year compared with about 22 in Aberdeen.

There is little that an Amenity Manager can do about this except restrict the area of grass. However, it is interesting to note that the mild climate of the South West is one of the reasons for the success which the Parks Manager of Plymouth has achieved in pioneering the use of the grass growth retardant: maleic hydrazide. Moist summers help to prevent the browning and scorching often caused by maleic hydrazide elsewhere.

The length of growing season also affects the amount of extension growth that woody plants will make, if other factors such as ground conditions and nutrient supply are adequate.

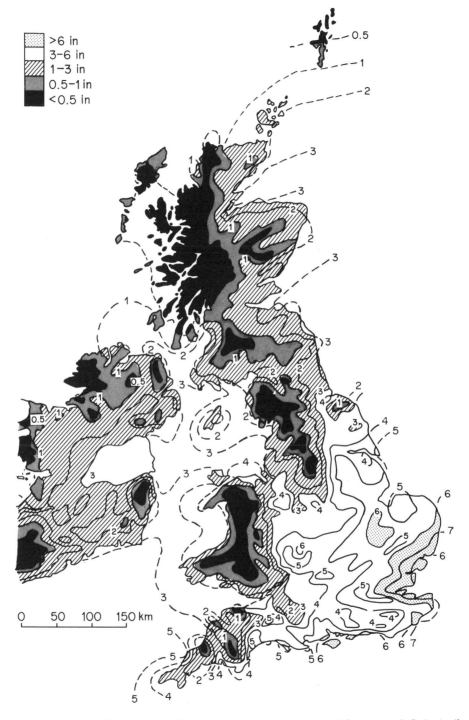

Figure 3.2 The annual average potential water deficit (soil moisture deficit) in the British Isles.

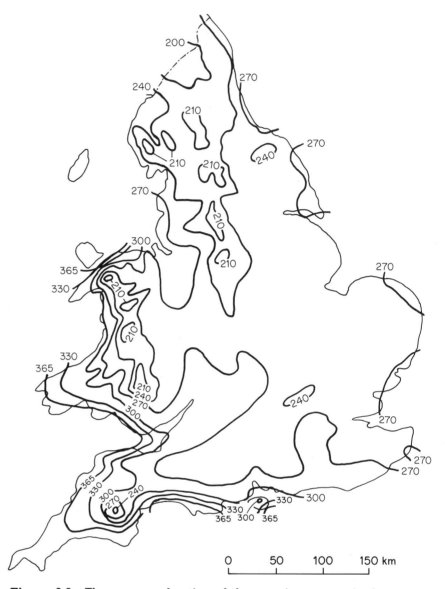

Figure 3.3 The average duration of the growing season in days over England and Wales.

EXPOSURE

Extension growth is also strongly affected by exposure to wind. The latter influences growth mainly by its drying effect on foliage and soil. The effects of wind are usually capable of being ameliorated by the creation of shelter. There is often a choice of methods including ground modelling, the construction of walls, screens or fences, the planting of hedges and shelter belts, the use of anti-transpirants and so on.

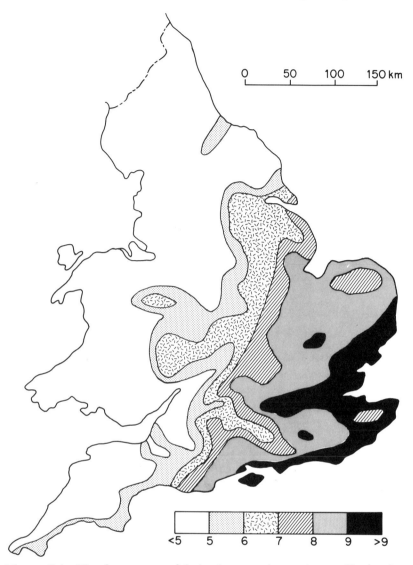

Figure 3.4 The frequency of irrigation requirement over England and Wales expressed as number of years in ten.

Foresters protect exposure-sensitive trees, such as oak and beech, from wind by using nurse species. Modern 'ecological' plantings speed up natural processes in a similar way. Hardy shrub or tree species are included so as to protect the more sensitive climax species. Planting densities are often increased on very exposed sites as a means of improving the micro-climate afforded at least to the interior rows.

There are many techniques by which exposed sites can be altered in favour of plant growth. The extent to which Amenity Managers will be willing to use resources to fight the natural climate will depend on the importance which is placed on quick growth and the establishment of a range of species. For example, the Liverpool Garden Festival of 1984 was an extremely prestigious and politically important event. The team responsible for creating the landscape only had 2 years in which to do so. Money was plentiful and the incentive to make plants grow quickly on the windy, salt-blasted reclamation site was very great. A range of techniques was therefore used including erection of webbing wind screens, use of anti-transpirant sprays, generous ground preparation with planting composts and deep mulching.

Foresters planting similar sites, but working to a longer time scale, are able to use much less expensive techniques because they can work with the processes and pace of nature. For foresters the speed of establishment may not be so important. Indeed final plant performance is likely to be better when a manager uses very small stock and thus has the resources to spend on essentials such as ground preparation, rather than on standard trees, stakes, ties and planting composts.

PRECIPITATION

The direct effect of soil moisture deficits on landscape management is seen most clearly where new plantings have been made. If site preparation, the choice and the care of plants, and planting techniques are right, many plants can establish successfully without irrigation even in quite dry seasons. However, faults in planting husbandry usually result in the drying out of plants. It is in these cases that irrigation is required. Estimates indicate that Amenity Managers in Britain may be wasting at least 50 million pounds a year by planting trees and shrubs which subsequently die (Insley, 1986).

Figure 3.4 indicates the frequency of irrigation required for agricultural crops in England and Wales. Crops differ, of course, in their requirement for irrigation according to whether they serve commercial or amenity needs. For example, in commercial horticulture only high value crops, such as fruit and intensive market garden crops, are normally irrigated. However, increasing numbers of growers are insisting on irrigation equipment for lower value field crops, such as cabbages and potatoes, since they have found it cost-effective to do so.

The need for irrigation varies from location to location, season to season and the nature as well as the age of the landscape features involved. Young and tender plants located in prestigious amenity areas are likely to be the pirme candidates. By far the largest resource requirements are associated with the provision and installations of the irrigation equipment. Running costs are said to represent a comparatively small proportion of the costs. Table 3.1, provided by Cameron Irrigation, a Division of Wright Rain Limited, gives some indication of the comparative resource requirements for the main landscape features most likely to require the installation of an irrigation system.

Table 3.1   The irrigation of prestigious landscape features: estimated resource requirements

Landscape feature and dimensions	Type of irrigation system	Approximate installation costs per m^2 or per unit	Maximum likely water need	Water supply requirement	Operating time man hours
Cricket square 27.50 m × 27.50 m	Portable sprinkler and hose; hydrants; water mains; pump/tank	3.00/m^2	17 m^3 per week	55 litres per minute (at 55 metre head at pump)	1 hour per week (5 hours watering time per week)
Cricket square 27.50 m × 27.50 m	Automatically controlled pop-up sprinkler system	6.00/m^2	17 m^3 per week	164 litres per minute (at 70 metre head at pump)	Nil (system operates for 15 minutes per night)
Bowling green 38.41 m × 38.41 m	Full/adjustable part circle, portable sprinkler and hose; hydrants; water mains: pump/tank	1.40/m^2	27 m^3 per week	55 litres per minute (at 50 metre head at pump)	2 hours per week (8.5 hours watering time per week)
Bowling green 38.41 m × 38.41 m	Automatically controlled pop-up sprinkler system	2.80/m^2	27 m^3 per week	164 litres per minute (at 65 metre head at pump)	Nil (system operates 24 minutes per night)
Mature trees 25 no in paved area at 10.00 m apart	Automatic, sub-surface drip system including a pump/tank	60.00/tree	180 litres per tree per week	10 litres per minute (at 21 metre head at pump)	Nil (system operates for 60 minutes per night)
Hanging baskets 25 no	Automatic drip (no pump/tank) required	3.00/basket (excludes supply of water to baskets)	7 litres per basket per week	2 litres per minute (at 21 metre head at baskets)	Nil (all baskets watered together for 15 minutes per night)
Shrubs 100 m^2	Micro sprays on stand pipes; no pump/tank manual control	0.30/m^2	2.5 m^3 per week	17 litres per minute (at 18 metre head)	1 hour per week (system operates for 20 minutes daily)
Shrubs 100 m^2	Automatic drip system	2.00/m^2	2.5 m^3 per week	27 litres per week (at 21 metre head)	Nil (system operates for 10 minutes per night)

Source: Cameron Irrigation – a division of Wright Rain Limited.

Further references to the need for irrigation are made in later sections of the book: principally those dealing with the cost-effective and the re-establishment of woody plants.

Particularly in the south and east of Britain Amenity Managers are likely to find that irrigation of both prestigious plantings and areas, where rapid establishment is desired, is cost-effective.

TEMPERATURE

Temperature is the most important factor influencing the choice of plant species. This applies particularly to the number and duration of periods when it falls below zero. Temperature is difficult to change significantly, although shelter, radiation from buildings, and so on, can create micro-climates which differ by many degrees from their surroundings.

In order to increase cost-effectiveness, therefore, the Amenity Manager should use plants which have a reasonable chance of success in their local climate. Replacement planting can be expensive and may be neglected in a busy organization to the detriment of the landscape. There is an enormous amount of knowledge readily available on the cultural requirements of plants suitable for landscape work (Clouston, 1977, 1989). Computer facilities and programs now exist which offer managers the opportunity to feed in their site conditions and requirements and which, in return, pro-duce a print-out of suitable plants.

OTHER CLIMATIC FACTORS

Factors such as salt winds and sunshine hours also affect the costs and benefits associated with providing and managing landscapes, chiefly through their effect on both the choice of species and the maintenance required.

Several lists (Royal Horticultural Society, 1969; Hilliers, 1988) of species adapted to a range of climatic factors and suitable for landscape use are published. These focus attention on what might be regarded as the 'Managers' friends' in that they are both attractive and grow successfully under a range of hostile conditions.

The use of species which thrive under local climatic conditions is likely to be most cost-effective, particularly where less prestigious landscapes are involved and where the expertise of staff is not very great. Plants which grow well and are healthy usually look better and are cheaper to maintain than seemingly more desirable but 'difficult' plants, which dislike the climatic conditions. For example, common species of willows or the native Buddleia have been used successfully on many urban reclamation sites to produce a mass of unpretentious greenery. More sophisticated shrubs such as laurel (*Prunus laurocerasus*) can be visually less pleasing, even though they are evergreen, because the harsh site conditions do not suit them.

There are situations in which an Amenity Manager may be both willing and required to experiment with plant species. This applies particularly in locations where climatic conditions are austere, e.g. reclamation sites, exposed coastlines or reservoir margins.

Extremes of weather undoubtedly put plant selection decisions to the test. The extent to which managers should 'play safe' in making their choice is an open question. Many plants which were considered to be totally hardy were cut to the ground by the winter of 1982/83: common cultivars of *Pyracantha* and *Cotoneaster*, *Ligustrum ovalifolium* and *Prunus laurocerasus*, for example. Inevitably this raised questions such as: should managers, like Water Engineers, design for the 1 in 100 year disaster? Should they restrict their palette exclusively to reliable plants or should they accept the possibility of occasional (say 1 in 20 year) damage to a proportion of their plants?

Most managers, who like plants, speculate with a few in order to see if they will succeed. Introductions of some unusual or expensive species into a standard landscape planting can help to maintain staff interest, increase their plant knowledge and give pleasure to landscape users. If such trials fail, the cost is usually relatively small. On the other hand by proving that they are successful under local conditions, a manager can then use them more widely with relative impunity.

EFFECTS OF CLIMATE ON MANPOWER

Rainfall and frost in particular restrict the operations which staff can carry out on site. Many direct works organizations do not ask their operatives to work out of doors in heavy rain or snow.

Hard winter frost and thick snow prevent planting from being carried out and snow makes difficult any work on or near the gound, such as path clearing or weed control. Jobs such as thinning and pruning are valuable because they can be carried out during snowy and frosty weather. Frosty conditions may in fact allow access over normally wet ground without causing damage.

Soil should not be worked in wet weather. Unfortunately the pressure to carry out contracts or to meet expenditure targets encourages people to continue working in unsuitable ground conditions. This is a major cause of soil damage and of other effects, such as waterlogging and plant failure, which can cause the Amenity Manager a great deal of difficulty and expense.

Wind has a major influence on weed control, since it makes application of herbicide sprays difficult. Even light winds may render the spraying of contact herbicides in planted areas too dangerous to risk. On very windy sites it may be impossible to spray chemicals, such as glyphosphate, near to plants. Consequently, other forms of treatment, using for example rope or wick applicators, may be necessary. Chemicals such as simazine, propyzamide and fluazifop butyl are valuable, partly because they can be sprayed in windy weather over crop plants without fear of damage.

3.3
Topography, relief, altitude and aspect

There is a close relationship between these physical factors and climate. These factors therefore tend to influence landscape management costs significantly.

EFFECTS ON MICROCLIMATE

Topography, altitude and aspect affect site conditions mainly through the influence they have on local climate. Quite different microclimates can be caused by shading on north slopes, by frost pockets, by local wind patterns and so on. If these effects cannot be ameliorated, landscape design and plant selections need to allow for their influence.

In creating new landscapes use is often made of mounding and ground modelling to create interesting land forms, shelter, noise attenuation zones and so on. This seems to be a growing trend. It is therefore important that the management implications of landforms are understood by those who create them.

Effects on other management costs

Slopes have a considerable effect on several aspects of amenity management. They restrict the type of machinery which can be used and may make it impossible to use large-scale cost-effective machinery. Tractors, for example, cannot work safely on slopes greater than 1 in 4 (14 deg).

All operations, whether on foot or using machinery, are made more difficult, tiring and potentially dangerous by steep slopes. The task of carrying a 4 gallon knapsack sprayer through plantings on a slippery 1 in 4 slope all day is hardly one to be relished. Both designers and administrators need to consider carefully the maintenance requirements of the landscape components which are used on slopes and more particularly how they will affect the staff who will be doing the work.

Steep slopes, both natural and man-made, suffer more from erosion and wear than gentler land forms. This results from the extra force which feet or wheels exert on sloping ground, and from the effects of rainfall. It may be difficult to establish vegetation, particularly from seed, on steep slopes because of weathering problems. Special techniques such as hydroseeding may be needed.

Some of the most attractive natural and semi-natural landscapes are in hilly or steeply sloping areas. In upland areas intensive use by visitors, coupled with heavy rainfall, often leads to erosion. This is one of the most serious problems confronting Amenity Managers in such areas.

3.4
Ground conditions

Of the three site variables, the condition of the ground is probably the one most readily amenable to change. This section provides a short review of both the substrates available and their respective properties.

SUBSTRATES

The substrate or growing medium used to establish and sustain both vegetation and public use on a site is of fundamental importance. It will usually have a long lasting influence upon the landscape or amenities provided. If not immutable, it will almost certainly be expensive to alter in any significant manner. The substrate may consist of a natural soil profile with or without the top soil. Alternatively it may be formed from imported or foreign materials, such as building rubble and industrial spoil.

There is often scope either for choosing an appropriate type of substrate from a range of materials available locally or for using those which may be present on site in imaginative and relatively low-cost ways to suit management objectives.

In many cases, substrates determine the type of vegetation which can be made to grow on them: species-rich herbaceous swards, for example, will succeed only on nutrient-poor substrates, such as chalk. Substrates also have a profound effect on user carrying capacity and resistance to wear.

Mismanagement of substrates – particularly during initial groundworks – can have a lasting effect upon the landscapes from which they are derived. This is one of the commonest causes of poor plant performance in 'built' landscapes.

The movement towards 'no-topsoil' techniques is now well established (Bradshaw, 1987); and the vegetation which can be successfully established and sustained on quite poor and difficult substrates through appropriate management is well documented by those who have been involved in the design and management of, for example, Warrington New Town landscapes (Ruff and Tregay, 1982).

It is therefore clear that an unbiased and opportunistic attitude towards substrate use and management can reap worthwhile benefits and make a profound impact on cost-effectiveness.

Some general points relating to cost-effective use of substrates are given in the sections which follow.

Inevitably the attention of many Amenity Managers is increasingly drawn towards the use of low fertility substrates. This is currently one of the areas where new technology and research offer exciting prospects, especially regarding the achievement of cost-effective results. However, it is important to retain a sense of balance. For thousands of years the prestigious components of amenity landscapes have depended upon the use of deep soils, treated regularly with ample supplies of organic matter. Important as the results undoubtedly are of new research into alternative substrates for use on hostile sites, the properties and values of the conventional growing medium should continue to command priority attention.

THE KEY PROPERTIES

Good structure and drainage are two of the most important characteristics which most substrates are expected to possess. Coarse textured substrates, such as sands, grits and gravel-based soils, are more resistant to compression and compaction than finer substrates containing high proportions of clay, silt or small particle organic matter. They therefore tend to retain their structure and drainage properties better under the wear of feet, hooves and wheels, thereby usually remaining usable or 'sightly' for longer under wet conditions. Soils developed over permeable or porous rocks, such as limestones or chalks, are also usually well drained.

A combination of coarse texture and good drainage characteristics usually results in nutrient losses through leaching. Such substrates therefore tend to be nutrient poor. They thus support some of the most attractive areas of natural and semi-natural vegetation in the country. It is noteworthy that, even in urban and urban fringe locations, many semi-natural areas have withstood intense public recreational pressure and have retained an attractive character under fairly minimal management up to the present day. Hampstead Heath and Blackheath (London) on sands and the Clifton Downs (Bristol) on limestone are examples of such areas.

Many substrates resulting from industrial activities such as colliery spoils and slate wastes are also coarse textured and, often, extremely poor in nutrients. In cities, building rubble is free draining, but usually contains significant quantities of all the macro-nutrients except nitrogen (Dutton and Bradshaw, 1982). Extremely coarse textured substrates do pose re-vegetation problems as their reclamation has shown. This is largely due to the poor retention of moisture and nutrients. However, less extreme spoils may in many ways be easier to reclaim, manage or use in modern land-scapes than topsoils. They are more conducive to the growth of unpro-ductive (low biomass) and hence low maintenance forms of vegetation than richer soils.

Also, they often withstand certain forms of wear better than finer soils. For many purposes they are worth using as growing media in their own right. Some amelioration of these substrates will probably be necessary, involving the additions of both bulky organic materials and inorganic fertilizers. However, this is usually far cheaper than covering the site with top soil.

Because of their free-draining characteristics, coarse textured substrates are also invaluable in both establishing and improving areas of sports turf. High quality professional and non-professional sports facilities are now usually constructed on a substrate consisting largely of coarse inorganic media (sands and gravels). The more intensively used or demanding areas of ordinary club or school facilities, such as golf greens, cricket squares and bowling greens, are also normally constructed in this way. Sand is now used extensively to improve the drainage of pitches suffering from com-paction. Application is by top dressing or by incorporation into the top surface through various forms of sand slitting or by slit drainage (Hunt and Rorison, 1980; Stewart, 1980).

In contrast, finer textured soils may be much harder to manage in amenity areas than coarse ones. Although better able to retain moisture and nutrients, they tend to deteriorate more easily under wear, especially in wet weather, and to become muddy, smeared and compacted. This is a major problem on heavily used sports turf areas.

The problems resulting from wear and bad drainage are well known (Natural Environment Research Council, 1977) to be among the most pressing of Amenity Managers. Mishandling of fine soils – typically clay subsoils – is also a major cause of plant failure, particularly in the case of woody plants on new landscape sites. Fine textured substrates are there-fore liable to need more careful management than those which are freely drained. Heavily used 'walked-upon' and 'played-upon' grass may need intensive remedial action to correct surface smear, compaction and destruction of free drainage. Typical remedial action includes harrowing, surface spiking, control of thatch, renovation of worn areas, sand slitting, grading to encourage run-off of surface water and the improvement or installation of sub-surface drainage systems.

There is also usually some scope for changing patterns of wear, since these are typically concentrated in certain areas, such as goal mouths and cricket wickets, and along desired lines. For example, the position of sports pitches on a field can be changed; wickets are normally moved across cricket squares and users can often be re-routed by various means, such as duckboards at Hidcote and nylon string at Danebury Hill Fort and Tarn Howes.

There are limits, however, to the extent that such actions can be cost-effective. At such points other measures may have to be taken, such as either restricting user numbers or changing the vulnerable landscape element to one which is more resistant, for example polypropylene mesh netting.

The previous paragraphs make some reference to the benefits of good drainage, as well as to the difficulties associated with poor drainage. However, in some situations it is possible to 'live with' bad drainage, to exploit it positively and even to create it deliberately. Some of Britain's vanishing wetlands are re-appearing unintentionally in many new landscapes. Such areas are being used in creative ways by some enterprising designers and managers.

Wetland habitats can add greatly to the interest and value of many informal recreation and landscape areas. They should not, however, be taken for granted. Like any other amenity features, they need to be incorporated into the user and maintenance requirements of the overall site. For example, if an area of moist grassland is to be managed for hay then the need for access and operation of the relevant agricultural machinery must be accommodated. 'Tidy-up' cuts of smaller areas may need to be carefully timed in relation to the restricted periods of the year when the ground is dry enough for machinery.

GROUND WORKS

Before presenting the guidelines for various landscape components it is essential that readers should have access to data on the resources required for typical ground preparation, periodic maintenance and renovation operations. Such operations are involved at some stage in maintaining most of the landscape components covered in later chapters. The standard man values provided in the tables which accompany those chapters do not include the times required for any of the ground works operations. Because of their almost universal application, it is considered that this introduction would not be complete without presenting readers with data on the typical manpower requirements involved. The data compiled for this purpose are displayed in Tables 3.2 and 3.3

Table 3.2 Ground preparation and cultivation: estimated resource requirements

Source	Operation	SMV	Unit
Sh	Clearing site of rubbish before cultivating	58.68–117.37	100 m^2
W	Rotavating ground with tractor-mounted rotavator	4.28	100 m^2
D	Rotavating ground with tractor-mounted rotavator	5.50	100 m^2
D	Cultivate ground with tractor-mounted Pirminter cultivator	4.00	100 m^2
H	Ploughing unrestricted area	3.17	100 m^2
H	Ploughing unrestricted area	5.90	100 m^2
W	Ploughing with 2 furrow reversible	4.32	100 m^2
W	Rotavate: Howard Gem	6.30	100 m^2
Sh	Rotavate: Howard Gem normal ground	15.00	100 m^2
Sh	Rotavate: Howard Gem high ground	18.00	100 m^2
D	Cultivate ground using pedestrian controlled 20″ machine	25.00	100 m^2
D	Ploughing open ground using Graveley tractor	12.00	100 m^2
H	Discing unrestricted area	0.66	100 m^2
H	Discing restricted area	1.30	100 m^2
Sa	Excavating by hand	80.00	1 m^3
D	Picking up soil using tractor bucket and taking to heap	3.00	100 m^2
D	Levelling topsoil from heaps using tractor and levelling bar or rear blade	1.50 or 30.00	tonne or 100 m^2
D	Levelling area with levelling bar, tractor mounted	7.00	100 m^2
Sh	Spreading soil from heaps and distributing on site	239.52–670.65	100 m^2
D	Chain harrowing ground	2.10	100 m^2
Sh	Rough rake into piles for collection	59.88	100 m^2
Sh	Grub out vegetation with mattock on spade	299.40	100 m^2
L	Dig over soil using spade/fork	377.00	100 m^2
Sh	Dig ground one full spit deep	371.26	100 m^2
Sh	Spread manure on beds	233.53	100 m^2
Sh	Dig in manure one spit deep	479.00	100 m^2
L	Dig over soil areas including incorporation of manure	606.00	100 m^2
W	Fork shrub beds, densely planted	366.00	100 m^2
FC	Ploughing rate proportional to length of furrow, bogging risk, slope, surface, roughness	2.60 6.70	100 m^2
FC	Digging drains: Whilock 110 Backactor on Bowen 60 Tractor in clay or peat soils	150.00 200.00	100 m^2

See Table 2.2 on p. 37 for details of sources.

Table 3.3   Drainage operations: estimated resource requirements

Source	Operation	SMV	Unit
a) *Construction*			
Sh	Excavate trench using Davis Task Force 200	59.88	100 m
Sh	Excavate trench by hand to 76 cm	106.00	1 m³
H	Dig trench manually variable soil conditions	56.5–109.5	1 m³
H	Remove spoil from trench bottom 7.5 cm–23 cm	200–260	100 m
H	Layout pipes along top of trench	16– 31	100 pipes
Sh	Lay 10 cm – 15.25 cm pipes	2.70	pipe
H	Lay pipes	0.31	pipe
Sh	Cut 10 cm – 15.25 cm pipes	18.80	junction
	Lay Lamflex	50.30	100 m
H	Backfill trench – soil	150.69	10 m²
	– ash	96.88	10 m²
	– limestone, chippings hardcore	102.26	100 m²

b) *Deepening*
Time in minutes per metre deepened

Soil type	Depth removed (cm)										
	5	7.5	10	12.5	15	17.5	20	22.5	25	27.5	30
i) Peat Peat and silt or silt	1.5	1.7	1.9	2.1	2.3	2.5	2.7	3.0	3.2	3.4	3.6
ii) Clay with few stones	1.9	2.2	2.5	2.8	3.0	3.3	3.6	3.9	4.1	4.4	4.7
iii) Clay mixed with stones	2.4	2.7	3.1	3.4	3.8	4.1	4.5	4.8	5.2	5.5	5.8
iv) Hard packed clay with many stones and shale	2.9	3.3	3.7	4.1	4.5	5.0	5.4	5.8	6.3	6.7	7.1

The peat and silt table (i) may be extended (at 2.0 minutes per metre for extra 2.5 cm of depth) to a maximum of 60 cm depth removed.

c) *Widening*
Time in minutes per metre

Width increase at top of drain (cm)	Up to 15 cm	15 to 30 cm	30 to 45 cm	45 to 60 cm
Minutes per metre	1.8	2.0	2.2	2.3

cont'd

Table 3.3 (cont'd)

d) *Ditch maintenance*		SMV	Unit
Sa	Clear out silt from bottom of ditch using shovel and dispose to bank	223	100 m
Sa	Cut and clear grass and weeds from side of ditch using hook/scythe and dispose of cuttings	113	100 m^2
H	Remove 25 cm of spoil from ditch bottom and trim sides	650	100 m

See Table 2.2 on p. 37 for details of sources.

COMMENT

It is primarily because of the physical (climatic, topographic and edaphic) factors described in this chapter that average or general guidelines on the resource requirements for each landscape element cannot be provided for universal application. The guidelines presented in Parts 2–5 inclusive should therefore be regarded as no more than indicators and should be used with appropriate care.

References   Bradshaw, A.D. (1987) Turf establishment on hostile sites. In *The Scientific Management of Vegetation in the Urban Environment.* (eds P.R. Thoday and D.W. Robinson) Acta Horticulturae, 195.

Clouston, J.B. (ed.) (1977, 1989) *Landscape Design with Plants*, 1st and 2nd edns, Heinemann, London.

Dutton, R.A. and Bradshaw, A.D. (1982) *Land Reclamation in Cities*, H.M.S.O, London.

Green, F.H.W. (1964) A map of annual average potential water deficit in the British Isles, *Journal of Applied Ecology*, **1**, 151–8.

Hilliers (1988) *Manual of Trees and Shrubs*, David and Charles, Devon.

Hunt, R. and Rorison, I.H. (1980) (eds) *Amenity Grassland – an Ecological Perspective*, John Wiley and Sons, Chichester.

Insley, H. (1986) Causes and Prevention of Establishment Failure in Amenity Trees. In *Ecology and Design in Landscape* (eds. A.D. Bradshaw, D.A. Goode, and E. Thorp) The 24th Symposium of the British Ecological Society, Blackwells, Oxford.

Natural Environment Research Council (1977) *Amentity Grasslands – the Needs for Research*, NERC Publications Series C, No 19, Swindon.

Nix, J.S. (1987) *Farm Management Pocketbook*, 17th edn. Farm Business Unit, School of Rural Economics, Wye College, University of London.

Royal Horticultural Society (RHS) (1969) *Dictionary of Garden Plants*

Ruff, A. and Tregay, R. (eds) (1982) *An Ecological Approach to Urban Landscape Design*. Occasional Paper No. 8., Department of Town and Country Planning, University of Manchester.

Smith, K. (1975) *Principles of Applied Climatology*, MacGraw-Hill (UK) Ltd.

Stewart, V.I. (1980) Soil Drainage and Soil Moisture In: *Amenity Grassland – an Ecological Perspective*. (eds R. Hunt and I.H. Rorison), John Wiley and Sons, Chichester.

Further reading   CLIMATE FACTORS

Blake, P. (1979) Plants for exposed gardens, *The Garden, Journal of The Royal Horticultural Society*, **104**, (4), 141–6.

Burrage, S.W. (1976) The microclimate of the garden, *The Garden, Journal of The Royal Horticultural Society*, **101**, (2), 91–5.

Caborn, J.M. (1965). *Shelter belts and wind breaks*. Faber and Faber, London.

Harding, R.J. (1979) Radiation in The British Uplands, *Journal of Applied Ecology*, **16**, 161–70.

Haworth Booth, M. (1962) *Effective Flowering Shrubs*. Collins, London.

MAFF (1900) *Agricultural Climate of England and Wales*. Technical Bulletin No. 35, H.M.S.O.

Searle, S.A. and Smith, L. (1958) *Weather-wise Gardening*, Blandford, Poole.

Wright, T.W.J. (1976) Microclimate and plant selection, *The Garden, Journal of The Royal Horticultural Society*, **101**, (7), 234–41.

GROUND CONDITIONS *

Taylor, J. (1980) A garden on mine waste, *The Garden, Journal of The Royal Horticultural Society*, **105**, (8), 307–10.

* Further references are given in Parts 2, 3 and 4.

Part Two

The Management of Amenity Grasslands

This part covers what is often the most extensive and costly component of amenity landscapes. Both nationally and internationally, the management of amenity grasslands accounts for a significant proportion of the total expenditure incurred in servicing public leisure and recreation facilities.

The first chapter, Chapter 4, identifies the four main categories of amenity grasslands, based on widely different uses. These range from highly manicured golf greens and lawns on the one hand to dunes and moorlands on the other. Both management motivations and public perceptions are reviewed as a basis for determining maintenance standards. The scope for changing both these standards, and indeed the roles of amenity grasslands, are examined. The cost implications and the main interacting factors determining the choice of management method are outlined.

Chapter 5 collates information on all of the various factors, such as climate, site characteristics and soils, layout, levels of wear, diseases and weeds, which influence the cost-effectiveness of different types of management.

Chapters 6, 7 and 8 describe the management of the main types of grassland. These respectively are: sports turf and other sports surfaces; low wear – low maintenance grasslands of, for example, motorways, rural parks, derelict areas and steep slopes; and semi-natural grasslands, which include moorlands and heathlands, chalk grasslands and sand-dunes.

The final chapter in this part provides management guidelines for what are termed problem, special and general areas. They include worn and over-used areas, obstacles, steep banks and areas of naturalized bulbs. Inevitably the importance of grassland species selection receives considerable attention in the section devoted to repair and restoration.

4

AMENITY GRASSLANDS:
GENERAL INTRODUCTION

**4.1
Introduction**

Amenity grassland was defined by the NERC Amenity Grasslands Committee of 1977 as 'all grass with recreational, functional or aesthetic value, and of which agricultural productivity is not the primary aim' (NERC, 1977). The Committee estimated that there were some 8500 km^2 of amenity grassland in the United Kingdom at that time, and subsequent estimates give even larger figures (Bunce, *et al*. Pers. Comm., 1986). These are displayed in Table 4.1.

Amenity grassland, including domestic lawns, represents about 4% of Britain's total area. It was calculated in 1973 that approximately £140 million of public and private money is spent on this resource each year. This approximates to £602 million in 1987.

'Amenity grassland' as defined by NERC is a rather loose term, since it includes not only 'all-grass' swards, but many forms of 'grassland' which contain few or no grass species: heather moorland for example. However, the term 'grassland' is used in this chapter to cover all those forms of low vegetation commonly called 'grass', 'turf', 'sward', 'heath', 'moor', etc.,' but with the reminder that the majority of grasslands contain many non-grass species of plant.

CHARACTERISTICS

Repeated management or wear of the above-ground parts of any vegetation – whether by mowing, grazing, burning, walking, wind or other agencies – usually results in a low carpet of plant species which are adapted to that type of treatment. In Britain plants which can tolerate this type of 'orderly disturbance' (Grime, 1979, 1986) are mainly non-woody, and include grasses and other monocotyledons, many species of broad-leaved plants, and mosses.

Some grasslands are created and maintained deliberately for amenity use. Most of the remainder are by-products of other land uses, of which agriculture is by far the most important.

Grassland also occurs in areas where the vegetation is largely unaffected by the activities of man, but is kept relatively short by natural factors such as wind, low temperatures, rabbit grazing, burning, etc.

Natural grasslands grade into other forms of vegetation such as low scrub from which they often cannot be clearly distinguished. However, from landscape design and user standpoints, the essential feature of grasslands is that they are *open*, and can be walked across or looked across with relative freedom.

Table 4.1 classifies amenity grasslands according to their main uses and types of ownership. Typical costs of maintenance per unit area are given, which reflect the intensity of management usually required.

Another useful classification is the one used in Table 4.2 which categorizes grasslands according to their main use or wear, and their average mowing height. The use and wear categories are similar to the 'untrampled open space,' and 'intensively managed' classes used by the NERC Committee.

GRASSLAND MANAGEMENT: IMPLICATIONS

Approximately 32% of amenity grassland in Britain is of the 'fine' and 'medium' class. It is well known, and has recently been reconfirmed by research results presented in Table 4.3, that the largest input required to maintain this type of grassland is cutting. For this reason managers regard fine-medium turf as a particularly important landscape component. In fact, manning levels in many maintenance organizations are dominated by the summer 'bulge' of labour needed to keep turf cut in the growing season. Because of the large total area of this class of grassland, and the associated expenditure, it is worth looking at management carefully in the light of user needs and expectations.

Table 4.1   Categories of amenity grassland – land ownership and relative management costs

Primary land use	Ownership[1]	Approximate size[2] Ha	Index of relative management costs per unit area[3]
Recreational		50,000	100 (L)
Sports grounds	Pu & Pr	1,700	87 (L)
Golf Courses	Pu & Pr		
Bowling Greens	Pu & Pr	4,500	2,895 (L)
Race Tracks	Pr	170	163 (L)
Lawns	Pr	12,860,800	107 (L)
Park Grassland:			
Urban	Pu	132,000	100 (L)

Table 4.1 (cont'd)

Primary land use	Ownership[1]	Approximate size[2] Ha	Index of relative management costs per unit area[3]
Country	Pu	6,000	2 (L)
National	Pr	N/A	(0)
Commons	Pu & Pr	32,000	(2–25)
National Trust, grounds and estates open to the public	Pr	92,200	(25–100)
Caravan, camp sites	Pu & Pr	5,824	4 (L)
Conservation			
Nature reserves, AONBs & SSSIs	Pu & Pr	63,000	0.1 (L)
Archaeological/ Historical sites	Pu & Pr	647	(2–25)
Chalk grassland	Pu & Pr	N/A	
Moors, heaths	Pu & Pr	N/A	(0.1–4)
Dunes, sea marshes	Pu & Pr	119–263	
Functional			
Road verges –			
Urban	Pu	25,000	125 (L)
Rural	Pu	101,000	24 (L)
Military training areas	Pu	N/A	24 (L)
Airfields	Pu & Pr	11,000	13 (L)
Undeveloped & 'by-product'			
– Buffer land	Pu & Pr	N/A	(0.1–100)
– Waterway, railway banks	Pu	25,000	5–40 (L)
– Pipe lines etc.	Pu & Pr	N/A	(0.1–100)
– Derelict, despoiled land	Pu & Pr	45,000[4]	–

Key

[1] Pu = Public
  Pr = Private
  NB The general public may have access to some private land
[2] = Estimates from Liddle/NERC, BCPC, DOE
[3] Calculated on the basis of urban grassland as 100% (1975 figures)
(L) = Liddle/NERC
[4] = Much of this derelict land has no vegetation.

Table 4.2   Amenity grassland types classified by management and height of cut

Category	Use	Average Height (cm)
Fine 'look-on'	– Prestigious 'Keep off the grass', e.g. college quads	1–2
	– As foil for other landscape elements in formal areas, public and private	1–3
Fine 'walk-on'	– Some private lawns	1–3
	– Grazed downland	0.5–5
Fine 'play-on'	– Bowling greens	0.5–1
	– Golf greens, cricket squares	0.5–1.5
	– Lawn tennis, croquet lawns	1–1.5
Medium	– Mown urban road verges	2–5
Medium 'walk-on'	– Most park and open space grassland	2–5
	– Urban (mainly gang mown)	2–5
	– Rural (may be grazed or mown	25+
	– Bridle tracks, footpaths	25
Medium 'play-on'	– Formal sports turf	1.5–5
	– Golf fairways	15–25
	– Race courses	
	– Sports out-fields	5–10
	– Informal 'kickabout' turf	5–10
Rough 'look-on'	– Road and motorway verges	10+
	– Rail and waterway banks	10+
	– Some nature reserves, etc. e.g. protected dunes, ancient hay meadows	
'Look-on'	– Some industrial and commercial landscaping	15–50
	– Airfields	15–50
Rough 'walk-on'	– Much extensively managed countryside, e.g. National Park rough grassland, moorland and heaths	2+
Rough	–Scrambling courses	10+

Note: Taking 8500 Km² as total area of amenity grassland.

Table 4.3 Average expenditure on amenity grassland management: relative importance of the main maintenance operations

Operation	Percentage of total costs
Mowing (including machinery costs)	59
Fertilizing (including material)	14
Weed control	5
Spiking (solid and hollow tine)	3
Rolling	2
Mole drainage	2
Disease control	2
Over-seeding (not including seed)	1
Top dressing (sand or compost)	1
Scarification and harrowing	1
Pest control	< 1
Growth retardants	< 1
Percentage of total costs not accounted for	10
	100

Note: Total costs include the costs of maintaining domestic lawns. Adapted from NERC.

Useful questions to ask are:

- For whom is this grass provided?
- Do they use it and, if so, how?
- Does the use justify the management and maintenance costs?
- Could it be maintained differently, or more cheaply?
- Would it be better to replace it with another type of landscape element?
- What are the implications of changing its management?

Some of these questions are discussed in the pages which follow.

4.2
How should grassland look – traditional attitudes

It is often assumed, particularly in urban situations, that grass should be green, short and consist exclusively of grass species.

Much grassland husbandry is therefore geared to producing vigorous mown grass 'monocultures', although strictly speaking there may be made up to half a dozen grass varieties. This is partly due to the traditional aesthetic vision of an 'ideal garden'. Monocultures in themselves have a certain unique attractiveness, particularly when the effect desired is one of orderliness.

Those responsible for maintaining areas of specialist sports turf are often obliged to produce turf that behaves in a predictable way, is level, largely free from weeds and regularly mown. This in turn must have contributed towards the public's perception of the necessity for, and desirability of, a close mown grass monoculture in municipal parks and gardens.

THE 'IDEAL' PRIVATE LAWN

Tradition, garden literature and product sales pressure encourage private gardeners to grow lawns which are visually uniform, green and short. Intensive husbandry, which includes eradication of species which are not grass or are the wrong sort of grass (e.g. daisies, plantain, annual meadow grass), fertilizer use, aeration, irrigation and frequent mowing to control the strong growth produced, is needed to achieve this. The resulting 'striped green velvet' is often treated as an ideal to be achieved whenever possible; indeed in public as well as private spaces.

THE 'IDEAL' SPORTS TURF

'Play-on' grass needs to provide a uniform playing surface and, in most cases, to be hard wearing as well. Broadleaves, mosses and certain grasses can disturb the uniformity of precision surfaces, may not stand up to the hard wear of players or the rigours of management (e.g. on cricket squares), can be slippery and dangerous, and may compete with the desirable grass species. The management of sports turf therefore involves a specialized type of husbandry designed to provide users with the kind of surface they want, and to maintain that surface under the stress of wear and tear. It usually requires intensive management which can greatly exceed that necessary to maintain less demanding types of grassland. This difference is highlighted in Table 4.1: for example, compare the cost per ha of maintaining bowling greens and rural road verges. However, Table 4.1 also shows that private lawns and sports areas make up a very significant proportion of the total area of amenity grassland. This, together with their popularity as areas of high use, may explain why their appearance tends to be taken as the standard for other areas. Nevertheless, there are no intrinsic reasons why grasslands should be all grass, all green, all the year round, or always short. Decisions on the type of amenity grass which a manager produces should therefore try to take into account both user needs as well as requirements and the management resources which are available; in short, expense should be related to consumer satisfaction. For example, it is well known that the 'ideal green velvet carpet' is:

- Relatively expensive to create and maintain per unit area compared to most other landscape elements; and
- Very much enjoyed by most members of the public.

This combination of high cost and high user enjoyment suggests that fine turf is worth having. However, we are no longer a rich country. Both public and private budgets are under attack. For this reason 'green velvet', though still very popular, is usually only found in restricted or prestigious areas. For example, in combination with carpet bedding, it is now often found on urban centre roundabouts where it is protected from wear and is the focus of many eyes.

There are some situations, such as rural and natural plantings, where a short mown monoculture is as inappropriate as a diverse sward community would be on a bowling green.

4.3
Could grassland be
managed differently?

Due to the abundance of fine and medium grass and the large inputs required to keep it short, Amenity Managers tend to look at this type of grassland first when trying either to make savings, or to increase cost-effectiveness.

THE SCOPE FOR CHANGE

Of course, many areas of grassland do need to be kept fairly short in order to fulfil their functions. These include 'play-on' areas, some parts of 'walk-on' areas, and other sites such as airfields and training grounds. However, much grassland is over-maintained in the sense that the cost of keeping it short does not seem to be repaid by benefits to users. The so-called 'green deserts' in many cities, such as Liverpool, Manchester, London and Bath, are of this nature. So are those 'looked-on' swards like rural road verges which are maintained to higher standards than those needed for functional or safety reasons.

However, where function does not dictate that the grass should be short, is there scope for changing management, and what are the implications of making changes?

A number of options are available for managing these grasslands more cost effectively. However, it needs to be borne in mind that savings are usually accompanied by a range of consequential effects. Changing short sward management probably offers the greatest scope for achieving savings in costs. Nonetheless, in these situations public attitudes cannot be over-looked. These, together with cutting methods, redesign and surface substitutions, are the main factors which strongly influence the degree to which change can be effected. A brief review of each of these factors follows.

PUBLIC PERCEPTIONS AND ATTITUDES

Public pressure to maintain certain levels of grass maintenance is very strong in Britain. On the whole the British public appreciates short, well-mown grass, particularly in urban areas. Like private lawns, these have many virtues, including their tidy appearance and their ability to provide a pleasant visual spectacle as a foil for other features such as paving, bedding, etc.

If the Amenity Manager wants to relax levels in towns by, for example, introducing 'differential mowing' or using rural methods by, say, allowing roadside vegetation to grow, cutting it infrequently with a flail and leaving the cuttings to lie, then considerable public resistance will probably be experienced (Parker, 1986). It is important to realize, however, that this does not apply everywhere. Close neighbours of the British, such as the

Dutch and Germans, appreciate and positively lobby for informal vegetation, especially close to buildings. We in Britain tend to have a much lower tolerance towards untidy vegetation than do the people of many other nations. Ironically this is in sharp contrast to public attitudes towards litter, which tend to be more lax in Britain.

The issue of tidiness was summed up by John Parker of Kent County Council when he wrote 'The Englishman takes a great deal of pride in mowing his lawns and this sense of pleasure is reflected by the professional gardener and groundsman. The scent of new mown grass and the sense of achievement in ordering the natural is obviously important, but as a result there is a danger that a good deal of mowing is done for the satisfaction of the gardener (Parker, 1982).

In some urban parks a zoned mowing regime has been successfully introduced. Areas of long grass are provided with closely mown boundaries, paths and clearings to improve access and use. These also help to provide the impression that there has not been a drop in standards, but rather just a more flexible approach to grass maintenance.

Other factors also militate against the success of 'rural' maintenance levels in towns. First, traditional soft landscapes have nearly all been established using topsoil. Consequently urban vegetation is usually growing in comparatively fertile conditions. If the grass on these soils is left uncut, it usually produces a vigorous stand of coarse growth and 'weeds'. Some of the latter are legally notifiable (dock, creeping thistle, ragwort) and most are unsightly.

Secondly, where urban sites have been reclaimed or re-vegetated without the use of top-soil, the seed mixes used are often inappropriate. They frequently contain much ryegrass which tends to look unattractive if it is left uncut.

Finally, the level of civic pride amongst some of the British population tends to be lower than in many other parts of Europe. Consequently long grass tends to become contaminated by litter, fly-tipping and so on. Whilst litter is dispersed by frequent mowing and hidden by the fresh growth of grass, there is a tendency for debris to accumulate in unmown swards, unless special corrective measures are taken. In areas where public cleansing operations are already over-stretched or ineffective it may not only be expensive but impossible to cleanse areas of longer grass. The 'natural' herbaceous vegetation can then become extremely unsightly. The effect of reduced mowing may also therefore be to transfer costs from the grounds maintenance department to a cleansing department causing friction within the overall organization.

CUTTING METHODS

The interaction between mowing costs and standards is complex. A reduction in the frequency of mowing may not only affect the visual appearance of the sward but may actually create additional problems and prove more expensive.

Trials and operating statistics show that in cities the most cost-effective way of keeping grass short is by frequent cutting with fast machinery which disperses the cuttings, i.e. tractor-mounted cylinder gang mowers. All other methods of cutting grass, mechanically or manually, are more expensive per cut as shown in Table 4.4.

If the cutting frequency for actively growing grass is less than every 10–14 days – presuming the climate and site fertility are suitable for continued grass growth – or if the grass is allowed to grow longer than about 10 cm, then the sward outgrows the capacity of most cylinder mowers. As a result, other machines, such as rotary mowers or flails, have to be used. These are slower than cylinder mowers, and they tend not to disperse the cuttings so well, but – particularly if grass is wet – can leave them in swathes or rucks. At worst these can be thick enough to kill the sward beneath. At best they are unsightly, and mean that on the occasion of the next cut, machines have to cope with the undispersed debris. Appreciable amounts of cut debris may be more unacceptable than the long grass itself. Thus if managers want to be able to leave mowings where they fall, fairly frequent cuts may be necessary although some pedestrian-operated rotary mowers such as Victas disperse cuttings reasonably well.

While rotary and flail cutters can tackle longer grass than cylinder mowers and can therefore in theory be used on a longer mowing cycle, this advantage has to be balanced against speed of work (shorter grass is quicker to cut) and the appearance of the cut herbage (longer grass is more unsightly). These points are summarized in Table 4.5. In addition if it is necessary to remove cuttings for visual reasons or to make further cuts easier, this extra operation can be very time-consuming. Forage harvesters can be used to remove grass in some situations, but usually raking is the only practical method. Raking a given area of grass usually takes longer than cutting it with a pedestrian mower, and much longer than gang mowing it. The figures in Table 6 for raking and removing grass, when compared with those for hand mowing in Table 4.4, show that this is so.

The type of grassland which is quickest and cheapest to maintain is often the one with layout, drainage, gradients and levels which facilitate the use of large sets of tractor-drawn gang mowers. The appearance of the grass is a direct result of this.

Low maintenance management is therefore not as simple as just cutting grass less often. However, there are many alternative ways of decreasing the maintenance load of grassland. These include allowing the grass to be cropped for hay or silage; grazing; using growth retardants or re-sowing with low maintenance grasses and/or wild flowers or changing to another landscape element altogether, such as trees and/or shrubs. All these, with the possible exception of grazing, can be used in urban areas; and some have extra advantages since they may earn money and increase the ecological and educational value of the grass. However, they all need to be properly planned for and managed, and there are many situations in which conventional mown grass is found to be the most appropriate type of 'landscape' (Rorison, 1980).

Table 4.4 Comparison between the times needed for different methods of cutting grass

Type of Machine	Verges	Open areas	Banks	Long grass	Unit
12″ hand	14.0	11.0	24.0	N/A	100m^2
14″ m/c	N/A	7.0	N/A	N/A	100m^2
18″ m/c	10.0	6.0	N/A	27.5	100m^2
Flymo 19″/21″	8.0	5.5	31.0 Roped	N/A	100m^2
	N/A	N/A	16.0 No Rope	N/A	100m^2
20″ m/c	8.0	6.0	10.0	N/A	100m^2
22″ m/c	N/A	6.0	10.0	N/A	100m^2
24″ m/c	8.0	6.0	16.5 Roped	N/A	100m^2
	N/A	N/A	8.5 No Rope	N/A	100m^2
26″ m/c	5.0	N/A	4.0 No Rope	N/A	100m^2
28″ m/c	N/A	4.5	N/A	N/A	100m^2
30″ m/c	10.0	3.0	N/A	8.0	100m^2
34″ m/c	N/A	3.0	N/A	N/A	100m^2
36″ m/c	N/A	3.0	N/A	N/A	100m^2
60″ m/c	N/A	1.5	N/A	N/A	100m^2
Turner flail	0.06/m	7.0	N/A	7.0	100m^2
Bomford B6	N/A	2.5	N/A	N/A	100m^2
Lupat	N/A	4.0	6.0 No Rope	N/A	100m^2
3 set gang	2.0	1.0	N/A	N/A	100m^2
5/7 gang	0.6	0.3	N/A	N/A	100m^2
Triple	1.5	0.8	N/A	N/A	100m^2
Junior Triple	N/A	1.0	N/A	N/A	100m^2
Wheelhorse	N/A	3.5	N/A	N/A	100m^2
Allen Scythe	9.0	5.0	N/A	9.0	100m^2
Allen Triple	N/A	2.0	N/A	N/A	100m^2

Cut rough grass using Hayter

	Verges	Open areas	Banks	Long grass	Unit
Osprey	N/A	N/A	N/A	4.5	100m^2

Hand Tools[1]

Tool	Verges	Open areas	Banks		Unit
Hook	N/A	74.0	61.0		100m^2
Scythe	29	22.0	N/A		100m^2
Shears	N/A	N/A	98.0		100m^2

Source: Devon County Council.
N/A: Not Available/Not Applicable.
[1]: Clearing to piles not included.

Table 4.5 Relationship between type of mower, frequency of cut, costs and finish

Mower Type	A Cost incl. operator (A) £ per hour	B Cutting rates hrs/ha (B) Hrs per ha	C Cost per hour (C = A × B) (C) £ per hour	D Cuts per year (D) No.	E Total annual cost/Ha (E = C × D) (E) £ per ha	F Relative costs (Gang mowing = 100%) (F) Index	Quality of finish
3.5m 5 Unit Gangmower	10.00	0.7	7.0	24	168	100	Med–good
1.7m Triple Cylinder Mower	6.00	3.7	22.2	12	266	158	Med–good
500mm Cylinder mower	5.30	12.6	66.8	24	1,603	954	Med–good
500m Cylinder mower (Cuttings boxed off)	5.30	14.5	76.8	24	1,844	1,098	Med–good
500mm Rotary mower	5.30	17.9	94.9	6	569	339	Med–good
450mm 'Hover' Rotary (On banks)	5.30	47.5	251.7	4	1,007	599	Rough–med
2.1m Tractor rear mounted flail	7.50	3.8	28.5	2	57	34	Rough

Source: Adapted from J. Parker (1982) *Cost Effective Amenity Landscape Management*.

REDESIGN

Opportunities do exist through redesign of grass areas for long-term cost savings without any reduction in maintenance standards. Examples include a reduction in the need for ancillary tasks such as edging and the rationalization of grass into large areas without steep slopes that can be maintained by large machinery. However, to be successful, such schemes need an awareness by the Amenity Manager, and his superiors, of the value of capital investment in the redesign of an existing landscape. This appreciation is not always easy to find.

SUBSTITUTE LANDSCAPE ELEMENTS

Small, oddly-shaped, inaccessible areas of grass are often most successfully treated by replacing them with other vegetation or even hard surfacing materials, which have a lower annual maintenance cost.

Table 4.6 Grass management – ancillary operations

Source	Operation	SMV	Unit
W	Raking grass and removing	11.00	100m^2
Sh	Raking grass and removing	15.57	100m^2
Sh	Edge off half moon	83.83	100m
W	Edge off half moon	90.00	100m
K	Recut kerb	31.86	100m
K	Recut border	74.25	100m
K	Trim edges with long handled shears	27.55	100m
Sh	Trim edges with long handled shears	27.55	100m
W	Trim edges with long handled shears	52.00	100m
Sh	Dig drainage channel adjacent to grass area	323.35	100m
Sh	Weed drainage channel adjacent to grass area	125.75	100m

Note: The cost of most of these operations can be reduced by thoughtful design and management.
See Table 2.2 on p. 37 for details of sources.

Of course, there are many variables that have to be borne in mind when determining the relative costs of different landscape treatments.

The most important of these is probably whether the new landscape will still meet the design requirements of the site. Grass is the only vegetation treatment that will withstand regular trampling, or indeed can be used for sitting. Removing it may mean that consideration will have to be given to providing seats and paths, and the end result may still not be as popular with the users.

The decision between different treatments will also vary depending on whether the grass area is existing or merely planned. If it is planned, the relative costs of shrubs or other treatment can be partly offset against the costs of seeding or turfing. For existing areas the capital cost of the new treatment will have to be recouped entirely by the reduced maintenance input. Calculated example figures are given in Table 4.7.

The time it takes to recoup the initial investment is a fairly simple equation that can be calculated on the basis of capital cost, new maintenance costs and the annual savings compared to the existing system. Shrub and groundcover plantings often have a high maintenance requirement over the first three years until the planting forms a complete weed suppressing canopy. Several years of undisturbed use will then be necessary to recover the costs. If the site is temporary or likely to be disturbed, grass will prove to be the cheapest treatment even if the mowing is far from efficient.

Small grass areas that have been cost-effectively designed with no edging costs and are free of steep slopes will be fairly inexpensive to maintain, even if mown by a pedestrian machine. Other considerations include the

Table 4.7   Landscape elements: some total capital and maintenance 'substitution' costs

Surface	Relative index of capital cost per unit area	Relative index of annual maintenance cost per unit area	'Break-even' point* (years)
Small 'lawn'	1.00	0.25	Not applicable
Ground cover	2.00	0.05	5–7
Shrubs	2.80	0.06	8–11.25
Hoggin	4.00	0.03	12–14
Concrete	5.00	–	14–16
Tarpaving	7.00	–	
Various pavings	12–20	–	> 20
Cobbled concrete	30.00	–	
Gang mown grass	0.25	0.02	Not applicable

* This is the number of years taken to recoup the additional capital cost, through reduced maintenance, compared with a small lawn established from seed.

Adapted from: J. Parker (1982) *Cost Effective Amenity Landscape Management*, adjusted for changing prices.

presence of machinery on site: whether the grass area is on a route that is served by a pedestrian team: and whether it is relatively isolated.

Probably for many Amenity Managers the final decision is based on whether the appropriate capital finances and labour can be found to perform the planting or surfacing. This illustrates again that consultation between those responsible for maintenance and design operations is essential before any money is spent on a new site.

The foregoing review outlines four of the main interacting factors which affect the choice of management method. In the next chapter all the various factors concerning the management of different *types* of grassland are collated and discussed. This includes such factors as soil, site layout and user wear and the influence which they have upon the cost-effectiveness of grass management.

References   Grime, J.P. (1979) *Plant Strategies and Vegetation Processes*. John Wiley and Sons, Chichester.

Grime, J.P. (1986) Manipulation of plant species and communities. In *Ecology and Design in Landscape* (eds A.D. Bradshaw, D.A. Goode, and E. Thorp,). The 24th symposium of the British Ecological Society. Blackwells, Oxford.

NERC (Natural Environment Research Council) (1977) *Amenity Grasslands – The Needs for Research* NERC Publications Series C. No. 19. Swindon.

Parker J.C. (1982) Mown grass: techniques, costs and alternatives. In *Cost Effective Amenity Land Management*. (eds C. Addison and P.R. Thoday) University of Bath, Bath.

Parker, J.C. (1986) Low cost systems of management. In *Ecology and Design in Landscape*. (eds A.D. Bradshaw, D.A. Goode, and E. Thorp) The 24th Symposium of the British Ecological Society. Blackwells, Oxford.

Rorison I.H. (1980) The current challenge for research and development In: *Amenity Grassland – An Ecological Perspective*. (eds R. Hunt, and I.H. Rorison) John Wiley and Sons, Chichester.

Further reading

Gilbert, O.L. (1983) The Capability Brown lawn and its management. *Landscape Design* **146**, 8.

Hunt, R. and Rorison, I.H. (eds) (1980) *Amenity Grassland – An Ecological Perspective*. John Wiley and Sons, Chichester.

Large R.V. and Spedding C.R.W. (1976) Agricultural use of amenity grassland. In: *Amenity Grassland*, (ed Wright S.E.) Wye College, University of London.

Parker, J. (1984) *Quality Grass for General Landscape Functions*. NTC Workshop Report No. 4, Bingley.

Parker J.C. (1985) Just keep on mowing for 300 years. In *Fifty Years of Landscape Design*. (eds S. Harvey and S. Rettig) The Landscape Press.

Patmore J.A. (1970) *Land and Leisure*. David and Charles.

Sanecki K. (1979) *The Great British Lawn*. GC & HTJ, 7th Sept.

Thompson, J.R. (1986) Roadsides: a resource and a challenge. In: (eds A.D. Bradshaw, D.A. Goode, E. Thorp) *Ecology and Design in Landscape*. The 24th Symposium of the British Ecological Society. Blackwells, Oxford.

Way, J.M. (1974) The management of grass. *Municipal Engineering* **151** (36), 1639–1642.

Way, J.M. (1977) Roadside verges and conservation in Britain: a review. *Biological Conservation* **12**, 65–74

Wells T.C.E. (1980) Management options for lowland grassland. In: (eds R. Hunt, and I.H. Rorison,) *Amenity Grassland – An Ecological Perspective*. John Wiley and Sons, Chichester.

Wright, T.W.J. and Parker, J. (1979) Maintenance and Conservation. In: *Landscape Techniques*, (eds A.D. Weddle) Heinemann, London.

5 GRASSLAND MANAGEMENT: MANAGING FOR COST-EFFECTIVENESS

5.1 Introduction

This chapter covers the principles and factors influencing the cost-effective management of amenity grassland. Since mowing is the main operation (Parker, 1980), much of the initial part of the chapter is devoted to factors which influence mowing costs. Thereafter the other factors which control the growth and performance of grass are covered: pressure of use, weed and pest control, fertilizer application, irrigation and the use of growth retardants.

5.2 Site characteristics

The main characteristics which influence both the growth rates of grass and related maintenance requirements are reviewed in this section.

CLIMATE

The effects of local climate and microclimate upon the length of the growing season are particularly important in the management of mown grassland. These, more than any other physical factors, control the number of times a year that the grass will need to be cut. On the whole, the length of the growing season increases with temperature and rainfall and is therefore greatest in the maritime south-west of Britain and shortest in the north and at higher altitudes. Microclimate can be considerably affected by aspect, relief, shelter and other factors, such as proximity to buildings and water.

SUBSTRATE

Substrate has a very great influence on grassland performance and management. It is difficult to change the characteristics of soils in existing landscapes. However, it is often possible to choose appropriate substrates when constructing new areas of grass. In these cases the use for which the grass is intended should determine the choice of substrate. For example, 'look-on' grass, which is not required to sustain much wear and which does not need to be of very high quality, can be constructed on 'no topsoil' substrates. (Bradshaw, 1980; Dutton and Bradshaw, 1982). Many subsoils, urban rubbles and industrial spoils, for example, can be managed so that they produce vegetation which is both attractive and cheap to maintain.

It is simpler to make a poor substrate productive than it is to make a rich soil poor. The chemical and the physical condition of poor substrates can be improved without adding greatly to their nutrient status. For example, the use of peat to improve structure makes it possible with lime and slow release fertilizers to grow attractive grassland on many 'sterile' subsoils. Situations where successful establishment has taken place include Warrington New Town and Ferry Meadows, Peterborough.

Removing clippings may be a long-term method for reducing fertility, or at least preventing its build-up in some sensitive sites.

In some rural and natural areas it will be worthwhile to investigate the option of removing and stacking topsoil before the amenity land is to be seeded and planted. If appropriate, this will reduce fertility and hence maintenance costs. It should also reduce the population of weed seeds present on site. The topsoil can be sold or used as a valuable source in other landscape situations.

Before this practice is adopted an investigation of the nature of the subsoil will be necessary to determine whether it is physically suitable. Care must be taken not to degrade severely the structure of the subsoil by the passage of heavy machinery in wet weather or to reduce the fertility of the site to a level where it needs treatment in order to support growth of the desired plants. Of course any site which contains an established desirable floral community should not be disturbed in this way.

SEED MIXES

Advances in seed breeding over the last decade have created new low maintenance mixtures which grow more slowly and have a smaller and finer habit. These offer the opportunity for Amenity Managers to reduce maintenance costs by approximately a third without any change in the design of the site or the maintenance standards (Moffat, 1980).

TEXTURE AND DRAINAGE

Two types of grassland in particular are likely to be troublesome. First, many existing areas of grassland are now subjected to heavier uses and less maintenance than they were designed to tolerate. This applies particularly to sports facilities. Secondly, many areas of new landscape are designed and constructed poorly so that difficulties are bound to ensue. For example, provision for drainage is often inadequate and earth-moving operations frequently destroy any soil structure and natural drainage, which existed before construction. This can give rise to many management problems. For example, tractor-mounted machinery needs firm, well-drained ground if it is to operate without damage to grass. Even pedestrian-operated mowers will mark very soft ground. If an area of grass is to be designed for quick and easy maintenance, therefore, good drainage must be part of the design 'package'. This will mean that gang mowers can usually operate whenever necessary during the growing season.

Normally, ground dries out as the growing season progresses, and firmer conditions usually coincide with the mowing season. However, if grass areas lie wet late into the spring so that they remain unmown, then they may outgrow the capability of the gang mowers.

These examples show that it is often essential to provide adequate capital inputs, in order to create landscapes which are cheap to maintain. They illustrate the importance of giving full consideration to maintenance requirements at the design and construction stages of a landscape scheme.

Working on soft ground causes soil compaction and may produce other undesirable effects, such as the rutting of playing fields. Built landforms which help surface water to run off can aid natural good drainage considerably. For example, although sports pitches need to have an even surface, a fall of up to 1 in 40 is acceptable for play and can help to shed surface water.

SLOPES AND GRADIENTS

Tractor-mounted mowers cannot work safely on slopes steeper than about 1 in 5.

Most pedestrian-operated cylinder mowers, and some rotary machines, cannot be used on slopes greater than 1 in 4 in the interests of operator safety and other factors, such as maintaining oil circulation in some machines. Slopes steeper than 1 in 2 (27 degrees) are difficult and dangerous for a pedestrian operator to mow mechanically. They are also tiring unless the machine is self-propelled. Use of a hover mower (e.g. Flymo type) lowered on a rope is common, but it is slow and can be dangerous.

The times required to mow banks compared with flat areas are given in Table 5.1 and earlier in Table 4.5. The mowing times shown there demonstrate how time consuming it is to mow banks compared to more level areas of grass.

LEVELS

Uneven, bumpy, rough or stony ground will damage cylinder mowers. Good quality ground preparation before seeding is therefore essential if a site is to be maintained to more than rough cut standard. Repeated disturbances of mown grassland by events such as building developments or statutory undertakers' repairs may result in areas that are too rough to be gang mown, and therefore need to be cut by slower, more expensive machines such as rotary or flail mowers. The cost implications of reduced

Table 5.1   Economies of scale: relationship between types of mower, size of grass unit and labour requirements

Mower and landscape category	Approx. annual labour requirement Hours per hectare
Tractor mowing on extensive areas	
Gang mower: 5 unit gangs @ 24 cuts per year	14–24
Flail mower: rear mounted @ 4 cuts per year	17–20
Pedestrian mowing on restricted areas	
Cylinder mower: 900mm @ 24 cuts per yr	340–1100
Ditto, cuttings boxed off	450–1300
Cylinder mower @ 24 cuts per yr	700–1400
Ditto, cuttings boxed off	800–1700
Rotary mower: 500mm @ 6 cuts per yr	250–400
Ditto on steep banks	500–800

Note: The range of annual labour requirements depends on the size, shape and accessibility of the areas.

Source: Adapted from T. Wright 'The Horticulturists Handbook'

operating speeds are indicated earlier in Table 4.5. Whilst flailing is relatively costly on an hour or area basis, this is often more than offset by the reduced number of cuts necessary each year. However, flailing produces a poor finish that restricts the flexibility of the machines. They are usually employed on swards which require cutting once or twice a year, and unless there are many such sites the capital costs of the machines will be hard to justify. A greater problem, on visually sensitive sites and those where the soil nutrition must by kept low, is the collection of the large quantities of cut material. The best solution is often the hire of agricultural machinery such as silage harvesters. Unfortunately their access requirements can often exceed the capacity of the site.

LAYOUT

In general, the more of a sward which can be cut by tractor-mounted equipment, the cheaper it will be to maintain. If a tractor can easily be operated without having to back into corners, turning tight corners, having to avoid obstacles, and so on, the mowing task will be quicker and more efficient. In addition the less grass which is missed by the tractor and needs

Table 5.2   The influence of grass unit sizes on mowing rates

Total area cut Ha	Grass units to be cut No. of units	Size of each unit m^2	Man hours required for mowing
1	1,000	10m^2	15
1	100	100m^2	12
1	10	1,000m^2	2
1	1	10,000m^2	1

Note: It is assumed that the units are 10 metres apart.

to be cut by smaller, slower equipment, the more efficient will be the layout. 'Design for tractor mowing' need not result in a dull landscape, but it requires a good knowledge and understanding of the operating characteristics of the machinery to be used, in particular turning circles, widths, versatility, etc.

GRASS UNIT SIZE AND NUMBER OF UNITS

Transporting a mower to site and preparing it for action takes as long for a site which is 10 m^2 as for one which is 10,000 m^2. It is therefore cheaper to maintain fewer, larger areas of grass because less time is spent on unproductive operations such as travelling, loading and unloading.

Tables 5.2 and 5.3 provide insights into the extent to which the work-rate values involved in managing grass areas are affected by size.

The number of individual units on a site can also affect many associated tasks as demonstrated by the worked example in Figure 5.1.

COMPLEX LAYOUTS

Complicated mowing areas, such as those which are often found in housing sites, can slow down work. This occurs not only because they are inconveniently located, but because machine operators take longer to become familiar with the layout.

OBSTACLES IN GRASS

Obstacles in grass, such as trees, bollards, lamp-posts, fences, raised manhole covers and the boundaries between grass and paths or walls, may reduce the speed of mowing. Special separate treatments may be required to prevent them from looking unkempt.

Woody plants in mown grass are prone to damage from machinery which is not handled carefully. Strimming round trees to remove long grass and weeds is liable to whip and even girdle young plants which have thin bark. If management or operator ability is likely to be less than good, obstacles –

Table 5.3 Large grass areas: estimated resource requirements

Source	Medium wear grass: operations	SMV	Unit	Typical frequency	Typical SMV/Ha/ Year
Sh	Gang mow (triple unit) depending on area	56.83–88.96	Ha	1/7–10 days	1364–2135
W	Gang mow (3 gang)	1.26	100m²	1/7–10 days @ 24 × yr	3024
D	Gang mow (3 gang)	1.00	100m²	1/7–10 days @ 24 × yr	2400
D	Gang mow 5/7 gang	0.30	100m²	1/7–10 days @ 24 × yr	720
K	Gang mow 5 gang: depending on size of area	34.96–84.76	Ha	1/7–10 days @ 24 × yr	839–2034
D	Aerate: 30″ Sisis	3.00	100m²	Depending on wear	300*
Sh	Aerate: 31″ Sisis	3.20	100m²	Depending on wear	320*
Sh	Spike: Paterson	5.99	100m²	Depending on wear	599*
S	Spike: tractor towed, 1.7m hollow tined	9.27	Ha	Depending on wear	57*
D	Roll grass: 72″ motor roller	1.00	100m²	Occasional, as necessary	100*
W	Apply fertilizer: tractor mounted Vicon	0.31	100m²	Occasional, as necessary	31*
K	Apply fertilizer: Quillot or Sisis Coultis	2.93	100m²	Occasional, as necessary	293*
W	Apply fertilizer: by hand	2.90	100m²	Occasional, as necessary	290*
W	Spray herbicide: tractor mounted sprayer and boom	1.76	100m²	Occasional, as necessary	176*
K	Topdress and re-seed worn area	33.47	100m²	Occasional, as necessary	1116†

Note: *The figures relate to the operation being undertaken once during the year.
       † The figure relates to the operation being undertaken once in three years.
See Table 2.2 on p. 37 for details of sources.

especially living ones – are best sited outside grass areas. This will usually make both management of grass easier and improve the growth of plants. Figure 5.2 provides a worked example to show how obstacles in grass increase the costs of mowing an area.

GRASS EDGES

The boundary between grass and other surfaces such as paths, beds or walls can be made nearly maintenance-free through the use of the right

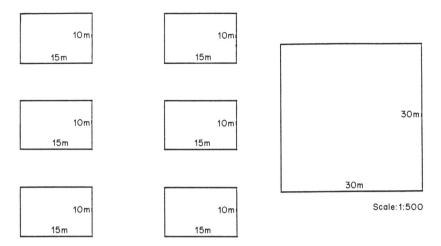

If a landscape scheme contains 900 m² of grassland laid out as one large square bed of 30 × 30 m then the total length of edge to maintain would be 120 m.

The same total areas of grass if laid out as six beds of 10 × 15 m would involve a total edge length of 300 m.

The time required to trim edges with long handled shears is taken as 23 min/100 m.

To maintain 120 m would therefore take 27.6 minutes.

To maintain 300 m would therefore take 69.0 minutes.

The choice of more units would involve a 2.5 times increase in labour requirements.

Figure 5.1 Effects of number of landscape elements upon labour requirements.

design, construction and management techniques. Otherwise grass edges can be time consuming to maintain and, if neglected, they can make an otherwise well-cared for landscape look scruffy and unkempt. Table 4.6 gives work rates for operations such as clipping edges. Figure 5.3 is a worked example which shows how much time can be saved through the use of low intensity maintenance techniques. Care in detailing edges is therefore worthwhile. In some cases capital invested in features such as mowing trims is cost-effective, although the high costs of hard materials will mean that the time for recouping the investment may be longer than expected. Figure 5.4 provides a worked example to demonstrate this.

Despite the long payback period indicated in Figure 5.4, there may be other less obvious reasons for using mowing trims, such as convenience. On a new scheme it may be particularly valuable to reduce all maintenance or revenue costs. Moreover, at this stage initial capital monies may be relatively easy to obtain.

The annual savings may also be much greater than indicated in Figure

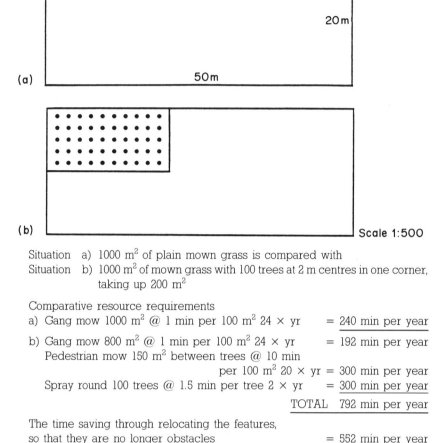

Figure 5.2   Effects of obstacles in grass on mowing costs.

5.4, if work schedules and labour deployment means that a worker would have to be sent quite long distances, 12 times a year, just to do the edging.

Again in the interests of cost-effectiveness, grass levels should always be slightly higher (10–15 mm) than the adjacent hard surfaces, such as paths or kerbs. This means that mowers can operate right up to the edge of grass without hitting hard edges.

Mowing trims are flat edgings to grass laid so that mowers can cut the edge of the grass while riding on the trim. They also prevent the need for frequent trimming of grass edges. Trims can be laid at the boundaries between grass and flower/shrub beds. For example, paving slabs forming a path between grass and bed also act as a mowing trim if laid slightly below the level of the grass. Trims can also be used where grass meets a vertical surface such as a wall, although herbicides can also keep this zone grass-free.

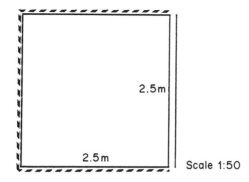

Operation	Quantity (a) m	Work rate (b) Min/100 linear m	(c) Frequency	Total annual (d) Labour rqmt, hrs per 40 m
1. Intensive maintenance:				
Trim edges with shears	40	23	20/yr	3 hrs
Weed and clean channel	10	105	6/yr	1 hr
Edge off with half moon	40	80	4/yr	2 hr
				6 hr/yr
				(= 9 min/metre)
2. Low maintenance:				
Spray edges	40	16*	2	0.2
Edge off with half moon	40	80	1/2 yrs	0.3
			(20 m/yr)	0.5 hr/yr
				(= 0.75 min/metre)

$$(d) = \frac{(a) \times (b) \times (c)}{100 \quad 60} \text{ hrs}$$

* derived from W value of 32.5 min/100² to spray a 500 mm strip

Figure 5.3 Effects of grass-edge treatments on maintenance costs.

By using the methods above, it is possible to dispense with time-consuming, old-fashioned techniques of edge maintenance, such as those involving the use of channels.

Table 5.6 and Figure 5.3 show how much time it takes to maintain channels.

Grass gradually encroaches on adjacent hard surfaces blurring the sharpness of the design and sometimes compromising the utility of paths. However, if the edge is well designed as a mowing trim the grass can be kept under control by regular passes with the mower and the encroachment is seldom serious.

Manual grass edging in many such landscape situations is really a symptom of poorly-defined design objectives. Alternatively it can represent a lack of flexibility in the allocation of investment between capital intensive redesign or, in the long term, more costly maintenance.

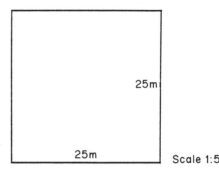

If there is an area with a grass edge of 100 m long, traditional high quality edging and sweeping undertaken 12 times per year (every alternate mowing) would require 5.4 hours annually. This is based on a time input of 27 minutes/100 m.

At an assumed labour cost of £7 per hour, the annual maintenance costs would be approximately £38 per year.

If, as an alternative, brick pavior edging is installed, the cost would total approximately £1,300/100 m. This is based on the cost of £13/m (Spon's Landscape Price Book, 1987).

The time taken to recoup investment in a brick pavior trim would be approximately 35 years.

Figure 5.4 Appraisal of mowing trim costs.

Sites that are highly prestigious with high quality turf and border planting, or those schemes that are designed to reflect a historic style of gardening, can possibly justify the constant maintenance demands associated with manual edging.

Medium quality sites where the design is intended to be reasonably permanent will both look better and be cheaper to maintain if mowing trims are provided.

Mowing trims represent a capital investment. They can be difficult to install in some situations once the construction phase has been completed. Unfortunately this applies even when it can be demonstrated that over the life of the landscape scheme they will save money. If possible, therefore, efforts should be made at the design stage to ensure that mowing trims are provided.

It is possible to have 'no maintenance' interfaces between grass and beds in landscapes where crisp edges between the trims are not required. For example, interfaces between shrub beds and lawns can be effectively maintained through the use of herbicides.

Clean edges are often required in more prestigious areas, and are always necessary around beds of display planting in fine turf. Regular clipping, usually with every second mowing, should produce the desired result. They also usually require occasional straightening with a half moon or similar tool. Consequently, as Table 5.6 shows, edges are relatively expensive to maintain. Fig 5.3 compares the maintenance costs of two plots of grass, one with intensively maintained edges and one without.

The length of edge increases in proportion to grass area as the size of grass or bed areas decreases and the number of beds increases. Therefore the length of grass edge which needs treatment can be reduced by restricting the number of beds and increasing the size of grass (and bed) units.

5.3
Usage factors

There are several factors which affect the amount of wear received by grass and which therefore influence the choice of the most cost-effective management approach. These are reviewed in the paragraphs which follow.

WEAR

The level of use which grass receives is a key factor in determining its management. Wear was identified as a major problem by landscape managers who answered the NERC Survey (NERC, 1977; Hunt and Rorison, 1980). Some aspects of this have already been mentioned and are discussed further in the sections on sports turf and dune systems.

LITTER AND FLY TIPPING

Gangmowers are easily damaged by stones and hard debris. If much time needs to be spent checking gang-mown or cylinder-mown grass for rubbish before cutting, it may be more cost-effective to use a slower but less vulnerable type of machine, such as a rotary mower. French drains and other sources of loose stones near to grass areas can be a great nuisance because they provide a convenient supply of 'missiles' for children who enjoy throwing them onto the grass.

Grassed areas are particularly vulnerable to fly tipping if they are flat and concealed, if there is a relaxed air of maintenance and if they are easily accessible to vehicles. Fly tipping can be an expensive problem, particularly in urban areas: it can really only be solved at source. This involves preventing access, as well as improving both public attitudes and behaviour. Whilst the former is usually expensive, the latter usually requires a sustained campaign over several years.

DOGS

Fouling by dogs is a very real and distressing problem, particularly in urban areas with a high ratio of dogs to open space. Landscape staff are the ones who suffer most particularly when mowing fouled grass, but dog fouling is unpleasant to everyone who uses these areas and can be dangerous to children. The introduction of dog pounds and loos in parks seems to be quite effective.

Dogs can be hazardous to stock in grazed areas. This is one reason why grazing is not usually a viable way of managing grass in towns. The experience of those managing grazed grassland on the edge of towns points to the need for good fencing and close 'shepherding' if losses are to be minimized. The extra expense is often not justified.

VANDALISM

Vandalism of grass, as distinct from other landscape areas, is confined mostly to the removal of turf and to firing long, uncut grass. The latter is particularly dangerous, but can usually be avoided by the adoption of suitable mowing regimes and, if possible, by ensuring that the areas are open to public view.

ANTI-SOCIAL SPORTS

There may be a need to ban some sports such as golf in public open spaces because they are dangerous. 'Rogue' golfers can be a nuisance, and may damage fine turf areas, for example cricket squares, by using them for practice swings.

ALIEN PARKING

Where parking space is scarce and in high demand, any accessible flat ground may be pressed into use for parking without permission. Considerable damage to grass and even to planted beds can result from this. Vehicles often need to be positively excluded from places where there is excessive pressure to park in a limited area, such as many hospitals. This can be achieved by the use of bollards, threats of immobilization, and so on. Otherwise the grounds are likely to be swallowed up or disjointed such that maintenance costs increase by continually expanding car parks.

There are certain substrate types, particularly sands and brick rubbles, and seed mixes, notably hard wearing *Lolium perenne*, that can be suitable for temporary overspill parking.

If there is regular maintenance input involved in protecting and reinstating damaged turf areas, there may be a long-term saving if the grass is reinforced by some means. One possible option is to use Wyretex mesh.

FIRE

Fires, whether natural, accidental or deliberate are a potential problem on any grassland which is left uncut. They can be particularly dangerous near busy roads. A late summer 'tidy-up' cut helps to prevent fires, since many start in spring on dry over-wintered litter. Other areas particularly at risk include infrequently cut semi-natural grasslands and heathlands.

5.4
Resource factors

Both the extent and type of resources which are available to an Amenity Manager have a profound influence upon the effectiveness with which amenity areas are maintained. The allocation of the annual maintenance budget between machinery, materials and labour resources and the choice of, say, particular machinery items or chemicals are thus amongst the most important management decisions. Some of the main factors which have a significant bearing on the use and selection of machinery, herbicides, fertilizers, irrigation equipment and growth retardants are outlined in the remainder of this chapter.

MACHINERY

The selection of grass cutting machinery is dependent on many factors, including site accessibility and topography, the intended frequency of use, the quality of finish and the size of the area to be mown (Farley, 1980; Jones, 1982).

For many maintenance organizations, mowers, of all the machinery items, involve the greatest capital outlay. The range of available models is without doubt the largest of any landscape equipment type. It is therefore important to determine exactly the machines that are required (Halford, 1984).

One of the most fundamental decisions, influencing machine selection, concerns the type of finish required (Parker, 1982). Cylinder mowing blades, if well maintained, provide the type of very fine cutting edge necessary for achieving a high quality finish. Such mowers usually give most precise control over the height of the grass, but often cannot be raised as high as other types of machine. They offer the greatest frequency of cut (60–70 cuts per metre are required for medium quality grass, 120–130 for top quality). However, they are not able to cope with very irregular ground, are less robust when hitting obstacles and cannot cut grass that is too long or which contains the occasional semi-woody weed.

Rotary mowers can handle much tougher cutting jobs and irregular ground. Many machines have blades which fold back when hitting a stone or solid edge. Although the cut tends to tear the grass more than in the case of cylinder mowers, it is adequate for most general-purpose swards. Rotaries take more power than cylinder mowers and are thus also usually noisier. Conversely, they are more versatile, macerate the cuttings more effectively thereby reducing the need for collection, are more versatile on banks and slopes and are more tolerant of wet conditions. There is also less need to maintain the blades by sharpening. The largest tractor-driven rotary mowing heads can be a metre wide.

Flail mowers or those that use a reciprocating cutting edge are suitable for the longest and most difficult grass. They are the essential machines for area such as wild flower grasslands and rural roadside edges which are only cut once or twice a year. Reciprocating cutters are best for long grass because the vegetation is not flattened before it is cut. Flail mowers are expensive and bulky. However, their performance and work rates can be very good, they are versatile and are capable of cutting back scrub and rural hedges as well as grass.

The type of power supply is also an important factor influencing machine selection. For small machines, which are only designed to travel short distances and to cut small areas, the power can come from either the person pushing or from electricity. Electric mowers have few starting or maintenance problems, but they are not very powerful and usually have a limited range. Thus it is more common for the energy supply to be a self-contained petrol or diesel engine. The engine size should match the degree of use expected.

Whereas the engine of a pedestrian mower is primarily used to provide the cutting action, it may also supply the motive power for a larger machine. Hover mowers represent an attempt to reduce the manual power required. They usually cover a cutting width of 30–60 cm.

Larger mowers can be of the ride-on type which are entirely self-propelled and steered like a small tractor. These typically can drive from 2 to 4 cutting heads to improve the rate and cost-effectiveness of the cut. Triple headed mowers are the most common and they can cut over 2 metres in width.

Tractor-powered mowers will drive five or sometimes seven mowing heads. Where there are large accessible areas to be mown they are by far the most cost-effective type of machine. This is due to a combination of the travel speeds and the total widths of cut achievable.

Some method of collecting the grass cuttings may be necessary. On fine quality turf a collection box and a rear roller will be required if the objective is a pristine 'striped' lawn effect. For medium quality turf, collection will not be necessary unless cutting is so infrequent that large quantities of dead material is left behind. This can look unattractive and can temporarily damage the grass beneath. Some types of rotary mower macerate the cuttings very effectively so that they decompose rapidly, removing the need for collection. However, in the case of most wild flower areas which are mown, the collection of cuttings is essential to prevent both a rise in fertility and a mulching effect that will favour undesirable coarse grass species.

Collection is a time-consuming task that can greatly increase the cost of the mowing regime. It is usually only possible with pedestrian mowers. In some circumstances collection may only be necessary in the periods of maximum grass growth, notably early summer.

If cuttings are not to be collected the direction in which these are dropped can sometimes be important. On narrow grass roadside strips it is usually important that the cuttings are deposited on the grass rather than on the adjacent road or pavement.

Particular requirements may include manoeuvrability; the weight of the machine on the tyres which is important in wet areas; a low centre of gravity and good grip for banks; floating heads for small undulations in the turf; the ease of transportability or speed if self-propelled; and the machine width for access to sites.

Less easy to determine from brochures or casual inspection are comfort, running costs, repair costs and the safety of the machine. Amenity Managers should, if possible, seek guidance from organizations which have similar requirements.

Safety is particularly important, as mowing accidents make up a disturbingly large percentage of the total accidents associated with maintaining the natural landscape. Machines should be chosen which provide shields to stop feet fitting beneath the blades. Extreme care is necessary when mowing on steep banks. It is essential that safety footwear is worn at all times. In order to avoid passers-by being hit by stones, it is important that machines should not be operated at lower than recommended mowing heights.

The decision on which machinery to purchase, and which if any to hire, will depend not only on the task in hand but the amount of work and the isolation of different sites. It may be more cost-effective to keep small mowers on a variety of widely separated sites than to move one large mobile machine between them.

The capital costs of more specialized equipment may not be justified if the machines are used infrequently. This applies particularly in the case of those types of flail mower which are used for annual or bi-annual cuts. Such machines may be more usefully hired or small areas may even be tackled with manual scythes.

Strimmers and shears will also be important ancillary equipment where the grass contains many edges and obstacles.

Tables 5.4 to 5.7 presented later in this chapter provide useful pointers for those faced with selecting the most appropriate machinery for maintaining amenity grasslands.

PEST, DISEASE, AND WEED CONTROL

If wildlife such as insects, fungi and weeds interfere with the functioning of a grassland area, they may need to be controlled. On the whole, however, systematic control of turf-grass pests, diseases and weeds is usually only necessary on fine grassland and sports turf. Fine 'play-on' grass in particular is often subjected to extremes of management or wear and this may make it less resistant to damage by pests. Medium 'play-on' grass usually requires fairly regular control of non-turf grass weeds which interfere with its playing qualities, but other medium to rough grassland usually needs little if any pest-control treatment. Managers therefore need to be clear about the function which an area of grass is expected to fulfil and the possible results of any treatment before embarking on a control programme (Fisher, 1977; Haggar, 1980).

For example, the primary purpose of grass on a bowling or golf green is to provide a playing surface, although the appearance of turf is also important to some less discerning users who may judge quality by appearance as much as by playing characteristics. Diseases such as fusarium, pests such as worms, and turf weeds disturb the uniformity of the surface and hence the main function of the green (Fisher, 1977). The disrupting factors therefore need to be controlled. The scope for cultural controls is often limited, since a practice which promotes a pest or disease may be essential to the general qualities of the turf. For example, certain fungal diseases are encouraged by high nitrogen and moisture levels in the swards, but these inputs are often required to keep the grass growing vigorously in the face of frequent mowing (Atkinson and White, 1977). Control is therefore necessary and chemical treatment is often used. Some of the pesticides used on fine amenity turf are quite toxic or persistent (chlordane, arsenic compounds, HCH, for example) and would not be acceptable in most other situations.

In contrast, management of most semi-natural grasslands is intended to encourage the greatest species diversity which is compatible with the site and its other amenity uses. Although this may entail controlling plants which threaten to lessen diversity, such as competitive bracken or invasive scrub and trees, intervention should be as minimal as possible. Control measures are likely to be cultural, physical or biological rather than chemical, and the use of persistent chemicals is particularly out of place in areas managed for conservation and wildlife.

Moss is often really a symptom of surface compaction and poor drainage. Thus applying moss killer may only be a temporary solution.

In many rural and natural settings which receive only occasional grass cutting, and particularly sites which have been neglected for some time, the most difficult type of weed to control may well be invading seedlings of woody plants. Scrub control of this nature is often performed manually. Flail equipment is probably the only grass cutting machinery that will deal with established woody plants. Typical manpower requirements are presented in Table 5.4.

In between these two extremes are very large areas of amenity grassland with a range of functions. These include many medium and rough 'walk-on' and 'look-on' swards including much urban and country park open space; road verges; the outfield and rough parts of formal sports areas etc. Action against the wildlife which makes its home in these areas will depend on how the Amenity Manager views the functions of that grassland, and upon the costs and benefits of the potential control measures (Anon, 1974; Francis, 1984).

For example, areas of formerly close-mown grass which have been converted to a less frequent cutting regime are likely to produce crops of unsightly or noxious weeds, such as docks and nettles. These need to be controlled for both aesthetic and legal reasons. The manager may decide to 'spot treat' them with herbicides. Again, some vigorous broad-leaved weeds, such as docks and dandelions, are remarkably persistent even under close-cut gang-mowing regimes. They may become so numerous on certain soils or in certain weather conditions that they compete seriously with the grass or become visually unacceptable. In such cases the manager may decide to take action against these pests which are disturbing the performance of the grassland.

Conversely worms, the casts of which are often regarded as unsightly on highly manicured turf areas, can have a valuable beneficial influence on the

Table 5.4   Grassland weed control: estimated resource requirements

Source	Operation	SMV	Unit
W	Knapsack: 'Spot treating' 10% of total area	3.00	100m²
Sh	'Spot' spray	3.71	100m² inspected
W	Overall grass with tractor and boom	1.76	100m²
K	Spray weeds with Mistifier	1.37	100m²
W	Overall grass with self-propelled sprayer & lance	32.50	100m²
Sh	Overall grass with self-propelled sprayer & lance	22.75	100m²
Sh	Overall grass with self-propelled sprayer & booms	5.99	100m²
W	Overall and knapsack sprayer	32.50	100m²
Sh	Overall and knapsack sprayer	20.36	100m²
CRC	Watering Can	12.00	100m²
W	Flail (long reach)	7.20	100m²
W	Scrub control – flail (rear mounted)	2.67	100m²
E	Scrub control – swipe	2.19	100m²

See Table 2.2 on p. 37 for details of sources.

structure and fertility of the grass. Removing them can increase drainage problems and lead to a less attractive grassland. They should only be controlled where an absolutely true playing surface is necessary.

Factors which may require consideration in assessing the need for action include:

- Unwanted side-effects from using pesticides;
- Availability of labour;
- Desirability of preventing unwanted species from spreading or seeding.

Table 5.4 provides figures for the time required to carry out some pest control operations on grass. Normally, however, no systematic programme of 'weed' or 'pest' control is needed in rough and ready grass areas.

FERTILIZERS AND TOP DRESSINGS

The same line of reasoning which was applied to pest control in the last section can also be applied to fertilizer use.

Some of the main questions which need to be considered by an Amentiy Manager include:

- Are fertilizers actually necessary on this piece of grassland?
- Can the grass perform properly without them?
- Is it in fact better without them?

Some reasons for using fertilizers are:

- *Biological*: to promote growth where substrates are inadequate for healthy grass production; for example, on some industrial spoils, or urban brickwastes, improvement of nutrient levels can be critical to the establishment and maintenance of a satisfactory sward;
- *Aesthetic*: to make grass green where this is thought to be desirable, as in the case of many 'look-on' swards;
- *Functional*: to produce wear-resistant growth in areas under heavy user pressure; to produce biomass for a hay/silage crop or for grazing animals, if normal growth is inadequate.

Reasons for not using fertilizers include the following:

- They will cost money;
- They will entail the need to cut grass more frequently;
- They will tend to reduce species diversity.

Fertilizers should not normally be used on any low maintenance areas, which are to remain largely or entirely uncut.

Fertilizers can be used 'differentially' within a site, in conjunction with substrates and seed mixes, for example to strengthen the growth on path ways and play areas. This is an adaptation of typical golf course grass management, and has been used, for example in Birchwood Brook Park in Warrington New Town (Roberts, 1986). This has the advantage of restricting vigorous grass growth to those areas where it is needed, while

Table 5.5   Fertilizer application: estimated resource requirements

Source	Operation	SMV	Unit
W	Hand Broadcast	2.90	$100m^2$
K	Hand Broadcast	5.10	$100m^2$
Sh	Pedestrian operated spinner type (Cyclone)	2.75	$100m^2$
K	Quillot or Sisis Coults	2.93	$100m^2$
K	Tractor mounted Vicon type	0.31	$100m^2$
H	Liquid feed – Applied from watering can. Boom sprayer	13.00	$100m^2$

See Table 2.2 on p. 37 for details of sources.

keeping other areas low maintenance. Table 5.5 gives some manpower figures for fertilizer applications.

Fertilizing is a fairly rapid operation even when done by hand. Its cost is therefore more in the purchase price of the materials themselves and in the creation of extra work caused by added grass growth.

The principal minerals that will need to be added are likely to be nitrogen and phosphorus. However, localized deficiencies in any of the necessary plant nutrients will weaken the grass and retard growth. Work undertaken by the Sports Turf Research Institute (Robinson, Moore and Murphy, 1977) shows that nitrogen is the most important nutrient when good wear tolerance is needed.

The need for fertilizing will be greater where cuttings are boxed off the site.

Topdressings include a range of organic and inorganic materials and are used on grass for a number of reasons:

- as mixtures of seed and soil to level uneven swards;
- as mixtures of soil, seed and fertilizer to reinstate areas damaged by sporting activities, excavating services, etc;
- as sand, to improve surface drainage, maintain sand slits, etc.;
- as fine loam, to provide a firm playing surface on cricket wickets;
- as a carrier and spreader for fertilizers, mosskillers, etc.;
- as loams, leafmould, sewage sludge, etc., to increase soil organic matter and nutrient content and to act as a reservoir of slow-release plant foods.

Grass cuttings and other organic litter, such as tree leaves, act as natural top dressings and return nutrients and organic matter to grass if they are left to lie. However, thick dressings can smother the grass beneath or change its composition through nutrient-enrichment. Thus, in some cases the cut herbage may need to be removed. The sections on heathland management and species-rich grassland in Chapter 6 cover this in more detail.

Burning of grasslands is a form of 'anti-mulching', as it destroys litter and disperses some of the nutrients in the ecosystem.

Fertilizer equipment again comes in a range of sizes from small, hand-propelled distributors up to tractor-mounted spreaders. Various different application systems are adopted, such as distribution by spinner or flicker plate. Extreme care should be taken over the selection of a spreader. Experience has shown that considerable wastage and over-lapping leading to excess application can occur when spinners rather than full width applicators are used.

LIMING

Heavily mown amenity grassland, particularly that which has the clippings boxed off and removed, rapidly loses calcium ions. On some soil types this tends to make the ground more acidic. Acidity in turn can reduce the activity of soil microorganisms which are responsible for breaking down dead organic matter. As a result the grass may start to develop a thatch of dead growth which affects the appearance and encourages shallow rooting. This also means that soil nutrients, particularly nitrogen, can remain locked up in an organic form limiting grass growth (Vick and Handley, 1975).

Liming of grassland can be extemely cost-effective in improving the growth, wear tolerance and appearance of the sward. Material costs are relatively low per unit weight. However, compared to most other fertilizers lime is required in considerable bulk, usually requiring a tractor-mounted spreader.

The need to lime will depend on many variables such as initial soil type, the cutting regime and rainfall. Thus the choice of application rate should be based on both soil analysis and inspection of the quality and nature of the turf species present.

IRRIGATION

Irrigation of amenity grassland is expensive in terms of equipment and labour. It can therefore only be justified in certain situations, such as prestigious landscapes and high quality sports facilities. Typical uses of irrigation are:

- To help the establishment of newly-seeded or turfed areas and the renovation of existing turf. Successful and speedy establishment may be vital both to owners of ornamental areas and to users who wish to make use of a grassed area as soon as possible.
- To keep demanding areas of turf in top quality condition during dry spells. Golf greens are usually supplied with built-in irrigation systems. Bowling greens and cricket wickets need irrigation to help stimulate grass under harsh management regimes. Professional sports turf areas require irrigation to maintain strong growth. Some new sports turf pitches are now being constructed using a sealed cell system, which combines under drainage with sub-surface irrigation and nutrition;

Table 5.6 Irrigation – estimated resource requirements

Source	Operation	SMV	Unit
D	Water bowling green with hose	45.00	Green
CRC	To set up oscillating sprinkler, move every 2–3 hrs and dismantle at night	30.00	100m^2
K	Water cricket square with seep hose	3.30	100m^2
H	Set up sprinkler and visit twice per run	20.00	Green

See Table 2.2 on p. 37 for details of sources.

- To keep prestigious fine turf areas green and evenly coloured during dry weather. However, it is important to realize that grass does not usually die under ordinary moisture stresses even if it turns brown. Irrigation of ornamental grass is therefore largely cosmetic.

Because it is so dependent on soil type and conditions, irrigation is an operation which is difficult to measure. Most work value booklets do not contain figures for watering. Table 5.6 does, however, provide a few. Manual watering is usually very slow. Automatic irrigation systems are labour-saving to operate, but expensive to install.

The choice of irrigation equipment will largely depend on the extent to which the need for irrigation is likely to be permanent. There is usually a roughly inverse relationship between capital investment and subsequent running costs: the cheapest need the most attention from operators.

The main types of irrigation equipment are summarized in Table 5.7 in order of their relative cost and flexibility.

GROWTH RETARDANTS

The chemical maleic hydracide (MH) has been on the market now for a number of years as a grass growth retardant. Its value has been proved and widely publicized for the Plymouth area by Waterhouse (Waterhouse, 1985). However, MH does not appear to have been taken up by other managers on the large scale which its properties might suggest would be appropriate. Though frequently written up in the amenity press as a panacea for the Landscape Manager, and a cure-all for grass cutting, it seems that in fact relatively little grass is being managed chemically in this way. Some reasons are suggested below and the properties of grass growth retardants currently on the market are described.

Inhibition of growth means that grass needs to be cut less often. This is particularly valuable in the early part of the year when grass growth coincides with the first flush of weeds, and some seasonal activities such as summer bedding-out. Cost savings of up to 60% have been obtained over conventional pedestrian mowing in Plymouth (see Table 5.8). Greater flexibility and freedom for labour deployment can be equally important benefits. Whilst it is likely that cost savings will be gained compared with the use of gang or triple mowers, the ability to spread the workload may

Table 5.7   Characteristics of grass irrigation equipment

Hose – cheap and with many proprietary designs of spray head which make it quite adaptable. Operators may be needed to provide almost constant attention for moving the hose and directing the water.

Seep Hose – releases water at a gentle rate along its entire length. It is not as cheap as a plain hose and is less flexible. However, once in place it can water an entire bed without attention.

Spray Boom or portable spray head – fixed and rotating semi-permanent spray heads fed by a hose; a boom will contain several heads. There are models which rotate under the water pressure to increase the area which is covered. They can be unwieldy to move and therefore are often used semi-permanently. They can give a wide and even local deposition.

Pop up sprinklers – permanently positioned heads with hoses hidden below ground. They make use of a clever hydraulic system to raise the sprinkler heads out of their underground recesses when the water is turned on. Permanent installations are capital intensive and are usually reserved for high prestige sports areas.

Flooding – used occasionally in very high quality and prestigious self-contained sports pitches such as bowling greens and tennis courts.

Tankers/bowsers – these have to be used where there is no local water supply. They are therefore usually reserved for capital intensive plantings such as shrubs or hanging baskets. Their use may include seed and turf establishment.

Table 5.8   Grass maintenance costs: comparison between mowing and chemical (maleic hydrazide) control

Mower type	Proportional costs per 1,000 m² Financial units*		Frequency of annual operations	Proportional costs per year	Financial index
Gang mower	1.0	@	20 cuts	20	100
Motor triple	1.25	@	20 cuts	25	125
Large rotary pedestrian mower, 22″	4.42	@	20 cuts	88.4	442
Flymo (19″)	5.86	@	20 cuts	117.2	586
Spray (operatives + lorry and driver)	8.14	@	3 sprays	24.4	122

* Cost of 1 cut by gang mower taken as 1.00 financial unit.

Source: Figures from Waterhouse (1985)

still be valuable. This applies especially at the beginning and end of the summer when strong flushes of grass growth can put pressure on the available equipment and manpower to ensure that grass does not get too long to be cut by conventional means.

The chemicals also reduce the bulk of grass clippings that are left following a cut.

Maleic hydracide (MH) is a growth regulator which acts by inhibiting plant cell division for about 5–8 weeks. It tends to be selective against coarser, more productive grass species in particular. It also produces a finer growth habit in treated plants.

MH is usually used in combination with cutting regimes. Spraying before cutting has been found to assist in preventing the formation of unsightly seed heads. The recommended time for spraying is mid-March to early May, i.e. after the main frost but before the spring grass flush, followed by

HE MUST HAVE OVERHEARD ME SAYING THAT WE WERE GOING OVER TO GROWTH RETARDENTS.

further applications as needed. In districts with long growing seasons three treatments per year, typically May, July, and September may be needed; one or two usually suffice elsewhere, depending on the type of control required. Late season applications in September to mid-October give control of grass for a few weeks in the following spring, which can also be very useful.

In the past MH has had a bad reputation for scorching or yellowing of grass and sometimes for failing to inhibit growth to the extent claimed by the manufacturers. Recent formulations have been improved, discolouration decreased and weather-proofing increased (Bauer, 1985).

The timing of application in relation to mowing is critical. Since the chemical is not completely rainproof, weather conditions are also critical. Precision in the timing of applications, combined with the need for spraying operations to be undertaken on a fairly large scale, may also be two of the reasons why the use of MH is not more widespread.

Two new chemicals are now available: mefluidide and PP333. Although there has been less time for them to be fully assessed, they appear to be equally as valuable as MH, and in some circumstances more so (Marshall, 1982a, b).

Mefluidide, which is usually sold as 'Mowchem', controls coarse grass better than fine species, like MH. However, it is much better than MH at controlling seed head formation. When grass does begin to grow again it is as fresh green vegetative growth. The subsequent reduction in thatch and dead seed heads can greatly reduce fire risk. The chemical is very fast acting and its effect lasts for about 5 weeks. In swards where the intention is to retain or encourage the growth of broadleaves, Mefluidide has less effect on these than MH or PP333. Conversely, broadleaved weeds will be more visible in fine turf.

PP333 seems to work better on fine grasses than the other two chemicals. It does not control heading, so a carefully timed cut will be important if this is desirable. It is slower to take effect than the others and is soil-acting, so its effect can actually be delayed if there is no rain to wash it into the soil. The effect can last for about three months although duration is dependent on the application rate. The best results are obtained by spraying during active growth rather than before.

Dikegulac, a growth retardant used to control woody plant or hedge growth, is too expensive for wide-scale grass application. Trials are under way for at least three new potential growth retardant chemicals.

The choice of which type to use is dependent on the grass to be controlled and the season. The ideal treatment in many situations is to use a cocktail of two or more of the above growth regulants, and possibly some selective herbicide treatment in the same spray. Such cocktails can be invaluable in overcoming or balancing the deficiencies inherent in any one of the chemical treatments alone. Because there are so many possible combinations, it is much harder to comment on the behaviour of cocktails compared with single chemicals. However, new research reports will doubtless emerge.

If a herbicide is used to eliminate broadleaves, some bare patches will result, but these are usually colonized by grass within about a year.

There is clear evidence that growth retardants do work and that their use is cost-effective particularly in certain defined types of area (Marshall, 1982a, b). Elsewhere conventional grass cutting may be as cheap or cheaper, or it may be simpler because the manager is accustomed and organized to undertake mowing operations. Also, although there is a reduction in operator maintenance time, there is not only a need for more skilled junior management but a greater involvement on its part in what was previously a routine operation. It seems likely that as more, improved and more heavily promoted retardants appear on the market, more managers will consider transferring resources from mechanical to chemical grass control.

The locations where growth retardants have proved their worth are:

- Grass areas containing many obstacles which preclude gang mowing. Graveyards and some verges are examples of such areas;
- Steep banks;
- Areas with very many obstacles, notably graveyards;
- Small isolated areas which are relatively expensive and/or inconvenient to mow.

Some representative cost savings are shown in Table 5.8.

In the past it would appear that the adoption of growth retardants has been inhibited due to:

- A lack of experience, and indeed a built-in resistance to the use of chemical sprays by management;
- Some Union opposition to the use of chemicals.

Use of contractors, skilled in handling and applying herbicides, is likely to be a sensible option for many public and private organizations. There are already several moves in this direction.

In future public resistance may prove to be the strongest obstacle to the implementation of chemical grass maintenance. In recent years there has arisen increased suspicion of the use of chemicals in the environment. Health and Safety requirements mean that the operators are frequently dressed like spacemen even if the chemical in its diluted state is confidently felt to be harmless. Strong reactions can be expected to any regular application routine in public places.

Table 5.9 summarizes the relative advantages and disadvantages associated with the use of growth retardants on grass areas.

5.5 Ancillary tasks

As well as mowing, there are a number of ancillary tasks that are associated with high to medium maintenance grassland, although they are more common on intensively used sports turf.

Aeration and infiltration of surface water is promoted by using equipment that removes cores or slots from the surface of the grassland. This

Table 5.9   Technical assessment: some of the main advantages and disadvantages of growth retardants

Advantages	Disadvantages
Average savings of 50–60% over conventional pedestrian cutting methods are achievable	Skilled labour and good supervision are needed
Drought resistance is increased	Grass looks 'long' for significant periods of time
Compatible with selective herbicides (but care is needed concerning drift)	Flowering is not inhibited if chemical is applied after mowing; seed heads can look unsightly (pre-mowing sprays can prevent flowering)
Labour profiles can be improved	Differential growth of grass and 'weeds' may look untidy, if weeds are untreated.
Steep and dangerous areas need not be mown	Appearance compared to mown grass, is less attractive
Appearance, compared to unmown grass, can be improved	Public and labour resistance may be high

is particularly important on turf that receives heavy winter wear but is subsequently expected to give a high performance, notably football, rugby and hockey pitches. If the pitch is particularly important, a major restructuring treatment of sand slitting will improve the wear tolerance and reduce maintenance costs.

Current thinking suggests that regular rolling of grass is only necessary on particularly intensively managed sports grounds, notably bowling greens and cricket squares, although other types of sports turf will usually receive an annual treatment.

Scarifying to remove dead thatch from the grass is usually performed when judged necessary by the groundsman. The requirement for this treatment depends on the site conditions, the vigour of the grass and often the soil type.

Harrowing is used to help aerate and level the turf.

The equipment to perform such tasks can be hired if there is not sufficient justification for purchase. Small models can often be obtained for use with ride-on-tractor-mowers.

Smaller-scale work includes brushing the turf to remove worm casts, leaves and litter and switches to remove dew.

Other ancillary tasks such as marking out of pitches are covered in chapter 6.

References   Anon (1974) Effective control depends upon identification. *Turf Management*, Oct.

Atkinson, D. and White, G.C. (1977) Soil management with herbicides, the response of plants and soils. Proceedings of the 1976 British crop protection conference – Weeds 873–884.

Bauer, J. (1985) The Sheffield Experience – pros and cons. In: *Growth Retardants*, (J. Shildrick, and J. Marshall) NTC Workshop Report No. 7., Bingley.

Bradshaw, A.D. (1980) Mineral nutrition In: *Amenity Grassland – An Ecological Perspective* (eds I.H. Rorison, and R. Hunt) John Wiley and sons, Chichester 101–17.

Dutton R. and Bradshaw A.D. (1982) *Land Reclamation in Cities*. HMSO, London.

Farley, R. (1980) *Handbook of Garden Machinery and Equipment*. Dent, London.

Fisher, R. (1977) The selective control of undesirable grasses in amenity grasslands. *Journal of the Sports Turf Research Institute* **53**, 11–30.

Francis, D. (1984) Grass wars. *GC & HTJ* **195** (2).

Haggar R.J. (1980) Weed control and vegetation management by herbicides. In: (eds R. Hunt, and I.H. Rorison) *Amenity Grassland – An Ecological Perspective*. John Wiley and Sons, Chichester.

Halford, D. (1984) Mower choice, *GC & HTJ* 6th March.

Hunt, R. and Rorison, I.H. (eds) (1980) *Amenity Grassland – An Ecological Perspective*. John Wiley and Sons, Chichester.

Jones, L. (1982) Cutting comments *GC & HTJ* **191** (17).

Lovejoy, D. (ed.) (1988) *Spon's Landscape and External Works Price Book*. E. & F.N. Spon London

Marshall E.J.P. (1982a) Chemical control of grass grown in rural amenity areas. In: (eds C.H. Addison and P.R. Thoday) *Cost Effective Amenity Land Management*, University of Bath, Bath.

Marshall, E.J.P. (1982b) *Managing Rural Amenity Sites with Chemicals*. Ninth report 1980–81, Weed Research Organisation, 71–7.

Moffat, J.D. (1980) *Grass Seed Mixes – Their Choice, Growth and Development*. Warrington New Town Development Corporation.

Natural Environment Research Council (1977) *Amenity Grasslands – The Needs For Research*. NERC. Publications series C. No. 19. NERC. Swindon.

Parker J.C. (1980) Management problems of mowing on an intensive scale. In: (eds R. Hunt, and I.H. Rorison) *Amenity Grassland – An Ecological Perspective*. John Wiley and Sons, Chichester.

Parker J.C. (1982) Mown Grass – techniques, costs and alternatives. In: (eds P.R. Thoday and C.H. Addison) *Cost Effective Amenity Land Management*. University of Bath, Bath.

Roberts from the BES conference.

Robinson, G.S., Moore K.K. and Murphy J. (1977) Effect of a number of standard and slow release nitrogenous fertilisers on the quality of fine turf. *Journal of the Sports Turf Research Institute* **53**, 74–84.

Rorison I.H. (1980) The current challenge for research and development.

In (eds I.H. Rorison and R. Hunt) *Amenity Grassland: An Ecological Perspective*. John Wiley and Sons, Chichester.

Vick, C.M. and Handley, J.F. (1975) The correction of soil acidification in urban parklands. *Journal of the Institute of Parks and Recreation Administration* **40**: 39–48.

Waterhouse, D. (1985) The Plymouth Experience – pros and cons. In: J. Shildrick, and J. Marshall, *Growth Retardants*. NTC Workshop Report No. 7, Bingley.

Further reading

Beard J.B. (1973) *Turfgrass: Science and Culture*. Prentice Hall.

Conover H.E. (1958) *Grounds Maintenance Handbook*. McGraw-Hill.

Dunball, A.P. (1983) Management of herbaceous vegetation on the sides of roads and motorways. In (ed. J.M. Way) *Management of Vegetation*, British Crop Protection Council Monograph No. 26. BCPC, Croydon.

Green B.H. (1980) Management of extensive grassland by mowing. In (eds R. Hunt, and I.H. Rorison) (1980) *Amenity Grassland – An Ecological Perspective*. John Wiley and Sons, Chichester.

Hawthorn R. (1977) *Dawson's Practical Lawncraft*. Crosby, Lockwood and Staples, London.

Hanson A.A. and Juska P.V. (eds) (1969) *Turfgrass Science*. American Society of Agronomy. Madison, Wisc.

Parker, J.C. (1986) Low cost systems of management. In (eds Bradshaw, A.D., Goode, D.A. and Thorp, E.) *Ecology and Design in Landscape*. The 24th Symposium of the British Ecological Society. Blackwells, Oxford.

Sharing, S.J. and Batch, J.J. (1981) Amenity grass retardation – some concepts challenged. In: *Chemical Manipulation of Crop Growth and Development*, 33rd Easter School in Agric. Science 23/27.

Willis, A.J. (1972) Long term ecological changes in sward composition following application of maleic hydrazide and 2, 4–D. Proceedings, 11th British Weed Control Conference, pp. 360–7.

GROWTH RETARDANTS

Johnston, D.T. and Faulkner, J.S. (1985) The effects of growth retardants on swards of normal and dwarf cultivars of red fescue. *Journal of the Sports Turf Research Institute* **61**: 59–64.

Peel, C.H. (1986) Trials of three growth retardants in a churchyard. *Journal of The Sports Turf Research Institute* **62**: 200–3.

Peel, C.H. and Shildrick, J.P. (1986) The effect of two grass retardants on eight perennial ryegrass cultivars. *Journal of the Sports Turf Research Institute* **62**: 153–71.

Peel, C.H. and Shildrick, J.P. (1986) The effects of three growth retardants, singly and in mixtures, on growth, colour and composition of lawn turf. *Journal of the Sports Turf Research Institute* **62**: 172–81.

Sports Turf Research Institute (1986) Growth retardants. *Sports Turf Bulletin* **152**: 2–4.

6

THE MANAGEMENT OF MAIN GRASSLAND TYPES: SPORTS TURF AND OTHER SPORTS SURFACES

6.1
Introduction

There are at least 98 000 ha of sports turf in Britain today (NERC, 1977) and the figure may be nearer 158 000 ha (Bunce, 1986, Pers. Comm.).

MANAGEMENT RESPONSIBILITIES

At least £191 million is spent on maintenance annually by managers in Clubs, Universities, Institutions, Local Authorities and the many other organizations responsible for looking after these surfaces.

Many sports councils and advisory committees provide Local Authorities with guidelines on the desired levels of sports provision for a given population. Whilst not binding, these represent some of the most organized pressures experienced by Local Authorities in exercising their open space responsibilities. Similar public pressures can be brought to bear by certain interest groups (Law and Bowen, 1973). Decisions concerning the allocation of budget resources for the maintenance of sports surfaces call for careful consideration. Public needs must be balanced against the required maintenance expertise, and the fact that sports activities are typically very difficult to reconcile with other land uses, either visually or in terms of user pressures.

Several questions need to be addressed: Are the Authorities allocating their budgets wisely and are their clients receiving the kind of services they want? Would some of the money previously spent on sports turf serve a better purpose if it were to be used on something else, such as a swimming pool or a floral clock? How can the Amenity Manager tell if the pitches are under- or over-used and if a change should be made to a synthetic surface? How should sports areas be managed in the most cost-effective way?

These are just some of the questions facing those Amenity Managers who are responsible for sports turf and sports areas in Britain today.

**6.2
Special characteristics
and requirements of
sports turf**

Sports turf is a specialized type of grass, whose sole job is to provide the right kind of surface for a game. This means that the construction and maintenance of sports turf areas have to be carried out in such a way that the surface fulfils the sporting requirements (Gooch and Escritt, 1975). Often the requirements of the sport are quite rigorous: the surfaces of bowling and golf greens and cricket wickets have to be as smooth, well rolled (firm) and as short as possible. The needs of the game, therefore, often conflict with the needs of the plants making up the turf. In addition, actual play is likely to damage the turf or the ground in which it is growing. Very active sports such as football can destroy the turf surface altogether, while sports such as golf and cricket create more localized damage in the form of divots and worn wickets.

Wear and damage increase both with greater use of the turf and when the ground is moist. Wear may eventually make the turf unusable (Shiels, 1981). One of the key problems in sports turf management is, therefore, the conflict between the biological needs of the grass and the requirements of players (Stewart, 1976).

Two added problems are that:

1.   Much sports turf is now being used more heavily than was intended when it was first laid down;
2.   Many managers have fewer resources than hitherto with which to maintain their sports areas.

Under-used sports turf also exists. Since it has to be maintained properly if it is to be used for sports at all, under-use represents decreased benefits with virtually no reduction in costs.

COSTS AND OPPORTUNITIES

The true cost of sports turf is the 'cost per use'; that being the amount of use obtained from an area compared to the cost of that area. This is comparable to the 'cost per wear' idea which has been used for clothes. Even expensive clothes can have a low 'cpw', if they are worn a lot, while cheap garments, if under-used, have high 'cpw's'.

The best value for money in sports provision is therefore obtained from surfaces which can be, and are, frequently used (Martyn, 1982). It is important that the surface should:

• Be able to support the use it receives: the wear tolerance of the grass imposes an absolute limit on the use of many sports grounds.
• Be used enough to make investment in its construction and maintenance worthwhile.

The evidence shows that in fact many sports areas are over-used and undermaintained, while others are under-used and yet have to be maintained to a reasonable level in order to meet demands as they occur.

These two problems were highlighted by the NERC's survey (NERC, 1977) which showed that managers of grassland thought that mowing, which is the most expensive part of maintenance, and wear, which causes a range of management problems, were the subjects most in need of research.

UNIT COSTS AND CHARACTERISTICS

The unit cost of a sports area is the total cost of construction, maintenance and of any other works such as sand slitting which have been undertaken during its lifetime, per hour of potential use per unit area.

Table 6.1 shows some typical costs which have been calculated for the first ten years in the lives of a range of sports surfaces, including hard and synthetic surfaces. Some of the typical management operations that would be involved over this period are detailed in Table 6.2. Estimated Resource Requirement figures are supplied in Table 6.3 and 6.4.

RELATIVE MERITS OF DIFFERENT SURFACES

Well managed turf is acknowledged to be the best surface for most sports, including football and cricket, as it combines firmness with some resilience.

Table 6.1 Sports surfaces: typical unit costs in the first ten years

	Construction costs £/acre[1]	Potential use hrs/week[2]	Anticipated maintenance cost £/yr	Unit cost/ hr of use (over 10 yrs) £/hour	Unit cost/ hr of use (over 30 yrs) £/hour
Natural turf – ordinary drainage	1,000				
Natural turf : native soil, sand slit system installed	12,500	15	1,000	5.00	3.1
Natural turf : sand/soil mix	50,000	30[3]	800	6.40 3.12	2.7 2.27
Hard porous	32,000	50	4,600	3.57	1.29
Hard porous : with special surface cover	120,000	70[3]	500		
Synthetic turf	280,000	80	500	7.12	2.46
All sand	8,000[4]				
Sand Slitting	2,000[4]				

Notes [1] Written off over 10 years
     [2] Calculated over 30 week/year for grass and 50 weeks/year for other surfaces
     [3] Potential capacity for use not yet fully known
     [4] From Stewart – date unknown

Source: Adapted from R. Newman, (1982) 'Which surface' *GC & HTJ*, 26 Feb, p. 21.

Hard and synthetic surfaces may have less bounce than natural surfaces and can jar players' limbs more severely. Their harsher surface texture can cause severe abrasions and burns to players who fall. However, well constructed and maintained non-grass surfaces have one great advantage over turf on a soil base: the latter suffers from damage by play in wet weather resulting in muddiness and poor drainage. Hard porous surfaces may not drain fast enough to permit play at all times, but many of the new special synthetic surfaces incorporate underdrainage which permits rapid

Table 6.2 Guideline management operations and methods for medium 'play-upon' grass

Operation	Objectives	Suggested methods
Control height	To maintain a playing surface	Gang mow to between 20 and 40mm in summer, 35 and 75mm in winter.
Correct compaction	To improve duration and drainage and hence sward growth and playability.	Spike regularly.
Control thatch	To improve surface drainage and grass growth and limit disease.	Harrow; rotarake; maintain pH and nutrients at adequate levels.
Feed	To maintain sturdy growth under mowing regimes and hard wear.	Apply fertilizer e.g. 20.10.10 at 250 kg/ha apprx in summer and more dressing if needed.
Level	To create a firm level playing surface after disturbance by frost heave, repair work, etc.	Harrow/roll when necessary and when soil is not wet.
Repair work	To maintain an intact playing surface; speed up natural regeneration, prevent weed ingress.	Cultivate work areas and reseed or turf badly damaged parts Top dress and overseed minor damage.
Improve drainage.	Minor	Spike; tine; top dress work sand; Cultivate sand into top horizon; sand slit; improve under drainage. Remake pitch
Control unwanted species	Major *See also* Correct compaction above. To remove broadleaves which may weaken sward, be slippery, compete with grasses.	Spray with suitable selective weedkiller once a year.

Table 6.3 Lawns and fine turf: estimated resource requirements

Source	Operation	SMV	Unit
K	Mow: 24″ machine: unboxed	4.25	100m^2
K	Mow: 34″ Atco (ride-on): boxed off	4.56	100m^2
K	Mow: 24″ machine: boxed off	5.28	100m^2
W	Mow: 17″ Atco: boxed off	5.36	100m^2
K	Top dress	53.46	100m^2
Sa	Lute topdressing into turf	1.90	100m^2
Sh	Lute topdressing into turf	29.94	100m^2
K	Roll: Aveling Barford C.A.	8.91	100m^2
Sa	Roll using Vibroll	7.61	100m^2
D	Roll 24″ light hand roller	23.00	100m^2
K	Fertilize by hand	5.09	100m^2
W	Fertilize small areas by hand	2.90	100m^2
W	Apply herbicides, etc., knapsack sprayer	32.50	100m^2
Sh	Apply herbicides, etc., knapsack sprayer	20.36	100m^2
Sh	Spike Sisis Turfman (hand machine) 32″	4.19	100m^2
Sa	Spike Sisis Autoturfman, solid tine	1.50	100m^2
Sh	Scarify Sisis Rotorake 19″	5.27	100m^2
Sh	Scarify/Rake: Horwood Powarake	4.19	100m^2
Sh	Rake grass off, e.g. after scarifying	15.57	100m^2
W	Rake and remove mowings	11.00	100m^2
Sh	Clip edges with long handled shears	27.55	100m
K	Clip edges with long handled shears	25.13	100m
W	Clip edges: long handled shears	51.90	100m
K	Edge off with half moon	68.03	100m
W	Edge grass with half moon	90.00	100m

See Table 2.2 on p. 37 for details of sources.

removal of water. Compared to natural turf on soil they are, therefore, true 'all weather' surfaces (Newman, 1982; Gunne and Robinson, 1985).

Sports can also be played on nonporous surfaces such as asphalt. Asphalt is tough and relatively cheap to lay and to maintain. Although it does not have the playing qualities of the more sophisticated hard surfaces or of grass, it is suitable for 'kickabouts' and general use areas which get a great deal of wear. Many such small pitches have been built in inner city areas which lack recreational facilities.

Synthetic turf has a very high capital cost. Although it is popular for football and baseball pitches in the USA, only one football pitch in Britain (Queens Park Rangers F.C.) have adopted this surface (in 1983) (Anon, 1983b). It may be that natural turf on a non-soil base built on the 'all sand' construction principle will become a more popular option for top quality pitches. Fulham F.C., for example, has had its pitch converted to all-sand construction, based on the cell system in which sub-surface drainage and irrigation are combined (Anon, 1983a). The pitch was built and seeded during the drought of 1983 and was ready for play by the 83/84 season. The

Table 6.4 Fine sports turf: estimated resource requirements

Source	Sport	Operation	Unit/time
D	Cricket	Cut table – 36″	4.6/100m^2
		Cut wicket – 18″ (double cut)	10.0/100m^2
		Cut outfield – 36″	1.8/100m^2
		Mark out wicket	15.0/occ
		Mark new boundary	53.4/occ
		Mark established boundary	21.2/occ
		Repair wicket	27.5/occ
		Cut lift and lay turves for table repair	32.4/m^2
		Erect posts and wire to protect table	18.8/occ
		Fertilize using 24″ spreader	3.4/100m^2
		Spray table	7.2/100m^2
		Scarify table	155.5/occ
		Rotorake	5.5/100m^2
		Brush table	16.0/table
		Brush pitch	97.9/occ
		Roll wicket (5 cwt)	4.4/100m^2
		Roll wicket (2 cwt)	3.8/100m^2
		Hollow tine with fork	21.0/10m^2
D	Bowling	Prepare for match	35.0/occ
		Put aside lines ready for cutting	13.0/occ
		Collect up lines for storage	21.0/occ
		Set out wet weather sheets	16.0/occ
		Cut grass	74.0/green
		Roll – light weight roller	35.0/green
		Roll – Savel Roller	131.0/green
		Check levels and correct with sands	786.0/occ
		Repair patches on green and reseed	14.0/10m^2
		Brush green with soft brush	45.0/green
		Water green with hose	45.0/green
		Scarify – 18″ Sisis	71.0/green
		Scarify by hand springbok	650.0/green
		Aerate using Sisis aerator	181.0/green
		Aerate using fork	8.0/10m^2
		Aerate using Paterson's Spiker	97.0/green
		Top dress by hand	880.0/green
		Apply fungicide using can	127.0/green
		Apply fungicide using sprayer	76.0/green
		Spray selective weedkiller	5.0/gall
		Drag green with mat	55.0/green
		Fertilize/spread chippings with cyclone spreader	19.0/green

See Table 2.2 on p. 37 for details of sources.

key to the provision of cost-effective sports pitches lies in efficient underdrainage facilities.

Conversion to all-sand requires complete removal of the original pitch. However, existing pitches on soil can be improved by sand slitting or by incorporation of sand into the soil profile, in order to improve drainage and wear characteristics. These techniques are also fairly new and their longer-term performance is not yet known. Besides initial capital costs the improved surfaces require continued maintenance to keep the drainage functioning and are not therefore cost-free panaceas for bad drainage. Poorly implemented sand slitting may produce little improvement in drainage. Since sand slitting is now being widely used to improve existing sports areas, Managers need to take care that investment in this technique is not wasted by poor construction methods. (Escritt, 1980; Drury, undated).

The sand used has to be graded to very precise requirements thereby ensuring that it provides the right combination of drainage and aeration together with the necessary resilience to the player's tread (Adams et al., 1971).

Table 6.1 compares the capital and maintenance costs of some of these surfaces and their unit costs for a predicted amount of use at 10 and 30 years. For the purposes of the table it is assumed that maintenance levels and costs stay the same over these lifetimes and that the surface will last 30 years without the need for major repair, improvement or replacement. If this proves to be so, some interesting points emerge.

First, it should be noted that, in all cases, maintenance cannot be reduced very much without also reducing the amount of use which the surface can accept. Increased levels of maintenance to produce a better quality surface are likely to be required for competition and professional sports. However, the resulting increased costs can usually be justified by the specialist needs of the players and by the revenue which they are capable of earning from spectators, promotions, and so on.

Sport of all types has increased tremendously in popularity during the last few years. Even previously minor sports, such as athletics, can now command a substantial audience. Increased expenditure on sports facilities for top quality players can therefore be cost-effective.

The cost per hour of use for grass on native soil remains relatively high compared with other surfaces, because of the high cost of maintenance and the low capacity for intensive use.

The very high maintenance costs of the hard porous surface, in relation to other surfaces, stands out. Nevertheless, because of its capacity for high wear, its unit cost per hour remains relatively low.

The unit cost of synthetic turf is comparatively high during the first ten years of its life. Although costs drop sharply thereafter, the life expectancy of these surfaces is not yet known. However, synthetic turf has been used mainly for top quality professional pitches where the quality of the playing surface is all-important.

For situations in which fine sports turf is considered to be the most appropriate playing surface, Tables 6.3 and 6.4 provide guidelines on the estimated resource requirements.

Where the requirements are less demanding, medium 'play-upon' grass comes into its own. Guidelines on the management operations and methods involved in maintaining this type of surface are provided in Table 6.2.

MONITORING SPORTS USE

Table 6.1 is based on the predicted annual use of different sports surfaces and the points which have just been noted refer to these levels of use. It is important to monitor actual use, in order to see how closely sports provision and sports use match each other. It is much easier to assess the performance of sports turf than it is, for example, to evaluate whether a park is doing its job. The number of satisified players can be used as a measure of the benefits derived from provision of the particular sports facility. It is much harder to assess use and satisfaction where the functions of a landscape area are less straightforward. Nevertheless, cost per unit per hour of play is not the only criterion which should be used in evaluating the cost-effectiveness of sports area management. Some further questions also need to be asked about the way money is spent. For example:

- Should players of a minority sport, which is costly to provide per unit area, be deprived of their game, because it is expensive per user? For example, should those who play bowls be catered for, even though the cost per user can be very high indeed?
- Are there other sports, or other recreation facilities, for which a demand but no facilities exist? Should they be catered for as well? Should the Manager try to discover the real requirements of his clients and satisfy them rather than providing the facilities which he expects people want?

If the Amenity Manager has considered the points made in the first part of this chapter, and is satisfied that the users needs are known, the next step is to determine how these needs can be satisfied in the most cost-effective way.

IMPROVING THE COST-EFFECTIVENESS OF SPORTS AREAS

Under-used areas
If monitoring of sports areas shows that some are under-used, the manager needs to consider how he can improve their cost benefits. The main options are reviewed in the paragraphs which follow.

Increasing use.   A large proportion of open space in cities is taken up by school playing fields. These are used in the day, but are often not used outside school hours because it is difficult to supervise them adequately. In addition, many recreation grounds in cities are under-used during the day when most people are at work or at school, although shared use schemes with local sports clubs have proved successful. It has been suggested that some under-used school playing fields should be sold off to be used for other purposes.

Time sharing of sports areas is therefore one way of increasing use and hence the cost-effectiveness of maintenance. This has been known to work in some Boroughs, but to encounter difficulties elsewhere.

Raising maintenance levels.   This may seem a paradoxical solution for an over-costly feature, but the provision and sustained maintenance of a better standard of surface may encourage more use and so improve cost-effectiveness.

Changing to another use.   The intensity of management and therefore the cost of maintaining different types of sports turf differ greatly. Bowling greens, for example, are particularly costly. If the turf is under-used it may be more sensible to consider converting it to another use. This could be another sport for which there is a greater demand, or another landscape feature altogether, such as an area of bedding or of simple 'walk-on' lawn.

It may be possible to pass the costs of maintenance on to another organization such as a club. Many bowling greens, for example, are maintained by members.

Charging fees for use can provide revenue, but someone must be available to take fees and charging can be counter-productive if fees are too high and people are discouraged from playing.

Over-used areas

Much sports turf suffers from over-use. However, many managers do not have the resources with which to combat wear and to cater for intensive use. Some of the factors which influence costs and some ways in which the Amenity Manager can use limited budgets, machinery, staff and materials in the most cost-effective way are discussed next.

Costs of heavily used sports areas maintenance are largely influenced by:

Soil/substrate type.   The type of soil or substrate on which the turf grows. The fact that modern pitches intended for intensive use and high quality performance are being built on pure sand shows how overwhelmingly important is good drainage of the substrate (Stewart, 1980).

It may be posible to use an in-situ sandy substrate for sports turf construction or to import one. This is likely to withstand wear much better than an ordinary topsoil. Construction undertaken without the use of topsoil will also usually be much cheaper. However extra feeding and possibly irrigation may be required.

Drainage.   Drainage is influenced heavily by substrate, by the fall of the sports area and by underdrainage. Falls of up to 1 in 40 are acceptable on most pitches.

Nearly all heavily used sports turf needs a good underdrainage system. Land drains at normal agricultural spacings of 3 to 4 metres are typical of older sports pitches, but are not usually adequate for intensive use. Play on wet pitches leads to compaction of the ground which in turn makes drainage worse and inhibits root growth. Soils become smeared and capped. Consequently the turf is more easily torn. Bad drainage therefore affects both growth of the turf and quality of the surface.

Many pitches are out of play for much of the winter due to bad drainage and this adversely influences their 'cost per use'. Bad drainage also makes maintenance more difficult and increases the need for repairs. The objective of a drainage system is to produce a surface on which play is limited by the wear tolerance of the grass rather than the ground. Drainage can be improved by a variety of means which range from routine operations such as spiking through sand slitting to installation of new drains and even a new pitch. Major capital works to improve drainage are very expensive and can subject the manager to additional maintenance as well, particularly additional weed control on the disturbed ground, interference with mowing cycles and extra wear on other pitches whilst reseeding is proceeding. The Amenity Manager, therefore, needs to assess carefully how much the turf can be improved by maintenance and repair techniques involving less financial outlay.

Low intensity improvements.   Experts (Escritt, 1980) consider that much sports turf could be maintained to an adequate standard if our current grounds maintenance knowledge and techniques were applied more thoughtfully. Sports turf maintenance is one of the most well documented fields in landscape management.

A great deal of written information is available in books and articles, from seed catalogues such as the one published by Johnsons, from machinery manufacturers, from the Sports Turf Research Institute and from others involved in the field. In addition the necessary resources, such as machinery and equipment, turf grass seeds, fertilizers and pesticides, are also available. Since the knowledge and the means are available, cost-effectiveness need not, and should not, be limited on their account. Indeed it seems that many of the limitations which do exist could be solved by better staff training and education, leading to better use of available techniques and equipment. Even so there is a minimum amount of time which must be spent in order to maintain sports turf adequately. Between 3 and 4 hectares have been suggested as the average area which one full-time maintenance worker can sustain. Even with the most cost-effective techniques (Parker, 1982) the standards of maintenance are likely to fall, if the work inputs are reduced. For example many school playing fields receive little more than gang mowing from a hard pressed local authority maintenance staff. It is not surprising that the turf degenerates steadily from year to year without the benefits of spiking or tining, feeding, reseeding or repair. Without adequate supervision many tractor drivers are inclined to mow grass too short partly because it 'looks nicer' and partly under the misapprehension that it will grow more slowly. Grass that is cut 'little and often' grows leaf more slowly, but retains a good root system and hence wear tolerance. Grass cut back too hard and infrequently can be severely weakened. Grass cut too low looks unsightly in drought.

Major improvements.   It is essential for a sports area to be able to sustain adequate use. If normal maintenance methods cannot bring about the improvements which are necessary, then the Amenity Manager may need to invest money in more capital intensive remedies, such as sand slitting. Table 6.1 shows that even the more expensive surfaces can be competitive with turf on soil, as long as they are well used and have been properly constructed (Daniel, 1969; Daniells, 1977; Shiels, 1982, 1984). Sand slitting is a 'half-way house' between standard maintenance methods and more drastic alterations to the turf. It has been used successfully on many sports areas. However, it is a relatively new technique and its long-term performance is not yet known. There are also many examples of pitches where sand slitting has not produced an improvement in drainage. Nevertheless, if well done, it can be a cost-effective way of improving wear without spending a very large amount of money.

Alternative pitch provision.   The 'honey pot' principle can be applied to sports turf management. For example, the provision of practice cricket wickets or informal football pitches can help to decrease pressure on main pitches.

The Amenity Manager may feel that construction of one or more 'all-weather' pitches is essential, in order to provide his clients with an adequate service (Tipp, 1983). Besides accepting a large amount of use itself, an 'all-weather' surface can help to take the pressure off natural turf facilities.

Supervision

Good supervision of sports turf and players is usually essential to ensure that the ground is not over-used, used without permission or otherwise abused. For example, golfers may use cricket squares as informal tees if not prevented. The presence of on-the-spot supervision is one of the advantages of having a resident groundsman in contrast to mobile maintenance staff, who only visit the site periodically.

Repairs and renewal

The Amenity Manager may need to carry out repairs to sports turf and other surfaces, and to renovate old or establish new sports areas. Some guidelines are provided in the paragraphs which follow.

Comparative manpower requirements.   The manpower required to carry out repairs involving reseeding and laying down new turf is given later in Table 9.9.

Some values for repair and renewal of hard surfaces are given subsequently in Table 23.7.

Table 6.5 Ancillary sports activities: estimated resource requirements

Sport Source	Operation	Frequency	SMVs
Tennis			
K	Sweep	1/week	$1.97/100m^2$
K	Roll	As nec	$8.91/100m^2$
D	Check nets	daily	2.00/court
Sh	Remove nets	1/year	6.00/court
Sh	Erect nets	1/year	18.50/court
D	Remark lines	2/year	23.00/court
Bowling Greens			
D	Check and make up levels	As nec	786.00/green
D	Prepare for match (set out mats etc)	1/match	35.00/green
D	Lay rainproof sheet	As nec	16.00/green
Sh	Clear channels	1/year	3.06/m
D	Light Roll	As nec	35.00/green
D	Heavy Roll	1/year	131.00/green
D	Brush	1/week	45.00/green
Cricket			
H	Brush pitch	4/year	92.90/pitch
K	Roll wicket	1/week	7.93/wicket
K	Rope off square	1/game	20.00/square
D	Mark new wicket	Once	101.00/pitch
H	Mark estab wicket	1/game	15.00/pitch
D	Renovate wicket	As nec	77.00/pitch
H	Mark outfield	1/game	21.20/pitch
Football[1] [2]			
D	Initial marking	once	375.00/pitch
D	Routine marking	1/week	27.50/pitch
Sh	Paint posts	1/year	4.00/m
Sh	Erect posts	1/year	112.00/pitch
Sh	Erect nets	As nec	24.00/pitch

Note: [1] Similar times are involved for most pitch sports.
[2] Many jobs such as net erection vary in frequency depending on whether the site is secure and whether there is likely to be vandalism between games.
See Table 2.2 on p. 37 for details of sources.

The material which the Amenity Manager chooses for a new or replacement sports surface will affect the surface's performance and the costs of maintaining it, as the tables detailed above show. The same is true of grass. The species and cultivars which make up sports turf have a strong influence on the performance, as well as on both the cost and maintenance.

Grass species and cultivars.   These affect such qualities as the capacity to withstand wear, winter hardiness, drought tolerance, growth rate and form.

·   During the last decade there has been a great deal of work on breeding grass cultivars for sports turf. A large range of cultivars is now available which are suitable for many different purposes. One of the most important advances has been the breeding of ryegrass cultivars which are both hard wearing and slow growing. 'Sprinter', 'Loretta' and 'Manhattan' are examples. These can reduce the number of cuts needed by sports turf by 25% or more and their price is comparable to faster growing cultivars.

Hard wearing characteristics affect the amount of renovation which the turf requires. The new cultivars have been said to be capable of reducing this by 30% for the same level of use (Gore, Cox and Davies, 1979).

The different characteristics of sports turf grasses are included in the tables given in Chapter 9 on 'Grassland Establishment', in particular Table 9.11.

Ancillary tasks

Because of the punishing wear and compaction that most sports turf undergoes certain tasks that are operated only occasionally on general purpose turf, such as spiking and scarifying, become very much more important and are performed at more frequent intervals.

Other ancillary tasks are of course associated with each particular sport – marking out pitches, erecting and maintaining nets, placing flags, and so on. Depending on the frequency of use and the security of the pitches these tasks may be infrequent or may in fact represent nearly as large a labour requirement as is needed for mowing.

Typical resource requirements are given in Table 6.5.

References   Adams, W.A., Stewart V.I. and Thornton D.J. (1971) The assessment of sands suitable for use in sports fields. *Journal of the Sports Turf Research Institute* **47**, 77–85.

Anon (1983a) Fulham FC plumps for all weather pitch. *Surveyor* **162** (4764)

Anon (1983b) Good grounds for artificial turf. *Surveyor* **162**(4759), 29.

Anon (1983c) *Synthetic Surfaces*, National Turfgrass Council Special Report No. 1, Bingley.

Daniel, W.H. (1969) The Purr-Wick rootzone system for compacted turf areas. Proceedings of the first international turfgrass research conference. Sports Turf Research Institute Bingley.

Daniells, I.G. (1977) Drainage of sports turf used in winter: a comparison of some rooting media with and without a gravel drainage layer. *Journal of the Sports Turf Research Institute* **53**, 56–72.

Escritt, J.R. (1980) Construction and maintenance of sports turf. In (eds I.H. Rorison and R. Hunt) *Amenity Grassland: an Ecological perspective*, John Wiley & Sons, Chichester.

Gooch, R.B. and Escritt, J.R. (1975) *Sports Ground Construction Specifications*, 2nd ed. National Playing Fields Association.

Gore, A.J.P. Cox, R. and Davies, T.M. (1979) Wear tolerance of turf grass species. *Journal of the Sports Turf Research Institute* **55**, 45–68

Gunne, S. and Robinson, J. (1985) On safer ground. *GC & HTJ*, 5th April.

Law, S. and Bowen, M. (1973) London's footballers need more pitches. *Sports and Recreation* (vol?)

Martyn, G. (1982) What Price Compaction, *GC & HTJ* **192** (2).

Natural Environment Research Council (1977) *Amenity Grasslands – The Need for Research*. Publications Series C. No. 19. NERC, Swindon.

Newman, R. (1982) Which surface? *GC & HTJ* **192** (2).

Parker, J. (1982) Mown grass – techniques, costs and alternatives. In (eds P.R. Thoday and C.H. Addison) *Cost Effective Amenity Landscape Management*. University of Bath, Bath.

Shiels, G. (1981) Mud glorious mud, *GC & HTJ* **191** (16).

Shiels, G. (1982) Towards an ideal, *GC & HTJ* **192** (2).

Shiels, G. (1984) All that's green, *GC & HTJ* **195** (1).

Stewart, V.I. (1976) Wallowing in mud. *Journal of Parks and Recreation* **41**, 38–51.

Stewart, V.I. (1980) Soil drainage and soil moisture. In (eds R. Hunt, and I.H. Rorison) (1980) *Amenity Grassland – An Ecological Perspective*. John Wiley and Sons, Chichester.

Tipp, G. (1983) *Sorting Out Synthetics*. Proceedings 2nd National Turfgrass Conference, NTC, Bingley.

Further reading

Adams W.A., Stewart V.I. and Thornton D.J. (1971) The construction and drainage of sports fields for winter games in Britain, In: *Welsh Soils Discussion Group Report No 12*, 85–95.

Baker, S.W. (1981) The effect of earthworm activity on the drainage characteristics of winter sports pitches. *Journal of the Sports Turf Research Institute*, **57**: 9–23.

Baker, S.W. and Isaac, C.P. (1987) The effect of rootzone composition on the performance of winter games pitches – sward quality and playing quality. *Journal of the Sports Turf Research Institute*, **63**: 57–81.

Bell, M.J., Baker, S.W. and Canoway, P.M. (1985) Playing quality of sports surfaces – a review. *Journal of the Sports Turf Research Institute*, **61**: 26–45

Canaway, P.M. (1980) Wear. In (eds R. Hunt, and I.H. Rorison) *Amenity Grassland – an Ecological Perspective*. John Wiley and Sons, Chichester.

Canaway, P.M. (1981) Wear tolerance of turfgrass species. *Journal of the Sports Turf Research Institute*, **57**: 65–83

Canaway, P.M., Colclough, T. and Isaac, S.P. (1987) Fertilizer nutrition of sand golf greens 1. Establishment and pre-wear results. *Journal of the Sports Turf Research Institute* **63:** 37–48.

Dury, P.L.K. (undated) *In the World of Cricket Pitches*. Nottinghamshire

County Council Education Department.

Evans, R. (1987) Make good and mend: routine winter renovation. *Horticulture Week*, 16th October.

Garelick, P. (1987) Changing waves of water. *Horticulture Week*, 10th April. Turf irrigation.

Garelick, P. (1987) Three way turf. *Horticulture Week*, 16th October.

Gibbs, R. (1987) Peak performance. *Horticulture Week*, 30th January.

Greenfield, I. (1979) Turf. In: *Landscape Techniques*, (ed. A.D. Weddle) Heinemann, London.

Greenfield, I. (1980) The modern approach to golfcourse construction. *Landscape Design*, **130**: 31–4.

Gunn, S. (1986) The moisture balance. *Horticulture Week*, 14th March. Grass irrigation.

Gunn, S. (1986) More than skin deep. *Horticulture Week*, 9th May. Pitch construction.

Gunn, S. (1987) Heavy use on fine turf. *Horticulture Week*, 8th May.

Hacker, J. (1987) Wear tolerance in amenity and sports turf – a review. In (eds P.R. Thoday, and D.W. Robinson) *Acta Horticulturae 195*. The scientific management of vegetation in the urban environment.

Hacker, J. (1987) Winning wickets. *Horticulture Week*, 16th October.

Harbridge, M. (1987) A sandy situation: the economics of sand slitting. *Horticulture Week*, 16th October.

Harbridge, M. (1987) Diagnosing drainage problems. *Horticulture Week*, 16th October.

Lawson, D. (1986) Healthy hibernation. *Horticulture Week*, 10th October. Grass fertilization.

Lawson, D.M. (1987) The fertiliser requirements of *Agrostis castellana/ Festuca rubra* turf growing on pure sand. *Journal of the Sports Turf Research Institute*, **63**, 28–36.

Mulqueen J. (1976) Aspects of the construction of sportsfields and recreation grounds in Ireland. In (ed. C.E. Wright), *The Next Decade in Amenity Grassland*. Queens University Press, Belfast.

Peel, C.H. and Shidrick, J.P. (1987) Preliminary trials of perennial ryegrass cultivars. *Journal of the Sports Turf Research Institute*, **63**, 116–35.

Robinson, G.S., Moore, K.K. and Murphy, J. (1977) Effect of a number of standard and slow release nitrogenous fertilisers on the quality of fine turf. *Journal of the Sports Turf Research Institute* **53**, 74–84.

Royle, D. (1986) Fighting fungus. *Horticulture Week*, 9th May. Grass.

Shildrick, J.P. (1985) Thatch: a review. *Journal of the Sports Turf Research Institute*, **61**, 8–25.

Sports Turf Research Institute (1983) Problems of dual purpose use. *Sports Turf Bulletin*, **142**, 8–10.

Sports Turf Research Institute (1983) Water and watering. *Sports Turf Bulletin* **142**, 10–12.

Sports Turf Research Institute (1983) Current disease problems on fine turf. *Sports Turf Bulletin*, **143**, 3–5.

Sports Turf Research Institute (1983) Thatch in fine turf. *Sports Turf Bulletin*, **143**, 5–7.

Sports Turf Research Institute (1984) Some principles on the use of fertilizers for sports turf. *Sports Turf Bulletin*, **146**, 8–10.

Sports Turf Research Institute (1985) Some maintenance problems on golf courses. *Sports Turf Bulletin* **151**, 10–12.

Sports Turf Research Institute (1986) Special issue on golf courses. *Sports Turf Bulletin*, **155**.

Sports Turf Research Institute (1986) Controlled droplet applications. *Sports Turf Bulletin*, **154**, 2–4.

Sports Turf Research Institute (1986) Low maintenance amenity grass. *Sports Turf Bulletin*, **154**, 4–7.

Sports Turf Research Institute (1986) Autumn and winter maintenance. *Sports Turf Bulletin*, **153**, 10–12.

Sports Turf Research Institute (1986) Drainage problems. *Sports Turf Bulletin* **153**, 2–5.

Sports Turf Research Institute (1987) The new pesticide legislation. *Sports Turf Bulletin*, **156**, 2–5.

Sports Turf Research Institute (1987) Storage and handling of pesticides. *Sports Turf Bulletin*, **156**, 5–7.

Sports Turf Research Institute (1987) Slow release fertilisers. *Sports Turf Bulletin*, **156**, 7–10.

Sports Turf Research Institute (1987) Research update in cultivars. *Sports Turf Bulletin*, **157**, 4–7.

Sports Turf Research Institute (1987) Research update on football pitches. *Sports Turf Bulletin*, **157**, 2–4.

Sports Turf Research Institute (1987) Special issue on bowling greens. *Sports Turf Bulletin*, **158**.

Stewart, V.I. (1973) Sportsfield drainage. *Playing Fields* **34**, 70–4.

Stewart, V.I. and Adams, W.A. (1971) *Lectures on Sportsfield Construction and Management*. University College of Wales, Aberystwyth.

7 THE MANAGEMENT OF MAIN GRASSLAND TYPES: LOW WEAR–LOW MAINTENANCE GRASSLAND

7.1 Introduction

FEATURES

The essential feature of low maintenance grasslands is that they receive little attention in terms of cutting on an annual basis. As will be apparent by now, small reductions in the frequency of cutting can create disproportionate problems when it comes to the use of existing machinery. Grass that has been left uncut for some time can only be handled by special flail or reciprocating cutter mowers which can be slow on an area basis. Such mowers only prove economic if there is a large enough area to mow to justify their hire or purchase, and the frequency of cuts is kept below about three times per year (Gilmour, 1982).

Estimates of the resource requirements for low maintenance grassland are provided in Table 7.1.

Low maintenance grass cannot usually be left completely uncut, although this is the approach adopted on motorways. Occasional maintenance is usually needed to prevent woody plant invasion or excessive build-up of thatch, which can be a fire hazard.

The question of whether grazing can be regarded as low maintenance is sometimes hotly debated, but the decision is usually based on the experience of the managing body and whether they have the resources required to handle livestock.

In some favoured sites, usually semi-rural in nature, grazing or hay cropping rights can be let to local farmers.

Unless grazing or grassland productivity is the objective, it is generally desirable that the grassland is not too fertile as the site may be swamped by large amounts of rank growth and unpleasant weeds (Grubb, 1977).

Table 7.1 Low maintenance and wild flora grassland: estimated resource requirements

Source	Operation	SMV	Unit
W	Cut rough grass: long reach flail	7.20	100m^2
W	Cut rough grass: Munro Bantam	1.54	100m^2
S	Mow-Allen scythe	15.07	100m^2
H	Cut grass general rough areas 30″ Turner flail	5.90	100m^2
K	Mow rough grass area: Mayfield	9.76	100m^2
W	Mow rough grass area: Condor		
D	Rake up long grass and load	33.50	100m^2
D	Rake grass to piles	11.50	100m^2
D	Fork cuttings to heaps and set alight	82.00	100m^2

See Table 2.2 on p. 37 for details of sources.

LOCATIONS

Typical sites where low maintenance grassland are found include:

- Motorways
- Neglected land
- Streamsides
- Steep slopes
- Rural parks
- Some commons
- Derelict land

For the most part low maintenance grassland, certainly in urban situations, only occurs where sites are inaccessible for machinery or have been neglected or regarded as somehow falling outside the jurisdiction of local councils. Occasional exceptions occur with certain areas of grassland that fall within the boundary of the town which are so large, or of a traditional rural character, such that they have not been managed in too intensive a form. Hampstead Heath, and Phoenix Park, Dublin, are two examples.

FUNCTIONS

In recent years, however, there has been a greater understanding of the value of such grassland, in economic, aesthetic and ecological terms.

Where there are areas designated as low maintenance grassland, a positive opportunity is presented to create effects that are normally made impossible by frequent mowing (Kelcey, 1977).

Normally this means that the grassland can be made, or encouraged to be, floristically rich. Usually there are two broad divisions of flower-rich grassland to consider. The first is naturalized ornamental bulbs which are often deliberately planted and may consist of entirely introduced species and man-made hybrids. The desired effect is essentially aesthetic only. The second is a grassland containing a diversity of flowering herbaceous perennials and biennials. These communities are usually intended to preserve or simulate natural species-rich meadows or grasslands. They have become increasingly important and are described below.

The other valuable function for infrequently cut grasslands is to act as a habitat for wildlife (Baines and Smart, 1984). They are often valuable as bird nesting and feeding sites or, depending on the species present, as dragonfly or butterfly reserves. Wet grasslands are particularly valuable in fulfilling this role.

7.2
Wild flower swards

TYPES OF SWARD

Wild flower grasslands can generally be divided into two separate types.

The first is any type of preserved natural rural plant community. Before management changes are introduced to such a site it will be valuable to obtain specialist advice on the relative importance of the existing species and the likely effects of planned operations. Seemingly quite innocent operations, even to land adjoining the site, can produce dramatic changes.

The second is artificially created floral mixtures. These do not usually concern the establishment of particularly rare and precious species, partly because of gaps in understanding, partly because of the fact that a rare plant often has demanding requirements and partly due to controls over the collection of seed material. The intention is usually to create an overall effect, aesthetic and educational, and to provide a general feeling for the life style of the plant or plants under threat.

ESTABLISHING A WILD FLOWER AREA

The degree of investment put into creating a wild flower area can vary greatly depending on the type of effect desired and the existing site conditions.

Site manipulation and topographical adjustment may be desirable to produce wet conditions. The stripping of topsoil or the deposition of subsoil serve to reduce the fertility of the site.

Many commerical seed mixes are available for the establishment of floral grasslands. Some of the cheaper mixtures actually consist of a collection of agricultural legume seed which are in no sense 'natural', are too vigorous and tend to increase the fertility of the site. More recent offerings from specialist seed houses are very much better (Wells, Bell and Frost, 1981).

If the site already contains vegetation, establishment may only be possible in disturbed ground or areas that have had small local application of non-residual herbicide. An alternative or complementary approach is to plant pot-grown plants or bulbs into the grass (Bisgrove, 1988).

Turf, introduced from natural sites or areas which are about to be developed, has sometimes been successful in acting as a source of natural colonization (Walthern and Gilbert, 1978; Gilbert, 1982).

**7.3
General principles
of 'ecological'
maintenance**

With the exception of specific natural habitats, such as sand dunes or marshes, there are typically three traditional forms of floriferous grassland and herbaceous habitats which can be emulated through appropriate management. These are:

1. *Abandoned fields or other disturbed sites.* Unless restrained by low fertility or re-disturbance, these can often evolve to a community of rank herbaceous plants and ultimately woodland;
2. *Grazed pastureland*, which typically favours low growing and rosette species of herbaceous perennials. Typically these do not flower prolifically unless the grazing pressure is relaxed. Often the best display is of buttercups and cowslips in early spring before the land is dry enough to support stock. Trial systems of rotational grazing to relax the pressure at other times of the year may be valuable;
3. *Hay meadows*, which typically contain the most spectacular and diverse communites of flowering plants. Evolution to climax woodland is controlled by the hay cutting at times of the year which allow herbaceous plants to grow tall and flower. This is the type most commonly emulated by a flail mowing regime.

The key principle of ecological management really involves just restricting the growth of the coarse species, in order to provide room for the more desirable ones (Grime, 1973). Many different methods are used to achieve this, ranging from control of nutrition (removal of clippings, soil stripping), use of herbicides and growth regulators, mechanical disturbance of the ground, mowing, grazing or burning. The latter three are the most common (Wells, 1982).

Although mowing can be controlled more precisely than the other two methods, it can also be more unifying and reduce the habitats available to some sward components. A single annual cut is all that is needed on poor soils. Unless the intention is to promote the growth of a certain species there is often no reason why this cannot be done in winter. If the cuttings need to be removed this may entail the hire of some form of silage harvester. Mowing is not appropriate on steep slopes.

Grazing presents problems in providing efficient enclosure and controlling the intensity. Livestock handling is beyond the experience and resources of many management authorities. Dunging can excessively increase site fertility.

Burning is often the best solution for steep slopes and simulates the past management of some limestone and chalk grassland pastures. Through this technique the removal of some invading plant species that livestock do not control can be achieved. It can contribute to soil impoverishment through the loss of N and P.

DERELICT LAND SWARD PROBLEMS

It is not appropriate to give more than a general review here of the problems of derelict land and their potential solutions. Reference should be made to specialist publications or to outside expertise. However, a summary of the typical problems that occur with different types of waste is provided in Table 7.2.

Initial establishment of swards on derelict land usually requires consideration of three stages: first the control of physical stresses; secondly the control of toxicity problems; and thirdly the build-up of appropriate nutrient levels.

Physical Problems
Physical problems can be broadly divided into the categories which follow.

Too little water retention
Normally this problem is rarely so severe that it is impossible to establish grasses and herbs, particularly if an autumn sowing is chosen. However it can limit the growth rate of valuable species, such as legumes, thereby compromising the success of the reclamation. If the need for treatment is accepted there are various solutions available, the choice of which will depend largely on the available resources and materials near the site. One option is to incorporate some form of material which either improves the structure of the substrate or itself can hold water. Examples are fine soil, overburden, or water holding polymers. An alternative approach is to alter the topography of the ground, so that the maximum rainfall is channelled to where it is needed. Where possible it is important to select drought-tolerant sward species.

Inadequate aeration
This problem usually results from standing water and poor drainage or methane gas production in the soil. The former can usually be solved by ripping the surface layers of the soil, but occasionally more widespread topographic and drainage adjustments need to be made. The methane problem can be best treated by piping off the methane from its source and ensuring an airtight cap between this and the sward (Parry and Brummage, 1981).

Concretion: poor root penetration
A variety of treatments from ripping to dynamiting have been attempted to overcome this problem. Usually herbaceous plants are good at finding and exploiting cracks in the soil pan and this, together with weathering, will eventually help to ameliorate the problem.

Erosion and instability
On areas where instant stability is crucial at any expense, various civil engineering methods such as Wyretex can be used to stabilize the soil.

Bitumen components in hydroseeding mixes can also help. In less sensitive situations a fast growing component in the seed mix, such as an agricultural hybrid rye-grass, will help to stabilize the soil until the other species have grown. Usually these agricultural components will not persist for more than a season (Foister, 1977; Gemmell, 1977).

Toxicity problems

Toxicity problems are also often predictable. These fall into two main categories:

Extreme pH.   The treatment of acidity is often simple on derelict land, because the sites often have a very low lime requirement due to a coarse structure and a lack of organic matter. Some types however, particularly colliery wastes, generate acidity through chemical breakdown of their components. Very high lime levels may be required in anticipation of this acidity generation. This high liming rate may in turn require high levels of phosphate to be applied to overcome the subsequent temporary shortfalls in the availability of this nutrient (Rorison, 1979).

Highly alkaline soils are less easy to treat, although incorporation of acidic organic matter can be successful. Often plant communities can survive extremely high pH substrates better than low ones. Wastes such as steel furnace slag, which is highly alkaline, can develop very valuable and spectacular wild flower colonies.

Heavy metal toxicity.   Resistant grass species are available which can survive in low to moderate concentrations of some metals (Bradshaw and Smith, 1972), specifically lead, zinc and copper. If concentrations are too high some form of capping will be essential to prevent the toxic ions from moving into the root zone. In some cases chemical treatment may be possible.

Nutrient problems

Nutrient build-up on derelict land sites can often be a much more long-term challenge. Most plant nutrients can be added very simply using artificial fertilizers.

Phosphate may be a problem simply because certain chemical conditions can make it immobile, but generally a slow-release application of Enmag, Slag or rock phosphate will be adequate.

The biggest problem is caused by nitrogen, which is so highly mobile that it is easily leached. Man-made slow-release fertilizers are expensive and short lived. Nitrogen can only be stored in the soil as organic matter, which slowly breaks down to release inorganic plant nutrients.

If an instant effect is required, organic matter can be added directly as sewage sludge or peat. Most other types of organic matter are unsuitable, because of their low nitrogen content which means that they can actually deprive the soil of nitrogen for a period.

Often a more successful approach is to establish nitrogen-fixing plants,

Table 7.2 The characteristics of derelict land sites inhibiting vegetation establishment and management

Ground material	Physical inhibitors											
	Instability of substratum	Steep slopes	Sheet and gulley erosion	Broken, uneven surface	Stoniness-absence of fines	Compaction or Consolidation	Cementation or iron pan	Wind turbulence, sand blasting	Poor drainage or flooding	Water Stress	Extremes of surface temp	Spontaneous combustion
Unburnt colliery spoil	**	**	**	*	*	**	–	*	*	*	**	**
Burnt (red) colliery spoil	**	**	**	*	*	*	–	*	*	*	*	–
Colliery washery waste	**	*	**	–	–	*	–	*	*	*	**	*
Metal mine spoil (non-ferrous)	*	*	**	*	*	*	–	**	*	*	**	–
Ironstone waste	*	*	*	*	–	*	–	*	*	*	**	–
Fluorspar mine waste	*	–	**	–	–	*	–	*	*	*	**	–
Blast furnace slag	–	**	–	**	**	*	**	–	–	**	*	–
Metal smelter waste (non-ferrous)	*	**	*	**	*	–	–	*	–	**	**	*
Chemical wastes	*	*	**	–	–	*	**	*	–	*	*	–
Gas works waste (spent oxide)	–	*	**	–	–	–	**	**	*	*	**	*
Pulverized fuel ash	–	–	–	–	–	*	**	**	*	*	*	–
Boiler and incinerator ash	–	–	*	*	*	–	–	*	–	**	*	–
Lime waste	–	*	*	–	–	–	*	*	*	*	–	–
China clay waste and pits	*	**	**	–	–	–	–	*	*	*	*	–
Quarry stone waste and pits	–	**	*	**	**	**	–	*	*	*	*	–
Clay pits and exposed clay	–	**	*	*	–	**	–	–	*	*	*	–
Sand and gravel workings	–	*	–	*	–	*	–	*	*	*	*	–
Slate and shale wastes	**	*	*	**	**	–	–	*	–	**	**	–
Demolition rubble	–	–	–	**	**	**	–	–	–	**	*	–
Domestic refuse	–	–	–	*	–	*	–	–	*	*	–	**
Sewage wastes	–	–	–	–	–	–	–	–	*	–	–	–
Peatland stripping	–	–	**	–	–	–	–	*	**	–	*	–
SCORE	14	22	25	18	13	18	9	20	16	25	27	7

** inhibitory factors very pronounced
 * inhibitory factors present
 – inhibitory factors negligible or absent

Source: Design and Management of Industrial Derelict Sites, Gemmell, R.P., (1979)
Ecology and Design in Amenity Land Management

| | | | | | | Chemical inhibitors | | | | | | | |
Acidity (low pH)	Potential acidity (Fe^2 S)	Alkalinity (high pH)	Salinity (osmotic effects)	Toxic cations present	Toxic anions present	Emission of toxic gases	Toxic organic compounds	Low nutrient (NPK) status	Phosphate fixation	Low ion exchange capacity	Low organic matter content	Absence of soil flora & fauna	
**	**	—	*	*	—	—	—	**	**	*	**	**	32
*	—	—	—	*	—	—	—	**	*	*	**	**	23
**	**	—	*	*	—	—	—	**	**	*	**	**	27
*	*	—	—	**	—	—	—	**	—	**	**	**	24
—	—	—	—	—	—	—	—	*	—	*	**	*	15
*	—	—	—	**	—	—	—	**	—	*	**	**	19
—	—	**	—	—	—	—	—	**	*	**	**	*	22
*	*	—	—	**	—	—	—	**	—	**	**	**	25
*	*	**	**	**	**	*	*	**	*	*	**	**	30
**	**	—	**	**	**	**	*	**	**	**	**	**	34
—	—	**	**	—	**	—	—	**	*	*	**	*	21
*	—	—	—	—	—	—	—	**	—	**	**	*	15
—	—	**	*	—	*	*	—	**	*	*	**	*	18
*	—	—	—	—	—	—	—	**	—	*	**	*	16
*	—	—	—	—	—	—	—	*	—	*	**	*	19
*	—	—	—	—	—	—	—	**	—	*	**	*	16
*	—	—	—	—	—	—	—	**	—	**	**	*	15
—	—	—	—	—	—	—	—	**	—	**	**	*	20
—	—	—	—	—	—	—	—	**	—	**	**	*	16
—	—	—	—	—	*	*	*	—	—	—	—	—	9
—	—	—	—	**	*	—	—	—	—	—	—	—	4
**	—	—	—	—	—	—	—	**	—	—	—	*	11
18	9	8	9	15	9	5	3	38	11	26	38	28	

which are not only able to tolerate the site deficiency but also build up nitrogen rich organic matter as they die or shed leaves and roots. To grow successfully, these may need liming or the addition of phosphate (Bradshaw *et al.*, 1981).

Other stresses not directly attributable to the derelict soil must also be controlled, such as overgrazing and trampling.

Most derelict land areas, even when successfully reclaimed, will never be particularly fertile. There is often a limited range of plants that can survive the hostile soil conditions. Non-grass components of the sward, especially nitrogen-fixing legumes, are essential for the successful growth of the grass. They are therefore unsuitable for anything but informal low maintenance mixed species swards. They are often very attractive, because the physical and chemical adversity limits the growth of overly competitive plants (Johnson, 1978).

In some situations the management required, particularly the cutting regime and fertilizing, will be aimed at maintaining adequate growth of the legumes. At least in the short term, grass growth is a secondary objective.

Clovers and many agricultural legumes require large levels of phosphate in the soil and a substrate that is not too acid. Whilst they may survive more adverse conditions, their rate of nitrogen fixation will suffer. Cutting height should not be so low as to weaken the legume but occasional cutting or grazing may be necessary to maintain an open sward for the legume to survive (Jeffries, *et al.*, 1981).

NATURALIZED BULB AREAS

These areas have superficially much in common with any early flowering mixed herbaceous and grass sward. There are however one or two critical differences that can greatly influence the management systems adopted.

Naturalized bulb areas, or areas planted to look natural, are often 'tolerated' as drifts amongst areas of traditionally mown general purpose grass. They also usually consist of species that complete their flowering and photosynthesis requirements early in the year. Traditionally, therefore, the system adopted has been to delay mowing until June, after which the area is cleared ready to be cut for the rest of the year, like the surrounding closely mown sward.

The result can actually be more expensive than normal gang-mown grass.

References   Baines, J.C. and Smart, J. (1984) *A Guide to Habitat Creation.* Ecology Handbook No. 2. GLC, London.

Bisgrove, R.J. (1988) Flower-rich grassland using wildflower plants and growth retardants. In (eds G. Taylor and J.P. Shildrick) *Wildflowers 87, NTC Workshop Report 14*, National Turfgrass Council, Bingley, West Yorks.

Bradshaw, A.D. and Smith, R.A.H. (1972) Stabilisation of toxic mine wastes by the use of tolerant plant populations. *Trans. Inst. Min. Metall.*, **81**, 230–7.

Bradshaw, A.D., Jeffries, R.A. and Putwain, P.D. (1981) Growth, nitrogen accumulation and nitrogen transfer by legume species established on mine spoils. *Journal of Applied Ecology*, **18**, 945–56.

Foister, J. (1977) Planting to stabilise steep slopes. In *Landscape Design with Plants*. (ed Clouston, B.) Heinemann. London.

Gemmell, R.P. (1977) Reclamation and planting of spoiled land. In: *Landscape Design with Plants* (ed. B. Clouston), Heinemann, London, pp. 179–97.

Gemmell, R.P. (1979) Design and Management of industrial derelict sites. In *Ecology and Design in Amenity Land Management*. (eds S.E. Wright and G.P. Buckley) Wye College, University of London.

Gilbert, O.L. (1982) Turf transplants increase species diversity. *Landscape Design*, **140**, 37.

Gilmour, W.N.G. (1982) The management of greenspace on a low budget. In: *Cost Effective Amenity Land Management*. (eds C.H. Addison and P.R. Thoday) University of Bath, Bath.

Grime, J.P. (1973) Control of species diversity in herbaceous vegetation. *Journal of Environmental Management*, **1**, 151–67.

Grubb P.J. (1977) The maintenance of species richness in plant communities: the importance of the regenerative niche. *Biol. Rev.*, **52**, 107–45.

Jefferies, R.A., Bradshaw, A.D. and Putwain, P.D. (1981) Growth, nitrogen accumulation and nitrogen transfer by legume species established on mine spoils. *J. Appl. Ecol.*, **18**, 945–56.

Johnson, M.S. (1978) Land reclamation and the botanical significance of some former mining and manufacturing sites in Britain. *Environmental Conservation*, **5**, 223–8.

Kelcey, J. (1977) Creative Ecology 1: selected terrestrial habitats. *Landscape Design*, **120**: 34–7.

Parry, G.D.R. and Brummage, M.K. (1981) Solid wastes: reclamation and management. *Landscape Research*, **6** (3), 15–18.

Rorison, I.H. (1979) The effects of soil acidity on nutrient availability and plant response. In *The Effects of Acid Precipitation on Terrestrial Ecosystems. (ed. T.C. Hutchinson)* Plenum Publishing, New York.

Walthern, P. and Gilbert, O.L. (1978) Artificial Diversification of grassland with native herbs. *Journal of Environmental Management*, 7, 29–42.

Wells, T.C.E., Bell, S. and Frost, A. (1981) *Creating Attractive Grasslands Using Native Plant Species*. Interpretative Branch, Nature Conservancy Council, London.

Wells T.C.E. (1982) Creating attractive grasslands in amenity areas — some problems and solutions. In *Cost Effective Amenity Land Management*. (eds C.H. Addison and P.R. Thoday) University of Bath, Bath.

Further reading

LOW MAINTENANCE GRASSLAND AND GENERAL
PURPOSE TURF

Colvin, B. (1968) Landscape Maintenance of Large Industrial Sites. *ILA Journal*, **84**, Nov.

Foister, J. (1977) Planting to stabilise steep slopes. In *Landscape Design with Plants*. (ed Clouston, B.) Heinemann. London.

Gemmell, R.P. (1977) Reclamation and planting of spoiled land. In:

Gaman, J.H. and Sayers, C.D. (1973) The amenity potential of low maintenance grasses. *Journal of Environmental Planning and Pollution Control*, **1** (4), 21–31.

Haggar, R.J. and Squires, N.R.W. (1979) The scientific manipulation of sward constituents in grassland by herbicides and one pass seeding. *British Grassland Society, Occasional Symposium* **10**, 223–34.

GENERAL PURPOSE TURF

Bradshaw, A.D. (1987) Turf establishment on hostile sites. In *The Scientific Management of Vegetation in the Urban Environment*. (eds P.R. Thoday, and D.W. Robinson) Acta Horticulturae 195.

Durry, S. (1986) An impressive line up. *Horticulture Week*, 9th May. Grass machinery.

Parr, T.W., Cox, R. and Plant, R.A. (1984) The effects of cutting height on root distribution and water use of ryegrass turf. *Journal of the Sports Turf Research Institute*, **60**, 45–53.

Porter, J. (1987) Cheap and Diverse. *Horticulture Week*, 8th May.

Shildrick, J.P. (1986) Mowing regimes and turfgrass regrowth. *Journal of the Sports Turf Research Institute*, **62**, 36–49.

Shildrick, J.P. and Peel, C.H. (1986) Turfgrass trials on city centre sites. *Journal of the Sports Turf Research Institute*, **62**, 182–99.

WILD FLOWER SWARDS

Baines, C. (1984) The wild garden and meadow gardening In *Classic Garden Design*. (eds R. Verey) Viking, London.

Bradley, C. (1982) An ecological approach. In: (eds A. Ruff, and R. Tregay) *An Ecological Approach to Urban Landscape Design*. Occasional Paper No 8. Department of Town and Country Planning, University of Manchester.

Cole, L. and Keen, C. (1976) Dutch techniques for the establishment of natural plant communities in urban areas. *Landscape Design*, **116**, 31–4.

Genders, R. (1976) *Wildlife in the Garden*. Faber & Faber, London.

Grime, J.P. (1972) The creative approach to nature conservation. In: *The Future of Man*, 47–54. (eds F.J. Ebling, and G.W. Heath) Academic Press, London.

Greenwood, R. and Moffatt, D. (1982) Implementation techniques for more natural landscapes. In *An Ecological Approach to Urban*

Landscape Design. (eds A. Ruff and R. Tregay) Occasional Paper No 8. Department of Town and Country Planning, University of Manchester.

Masters, P. and Lancaster, I. (1980) *Wildlife Areas for Schools*. Durham County Conservation Trust.

Ruff, A. (1986) Running wild. *Horticulture Week*, 28th March.

Walthern, P. and Gilbert, O.L. (1978) Artificial diversification of grassland with native herbs. *Journal of Environmental Management*, **7**: 29–42.

Wells, T.C.E. (1987) The establishment of floral grasslands. In *The Scientific Management of Vegetation in the Urban Environment*. (eds P.R. Thoday, and D.W. Robinson) Acta Horticulturae 195.

Wilson, R. (1981) *The Back Garden Wildlife Sanctuary Book*. Penguin, Harmondsworth.

DERELICT LAND SWARDS

Banerji, Shanka, K. (ed.) (1977) *Management of Gas and Leachates in Landfill*. USEPA 500/9–7/626.

Bradshaw, A.D. (1982) The biology of land reclamation in urban areas. In *Urban Ecology*. (eds R. Bornkomm, J.A. Lee, and M.R.D. Seaward), Blackwells. Oxford.

Bradshaw, A.D. and Chadwick, M.J. (1980) *The Restoration of Land: The Ecology and Reclamation of Derelict and Degraded Land*. Studies in Ecology, 6 Blackwells. Oxford.

Bradshaw, A.D., Costigan, P. and Gemmell, R.P. (1981) The reclamation of acidic colliery spoil. 1. Acidic production potential. *Journal of Applied Ecology*, **18**, 865–78.

Bradshaw, A.D., Roberts, R.D., Marrs. R.H., Skeffington, R.A. and Owen, L.D.C. (1981) The importance of plant nutrients in the restoration of china clay and other mine wastes. *Trans. Inst. Min. Metall.*, **91**, 42–50.

Chadwick M.J. and Goodman S.T. (eds) (1972) *The Ecology of Resource Degradation and Renewal*. Blackwells Scientific Publications, Oxford.

Coppin, N.J. and Bradshaw, A.D. (1982) *Quarry Reclamation*. Mining Journal Books, London.

Davis, B.N.K. (ed.) (1982) *Ecology of Quarries*. ITE, Cambridge.

Dennington, V.N. and Chadwick, M.J. (1983) Derelict and waste land: Britain's neglected and resource. *Journal of Environmental Management*, **6**, 229–39.

Dutton, R.A. and Bradshaw, A.D. (1982) *Land Reclamation in Cities*. HMSO, London.

Flower, F.B., Gilman, E.F. and Leone, I.A. (1981) Landfill gas, what it does to trees and how its injurious effects may be prevented. *Journal of Arboriculture*, **7** (2), 43–52.

Gemmell, R.P. (1977) *Colonisation of Industrial Wasteland*. Edward Arnold, London.

Greenwood, E.F. and Gemmell, R.P. (1978) Derelict land as a habitat for rare plants in S. Lancs. and W. Lancs. *Watsonia*, **12**, 33–40.

Hackett, B. (1978) *Landscape Reclamation Practice*. IPC Science and Technology Press.

Hayward, S. (1974) *Quarries and the Landscape*. British Quarrying and Slag Federation, London.

Kelcey, J.G. (1975) Industrial development and wildlife conservation. *Environmental Conservation*, **2**, 99–108.

Pankhurst, E.S. (1973) The effects of natural gas on trees and other vegetation. *Report No. 14 of the Welsh Soils Discussion Group*, pp. 116–30.

University of Newcastle-upon-Tyne (1972) *Landscape Reclamation*. Vols I & II. IPC Business Press, Guildford.

Williamson, N.A., Johnson, M.S. and Bradshaw, A.D. (1982) *Mine Wastes Reclamation*. Mining Journal Books, London.

8 THE MANAGEMENT OF MAIN GRASSLAND TYPES: SEMI-NATURAL GRASSLANDS

8.1 General characteristics

Semi-natural grassland is used here as a general term to include such landscape types and habitats as chalk grassland, lowland and upland heaths, moors and peatlands, coastal flats and sand dunes, footpaths and green lanes, and relatively unmanaged derelict, buffer and transport corridor land including verges, pipelines, wayleaves, etc.

Estimates of the areas of these landscape types and habitats is provided in Table 8.1. The relative costs involved in their management are indicated in Table 8.2.

General principles relating to the low-cost informal or ecological management of grasslands have been discussed above. Management of chalk grasslands, heathlands and moorlands have certain elements in common which separate them to some extent from other forms of grassland and are discussed in the pages which follow. An excellent publication by the Countryside Commission (Lowday and Wells, 1977) gives detailed guidelines on grassland and heathland management in country parks, most of which are relevant here.

Traditionally these open areas have been managed for extensive grazing, largely by sheep. Management has been aimed at promoting the growth of forage material and preventing the development of competing vegetation. This has been accomplished chiefly by a combination of grazing pressure and burning. These processes, which systematically deplete these extensive areas of nutrients, have tended to maintain them as biologically unproductive, ecologically rich and attractive open areas (Harpur, 1971; Grime, 1980, 1986).

Heathland and moorland, whose vegetation is dominated by heath-type dwarf shrubs, are usually less rich in species than the notably diverse chalk grasslands. However, these extensive areas of open land are usually highly attractive as areas of informal recreation and are the dominant landscape types in most national and some country parks. Management of grassland and heathland in such 'wildscape' amenity areas is usually geared towards

Table 8.1 Estimated areas of natural and semi-natural grasslands in Great Britain

Habitat	Area hectares × 10³ (rounded)	Source*/year
Coastal (mud flat, marsh, dune, shore, shingle beach)	119–263	Hubbard, J.C.E. (1960s) Nature Conservation Review (1977)
Lowland grass (institutional ownership)	289	Liddle, M.J. (1974) (adjusted)
and heath (road verges and green lanes)	214	NCR (1977)/Dunball, A.P. (1980)
Peatland	63	NCR (1977)
Upland grass and heath	1500–4057	Thomas, B. (1956) Bunce, R.G.H. (1982)
Other (railway verges and tracks)	20	NCR (1977)
(pipelines, wayleaves, mineral workings and tips, non-urban wasteland)	421	DOE (1979)

* Where a range of areas is given the source of the lower one is quoted first.

Source: Cobham (1983)

maintaining both ecological and recreational values, and combining these with the needs of farming, shooting, etc., where applicable. The requirements of areas managed largely for conservation and recreation tend to be significantly different from those managed for more commercial ends (Duffey *et al.*, 1974; Green, 1983); in particular a smaller scale pattern of diversity is usually desirable, while fire risks both to and from visitors is greater and tends to impose restrictions on management (Green, 1986).

8.2 Moorlands and heathlands: management operations

Heathlands have developed largely on leached acid, nutrient-poor soils. Under traditional management the aim has been to promote the growth of a heather dominated vegetation, so as to provide grazing for sheep. Heath vegetation is largely shrubby, and if allowed to develop naturally under normal grazing pressures it tends to become large and woody and to produce less of the young growth which is nutritious and palatable to sheep and grouse (Grant, 1971).

In order to prevent this, heather moors are rotationally burnt every 10 to 15 years, so that new young stands are periodically created, and the oldest stands destroyed. The aim of burning is to remove top growth without subjecting the lowest branches or the ground with its seed bank to lethally high temperatures. The regenerative strategies, vegetative and sexual, of heather are adaped to fire. Correctly burnt stands are rapidly recolonized

Table 8.2 The management of semi-natural areas approximate relative variable costs

Element	Cost index	1977/78 £ per ha
Short grass	100	185
Long grass	12	23
Heath	20	38
Scrub	15	28
Woodland	35	65

Source: Warren and Harrison (1978)

by seedlings and new shoots from the old plants, if weather conditions are right (Gimmingham, 1972).

The temperature of a burn can be limited by burning downwind in February to March when the ground is still wet and the vegetation will not get too hot. This type of burn also tends to skip small tussocks which are beneficial for insects and animal life. Exhaustive precautions must be taken to control the fire spread. Firebreaks should be made, and there should be provision to have beaters standing by to control the spread. Sometimes alginure sprays are used to protect areas that are to be preserved.

Fires which become too hot may kill the lowest nodes and roots of heather plants, destroy seeds in the litter and soil layers, and at worst actually set the litter layer alight. This can cause prolonged and extremely damaging smouldering fires which destroy organic soil horizons, and may burn down to the mineral layers beneath, leading in some cases to serious soil ersion.

Fires which burn into the wind tend to be slower and hotter than those which burn before the wind. Older, woodier stands produce hotter fires.

Burning is usually done in early spring when conditions are dry, although the permitted burning season runs from October to April in most areas. Patterns of burning vary with management aims. For sheep, strip patterns of less than 2 ha are recommended. For grouse and wildlife conservation smaller square or circular areas are preferable. Where many visitors are normal it may be necessary to burn or cut firebreaks to help the control of accidental or intentional fires (Ward, 1972).

The other traditional and still lucrative activity on heath and moorland is management for grouse. Grouse feed largely on young heather, but unlike sheep they require older stands in which to breed. Heathland management for grouse is also traditionally accomplished by periodic burning, but the areas burnt are on a smaller scale and the cycles of regeneration tend to be longer.

Grazing pressures may have to be relaxed to aid regeneration, although the exact timing required will depend on unknown variables such as weather patterns (Welch, 1977).

Feasibility of burning is affected by availability of manpower and of

Table 8.3   Heather moorland management: estimated resource requirements

Source	Operation	Time (minutes)	Unit	Typical frequency
CRC	Burning	1.42	100m²	12–15 yrs (2)
CRC	Cutting Turner flail	0.60	100m²	12–15 yrs (1)
CRC	Cutting; Jungle Buster and 4 wheel drive tractor	0.47	100m²	12–15 yrs (2)

Sources: 1. (1981) 'Heather Management on Ottercops & Raechester Farms' Countryside Commission: Demonstration Farms Project Topic Sheet.
2. Personal communication: Game Conservancy (1979).

suitable weather: dry days with suitable wind strengths and speeds are needed. Burning is labour-intensive and can therefore be expensive. It may be hard to organize in remote areas as a supply of manpower is needed at short notice when weather conditions are right.

Representative resource requirements are given in Table 8.3.

It is possible to manage heathland mechanically by cutting with a swipe or similar type of machine. This may be cheaper where mechanical access is possible since the process is considerably faster than burning. However, it is not feasible on very steep, rocky or boggy ground which may comprise much of the terrain in many of these heathland areas. Furthermore regeneration from beneath a mulch of cut debris tends to be slower than recovery after controlled burning (Auld, 1983).

RE-ESTABLISHING UPLAND HEATHS

Upland heath vegetation is for the most part relatively unproductive. Nutrient levels are low and the growing season is short. Such areas are, therefore, particularly prone to erosion from running water, trampling or overgrazing. A percentage of exposed ground is natural component of such habitats and should be accepted. However, where it occurs as a result of unusual pressures or disturbance remedial measures may be necessary.

Natural regrowth on such sites may be very slow and, to control further erosion, fencing together with artificial seeding may be required. Any plant material so used should of course match the local vegetation. One of the most successful techniques has been to collect litter from beneath existing upland heather stands for spreading on the bare areas. This litter contains a large number of viable seeds which germinate upon exposure to the light (Putwain, 1983).

To encourage rapid germination and growth of the seedlings some experts recommend that light lime and fertilizer dressings should be applied to the exposed soil (Tallis and Yaldon, 1983). Excessive treatments should be avoided as they may produce a residual effect that changes the natural character of the vegetation.

Where the cause of erosion is severe and repetitive, the above treatment may be insufficient. To prevent further poaching or erosion of surrounding soils, some form of more permanent soil improvement may be required. Laying Wyretex, fertilizing the soil and re-seeding with grasses may be an option. In some circumstances conversion to a low cost hard surface, which blends well with the surrounding geology, has had to be accepted.

8.3
Chalk grasslands: management operations

In the main these grasslands have developed on nitrogen-impoverished, alkaline soils that traditionally have been subjected to grazing by sheep and rabbits. Any management regime, which both defoliates the vegetation closely and regularly, and impoverishes the substrate, can produce a similar type of grassland. Where sheep grazing has stopped, chalk grasslands tend to accumulate biomass, to become dominated by coarse, slow-growing litter-forming grasses such as tor and brome grass, and eventually by scrub. Diversity decreases as these successions take place, because the typical small grassland species adapted to a regime of defoliation are displaced or smothered by the more productive grasses and woody plants. Before the advent of myxomatosis rabbit grazing arrested this succession in some areas (Wells, 1971b, 1973).

Management of a neglected chalk grassland may be a two stage process of:

1. Reclamation to reduce nutrients and litter; and
2. Action to maintain a low, nutrient-poor sward.

Fairly drastic action may be needed to counteract the decline of misman-aged chalk grassland. Where controlled burning is compatible with other local interests, it may be the most cost-effective method of reclamation. It disperses much of the nutrient content accumulated in foliage and litter, and destroys litter itself (Green, 1972). It can, if required, be used on a small scale to deal with colonies of coarse grasses, and has been found to be effective in controlling tor and brome grass.

Cutting with or without removal of cut debris can also be used in grassland reclamation. There appears to be some doubt about the need to remove cuttings, and there is evidence that leaving grass cuttings does not always significantly affect subsequent nutrient levels. Where scrub, partic-ularly nitrogen rich gorse or broom, is cut, however, it appears advisable to remove or burn it (Wells, 1971a)

Timing of the cuts is important if the flora present in the sward is to be preserved. It is desirable to imitate the traditional pattern of cropping as much as possible even if this means cutting some species in mid-flowering. This may be essential to prevent them from becoming too dominant.

Experiments in delaying cutting may be useful to improve the visual effect of the swards. However, careful account must be taken of both the changes in species composition and the reduced ease of management before any different cutting regime is adopted on a wide scale. Even so, it is inevitable that cutting will lead to some change in species composition, because it is less selective and more unifying than grazing.

The compatibility of burning with the conservation of fauna is not as well understood as we might wish, so there may be need for caution in the use of this technique on a large scale. Low intensity burns, i.e. downwind in winter, will tend to skip some tussocks which act as safe refuges for some animals. Smaller scale rotational burning is preferable to allow re-colonization of the animals from unburnt areas.

Once biomass has been reduced above ground, maintenance is required to keep productivity in check. Where grazing is not feasible, regular cutting has been shown to maintain typical chalk grassland as a species-rich community.

OTHER MANAGEMENT OPERATIONS

The use of conventional top dressings is neither necessary nor desirable in the case of chalk grassland. Species-rich grasslands and heathlands are attractive and interesting due to the low nutrient status of the substrates on which they have developed.

Farmland manure can be applied at normal rates to chalk grassland, without necessarily disturbing the ecosystem. Artificial fertilizers, how-ever, are more liable to cause unwanted changes in species composi-tion and diversity. Thus they are not recommended.

Use of herbicides is not normally desirable except in the form of spot treatments to control specific areas of unwanted vegetation. Physical, mechanical or biological control methods are preferable wherever possible, particularly where wildlife conservation is an important aim of management. Asulam is perhaps an exception. It has proved helpful in controlling bracken in some situations without apparent detriment to the ecosystem.

Tables 8.4. and 8.5. provide a guide to the level of machinery and associated manpower resources required to undertake the main operations entailed in the management of rough grassland and scrub areas.

8.4
Sand dunes: main
problems and
operations

Sand dunes are dynamic habitats characterized by a throughput of sand. The long-term stability of the environment relies on the continued supply of sand to the system, usually from the sea or along the shore, and its passage through the dunes. There are a number of distinct zones within the classical dune system which can be summarized as foreshore, foredune (white dune), rear dune (grey dune), slack and links (East Lothian C.C., 1970; Brown *et al.*, 1985).

However, this assemblage of landform and associated vegetation communities is sometimes modified with one or more of the elements missing.

Table 8.4 Rough grassland and scrub management: estimated resource requirements

Source	Operation	Time input	Unit	Typical frequency	Typical man hrs/ha/yr
FMH	Cut and clear with chainsaw and flail	2.00 hrs	100m^2	1/5–10 yrs	20–40
H	Rip hook brambles, etc.	5.68 hrs	100m^2	1/5–10 yrs	57–114
Sh	Fuji brush cutter – open areas	1.19 hrs	100m^2	1/5–10 yrs	12–24
FMH	Clear wet grass land and hand flail	2.10 hrs	100m^2	1/5–10 yrs	21–42
VC	Chalk grassland scrub clearance and stump treatment	16.00 hrs	1000m^2	1/5–10 yrs	16–32
VC	Grassland scrub clearance and burning	12–20 hrs	1000m^2	1/5–10 yrs	12–40
Sa	Grub hedge and burn to dispose	5.02 hrs	100m^2 of face	As necessary	NA
CRC	Burn heather	30.00 hrs	1 ha	1/10–15 yrs	2–3
RB	'Meadow' (1 cut and raking off and rotary triple and tr) (NB. Same as grass cut/7–10 days)	1.00 hr	100m^2	1/year	100
E	Swipe (wooded areas)	2.93 hrs	1 ha	1/yr	3
	Swipe (rides)	0.04 hrs	100m^2	1/yr	4
Sa	Riphook grass, rake up and dispose	1.88 hrs	100m^2	1–2/yr	94–188
Sa	Hand scythe grass, rake up and dispose	1.62 hrs	100m^2	1–2/yr	81–162

See Table 2.2 on p. 37 for details of sources.

Dunes are attractive for recreation, as they are close to the sea and have a 'natural' vegetation cover which is often aesthetically pleasing, but they pose considerable management problems in many parts of Britain and elsewhere, because of their inherent fragility.

Management and maintenance problems in sand dunes can be caused by a number of changes in the environment. Some of these changes may be natural and some induced by man's activities (Metcalfe, 1979).

Natural changes arise through modifications in climate, alterations in sea level, cessation of source of supply of material along shore or from seabed and subsequently storms can cause major and sudden changes to a dune system.

Man-induced changes likewise arise from many sources, notably:

- Recreation pressures;
- Coastal construction causing a change in supply of sand;
- Changes in the drainage bowl causing a change in the supply of fine riverine material to the beach and sea;
- Changes in off-shore contours due to dredging, etc.;
- Changes in grazing pressures of sheep and rabbits etc.;
- Construction of buildings and so on close to the dures;
- Loss of sand for construction;
- Introduction of alien plant species.

Dunes may serve a number of complementary functions such as coastal protection, nature conservation, recreation and the protection of water supplies.

Table 8.5 The management of rural general-purpose grassland (e.g. country park): estimated resource requirements

Source	Operation machine operation	Time inputs hours	Unit	Typical freq/yr × per yr	Typical man hrs/ ha/yr
FMH	Cut: tractor and forage harvester and trailer and remove grass	20.00	1 ha	2	4.4
FMH	Cut: tractor and flail	20.00	1 ha	2	2.4
Sa	Mow: Allen Scythe	25.12	1 ha	2	50.2
FMH	Harrow: tractor and harrow	1.00	1 ha	1	1.0
FMH	Roll: tractor and roller	1.00	1 ha	1	1.0
FMH	Fertilize: tractor and spreader	0.70	1 ha	1	0.7
W	Fretilize: tractor and speaker (vicon)	0.50	1 ha	1	0.5
	Manual Operation				
Sa	Riphook grass	1.62	100m^2	2	324.0
Sh	Hand cut with sickle	1.12	100m^2	2	224.0
Sh	Cut grass with hand shears: flat ground	2.71	100m^2	2	271.0
W	Rough cut: hook/scythe/ hand shears	1.95	100m^2	2	390.0
D	Hook open area	1.23	100m^2	2	246.0
D	Scythe open area	0.37	100m^2	2	74.0
Sa	Scythe grass	1.32	100m^2	2	264.0
K	Hand cut weeds between trees	0.75	100m^2	2	150.0
H	Rip hook banking (approx 45°)	2.00	100m^2	2	400.0
D	Hook banks	1.02	100m^2	2	204.0
D	Shear banks	1.63	100m^2	2	327.0
W	Weedeater	0.27	100m^2	2	54.0
W	Weedeater in densely planted areas	0.09	100m^2	2	18.0
H	Rip hook dense undergrowth	5.68	100m^2	1	568.0

See Table 2.2 on p. 37 for details of sources.

Table 8.6 Dune restoration and management: estimated resource requirements

Source	Operation	Manpower Requirements	Unit
SCS	Collect and plant marram	1–2 days	100m^2
SCS	Thatch dune with brush wood	3–5 hrs	100m^2
SCS	Brush wood fencing	2–3.5 days	100m
SCS	Post and wire fencing	4 days	100m
SCS	Chestnut paling (£1.50/m in 1984)	2–4 days	100m
SCS	Boardwalk construction in situ (not pre-prepared)	16 days	100m
SCS	Footpaths – cut, fill and edge	8 days	100m
SCS	Footpaths – surface and roll	4 days	100m
NT	Brash collection – open work	62–125 hrs	Ha
NT	Brash collection – closed work	187–375 hrs	Ha
NT	Grass collection – open	58–112 hrs	Ha
	– closed	42–85 hrs	Ha
NT	Transport brash – open	21–32 hrs	Ha
NT	Transport brash – closed	62–94 hrs	Ha
NT	Transport grass – open	7–10 hrs	Ha
	– closed	5–7 hrs	Ha
NT	Planting – open work	200–300 hrs	Ha
	– closed	300–500 hrs	Ha

Note: 1. Open work refers to situations where only heavily eroding faces are protected by brash and straw. Closed work is where all the site is covered. In the latter case operations take longer, but less grass material is needed.
2. These estimated resource requirements relate to the performance of the various operations by motivated workers, e.g. MSC rangers, keen volunteers.

Source: J. C. Bacon, Northumberland Coast Warden, National Trust.
See Table 2.2 on p. 37 for details of sources.

If the dunes are accreting, i.e. continually expanding, then the management problems are usually simpler. The primary edge of dune habitats will be constantly forming and the areas inland which are passing onto a more normal soil structure and climax vegetation are reasonably able to withstand any land use designated.

If the dune area is slowly eroding, either through climatic or geographical changes or through increased human pressure, much greater efforts may be needed to preserve the desirable habitats. The need for this is not only for the sake of conservation but because all of our coastal areas serve as a form of natural defence from the sea. In the past many devastating inland floods and sand storms have been attributed to the loss of stable beach systems.

This may include the deliberate control of the encroachment of climax or colonizing vegetation and sometimes the creation of large-scale artificial disturbance to the dunes to prevent over-stabilization, loss of dune slacks and so on (Brooks, 1979; Gunney, 1984; Anon, continuing publication).

The following paragraphs are concerned with the general management of dune systems, in order to maintain their continued existence and attractiveness. Certain general principles apply:

- A continued supply of sand must be maintained or, if not, artificially introduced;
- It is not possible to stabilize and vegetate the entire system. A certain amount of erosion and bare sand is a natural part of this dynamic habitat;
- Events on the foreshore or at a distance along the coastline from the site can be as important or more important than processes within the dunes themselves;
- It is advisable to channel people along strengthened pathways through the dunes to protect foredunes from excessive trampling. As with mown grass, zoned fertilization can improve wear tolerance;
- The position of car parks and access points are critical in influencing the distribution of users;
- Compaction of the foreshore can cause less infiltration of sea water into the beach, a higher wash and potential erosion of the toe of the foredunes;
- Grazing animals and rabbits may be significant management problems causing erosion and instability. However, dunes in recent years, like many chalk grasslands, experienced reduced grazing pressure. Mowing may be necessary to control the species composition and to produce grazing areas for wild fowl;
- Plant material can be introduced to help in trapping and stabilizing sand, but such action needs to be taken with care. Sea buckthorn, for example, can spread uncontrollably. It is generally best to use only species which are natural to the site such as: Sea lyme grass and marram grass, which are the most commonly planted species in Britain's dune systems. Sea buckthorn can play a valuable role in acting as a barrier to people and by building up soil nitrogen. Its spread can be limited by mowing the suckers and planting male-only plants, so that no berries form;
- It is possible to use fences (chestnut paling is common) and brushwood to trap sand, particularly on the foreshore;
- It is important to record and repair all damage as soon as possible before serious erosion problems occur.

In order to assess the necessity and frequency of maintenance tasks, the manager should keep a careful note of:

- Areas of sand accumulation where stabilization may be necessary;
- Pressure areas where potential erosion may call for preventive measures;
- The behaviour of visitors: informative and interpretive signs can be used to promote appropriate visitor response to management action;
- Nature plus growth of colonizing vegetation.

Dunes need regular maintenance where recreation pressures are experienced (Hewett, 1973) or where a sea defence function is recognized. A publication by the British Trust for Conservation Volunteers (Brooks, 1979) summarizes the main requirements for coastland management.

Maintenance can be classified as that required:

- To stabilize dunes and prevent blow-outs;
- To control public access and use;
- To manage vegetation and wild life.

Figure 8.1. shows the major influences and phases of dune management with the accepted methods of maintenance and control.

It is desirable to take specialist advice before embarking on any potentially devastating operations.

RE-ESTABLISHING DUNES

There are several steps that can be taken when attempting to re-establish dunes by changing the natural balance of dune accretion and loss in response to the damage caused by increased or unusual pressure. These are summarized in the sections which follow.

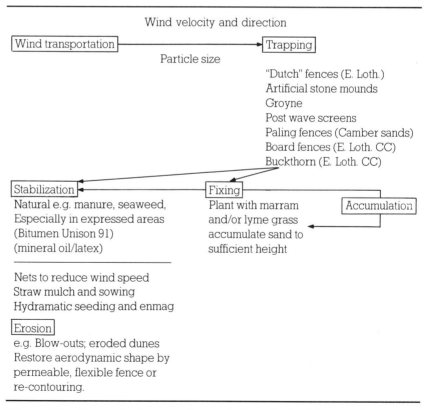

Figure 8.1   The main stages and accepted methods of dune maintenance

SAND FENCING

Where the site receives wind-blown sand, fencing can be used to trap this and either to build up a new dune system or to repair a damaged existing one. The fences used should ideally have a 40 per cent porosity. Fences of greater porosity will be less efficient at trapping sand. More solid fences will cause problems of wind eddying.

The dune that is formed will extend for about 16 times the height of the fence, on its windward side. High fences, however, need to be more wind resistant. Several lines of fencing may be required.

The cheapest form of fencing is to use brushwood, possibly restrained by posts and wires. This system is not suitable for very tall fences and alternatives include chestnut paling or timber slat fencing, although they may only be cost-effective over large areas.

The primary use for fences is to trap sand on a site which will subsequently be re-vegetated or otherwise stabilized. Fencing will not be applicable where existing sand is to be stabilized, unless that sand needs to be re-distributed on site. In the latter case, sand movement by machine may be equally, or more, cost-effective. Once the fences have been almost engulfed, with the result that no more dune accretion takes place, the dunes can be stabilized by planting.

There are two broad approaches that can be taken towards stabilizing existing very exposed areas of sand. These are geared to providing a longer-term solution to the erosion problem through the effective establishment of vegetation.

First, chemical stabilizers can be applied using hydroseeding applicators. There are two broad types: 'glues', such as alginure, that soak into the sand surface and 'mulches' of fibrous material that protect the surface. The stabilizers must be resistant to wind and wind-blown sand, and flexible enough to allow for sand movement or occasional trampling.

When applying the material many of the familiar problems that occur with all amenity spraying tasks become important. Correct care of equipment, reasonably skilful operators, some estimate of application rates and a supply of fresh water are all required.

Alternatively there is the traditional system of sand stabilization, which is to thatch the sand with brushwood to give a 75 per cent porosity. This method is more reliable than chemical stabilization and has the advantage that it is both more resistant to heavy public pressure and also forms more of a deterrent to trampling.

Fresh brushwood that will take longer to rot is desirable, although material with leaves should be avoided as it is bulkier to transport. If the latter has to be used, adjustment should be made to the density of laying in order to achieve the desired porosity once leaves have dropped. The brushwood should be wired to secure pegs thereby preventing loss in winds (Aaron, 1954).

This approach is extremely labour intensive and can be costly, as the material is so bulky to transport and lay. The costs are obviously highly dependent on transport distances.

Planting to provide long-term stabilization may be much more difficult on thatched or 'closed' dunes. One possible approach is to plant before the thatching is done, if the labour can be organized at the correct time of year.

DUNE PLANTING

Long-term stabilization of dunes can only be achieved by aiding the colonization of the natural vegetation on bare sand. In essence, this is simply achieved by collecting marram or sea lyme grass from nearby successful stands and planting them where the sand is to be stabilized. Familiar plant husbandry options operate as much on sand dunes as on any habitat. Excessive trampling and grazing must be avoided. Areas which are accumulating a depth of sand at a great rate should not be planted until the system has stabilized. Where erosion is greater than can be tolerated by even sand dune plants, stabilization by thatching or chemical will be necessary.

Plants should be handled carefully, not left exposed to the air when collected or prior to planting. Heeling them into sand is the best solution. Optimum planting times seem to be early to mid-spring. Initial fertilizer application, particularly with nitrogen, will aid rapid establishment.

Away from the main dunes the grass species mentioned above, which are especially adapted to areas which slowly accrete sand, will tend to lose vigour. Seeding of ordinary turf grasses, especially the fescue species, which can tolerate salt spray, will be the best solution. The husbandry of these grasses will be similar to that required in any low productivity area. Fertilizer application or sand amelioration with topsoil or organic matter may be required. The incorporation of nitrogen-fixing legumes into the sward may prove to be a better solution. Mulches may aid germination where rainfall is low.

Careful control of erosion and user pressure will be necessary for at least two years. Adequate fencing will be required. On areas where user pressure is expected to be high and unavoidable, for example on paths, the addition of top soil to encourage vigorous growth will be beneficial.

The estimated resource requirements for some of the cost-effective operations involved in managing sand dune systems, and especially for their re-establishment, are presented in Table 8.6. They are very variable figures and are much influenced by outside factors, which may vary greatly from site to site. Some operations, such as re-firming shrubs, will become unnecessary after 5–6 years. However, this decrease in work load may be compensated by the deterioration of permanent structures which require more maintenance.

More specific advice on vegetation and wildlife management can be obtained from the Institute of Terrestrial Ecology.

Because of the potential fragility of dune systems, it is not usually desirable to use heavy machinery for maintenance work. As a result, most of the tasks are labour-intensive and correspondingly expensive. Much erosion control in British dunes is therefore done by voluntary groups or under Government-assisted schemes rather than by contract or direct labour.

References   Aaron, J.R. (1954) The use of forest products in sea and river defense in England and Wales. *Forestry Commission Forest Record*, **29**.

Anon (continuing publication) *Plants and Planting Methods for the Countryside*. Countryside Commission for Scotland, Battleby.

Auld, M.H.D. (1983) Heather flailing and burning on the North York moors. In *Heathland Management in Amenity Areas* (ed. J.L. Daniels). Conference summary. Countryside Commission CCP 159, Cheltenham.

Brooks, A. (1979) *Coastlands*. BTCV, Oxford.

Brown, I.H., Wathern, P., Roberts, D.A. and Young, S. (1985) Monitoring sand dune erosion on the Clwyd Coast. *Landscape Research*, **10** (3).

Cobham, R.O. (1983) The economics of vegetation management. In *Management of Vegetation*, (ed J.M. Way) British Crop Protection Council, Number 26. BCPC Croydon.

Duffey, E., Morris, M.G., Sheail, J., Ward, L.K. *et al.* (eds) (1974) *Grassland Ecology and Wildlife Management*. Chapman & Hall, London.

East Lothian County Council Planning Department (1970) *Dune Conservation*. North Berwick Study Group Report.

Gimmingham, C.H. (1972) *The Ecology of Heathlands*. Chapman and Hall, London.

Grant, S.A. (1971) Interactions of grazing and burning on heather moors. *Jl. British Grassland Society*, **26**, 173–82

Green, B.H. (1972) Practical aspects of chalk grassland management in the Nature Conservancy's South East Region. In *Chalk Grassland: Studies on its Conservation and Management in South East England*, (eds A.C. Jermy and P.A. Stott). Kent Trust for Nature Conservation, Maidstone, pp. 42–6.

Green B.H. (1980) Management of extensive grassland by mowing. In: *Amenity Grassland – An Ecological Perspective*. (eds R. Hunt, and I.H. Rorison) John Wiley and Sons, Chichester.

Green, B.H. (1983) Management of vegetation for wildlife conservation. In *Management of Vegetation*, (ed. J.M. Way) British Crop Protection Council Number 26. BCPC, Croydon.

Green, B.H. (1986) Controlling ecosystems for amenity. *Ecology and Design in Landscape*. (eds A.D. Bradshaw, D.A. Goode, and E. Thorp) The 24th Symposium of the British Ecological Society. Blackwells, Oxford.

Grime J.P. (1980) An ecological approach to management. In *Amenity Grassland – An Ecological Perspective* (eds R. Hunt and I.H. Rorison). John Wiley and Sons, Chichester.

Grime, J.P. (1986) Manipulation of plant species and communities. In: *Ecology and Design in Landscape* (eds A.D. Bradshaw, D.A. Goode, and E. Thorp). The 24th Symposium of the British Ecological Society. Blackwells, Oxford, pp. 175–94.

Gunney, B.C.J. (1984) Sefton Coast Management Scheme, ILAM, March.

Harpur J.L. (1971) Grazing, fertilisers and pesticides in the management of grasslands. In *The Scientific Management of Animal and Plant Communities for Conservation* (eds E. Duffey and A.S. Watt). Blackwell, Oxford.

Hewett, D.G. (1973) *Human Pressures on Soils in Coastal Areas*. Welsh Soils Discussion Group Report No. 14.

Lowday, J.E. and Marrs, R.H. (1980) Bracken and scrub control on lowland heaths. *ITE Annual Report* **979**, 8.

Lowday, J.E. and Wells, T.C.E. (1977) *The Management of Grassland and Heathland in Country Parks*. CCP 105. Countryside Commission, Cheltenham.

Malone, C.R. (1970) Short term effects of chemical and mechanical cover management on decomposition processes in a grassland soil. *Journal of Applied Ecology*, **7**, 591–601.

Metcalfe, R.E. (1979) The management of the Camber sand dunes, Sussex. In *Ecology and Design in Amenity Land Management* (eds. S.E. Wright, and G.P. Buckley). Wye College, University of London.

Putwain, P. (1983) Restoration of heather cover. In *Heathland Management in Amenity Areas* (ed. J.L. Daniels). Conference summary. Countryside Commission CCP 159, Cheltenham.

Tallis, J.H. and Yaldon, D.W. (1983) *Revegetation Trials*. Peak District Moorland Restoration Project. Peak Park Joint Planning Board, Bakewell.

Ward, S.D. (1972) The controlled burning of heather, grass and gorse. *Nature in Wales*, **13**, 24–32.

Warren, A. and Harrison, C.M. (1978) Ecological information and the allocation of resources to recreation: experience in the South London Green Belt. In: *Proceedings: Ecological impact of countryside recreation – priorities for research*, (Ed J.P. Shildrick). Recreation Ecology Research Group, Report No 3, pp. 17–28.

Welch, D. (1977) Effects of grazing on moorland. *ITE Annual Report 1978*, **66**.

Wells, T.C.E. (1971a) Botanical aspects of conservation management of chalk grasslands. *Biological Conservation*, **2**, 36–44.

Wells, T.C.E. (1971b) A comparison of the effect of sheep grazing and mechanical cutting on the structure and botanical composition of chalk grassland. *Symposia of the British Ecological Society*, **11**, 497–515.

Wells, T.C.E. (1973) Botanical aspects of chalk grassland management. In *Chalk Grassland: Studies on its conservation and management in SE England* (eds A.C. Jermy and P.A. Stott). Kent Trust for Nature Conservation, Maidstone.

Further reading   SEMI-NATURAL AREAS

Benson, J.F. (1981) Animal communities in an urban environment. *Landscape Research*, **6**, 8–11.

Bradshaw, A.D. (1982) The biology of land reclamation in urban areas. In *Urban Ecology* (eds R. Bornkamm, J.A. Lee, and M.H. Seeward) Blackwell, Oxford.

Bradshaw, A.D. (1983) The reconstruction of ecosystems. *Journal of Applied Ecology*, **20**, 1–17.

Cole, L. (1982) Does size matter? In *An Ecological Approach to Urban Landscape Design* (eds A. Ruff and R. Tregay). Occasional Paper No. 8. Department of Town and Country Planning, University of Manchester.

Duffey, E. and Watt, A.S. (eds) (1971) *The Scientific Management of Animal and Plant Communities for Conservation*. Blackwell Scientific Publications, Oxford.

Dyne G.M., van (ed.) *The Ecosystem Concept in Natural Resource Management*. Academic Press, New York.

Fryer J.D. (1958) The potential value of herbicides in nature reserves. *Proceedings of the Linnaen Society*, **199**, 107–10.

Gemmell, R.P. (1982) The origin and botanical importance of industrial habitats. In *Urban Ecology*, (eds R. Bornkamm, J.A. Lee, and M.H. Seeward) Blackwell, Oxford.

Gemmell, R.P., Connell, R.K., and Crombie, S.A. (1983) Conservation and creation of habitats on industrial land. In *Reclamation 83*. Proceedings of the international land reclamation conference. Grays, Essex.

Green B.H. (1980) Management of extensive grassland by mowing. In: *Amenity Grassland – An Ecological Perspective* (eds R. Hunt, and I.H. Rorison), John Wiley and Sons, Chichester.

Green, B.H. (1981) *Countryside Conservation*. George Allen and Unwin, London.

Hookway, R.J.S. (1967) *The Management of Britain's Rural Land*. Countryside Commission.

Luke, A.J. (1987) Landscaping with Lupins. *Horticulture Week*, July 31st.

Marren, P.R. (1975) *Ecology and Recreation. A Review of European Literature*. University College, London.

Spedding C.R.W. (1971) *Grassland Ecology*. Oxford University Press, Oxford.

Thomson, J. (1986) Erosion Control. *Landscape Design*, August, pp. 41–4.

Warren, A. and Goldsmith, F.B. (1974) *Conservation in Practice*. John Wiley & Sons, Chichester.

Wright, T.W.J. (1979) Design and management of semi-natural areas in historic gardens and parks in Great Britain In: *Proceedings: Ecology and Design in Amenity Land Management*. (eds S.E. Wright and G.P. Buckley). Wye College, University of London, pp. 216–24.

HEATHS

Anon (undated) *Grouse Management*. The Game Conservancy Booklet 12.

Chadwick, L. (1982) *In Search of Heathland*. Dennis Dobson, London and Durham.

Countryside Commission (1974) *Upland Management Experiment*. HMSO.

Daniels, J.L. (ed) (1983) *Heathland Management in Amenity Areas*. Countryside Commission Conference Summary. CCP 159. Countryside Commission, Cheltenham.

Mercer, I.D. (1983) The management of upland vegetation for amenity and recreation. In *Management of Vegetation* (ed. J.M. Way). British Crop Protection Council Monograph No. 26. BCPC, Croydon.

Peel, Earl (1983) Integrated management of upland environment. In: *Management of Vegetation* (ed. J.M. Way). British Crop Protection Council Monograph No. 26. BCPC, Croydon.

Tubbs, C.R. (1974) Heathland management in the New Forest, Hampshire, England. *Biological Conservation*, **6**, 303–6.

CHALK GRASSLAND

Gay, P.A. and Green, B.H. (1983) The effects of cutting on the growth and litter accumulation of coarse grass swards on chalk soils. *South East Soils Discussion Group*, **1**, 140–52.

Large, R.V. and King, N. (1978) The integrated use of land for agricultural and amenity purposes: lamb production from Soay sheep used to control scrub and improve the grass cover of chalk downland. Grassland Research Institute, Hurley.

Lloyd, P.S. (1968) The ecological significance of fire in limestone grassland communities of the Derbyshire Dales. *Journal of Ecology*, **65**, 811–26.

Smith, C.J. (1980) *Ecology of the English Chalk*. Academic Press, London.

SAND DUNES

Anon. (1970) *The Coastal Heritage*. Countryside Commission. HMSO.

Bache, D.H. and Macaskill, I.A. (1981) Vegetation in coastal and stream bank protection. *Landscape Planning*, **8**, 363–86.

Boorman, L.A. and Fuller, R.M. (1977) Spread of Rhododendron on Sand Dunes. *ITE Annual Report 1976*, 40.

Liddle, M.J. (1975) A survey of tracks and paths in a sand dune ecosystem. II. Vegetation. *Journal of Applied Ecology*, **12**, 909–30.

Liddle, M.J. (1975) A selective review of the ecological effects of human trampling on natural ecosystems. *Biological Conservation*, **7**, 17–36.

9 MANAGEMENT GUIDELINES: PROBLEM, SPECIAL AND GENERAL AREAS

**9.1
General
characteristics**

The successful provision of public open space does not rely solely upon the single profession of amenity management. Instead it calls for a range of professions working in concert. Thus many of the problems encountered by Amenity Managers cannot be solved independently. They call for design, horticultural, mechanical, financial, scientific and other skills. Nowhere is this inter-dependence better illustrated than in the case of the problem grass areas.

Tables 9.1 to 9.4 and Figure 9.1 present ameliorative guidelines covering many of the problems which frequently beset the managers of amenity grassland areas. Inevitably the guidelines are indicative rather than exhaustive. They cover problem and special areas characterized by:

- Green deserts;
- Worn and over-used areas;
- Obstacles in or against grass;
- Naturalized bulbs in grass;
- Many separate small areas of grass;
- Steep banks, which are to remain grass covered;
- Steep banks which are too difficult, dangerous or expensive to mow;
- Areas of poor drainage which are difficult to mow;
- Awkward corners with difficult access;
- Areas where occasional or light vehicular access is required.

Where data exists, estimates of the resources required in overcoming the problems, as well as in managing the special areas, are presented in Tables 9.5 to 9.9 inclusive.

Table 9.1   Problem/special area guidelines: "Greenbelts". Trampled grass and obstacles

Problem/special area		Possible management solutions	Comments
Green deserts and worn grass			
Large, under-used, fairly flat and intensively maintained areas, e.g. many urban parks, recreation grounds, interim treatment land	1.1	Remodel ground to increase interest of relief	Costs may depend on availability of fill to create mounds
	1.2	Introduce differential mowing i.e. cut some parts on longer growing cycles. Mow short paths through these, if required	Mown trims to hard paths, etc. recommended. Control long grass growth near to plant beds
	1.3	Introduce woody plantings to add the third dimension, enclosure, ecological interest, etc.	
	1.4	Invite ideas from and encourage local communities to develop features they require	
Worn, over-used, trampled grass			
Highly popular routes or places used by people, vehicles or livestock	2.1	Replace with hard surfacing	Expensive
	2.2	Lay 'stepping stones' over grass	
	2.3	Lay duckboards over grass (e.g. Hidcote)	
	2.4	Strengthen with synthetic net, such as Wyretex (e.g. National Exhibition Centre)	
	2.5	Re-route users, repair, use again when sward re-established	
	2.6	Prevent unwanted access by using knee rails, or temporary fencing	May make mowing more awkward
	2.7	On fragile substrates spread sewage sludge, and seed; inform public of action taken	Acts as a natural deterrent. Used successfully in dune restoration work. Use only when a strong sward required
Obstacles in or against grass			
Obstacles include trees, lampposts, seats, litter bins, and other street furniture, fences and walls	3.1	Establishing trees: spray out at least 1m diameter circle round base, and keep weed free with contact and/or residued herbicide until plant is established	Do not strim—may damage bark Do not mow too close to plant
Living 'obstacles' (e.g. standard trees)	3.2	Established trees: keep vegetation round base, which mowers miss, clear by:	Do not mow too close to plant

cont'd

Table 9.1 (cont'd)

Problem/special area		Possible management solutions	Comments

		– strimming.
		– and/or herbicide e.g.
		  – dichlobenil
		  – simazine (strong)
		  – paraquat	

Non-living obstacles and interfaces	3.3	Strim off unwanted vegetation.
		Treat areas which mowers cannot reach with:
		  – dichlobenil
		  – Strong (2–4 × normal strength) simazine
		  – Other persistent weedkillers
			Lasts at least 1 year but may run on slopes

Table 9.2   Problem/special area guidelines: boundaries and naturalized bulbs in grass

Problem/special areas		Possible management solutions	Comments
1. Boundaries between grass and planted areas			Expensive but looks attractive
A Prestigious or intensively maintained areas	1.1	Lay brick or hard edging at boundary	Reduces maintenance costs
B Less formal areas	1.2	Strim off untidy grass as necessary	
	1.3	Spray off growth encroaching from grass side with contact herbicide (paraquat, alloxydim-sodium)	
2. Naturalized bulbs in grass[1]	2.1	Bulbs for naturalizing in grass must be allowed to photosynthesize adequately in the early growing season. This means that their foliage must not be cut off until it starts to die naturally—usually in early—mid June	Unmown areas can look unsightly in early summer. Tedious and expensive to 'tidy up' if growth is long
	2.2	Cut in early summer with rotary or flail mower and remove mowings. Cut again if necessary and resume normal mowing pattern	For rough informal areas only

[1]   These guidelines include bulbs in other 'uncut' or meadow areas mown for hay or silage if acceptable to farmers.

Table 9.3   Problem/special area guidelines: small areas and steep banks

Problem/special areas		Possible management solutions	Comments
Many separate small areas of mown grass			
These include any housing and industrial estates, some urban verges which are accessible, but time consuming to mow	1.1	Replace grass with perennial ground cover	Beware of sight lines in relation to mature height of ground cover
	1.2	Replace selected areas with appropriate hard surface, e.g. desire lines; corners subject to trampling	
	1.3	Simplify grass areas by amalgamation, removal of obstructions, etc.	Possibly little scope for this because of paths, drives, roads, etc.
Steep banks which are to remain grass covered	2.1	Flymo	Only suitable for small areas Only handles short grass well, so finish may be over formal.
	2.2	Flymo let down on a rope for slopes over 1 in 3	Dangerous Slow
	2.3	Low centre of gravity, self propelled rotary mower, e.g. Hayter Condor, Toro, Mayfield, for slopes less than 1 in 3	Can handle fairly long or rough grass
	2.4	Tractor mounted side arm flail	Large models have a reach up to approx. 7m. No limit to slope handled by cutting head

	2.5	Manual methods
		    strimmer
		    sickle, hook
		    shears (only for very small areas)
			Only suitable for small areas e.g. up to $1,000m^2$ as a 'one-off' or $200m^2$ on a regular basis

	2.6	Treat with growth retardant in combination with Flymo	
Steep banks which are too difficult, dangerous or expensive to mow	3.1	Regrade to a mowable slope and re-seed preferably with a low-productivity mix	
	3.2	Spray out grass with glyphosate. Plant up with un-demanding woody plants	

Table 9.3 (cont'd)

Problem/special areas	Possible management solutions	Comments
	3.3 Leave grass uncut and allow to develop. Fire may be a hazard naturally	
	3.4 Spray with growth retardant	
	3.5 Burn if location permits	
	3.6 Graze if feasible	
	3.7 Replace with retaining wall	

Table 9.4 Problem/special area guidelines: poor drainage areas, awkward corners and occasional access areas

Problem/special area	Possible management solutions	Comments
Areas of poor drainage which are difficult to mow	1.1 Improve drainage if use demands this, e.g. by underdrainage	Expensive
	1.2 Manage for hay and silage, i.e. remove crop when ground is firm in summer	Fair size plots only Adequate access essential Litter may be a problem
	1.3 Exploit and/or encourage wetness and manage for wildlife as wet grassland	Probably only acceptable in certain locations
Awkward corners with limited access, which are difficult to mow or manage effectively, e.g. very small areas of grass; areas cut off by other features (beds, fence, kerbs)	2.1 Replace sward with i Low maintenance ground cover – shrubby and herbaceous ii Hard surface e.g. cobbles, pebbles, or decorative mulch in very small areas and keep weed free with total herbicides	
Areas where occasional/light vehicle access is required with a 'soft' landscape appearance	3.1 Strengthen sward with synthetic net 3.2 Lay rigid units which can be seeded through, e.g. 'fire path pots', mono-beegee blocks	Expensive

9.2 Repair and restoration

Even under the best management it is almost inevitable that some grassland areas will require re-establishment (Brooks, 1983). In such situations various options exist for the Amenity Manager. These are reviewed in the paragraphs which follow.

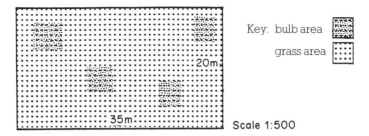

Key: bulb area

grass area

Scale 1:500

Savings made
Bulb areas uncut until end of June

Say 10 cuts saved @ 1 min per 100 m^2 per cut
Total saving = 10 min per 100 m^2

Extra costs incurred
When uncut grass and bulb foliage is mown it is hard to cut and therefore slow,
and usually needs cutting and raking off twice.

		min per 100 m^2
1st	Cut 1 @ 8 min per 100 m^2 (eg Condor or Mayfield)	8.0
1st	Rake 1 @ 20 min per 100 m^2	20.0
2nd	Cut 2 @ 6 min per 100 m^2	6.0
2nd	Rake 2 @ 15 min per 100 m^2	15.0
		49.0

Total costs therefore = 49 min − 10 min
Say 40 min per 100 m^2 per year extra spent on naturalized bulbs in grass

Figure 9.1 Naturalized bulbs in grass: estimated annual maintenance costs.

RE-ESTABLISHMENT

Re-establishment of grassland may be necessary wherever there has been disturbance through building work, removal of alternative landscape features, or excess wear.

Table 9.4 contains guidelines for those managers who elect either to restore on a like-to-like basis or to adopt an alternative.

The choice of site treatment will depend on whether the cause of the disturbance was a unique event or likely to be repeated, necessitating thought about re-design of the landscape (Countryside Commission, 1978, 1985).

GRASSLAND SPECIES: SELECTION

A range of suitable species and cultivars for various amenity uses is available. Correct selection can be of importance in achieving cost-effective management. This is not just a matter for the design stage, as it may be worthwhile at any stage to consider re-seeding existing grass areas and/or adopting management techniques which favour the development

Table 9.5   Obstacles in grass: estimated resource requirements

Source	Operation	Man Hrs/ year	Unit
K	Fence lines; annual weed spray, and rotary cut long grass	180 660	100 linear metre 1,000 linear metre
		SMV	Unit
K	Hand cut weeds between trees: scythe/hook	45.09	100m^2
Sh	Hand cut round obstacles in grass: sickle	37.00	100 no
Sa	Trim up round obstacles and edge of mown areas: hand sickle	4.31	100m^2
W	'Weedcut' round obstacles in grass	48.00	100m^2
W	Weedcut along fence lines, grass edges, etc.	16.00	100 linear metres
H	Clear weed from fencing: Rip hook	73.00	100m
D	Cut grass with hand shears at base of hedge, wall, fence	24.00	100m
Sh	Cut grass with hand shears by walls, fences, etc.	57.98	100m
D	Cut grass with hook by walls, fences, etc.	58.00	100 linear metres
W	Knapsack spray around standard tree	1.36	1 no
Sh	Knapsack spray around obstacles	0.60	1 no
K	Spray around obstruction	0.20	1 no

See Table 2.2 on p. 37 for details of sources.

Table 9.6   Bulbs in grass: estimated resource requirements

Source	Operation	SMV	Unit
	Rake up		
D	Rake up long grass and load	33.50	100m^2
W	Rake (sweep) and remove	11.00	100m^2
Sh	Rake (sweep) and remove and load	15.57	100m^2
	Cut rough grass in early Summer (two cuts may be needed)		
K	Cut with Mayfield	9.76	100m^2
D	Cut with Allen Scythe	5.00	100m^2
W	Cut with Hayter Condor	6.20	100m^2
	Planting		
Sh	Plant naturalizing bulbs in grass	52.00	100 no.
D	Plant out bulbs	38.00	100 no.
	Bulbs in beds		
Sh	Plant large bulbs (tulips, daffodils hyacinths)	15.30	100 no.
D	Plant out bulbs	18.00	100 no.
Sh	Plant small bulbs	7.70	100 no.

See Table 2.2 on p. 37 for details of sources.

Table 9.7   Grass banks: estimated resource requirements

Source	Operation	SMV	Unit
W	Flail mow: Long reach	7.20	100m^2
W	Pedestrian mow: rotary 30″ self propelled	5.00	100m^2
Sh	Pedestrian mow: Allen	7.78	100m^2
W	Pedestrian mow: Flymo 19″	14.40	100m^2
D	Pedestrian mow: Flymo 19″	16.00	100m^2
D	Pedestrian mow: Flymo 19″ roped	31.00	100m^2
K	Pedestrian mow: Flymo 19″ roped	28.74	100m^2
W	Weedeater	16.00	100m^2
W	Rough-cut: Hook/Scythe/Shears	117.00	100m^2
D	Rough-cut: Hook	61.00	100m^2
D	Rough-cut: Shears	98.00	100m^2
Sa	Riphook grass	76.88	100m^2

See Table 2.2 on p. 37 for details of sources.

and growth of certain species at the expense of others. The cost of grass seed is relatively small compared with the cost of maintaining an inappropriate mix. Time and care spent in selection and initial expenditure on seed will be justified if later savings in maintenance are significant. More importantly the extra cost of, not just the seed, but the re-establishment operations may well be justified in terms of cost-effectiveness.

Cultivars of most of the common turfgrass species are now available and appropriate mixtures of them can be selected for a wide variety of situations. For example, mixtures can be selected for high resistance to

Table 9.8   Grass re-establishment repair and restoration: estimated resource requirements

Source	Operations	SMV	Unit
D	Level areas: tractor mounted levelling bar	7.0	100m^2
D	Chain harrow	2.1	100m^2
D	Roll ground: 20″ rollers	1.4	100m^2
Sh	Rake to tilth and firm	62.9	100m^2
D	Rake prior to seeding	68.0	100m^2
D	Cultivate and seed new area	270.0	100m^2
D	Sow seed: tractor mounted seed box	2.0	100m^2
Sh	Sow seed by hand	21.53	100m^2
D	Sow seed by hand	10.0	100m^2
W	Repairs to damaged areas of grass: prepare and re-seed	271.0	100m^2
H	Prepare surface for turfing	730.0	100m^2
D	Lay turf	600.0	100m^2
H	Lay turf on playing fields, parks, etc.	360.0	100m^2
W	Prepare ground and lay turf	848.0	100m^2
H	Lay turf on ornamental lawns	1610.0	100m^2

See Table 2.2 on p. 37 for details of sources.

Table 9.9 Guideline grass mixtures and costs

Grass type	Ht (mm)	Sowing rate (kg per Ha)	Cost per Kg Relative index	Typical contents
Low maintenance Bowling green	13–50	250–350	13.7	60% PR (dwarf type) 35% SCRF 5% BB
Golf green	5	350	14.4	80% CF 20% BB
Fine lawns and tennis	8–12	350–500	11.9	65 CF 25 CRF 10 BB
Low maintenance Landscape	13	250–500	10.7	75 CRF 20 SSMG 5 BB
Conservation parkland	13	170–350	11.3	40 CRF 30 CF 25 HF 5 BB
Cricket square	5	350–500	12.7	40 PR 50 CF 10 BB
Sportsground	25	190	12.9	50 PR 20 SSMG 20 CF 10 BB
Golf tees	10	350–500	12.4	30 CF 40 CRF 20 SSMG 10 BB
Fairway	13	125–250	12.1	40 CF 35 CRF 15 SSMG
Rough	As necessary	125	12.1	40 SSMG 50 CRF 10 BB
Reclamation	–	80	12.3	42 PR 15 CRF 15 SSMG 20 FMG 5 BB 3 Clover
Country Parks	–	80–190	11.9	20 HF 20 SF 35 CRF 15 FMG
Legume and clover	–	20	41.5	Mixed
Road Verge	–	56	10.00	10 PR 60 CRF 12.5 FMG 10 SSMG 5 BB 2.5 Clover
Housing Estate	13	250–350	11.2	30 PR 25 CRF 40 CF 5 BB

KEY PR = Perennial Rye Grass, CF = Chewings Fescue, CRF = Creeping Red Fescue, SSMG = Smooth Stalked Meadow Grass, BB = Browntop Bent, SF = Sheeps Fescue, FMG = Flattened Meadow Grass, SCRF = Slender Creeping Red Fescue, HF = Hard Fescue.

wear coupled with a low rate of vertical growth and good tillering, so that less frequent mowing is required and turf can accommodate heavier use. The consequent savings can be up to 30 per cent. In situations where heavy use is not experienced, different species or cultivars may be chosen for their slow-growing characteristics: it is possible to halve the frequency of cuts by this means (Gaman and Sayers, 1973; Moffat, 1980). A range of wild flower seed mixtures is commercially available. However, in some cases it may be feasible to harvest or grow seed 'in house'. Regard should be given to the Wildlife and Countryside Act in this respect.

In situations where lack of nitrogen is a restriction on grass growth,

Yes, our only variety that's 40% Acrylic. No cutting, just use carpet shampno.

legumes can be used successfully to supplement swards (Haggar and Squires, 1979). Wild white clover is best, as it is low growing and does not require frequent cutting. Agricultural clovers are sometimes used but are too vigorous in most situations.

LOW MAINTENANCE GRASS MIXTURES

Traditional amenity grass mixtures may need cutting anything up to 30 times a year. Several low maintenance mixtures are now available which depend on slow-growing, fine-leaved grasses for areas of low wear, sometimes mixed with specially bred, slow-growing, prostrate rye-grass cultivars for areas of high wear (Shildrick, 1980). Recent EEC legislation has brought the prices of traditional mixtures up to levels not far short of the previously much more expensive low maintenance mixtures.

Some typical compositions and comparative prices are shown in Table 9.9. It is claimed that, depending on the situation and on the cutting machinery available, mowing costs may be reduced by 30–50 per cent. One problem that may arise, however, is the dilution of these low maintenance swards, after a few years, with local strains of native species which may require more frequent mowing to maintain the standards desired.

Further information on the characteristics and relative performances of

Table 9.10   Summary of main management guidelines for the principal types of grass

Type of grass	General purpose sown grass	Sports turf	Fine turf	Amenity lawns	Semi-controlled/ natural
Typical situations	Urban road verges Recreation ground Informal play areas	Football and rugby pitches Playing fields	Tennis courts Bowling greens	Private gardens Building surrounds	Rural road verges Open downland River banks
Main plant species	Perennial rye grasses Smooth stalked and annual meadow grasses Fescues and bents Clovers and other low growing herbs	Perennial rye grasses Smooth stalked meadow grass Fescues and bents		Smooth stalked and annual meadow grasses Fescues and bents	Rye grasses Meadow grasses Many other grasses and herbaceous species
Mowing length	2 in (5.1cm)	$\frac{1}{2}$–2in (1.3–5cm)	$\frac{1}{4}$–$\frac{1}{2}$ in (c 1cm)	$\frac{1}{2}$–1m (c 2cm)	5in (12.7cm)
Frequency of cut/yr	10–15	15–25	20–40	15–25	1–4
Mowing machinery	Rotary or cylinder	Cylinder	Cylinder	Cylinder Rotary on some occasions	Flail cutter bar or rotary
Cuttings removed	No	No	Always	Usually	Sometimes
Weed killer application	No regular applications	Maximum of once a year	Once or twice a year	Maximum of once a year	No general application. Spot treatment only (for pernicious weeds)
Fertilizers application	Occasional application to new swards if needed	Maximum of once or twice a year	Two or three times a year	Maximum of once a year	None
Special drainage requirements	None usually justified	Under drainage on most soils. Slit drains on many. $\frac{1}{2}$–4 in drainage rate per day		Cut off drainage from surrounding hard areas	None

Adapted from T. Wright, *The Horticulturalist's Handbook* (Instalment 3/October 1982).

Source: J. Parker, Kent County Council.

Table 9.11 Comparison of grassland management methods: cutting, grazing, burning

Type of management	Advantages	Disadvantages	Examples of situations when appropriate
1. CUTTING General	Management has control over the type of finish on the grass, time and frequency of cut	Usually no income can be generated only costs incurred	'Walk' and play-on areas
	Can be used at all intensities of public use	Produces relatively uniform and uninteresting sward. (Ground must be fairly level)	Areas of high public pressure
	Sometimes saleable product/rent from cutting rights to farmers	Needs to be cut fairly regularly gang mowers cannot cope with over-long grass	Certain rural picnic areas
		Nutrients usually returned to sward	
Amenity methods			
Cylinder gang mowers (tractor mounted or ride-on)	Can cover large areas quickly Leaves good finish for sports areas, etc.		
Flail, or rotary mowers (tractor mounted)	Can maintain large areas of rough grass in once/twice yearly cuts	No income generated	Topping informal swards
	Can cope with long coarse grass or scrub	clippings left on ground	Light medium scrub control
	Side arm flails can be used on many awkward areas	Can leave uniform and uninteresting appearance	
Pedestrian operated mowers	Can be used in places where tractor powered machinery is unsuitable	low cutting rate	
Cylinder Rotary			Fine medium turf Medium–rough turf banks, etc.
'Hover' Strimmer			Steep banks Round obstacles in grass, very steep or awkward areas

cont'd

Table 9.11 (cont'd)

Type of management	Advantages	Disadvantages	Examples of situations when appropriate
Portable bush saw			Clearing scrub off steep slopes
Agricultural methods	Reduce costs of grassland maintenance	Lack of precise management control	Former 'green deserts' and other underused open space of fairly productive grass
	may provide income – sale/rent	Litter or ragwort, may be incorporated into livestock feed	
	Feed value of grass can be utilized or nutrients removed from site	Needs to be left to grow longer than might otherwise be desirable	
Hay making equipment/cutter bar, tedder, baler, trailer for carting bails	Traditional technique may be vital for maintaining floristic interest of sward	Bales may be subject to vandalism.	
Forage harvester	Can be used more regularly, e.g. every 6 weeks in growing season		Medium rough grassland on terrain suitable for the machinery
2. GRAZING	Attractive feature in country parks	Requires experienced labour, fencing, additional machinery, etc.	Grassland with water and fencing, where visitor pressure is not too great and there is not a dog problem
	Potential source of income	Potential risk of stock fatalities (litter and dogs)	
	Saves cost of cutting	Livestock can produce mud, smell, flies, etc.	
	Can be used on steep slopes, where cutting is impossible		
Sheep	Maintain floristic diversity	Susceptible to dog worrying	Chalk limestone grassland especially steep slopes
	Safe with people	High level of husbandry required, especially when breeding	As component of mixed grazing on meadow, parkland, rough grazing

Table 9.11 (cont'd)

Type of management	Advantages	Disadvantages	Examples of situations when appropriate
	Attractive feature of interest for visitors, especially lambs	Disease prone on wet poorly drained areas	Low-medium public use, or intermittently on high public use areas when alternative grazing is available
	Traditional animal on certain grassland types	Unsuitable on very productive grass swards over 10cm	Ancient earthworks, hill forts, etc.
	Saleable products – animals, carcase, wool		
Cattle	Maintain floristic diversity	Calves susceptible to dog worrying	Chalk/limestone grassland, not steep slopes
	Safe with people. (Attractive feature in landscape)	Minority of public may be scared by their inquisitive behaviour	Meadow land
	Saleable products – animals, carcase, hides	Can poach grass in wet weather	Control of long coarse grass
	Attract subsidy in certain cases	Can damage cars	Reclamation management
	Certain breeds ideal for reclaiming rough pasture		
Deer	Exceptionally attractive feature in county parks. (Docile and harmless to public. Less susceptible to dog worrying)	Very high costs involved in maintaining deer fence and woody plant protection	Established parkland with deer fence
	Very hardy requiring minimum maintenance	Requires specialized labour with knowledge of deer husbandry	
	Saleable products – venison, hides, antlers	Tends to reduce floristic diversity	
		Occasional rogue stag may be potentially dangerous in latter stages of rut	
Horse	Attractive feature in parks	Temperamental behaviour, especially if	Confined to paddock with public/horse interface at

cont'd

Table 9.11 (cont'd)

Type of management	Advantages	Disadvantages	Examples of situations when appropriate
GRAZING *cont'd*		annoyed – may kick or bite.	fence
	Can be used for public riding and hence bring in revenue	Very selective grazer; (behavioural habits associated with dunging) can spoil floristic composition of sward	Larger open areas where they can retire away from public
		High initial expense	
		Can poach grass	
3. BURNING	Cheap potentially (useful when in certain situations)	Potentially steep, dangerous if gets out of control	Cheap unfenced rural grassland where grazing/ cutting impractical
	(Traditional method for maintaining heathland, and certain grassland areas)	Temporarily unattractive (burnt area)	In old stands heathland (for regeneration)
	Can reduce risk of accidental fires	Regeneration after fire may favour potentially undesirable species, e.g. bracken, purple moorgrass	Control of bracken litter
		Limited period of year when safe or useful (February–March)	

the different species are to be found in the Turfgrass Seed Report published regularly by the STRI and the catalogues of the various seed suppliers, such as Johnsons.

ASSOCIATED OPERATIONS

Before seeding it is sensible to treat the ground with a broad spectrum non-residual herbicide. Stonepicking and fertilizing may be necessary, although less so than when establishing new grassland. Light rolling will improve soil/seed contact. Watering may be required if seeding is carried out in summer.

Steep banks which have eroded may be more profitably seeded by specialist hydroseeding contractors in which case fertilizing is often carried out under the same contract.

TURFING

For rapid repair of prestigious relatively level areas turfing is often preferable to seeding. Turves should be bought from a reliable source and checked that they are free from weeds. With the exception of one or two specialist companies, turf suppliers rarely offer the Amenity Manager the same control over the grass species and varieties present that can be attained with seed.

Turves should not be stacked or left folded longer than ten days.

Unless they are laid in autumn or winter watering will be required. Once laid they should be brushed with good quality soil to fill in any gaps. They should be kept free of wear until established.

GENERAL AREAS: SUMMARY OF MANAGEMENT TECHNIQUES

A summary and comparison of the main management guidelines for the principal types of grass is given in Table 9.10. Table 9.11 contains a detailed comparison of the merits and demerits of the different grassland management methods, cutting, grazing and burning.

References   Brooks, A. (1983) *Footpaths*. BTCV, Oxford.

Countryside Commission (1978) *Tarn Hows – an approach to the management of a popular beauty spot*. CCP 106. Countryside Commission, Cheltenham.

Countryside Commission (1985) *Restoring Vegetation at Informal Carparks*. Cannock Chase Technical Report. CCP 185. Countryside Commission, Cheltenham.

Gaman, J.H. and Sayers C.D. (1973) The amenity potential of low maintenance grasses. *Journal of Environmental Planning and Pollution Control*, **4**.

Haggar, R.J. and Squires, N.R.W. (1979) The scientific manipulation of sward constituents in grassland by herbicides and one pass seeding. *British Grassland Society, Occasional Symposium*, **10**, 223–4.

Moffat, J.D. (1980) *Grass Seed Mixes – Their Choice, Growth and Development*. Warington New Town Development Corporation, Warrington.

Shildrick, J.P. (1980) Species and cultivar selection. In *Amenity Grassland: An Ecological Perspective* (eds I.H. Rorison, and R. Hunt). John Wiley and Sons, Chichester.

Further reading
Barletta, M. (1987) Repairing damage, *Horticulture Week*, 8th May.

Barrow, G. (1979) The restoration and subsequent management of countryside recreation sites. In: *Ecology and Design in Amenity Land Management* (eds S.E. Wright and G.P. Buckley). Wye College, University of London.

Bell, R., Bradshaw, A.D. and Holliday, R. (1980) *Grassland Establishment in Countryside Recreation Areas*. Countryside Commission Advisory Series No. 13.

Bradshaw, A.D. and Handley, J.F. (1972) Low cost grassing of sites awaiting redevelopment. *Landscape Design*, **99**: 17–19.

Canoway, P.M. (1985) The response of renovated turf of *Lolium perenne* to fertiliser nitrogen. *Journal of the Sports Turf Research Institute*, **61**, 92–110.

Countryside Commission (1980) *Grassland Establishment in Countryside Recreation Areas*. Advisory Series No. 13.

Haggar, R.J. (1974) Legumes and British grassland: new opportunities with herbicides. *Proceedings of the 12th British Weed Control Conference*, **1**, 771–7.

Haggar, R.J. (1977) Herbicides and low cost grassland establishment with special reference to clean seed beds and one pass seeding. In *Proceedings of the International Conference on Energy Conservation in Crop Production* (ed. C.J. Baker). Massey University, Aukland.

Humphreys, M.O. (1980) Grass breeding: objectives, principles and potentials. In *Amenity Grassland: An Ecological Perspective* (eds I.H. Rorison and R. Hunt). John Wiley and Sons, Chichester.

Huxley, T. (1968) *Footpaths in the Countryside*. The Countryside Commission for Scotland.

Pascal, J.A. and Sheppard, B.W. (1977) Development of a sod seeder for introduction of clover into hill pastures. *ARC Research Review*, **3**, 74–8.

Rorison, I.H. (1977) Selection and establishment of species in relation to soil conditions. *Journal of the Sports Turf Research Institute*, **53**, 103–4.

Shildrick, J.P. (1977) What qualities are needed in turfgrasses? *Journal of the Sports Turf Research Institute*, **52**, 38–51.

Shildrick, J.P. (1977) *Less Work and More Play – Trends in Turf Grasses*. Report of the 17th Askham Bryan Horticultural Technical Course, Jan.

Sports Turf Research Institute (1986) Spring renovation. *Sports Turf Bulletin*, **153**, 6–10.

Stansfield, D. (1986) Repairing the damage. *Horticulture Week*, 10th January.

Part Three

The Management of Woody Plants

Woody plants, in a variety of forms, are vital components of amenity landscapes. Part Three is devoted to their management and maintenance.

Chapter 10 specifically describes the operations involved in the effective management of amenity woodlands. These are defined as those woodlands in excess of 0.25 ha. All phases of the life-cycle are covered: the mature, senile and re-establishment phases.

The second chapter in this part provides a brief review of the characteristics of woody plants in general: trees, shrubs, ground covers, wall plants and climbers. It covers their functions and contributions, as well as the management problems which they can cause.

Chapter 12 deals with the management of massed tree and shrub communities with an area of 0.25 ha or less. Each of the main conservation and commercial management operations, including weed control, growth regulation, fertilizer application, mulching, irrigation, interplanting etc. is covered. Again, important distinctions are made between the mature, senile and re-establishment phases. Extensive guidelines are provided on weed control methods.

Chapter 13 describes respectively the management operations and resource requirements of trees and shrubs grown as individual or specimen plants.

In Chapter 14, the more specialist maintenance operations, covering shrub plantings and bedding roses are described.

Chapter 15, which covers hedge maintenance operations, completes Part Three. Resource guidelines are provided for both cutting and chemical control methods.

10 THE MANAGEMENT OF WOODY PLANTS: AMENITY WOODLANDS

10.1 Introduction

Inevitably there is some overlap between the guidelines given here for amenity woodlands and those given later for the management of amenity tree and shrub plantings during their mature, senile and re-establishment phases, since there are many similarities despite differences in scale. The distinction between woodlands and amenity plantings used in this book has, for the sake of convenience, been taken as that adopted by the Forestry and Countryside Commissions in defining grant aid eligibilities, namely:

- Woodland areas are those in excess of 0.25 hectares;
- Amenity plantings are those of 0.25 hectares and under.

Readers concerned with the operations and resource requirements which are involved in the management and maintenance of amenity plantings should refer to Chapters 12 and 13 in particular.

Many of the inputs required for the effective management and maintenance of amenity woodlands are similar to those which are needed in the case of commercial woodlands and forests. The management operations involved throughout the life cycles of commercial broadleaved and mixed woodlands are well documented (Blatchford, 1978; Evans, 1984; Watkins, 1983) Consequently they are not repeated here.

However, there are certain important qualifications to be borne in mind due to the many ways in which amenity woodland differs from commercial woodland. These differences have far reaching implications for management.

It is not long since the idea of managing woodlands would have seemed completely foreign to most Amenity Managers. Sharper divisions used to exist between the foresters and estate managers, concerned with the production of usable timber or game for financial return, and the Amenity Manager who, by definition, was primarily concerned with managing landscapes for the greater benefit of society.

However, over the last decade there have been profound and far reaching changes which have blurred many of these distinctions.

10.2 Britain's new woodlands

Britain is entering a period when significant changes in land use are expected. Agriculture is no longer economically and financially viable in many rural areas. Certainly, it can rarely be justified as an objective for the improvement of marginal and derelict land. Partly because the UK is so far from being self sufficient in timber products (some 90% of domestic needs is imported), farmers are turning to forestry and woodland management as a possible means of obtaining a return on land previously used for arable or dairy production (National Farmers Union, 1987).

In marginal areas, particularly around urban fringes, the incentives for maintaining agricultural production are no longer sufficient to outweigh the associated problems of trespass, vandalism and fly tipping. Woodland is increasingly proposed as a new land use in such areas (Kendle, 1987).

At the same time most inner cities contain large areas of land which are going to waste. Factory sites have been made functionless by the decline in traditional industries. Housing stock is losing its attractiveness as developers move into the less sacrosanct green belts and rural areas. At the same time high book rents and rates inhibit many new land uses.

Urban forestry is again being considered as an option to provide employment and to provide a relatively cost-effective means of greening of waste sites. Such sites could be sacrificed if in time over-riding needs arise (Reid, 1981; Thornton, 1971).

Parallel with these changes has been the dramatic rise in the 'ecological landscapes' movement. Designers, planners and the public are no longer satisfied with sterile grass tracts, rose beds and standard trees. A richer, more elaborate and diverse style of landscape is demanded, in which woodland plays a vital role (Baines, 1986).

Simultaneously, greater importance is attached to wider issues in managing the traditional commercial woodlands of our rural landscapes, namely the integration of amenity uses, good design and wildlife conservation, with financial interests.

The broadleaved woodlands policy of the Forestry Commission is having an effect on the provision of grants and felling licences through greater control of the species mixtures and the cropping systems that are eligible.

Increasing numbers of Amenity Managers are therefore finding that the care and management of woodland for multiple purposes is becoming an ever greater part of their work and responsibility.

Whilst the need to produce a financial return varies considerably between woodland sites there is, to some degree, a common need to consider objectives other than those which relate solely to profits. These wider objectives point towards the need to develop a new style of woodland management. This inevitably draws upon the lessons of forestry and silviculture but it is not the same as commercial forest management. The emphasis tends to be on providing a living resource for people and not on timber yield classes. In many circumstances a return on investment is desirable but, by definition, it is not the primary management objective for amenity woodlands.

There are many important factors to consider. These include the aesthetic impact of the woods; their contribution as wildlife habitats; their ability to allow and encourage recreational uses; their ability to accommodate public pressure; their interaction with urban environments and their role as a teaching resource both for learning new skills and to gain a better understanding of the environment.

At present the Amenity industry is struggling to come to terms with these new challenges. For the most part there has been a lack of definition of the new skills and techniques that need to be developed. Many gaps in the knowledge exist.

The Forestry Commission is the source for estimates of the resource requirements needed in amenity woodland management, given in the tables. This suggests that there have been attempts by the amenity industry to learn the lessons that can be taught by commercial timber producers. However, it must be stressed that the figures are to be read and interpreted with care. In the absence of specific research and experience such guidelines are all that exist. It must be appreciated that there are many situations in which the techniques and goals of commercial foresters are of limited value to Amenity Managers.

The planting densities appropriate for amenity woodlands tend to be completely different from those adopted for commercial production. Foresters usually plant at uniform spacings designed to maximize stem production and to minimize branch growth through self shedding.

The latter densities are likely not only to be too close both for public comfort and for wildlife use, but to be too wide for providing a rapid visual screen or forming an access barrier.

Self shedding of branches is seldom likely to be of importance in amenity woodlands. Often, in natural woodlands it is the trees and individuals with the best developed branch system that are most highly valued for visual and wildlife purposes. It is a challenge to designers and managers to find techniques whereby such natural forms can be encouraged and created in artificial plantations.

For similar reasons there is often a need to encourage a wide age distribution in amenity woodlands. This also helps to encourage a more stable and self-perpetuating tree population.

In amenity woodlands individual specimens or groups may be considered to be so important for design reasons that their failure or poor growth cannot be tolerated. During the design and planting stages these plants often justify specific care and attention. For example, inspection of the resource requirement tables presented later in the chapter illustrates that the labour requirements for planting forestry transplants are significantly lower than those required for establishing an equivalent plant on an amenity site.

Amenity woodland is often established on more fertile land than is the case with traditional forestry plantations. The vigour of growth of ground flora in these circumstances may mean that greater efforts are required to control competing ground vegetation.

Design considerations often call for use of a much wider range of species than are encountered or encouraged in traditional forestry. With the exception of introduced exotic conifers, there are relatively few species that are capable of generating an economic return from timber. In an 'ecologically designed' woodland, in particular, those species which foresters would regard as being of 'poor' form and slow growth, may in fact be those which are most highly valued.

It is also likely that the understorey vegetation is regarded as being as important as, or more important than, the actual trees. Spacing, thinning, felling and brashing may all be geared towards the early promotion of such undergrowth. There may be a need to stop the weed control regime long before timber production requirements would suggest (Peterken, 1975).

In many amenity plantings there is sometimes a need to provide a high initial impact prior to the development of the long term vegetation. This may involve the use of plant mixtures and densities that, without intensive management, would quickly suppress the slower growing species.

Of course, there is likely to be a range of complementary and conflicting needs in woodlands across the country. The greater the need for achieving financial returns, relative to other objectives, the more likely it is that traditional planting and management systems should be chosen.

Where amenity management practices and skills overlap with those of traditional forest management, reference should be made to the many excellent Forestry Commission publications, in particular to Forestry Commission Research and Development Paper 62, 'The silviculture of broadleaved woodland'.

The following pages are intended to give guidance where it is felt that the objectives of amenity woodland management are likely to differ from those established practices.

10.3
Amenity woodlands: the mature and senile phases

OPERATIONS

In the post-establishment and senile phases of the woodland life-cycle the principal woodland management operations are thinning, coppicing and felling.

THINNING

Thinning is an operation very similar to that of selective felling. The essential differences are that the work is carried out on younger trees, is less hazardous and probably also less profitable.

The only potential saleable value of most thinnings is as fire or pulp wood. If these markets do not exist, the thinnings may have to be left as deadwood or chipped on site. Alternative approaches include trunk injections of herbicide which kills the tree where it stands. Such deadwood is in fact extremely valuable as a habitat for wildlife, although where public access is also allowed it is advisable to fell the trees rather than to leave dead timber standing.

Early thinning is essential to produce both wind-firm trees on exposed sites and shelter belts. It is also important when feathered stems are required, as mutual shading between close trees will tend to suppress side branches. If thinning is neglected, there may be increased disease problems.

The necessary frequency of thinning will depend on the desired density and species of tree. Thinning is more likely to be necessary in a densely planted amenity woodland than in forestry.

COPPICING

Species such as hazel and sweet chestnut, and less commonly ash, oak, sycamore, alder, hornbeam and birch, can be coppiced, typically on 10–15 year cycles and, if necessary, on longer cycles. Commercial foresters are investigating the use of fast growing clones to be harvested on shorter rotations. These are most likely to be successful on highly fertile lowland sites, and it is also here that they are needed most to provide a possible new crop for marginal farmland without long periods prior to the return on investment. In amenity sites it may also be valuable to shorten rotation lengths where growth of the ground flora is as important as the coppice itself.

The density of coppice stools usually ranges from 50–120/Ha. Again wider spacings may be more valuable in amenity situations to promote the understorey. Longer rotations may be valuable if there is a desire to increase wildlife that actually lives in or on the coppiced wood. The productive life cycle of coppice stools is usually about 50–100 years. A variation is 'coppice-with-standards' whereby a matrix of large trees is left to grow to maturity amongst the coppice stools.

It may be desirable to extend the range of habitats in an amenity wood and to provide a more recognizable woodland structure for public use. This system relies on avoiding coppice species that are shade tolerant such as birch and sweet chestnut.

FELLING

Managers have recourse to four methods of felling. These are described in the paragraphs which follow.

Clear felling is not always appropriate. Alternatives may be required, particularly if the woodland is in an area where the management functions would have visual or wildlife repercussions. Clear felling may be replaced by a system of rotational felling. Removal and any subsequent replanting needs to be sensitive to considerations such as the skyline, the local vegetation patterns and the underlying topography.

Rotational felling also provides the opportunity for wildlife and understorey vegetation to survive the felling operations and to spread into newly replanted blocks. The remaining trees serve to provide both shelter for the new transplants and a seed source as well as to limit soil erosion.

The scope for rotational felling can be limited where there are strong winds, as the trees, which were originally within the canopy and now form part of the new edge, may die from exposure or be thrown.

Selective felling is a third option. There are essentially two approaches. In a woodland of mixed species and age diversity individual mature trees can be removed, leaving the remainder largely undisturbed, although there will be some resulting damage. There is the advantage that income from the woodland remains fairly constant. A variant of this involves select felling on a group rather than an individual basis. While the former has proved highly successful on the continent, group selection is generally more popular in the UK.

Alternatively the majority of the standing timber can be removed leaving just a matrix of large specimens that provide visual cover and shelter for new plantings or natural regeneration. As the new crop grows, further fellings can be performed to increase the room available for the new trees.

A hybrid system of selection and clear felling is sometimes adopted, whereby some trees are left to retain cover and preserve soil but where no income is expected from them.

Safety considerations should be of paramount importance during felling. Both skilled advice and skilled operators are essential, as is insurance cover.

In woodlands with a more commercial emphasis the size of the felling area will ultimately be determined by financial considerations. The amount of timber produced for sale may have both to justify the administrative costs of organizing and transporting labour to the site, including the costs of equipment hire, and to meet the need to produce an attractive amount of saleable material.

In the next few years there is likely to be a 'revolution' in the establishment of woodlands on land formerly used for agriculture. The nature of the above constraints is likely to change dramatically. There are likely to be more markets as well as an improved infrastructure for using timber products that were previously too isolated to be valuable.

RESOURCE REQUIREMENTS

The Forestry Commission provides guidelines on clearance, thinning and clear felling operations. These are reproduced in Tables 10.1 and 10.2. For an understanding of the system used in determining timber volumes, readers should consult the *Forest Mensuration Handbook*.

Table 10.1   The management of beech woodland: clearing and thinning: estimated resource requirements

| Average volume m³ | Time per tree in standard minutes | |
	Beech understorey clearance	Beech thinning
0.04	5.24	–
0.06	6.17	4.96
0.08	7.07	5.71
0.10	7.94	6.44
0.12	8.80	7.16
0.14	9.63	7.88
0.16	10.45	8.59
0.18	11.24	9.29
0.20	12.02	9.98
0.22	12.79	10.66
0.24	13.54	11.33
0.26	14.27	11.99
0.28	14.99	12.65
0.30	15.70	13.29
0.32	16.40	13.92
0.34	17.09	14.55
0.36	17.77	15.16
0.38	18.45	–
0.40	19.11	–
0.42	19.77	–
0.44	20.43	–

N.B. Interpolate where necessary

Source: Forestry Commission.

10.4
The re-establishment phase

This phase covers all of the operations following the completion of clear felling through to the successful establishment of a young stand of broad-leaved or mixed woodland. Thus it can include, in some cases, scrub clearance and burning as part of the site preparation works. The principal operations involved during this phase are restocking, weed control and clearing.

OPERATIONS

Many sites traditionally selected for, or left as, woodland are too wet, too steep or too infertile for intensive agriculture. Other operations may therefore be necessary at the planting stage, especially if timber production rates are important. These may include the improvement of drainage and soil structure by ripping and mounding or large-scale ground modelling. Open

Table 10.2   The management of broadleaved woodland: clear felling and estimated resource requirements

Species	Oak	Time per tree in standard minutes		
		Trees without ivy		Trees with ivy	
Average volume (m³)	Fell, convert	Fell only	Fell, convert	Fell only
0.01	2.16	1.38	2.61	1.82
0.02	2.84	1.76	3.49	2.59
0.04	4.15	2.48	5.20	4.05
0.06	5.38	3.17	6.86	5.38
0.08	6.52	3.82	8.45	6.59
0.10	7.59	4.45	9.98	7.73
0.12	8.58	5.04	11.45	8.75
0.14	9.51	5.60	12.87	9.71
0.16	10.38	6.13	14.24	10.59
0.18	11.15	6.62	15.55	11.41
0.20	11.90	7.09	16.82	12.18
0.22	12.57	7.54	18.04	12.90
0.24	13.20	7.95	19.22	13.58
0.26	13.76	8.34	20.35	14.24
0.28	14.28	8.70	21.43	14.90
0.30	14.76	9.06	22.48	15.52
0.32	15.19	9.38	–	–
0.34	15.59	9.68	–	–
0.36	15.94	9.95	–	–
0.38	16.27	10.21	–	–
0.40	16.57	10.45	–	–
0.42	16.83	10.69	–	–
0.44	17.08	10.90	–	–
0.46	17.31	11.09	–	–
0.48	17.53	11.26	–	–
0.50	17.73	11.44	–	–
0.52	17.91	11.60	–	–
0.54	18.09	11.74	–	–

N.B. Interpolate where necessary.

Source: Forestry Commission.

drains are often used to intercept ground water so that they cannot be blocked by plant roots. Fertilizing may also be required. Drainage could also be valuable to improve the usefulness of a site intended for public recreation. However, it is more common in amenity situations that such differences are welcomed as a means of extending the range of habitats.

RESTOCKING

This can be achieved through planting or natural regeneration, or a combination of both.

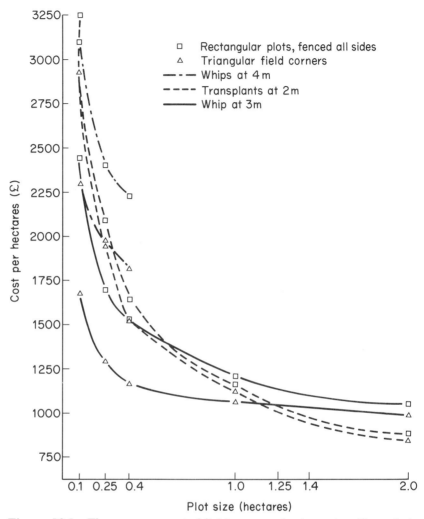

Figure 10.1   The management of field corner plantings: the effect of plot size and shape on costs (reproduced courtesy of M.J. Penistan and J.R. Laing Brown, Landscape Design).

PLANTING

Many issues of tree transplant establishment are dealt with in more detail later in this book.

The species chosen for replanting, as well as the degree of site amelioration that takes place before planting, depends upon one main consideration: how importantly timber production is regarded compared with the desire to create a woodland that is in keeping with the local vegetation character. For example, an open grown conifer such as cypress will quickly reach a saleable size with little branch growth relative to the main trunk. The opposite would be true with widely spaced oaks for example. Broadleaved trees may only be profitable if there are good local markets for fuelwood or pulp, which can provide a return on the branch growth (Savill, 1986).

The density of replanting depends on the intended afteruse, the growth rate of the species, the economics, the desired persistence of side branches and site conditions, such as exposure. Dense plantings rapidly suppress weeds but require a greater capital investment and need thinning. The choice may again depend on whether a local economic use for the thinnings is available. If density and uniform growth are important, beating-up may be necessary in subsequent years.

The speed of planting will depend on the soil type, site weediness, the presence of existing stumps, the weather, the size of plants and the method of transporting the plants to the planting site. Almost without exception, woodland planting is performed using small seedlings which can be easily carried in shoulder pouches. They are usually planted into 'notch' holes made with a mattock or a spade. Pit planting is very much slower but is more usual in amenity situations. It is also common that, for design reasons, the layout and species mixture is both more elaborate and more critical.

It may also be the case in amenity woodlands that certain larger individuals are planted, either to provide immediate impact or because of their selected form. This will dramatically increase the planting time required. Certain unusual components in the mixture, particularly broad-leaved evergreens such as *Ruscus* or *Buxus* that may be required in the under-storey, are more likely to be made available as containerized plants. These again will delay the speed of planting and the problems of stock transport.

Planting rates are therefore usually much higher on forestry sites than in amenity woodlands. The figures given later in Table 10.3 should be regarded as an upper estimate only, covering a simple species mix, planted in rows at even spacing.

Rides or clearings may need to be left as firebreaks, particularly if the woodland species include conifers. Rides also make inspection, felling and extraction easier. Booklets such as Forestry Commission Bulletin 14, 'Forestry Practice', give more details on such subjects.

In the case of large-scale plantings, fence protection against grazing animals may be cheaper and more effective than individual guards. Guidelines are provided by Figure 10.1.

NATURAL REGENERATION

Natural regeneration can be a valuable and cheap method for the restocking of amenity woodlands. Selected individual trees should be left on site to provide shelter and a seed source. Light is also necessary for adequate germination and growth. Thus, following seedling establishment, more mature trees may be felled.

Most trees seed every 1 to 4 years. Beech may go for ten or more years without masting.

The presence of grass, bracken or undecomposed leaf litter may inhibit germination so disturbance or scarification of the soil may be necessary. Selective felling and extraction may help towards this.

Protection from grazing animals is often essential before natural regeneration can be successful.

Thinning or beating-up may be necessary to produce the desired densities.

WEED CONTROL

Controlling weed competition is fundamental to the successful establishment and initial growth of woodland plantings. However, in wet upland areas weeding appears to be·less important than on lowland fertile sites. There is more water present, low soil fertility tends to reduce weed vigour and they may afford increased shelter to the transplants.

Depending on the weed species present, hand clearing may not be effective. The rapid regeneration from roots or other storage organs will only be inhibited if these organs are themselves killed by herbicides. Some invasive perennial weeds such as *Rhododendron ponticum* or *Polygonum japonicum* are likely to need repeated herbicide treatment.

Initial ground clearance by ploughing is rarely possible on sites that have

Table 10.3   The site preparation and planting of nursery stock for a variety of conditions and commercial woodland types: estimated resource requirements

Source	Operations	Input Days/Mins	Unit
FC	Step and notch planting on peat or peat mineral soils. Varies with slope of ground, soil etc.	25.50–35.90 mins	100 no
FC	Planting tubed seedlings into peats. Varies with walking conditions, types of soil, and experience of worker.	8.10–16.40 mins	100 no
FC	Notch planting on ploughed ground Varies with plant spacings (1.8m × 1.8m–2.1m × 2.1m) soil types, slope etc.	5.28–8.56 mins	100m^2
VC	Scrub clearance and burning	1.5–2.5 days 15–25 days	1000m^2 1 ha
VC	Rhododendron clearance and burning	4.5 days	1000m^2
VC	Pine and birch clearance and stump treatment (no burning)	2–6 days	100m^2
VC	Coppice woodland restoration: with burning with stacking	15–18 days 5–6 days	1000m^2 1000m^2

Note: It should be borne in mind that the above figures relate primarily to the planting of a single species or of two species mixtures in rows. Most amenity plantings involve a wide range of species. Furthermore, amenity planting rates are often significantly lower.

See Table 2.2 on p. 37 for details of sources.

Table 10.4 Woodland weed control: estimated resource requirements

Source	Operation	Time input minutes	Unit
FC	Spray herbicide with knapsack sprayer	8.00–16.74[1]	100m²
FC	Spray using ULV sprayer with knapsack refill system.		
	5 litres per hectare	0.60–1.00	100m²
	15 litres per hectare	1.90–3.10	100m²
FC	ULV spray using sprayer with 1 litre bottle with knapsack refill system		
	5 litres per hectare	0.50–2.20	100m²
	15 litres per hectare	1.50–6.70	100m²
FC	Spray using tractor mounted controlled droplet applicator to forestry row plantings at a speed of 60 metres per minute	47.90–75.50[2]	1 hectare
FC	Foliar spraying using Victair tractor—mounted mistblower (forestry model)	16.00–40.00[3]	1 hectare
FC	Weeding using tractor powered brush	1.40–3.70[4]	100m²

[1] The time input varies with the slope of the site, application rate, etc.
[2] The time input varies with length of row and distance between rows.
[3] The time input varies with output rate (100 litres per hectare – 150 litres per hectare), width of strip treated (10–15m), and tractor speed (2–4 kilometres per hour).
[4] The time input varies with row spacing, type of vegetation, length of 'weeding run'. Increase time for obstacles, poor visibility of trees very heavy woody growth.

See Table 2.2 on p. 37 for details of sources.

recently been clear felled because of the presence of stumps and roots. Similarly mechanical clearance may not be easy.

Some weed control is essential for the establishment of young trees even where the principal long-term objective is to encourage growth of the understorey. On sites, where the existing vegetation is of a desirable type, weed control restricted to a small area at the base of each tree should be sufficient, allowing much of the groundstorey to remain undisturbed. Physical mulches such as black polythene may be preferable, as these tend to suppress seed germination, relative to bare soil. A larger number of seeds may therefore survive until such time as the weed control can be relaxed.

CLEARING

Within the first ten years after establishment it is likely that, particularly on sites that have previously carried woodland, work will be needed to control unwelcome woody weeds, such as *Rhododendron ponticum*, or aggressive climbers, such as *Clematis vitalba*. Such weeds are not likely to be suppressed by the growing tree canopy and the period of control may have to be much longer than would be the case with lower growing plants.

Table 10.5 Chemical weed control: spot spraying using knapsack sprayers fitted with a guard – estimated resource requirements

| Tree spacing in metres | Number of trees per hectare | Standard minutes per hectare | | | | | | | |
| | | Using tree guard | | Using guarded nozzle | | | | | |
		0.9m* (42cc)	litres applied per ha	0.9m* (42cc)	litres applied per ha	1.2m* (63cc)	litres applied per ha	1.5m* (84cc)	litres applied per ha
1.4 × 1.4	5102	742	214	557	214	693	321	767	429
1.5 × 1.5	4444	689	187	524	187	646	280	717	373
1.6 × 1.6	3906	639	164	491	164	601	246	670	328
1.7 × 1.7	3460	588	145	461	145	558	218	626	291
1.8 × 1.8	3086	540	130	430	130	517	194	583	259
1.9 × 1.9	2770	492	116	401	116	477	175	542	233
2.0 × 2.0	2500	445	105	373	105	437	158	501	210
2.1 × 2.1	2268	398	95	344	95	398	143	465	191

* Diameter of the area treated around each tree (equivalent dosage per tree in brackets).

Note: Where tree spacings are other than those shown above, entry to the table should be made using the appropriate number of trees per hectare and interpolating where necessary.

Source: Forestry Commission.

These clearance operations can often be coordinated with the first thinnings and, if timber is a prime requirement despite wide spacing, brashing of side branches can be performed.

RESOURCE REQUIREMENTS

Tables 10.3 to 10.8 draw heavily upon the guidelines published by the Forestry Commission, concerning planting, weed control and cleaning. By comparison Table 10.9 is based on local authority timings. Most figures for amenity woodland are likely to lie between these two extremes.

THE FUTURE FOR AMENITY WOODLANDS

The UK imports roughly 90% of home timber needs. Despite the rapidly increasing interest in the establishment and cropping of woodlands on farms, surpluses are unlikely to be achieved. Indeed there are likely to be radical changes in the distribution of wood markets and timber mills. In order to encourage early returns on the new woodland investment, research is needed. Initiatives are also required to develop new techniques which will enable commercial use to be made of woodland products that were formerly regarded as worthless, i.e. early thinnings and short rotation coppice. It is likely that cooperative ventures will be established to help in coordinating the sale of produce from small isolated sites.

Table 10.6　Chemical weed control: knapsack sprayer requirements

Output

The following output can be expected in a full working day of 480 minutes.

Where rows are easily visible, walking conditions good and average distance each way to refill is:	Number of sprayers-full per day (1 sprayer = 18 litres)
50 metres	19–21
100 metres	17–19
150 metres	15–17

Modification and variations

N.B.　These modifications and variations are only to be applied when the prevailing conditions or job specification differ from those listed in paragraphs 1 and 2 of the publication.

i)　Ground conditions
Where there are impediments to movement necessitating considerable avoiding action, output is likely to be reduced by 1 or 2 sprayers-full per day.

ii)　Rows difficult to follow
Where rows are indistinct output is likely to be reduced by 1 or 2 sprayers-full per day.

iii)　Steep slopes
Where steep slopes are encountered and walking speed is reduced to 1.5Kph output will fall as follows:

Where the average walking distance each way is	Number of sprayers-full per day
50 metres	13–14
100 metres	11–13
150 metres	9–11

iv)　Reduced quantity carried
The capacity of the sprayer is 18 litres. Where circumstance demands that less is carried, the effect on output is as follows:

Volume carried	Average distance	Number of sprayers-full per day
$\frac{3}{4}$ full (14 litres)	50 metres	23–25
	100 metres	20–22
	150 metres	18–19
$\frac{1}{2}$ full (9 litres)	50 metres	29–31
	100 metres	25–27
	150 metres	21–23

v)　Spot treatment
If the technique is practicable, the following outputs will apply:

Average walking distance	Treating $\frac{1}{2}$ of row Numbers of sprayers-full	Treating $\frac{3}{4}$ of row Numbers of sprayers-full
50 metres	$12\frac{1}{2}$–$13\frac{1}{2}$	16–17
100 metres	12–13	14–15
150 metres	11–12	13–14

Source:　Forestry Commission

Table 10.7   Chemical weed control: granular and foliar spray application, and estimated resource requirements

---

i) *Application of granules (e.g. Chlorthiamid) with powered Knapsack Distributor and Fishtail Nozzle*

Average distance between refill point and midpoint of area to be treated (metres)	Output in full day	
	kgs	hectares (net)
50	80–90	1.30–1.45
100	75–85	1.20–1.35
150	70–80	1.15–1.30

Modifications and variations

N.B. These modifications and variations are only to be applied when the prevailing conditions or job specification differ from those listed in paragraphs 1 and 2 of the publication.

Obstacles and short rows

- Where there are obstacles to avoid, or short rows output will be reduced, in relation to their significance by up to 10%.
- *Sport treatment* Where spot treatment is practicable and 50% of each row is treated, these outputs may be anticipated.

Average distance between refill point and midpoint of area to be treated metres (net)	Output in full day	
	kgs	hectares
50	42–50	0.68–0.81
100	41–49	0.66–0.74
150	40–48	0.64–0.77

ii) *Foliar Spraying with Victair Tractor Mounted Mistblower*
Output table

Tractor speed (km/h)	Output in hectares per hour			
	100 litres/ha		150 litres/ha	
	10m strip	15m strip	10m strip	15m strip
2	1.64	2.27	1.51	2.03
3	2.27	3.03	2.02	2.60
4	2.79	3.65	2.43	3.04

Source: Forestry Commission.

Most of even the fastest growing conifers do not provide the bulk of their revenue for at least 40 years. Thus changes in grant aid have been introduced to help farmers to remain solvent throughout this long investment period.

The net effect of all these changes is that the opportunities for obtaining some return on produce from amenity woodlands will increase. Under

Table 10.8 Manual and mechanical weed control: estimated resource requirements

i) Weeding by hand tools – Time per hectare in standard minutes

Weed group	Grade	Plant spacing (metres)							
		2.1 × 2.1	2.0 × 2.0	1.9 × 1.9	1.8 × 1.8	1.7 × 1.7	1.6 × 1.6	1.5 × 1.5	1.4 × 1.4
Herbs, bracken and most soft grasses e.g. foxglove, willow herb, meadow sweet, sorrel and thistle and other wild flowers. Grasses e.g. agrostis, holcus, cocksfoot, non tussocky molinia, etc.	1	560	590	630	670	710	750	800	850
	2	1,000	1,040	1,090	1,150	1,210	1,290	1,380	1,490
	3	1,630	1,710	1,800	1,900	2,020	2,150	2,290	2,440
Coarse grasses and rush e.g. deschampsia caespitosa, clamagrostis, tussocky molinia, etc.	1	900	950	1,010	1,070	1,130	1,200	1,270	1,340
	2	1,330	1,390	1,470	1,560	1,660	1,770	1,900	2,040
	3	2,070	2,160	2,270	2,400	2,550	2,710	2,890	3,090
Climbers Principally bramble, briar also honeysuckle, clematis.	1	1,190	1,240	1,300	1,380	1,460	1,560	1,660	1,780
	2	1,950	2,050	2,160	2,290	2,430	2,590	2,760	2,950
	3	2,490	2,530	2,580	2,650	2,740	2,850	2,970	3,100
Woody weeds Coppice and seedlings, gorse and broom included	1	1,410	1,470	1,540	1,630	1,730	1,830	1,950	2,090
	2	2,490	2,530	2,580	2,650	2,740	2,850	2,970	3,110
	3	3,350	3,390	3,480	3,620	3,800	4,030	4,320	4,650
Areas not requiring any cutting		150	155	160	170	180	190	200	210

N.B. Interpolate between grades where necessary.

ii) Weeding by portable brushcutter – Time per hectare in standard minutes

Weed group	Grade	Plant spacing (metres)							
		2.1 × 2.1	2.0 × 2.0	1.9 × 1.9	1.8 × 1.8	1.7 × 1.7	1.6 × 1.6	1.5 × 1.5	1.4 × 1.4
Herbs, bracken and most soft grasses) e.g., foxglove, willow herb, meadow sweet, sorrel and thistle and other wild flowers.	1	720	770	820	870	920	970	1,030	1,080
	2	840	910	980	1,050	1,120	1,190	1,250	1,320
	3	1,040	1,120	1,200	1,280	1,350	1,430	1,500	1,570
Grasses, e.g. agrostis, holcus, cocksfoot, non tussocky molinia, etc.									
Coarse grasses and rush, e.g. deschampsia caespitosa, clamagrostis, tussocky molinia, etc.	1	620	720	820	910	1,000	1,100	1,180	1,270
	2	1,010	1,100	1,180	1,260	1,340	1,420	1,490	1,550
	3	1,210	1,310	1,400	1,500	1,600	1,690	1,780	1,870
Climbers Principally bramble, briar, also honeysuckle, clematis.	1	960	1,030	1,100	1,170	1,250	1,310	1,380	1,450
	2	1,240	1,330	1,420	1,510	1,610	1,710	1,810	1,910
	3	1,530	1,650	1,770	1,890	2,020	2,140	2,260	2,380
Woody weeds Coppice and seedlings, gorse and broom included	1	1,040	1,120	1,200	1,280	1,350	1,430	1,500	1,570
	2	1,530	1,650	1,770	1,890	2,020	2,140	2,260	2,380
	3	2,030	2,180	2,340	2,490	2,650	2,800	2,960	3,120
Areas not requiring any cutting.		150	155	160	170	180	190	200	210

N.B. Interpolate between grades where necessary.

Source: Forestry Commission.

Table 10.8 (cont'd)

i) Cleaning by hand tools – Time per hectare in standard minutes

Weed group	Grade	Plant spacing (metres)							
		2.1 × 2.1	2.0 × 2.0	1.9 × 1.9	1.8 × 1.8	1.7 × 1.7	1.6 × 1.6	1.5 × 1.5	1.4 × 1.4
Climbers									
Principally bramble, briar also honeysuckle and clematis	4	2,620	2,710	2,810	2,900	3,000	3,100	3,210	3,310
	5	3,460	3,590	3,720	3,850	3,980	4,110	4,250	4,380
	6	4,770	4,970	5,170	5,370	5,560	5,760	5,950	6,130
Woody weeds									
Coppice and seedlings, gorse and broom included	4	4,500	4,680	4,860	5,040	5,220	5,400	5,580	5,760
	5	6,570	6,840	7,110	7,380	7,640	7,910	8,170	8,420
Areas not requiring any cutting.		150	155	160	170	180	190	200	210

N.B. Interpolate between grades where necessary.

ii) Cleaning by portable brushcutter – Time per hectare in standard minutes

Weed group	Grade	Plant spacing (metres)							
		2.1 × 2.1	2.0 × 2.0	1.9 × 1.9	1.8 × 1.8	1.7 × 1.7	1.6 × 1.6	1.5 × 1.5	1.4 × 1.4
Climbers									
Principally bramble, briar, also honeysuckle and clematis	4	1,940	2,010	2,070	2,130	2,200	2,270	2,340	2,410
	5	2,420	2,550	2,670	2,780	2,890	2,990	3,090	3,180
	6	3,360	3,530	3,700	3,850	4,000	4,140	4,270	4,400
Woody weeds									
Coppice and seedlings, gorse and broom included	4	3,280	3,410	3,540	3,670	3,800	3,940	4,070	4,210
	5	4,820	5,000	5,190	5,370	5,550	5,730	5,920	6,100
Areas not requiring any cutting.		150	155	160	170	180	190	200	210

N.B. Interpolate between grades where necessary.

Source: Forestry Commission.

Table 10.9 General operations: estimated resource requirements

Source	Operations	SMV	Units
D	Clear undergrowth and underwood, hook and saw	320.00	100m²
W	Rough cut: hook/scythe/shears	117.00	100m²
K	Scythe/hook between trees	37.70	100yd²
D	Fork cuttings to heap and set alight	82.00	100m²
H	Cut grass in woodland area (30% density)	7.10	100m²
T	Pedestrian mow	9.00	100m²
FMH	Clear wet grassland and scrub and clear to heaps	960.00	1 ha
CRC	Cleaning, thinning, cut down saplings and burn	5 days/ha	
W	Saw down thin trees	7.40	1 no
Telf	Brash 8-year-old trees: Larch	172.00	100 no
	Ash, Chestnut, Sycamore	45.00	100 no
	Elm	117.00	100 no
CRC	Stump treatment with knapsack spray	50 hr	Ha
Salop	Grub out roots (15cm × 10m) and dispose	68.50	1 no
GLC	Plant small trees in cleared woodland	400	100 no

See Table 2.2 on p. 37 for details of sources.

these circumstances some profit may even be possible without the need to compromise in terms of species, densities or age distribution.

References

Baines, J.C. (1986) Design considerations at establishment. In *Ecology and Design in Landscape* (eds A.D. Bradshaw, D.A. Goode, and E. Thorp). The 24th Symposium of the British Ecological Society. Blackwells, Oxford.

Blatchford, O.W. (1978) *Forestry Practice*. Forestry Commission Bulletin 14.

Edwards, P.M. (1983) *Timber Measurements: a Field Guide*. Forestry Commission Booklet 49. HMSO, London.

Evans, J. (1984) *Silviculture of Broadleaved Woodland*. Forestry Commission Research and Development Paper 62.

Foresty Commission (1978) *Standard Time Tables and Output Guides*. Forestry Commission Booklet 45. HMSO.

Kendle A.D. (1987) A New Direction. *Horticulture Week*, 11th September.

National Farmers Union (1987) *Farm Woodlands. A discussion paper*. NFU, London.

Penistan, M.J. and Laing-Brown, J.R. (1979) Copse and spinney. *Landscape Design*, **127**, 26–29.

Peterken, G.F. (1975) Coppiced woods — restored for wildlife? *Conservation Review*, **10**, 4–5.

Reid, S. (1981) Woodland management in the urban setting. *Landscape Research*, **6** (3), 22–24.

Savill, P. (1986) Unpublished presentation, Woodland Management Conference Oxford Arb. Ass. 15th November.

Thornton, P.P. (1971) Managing urban and suburban trees and woodlands for timber products. In: *Trees and Forests in an Urbanizing Environment*. University of Massachussetts, Mass., pp. 129–32.

Watkins, C. (1983) Planting and management of small roadside plantations. *Quarterly Journal of Forestry*, **LVII** (3), 179–84.

Further reading   WOODLANDS

Anon (1956) *Utilisation of Hazel Coppice*. Forestry Commission Bulletin 27.

Anon (1983) *Broadleaved Woodland Establishment*. Economic survey of private forestry in Southern and Eastern England. Economics Section, Dept. of Forestry, University of Oxford.

Anon (1984) *Aspects of Applied Biology 5. Weed control and vegetation management in forests and amenity areas*. Assc. of Applied Biologists, Warwick.

Bamford, R. (1986) Broadleaved edges within conifer forest — the importance to bird life. *Quarterly Journal of Forestry*, **LXXX**, 115–21.

Berry, P.M. (1983) The landscape, ecological and recreational evaluation of woodland. *Arboricultural Journal*, **7**, 191–200.

Brazier, J.D. (1985) Growing hardwoods — the timber quality viewpoint. *Quarterly Journal of Forestry*, **LXXIX**, 221–6.

Brotherton, I. and Devall, N. (1987) More forestry: problem or opportunity? *Landscape Design*, **169**, 49–52.

Brown, I.R. (1984) *Management of Birch Woodland in Scotland*. Countryside Commission for Scotland, Battleby.

Brown, R.M. (1975) *Chemical Control of Weeds in the Forest*. Forestry Commission Booklet 40.

Campbell, D. (1987) Landscape design in forestry. *Landscape Design*, April, pp. 31–6.

Crowther, R.E. and Patch, D. (1980) *Coppice*. DOE Arboricultural Advisory Note 21/80/SILS.

Crowther, R.E. and Toulmin-Rothe, I. (1963) *Felling and Converting Thinnings by Hand*. Forestry Commission Booklet 9.

Currie, F.C. and Bamford, R. (1982) The value to birdlife of retaining small conifer stands beyond normal felling age within forests. *Quarterly Journal of Forestry*, **LXXVI**, 153–9.

Driver, C. (1985) Charcoal – another market for neglected woodland. *Quarterly Journal of Forestry* **LXXIX**, 29–32.

Edlin, H.L. (1973) *Woodland Crafts of Britain*. David and Charles.

Follis, A. (1980) *Hand Tools*. British Trust for Conservation Volunteers.

Garfitt, J.E. (1977a) Management of motorway plantations. *Quarterly Journal of Forestry*, **LXXI**, 162–4.

Grafitt, J.E. (1977b) Irregular silviculture in the service of amenity. *Quarterly Journal of Forestry*, **LXXI**, 82–4.

Garthwaite, P.F. (1977) Managing and marketing of hardwoods in S.E. England. *Quarterly Journal of Forestry*, **67**, 144.

Gill, R.M.A. (1985) The susceptibility of tree species to bark stripping by grey squirrels. *Quarterly Journal of Forestry*, **LXXIX**, 183–90.

Goldsmith, F.B., Harding, J., Newbold, A. and Smart, N. (1982) An ecological basis for the management of broadleaved forest. *Quarterly Journal of Forestry*, **LXXVI**, 237–46.

Gunn, D.J.P. and Naish, E.F.E. (1986) Grazing with standards. *Quarterly Journal of Forestry*, **LXXX**, 82–4.

Hamilton, G.J. *Aspects of Thinning*. Forestry Commission Bulletin 48. HMSO, London.

Hamilton, G.J. and Christie, J.M. *Influences of Spacing on Crop Characteristics and Yield*. Forestry Commission Bulletin 52. HMSO, London.

Hanson, D. (1987) Cherish your chainsaw. *Horticulture Week*, 19th June.

Helliwell, D.R. (1979) Economic aspects of amenity woodland management. *Arboricultural Journal*, **3**, 540–6.

Hilton, G.M. and Packham, J.R. (1986) Regional variation in English beech mast. *Arboricultural Journal*, **10** (1), 3–15.

Jobling, J. and Pearce, M.L. (1977) Free growth of oak. *Forestry Commission Forest Record*, **113**, 8.

Kirby, K.J. (1984) *Forestry Operations and Broadleaf Woodland Conservation*. Nature Conservancy Council Focus on Nature Conservation 8, NCC.

Lorrain-Smith, R. (1977) Economic problems of growing hardwoods in Great Britain 1. The basic economic approach. *Arboricultural Journal*, **3**, 165–9.

McCluskey, J. (1986) Shroud for the Scottish landscape. *Landscape Design*, **164**, 48–51.

McNaught, K. and Lorrain-Smith, R. (1980) The place of hardwoods in British forestry. *Arboricultural Journal*, **4**, 74–136.

Miles, J. and Kinnaird, J.W. (1979) The establishment and regeneration of birch, juniper and Scots pine in the Scottish Highlands. *Scottish Forestry*, **33**: 102–19.

Miller H.G. (1981) Forest fertilisation: some guiding concepts. *Forestry*, **54**, 157–67.

Neustein, S.A. (1968) *Restocking of windthrown forest*. Forestry Commission Research and Development Paper 75.

Nuttall, A. (1977) Kerb granules – a safe weedkiller for forestry. *Quarterly Journal of Forestry*, **LXXI**, 237–8.

Orde-Powlett, P.C. (1977) When to fell and thin. *Quarterly Journal of Forestry*, **LXXI**, 51–4.

Orrom, M.H. and Mitchell, A.F. (1972) *Silviculture and Good Landscapes in British Forestry: the improvement of planning and practice*. Forestry Commission Research and Development Paper 91. Forestry Commission, Edinburgh.

Palmer, C. (1983) *Weed Strategies for Hardwoods*. Forestry and British

Timber. April.

Patterson, G. (1986) Forestry Design. *Landscape Design*, February, 29–31.

Peterkin, G.F. (1972) Conservation coppicing and the coppice crafts. *Quarterly Journal, Devon Trust for Nature Conservation*, **4**, 157–64.

Pepper, H.W. and Tee, L.A. (1972) Forest fencing. *Forestry Commission Forest Record*, **80**.

Poore, A. (1982) Coppice management in East Anglian woodlands and its application in urban fringe nature conservation. *Arboricultural Journal*, **6**, 81–94.

Price, C. (1985) The distribution of increment and the economics of thinning. *Quarterly Journal of Forestry*, **LXXIX**, 159–68.

Price, C. (1987) Further reflections on the economics of thinning. *Quarterly Journal of Forestry*, **LXXXI**, 85–102.

Rorison, I.H. and Sutton, F. (1976) Climate topography and germination. In *Light as an Ecological Factor II*. (eds G.C. Evans, R. Bainbridge and O. Rackham) Blackwell Scientific Publications, Oxford.

Russell, B.P. (1985) Why invest in private woodlands. *Quarterly Journal of Forestry*, **LXXIX**, 169–74.

Seymour, W. (1979) The problems of the landowner in private forestry. *Arboricultural Journal*, **3**, 446–51.

Shaw, M.W. (1974) The reproductive characteristics of oak. In *The British Oak* (eds M.G. Morris and F.H. Perring) Classey, Faringdon, pp. 162–81.

Small, D. (1983) Management of woodland and woodland vegetation for amenity and recreation with particular reference to the New Forest. In *Management of Vegetation*, British Crop Protection Council Monograph No. 26. (ed. J.M. Way) BCPC, Croydon.

Smart, N. and Andrews, J. (1985) *Birds and Broadleaves Handbook: a Guide to Further the Conservation of Birds in Broadleaved Woodland*. RSPB.

Steele, R.C. (1972) *Wildlife Conservation in Woodlands*. Forestry Commission Booklet No. 29. HMSO, London.

Steele, R.H. (1983) Management of woodland and woodland vegetation for wildlife conservation. In: *Management of Vegetation*, British Crop Protection Council Monograph No. 26. (ed J.M. Way) BCPC, Croydon.

Sykes, J.M. and Horrill, A.D. (1985) Natural regeneration in a Caledonian Pinewood: progress after eight years of enclosure at Collie Coire Chuile, Perthshire. *Arboricultural Journal*, **9** (1), 13–24.

Towler, R.W. and Barnes, G.C. (1983) What future for broadleaved farm woodlands in East Anglia. *Quarterly Journal of Forestry*, **LXXVII**, 149–61.

Trower, J.P. (1977) When to fell and thin. *Quarterly Journal of Forestry*, **LXXI**, 175–6.

Watkins, C. (1983) The planting and management of small roadside plantations. *Quarterly Journal of Forestry*, **LXXVII**, 179–84.

Watt, A.S. (1919) On the causes of failure of natural regeneration of British Oakwoods. *Journal of Ecology*, **7**, 173–203.

Wittering, W.O. (1974) *Weeding in the Forest*. Forestry Commission Bulletin 48. HMSO. London.

Wood, R.F., Miller, A.D.S. and Nimmo, M. (1967) *Experiments onthe Rehabilitation of Uneconomic Broadleaved Woodlands*. Forestry Commission Research and Development Paper 51.

11 THE MANAGEMENT OF WOODY PLANTS: TREES AND SHRUBS

11.1
Introduction

The woody plants described in this chapter include trees, shrubs, ground covers, wall plants and climbers. Along with grasslands they are the most important landscape components, both in terms of area and maintenance costs.

Trees, shrub beds and woody ground cover on average take up between 35 per cent and 45 per cent of 'man-made' landscapes. In the countryside woodlands and scrub cover about 12 per cent of rural areas.

The purpose of this introductory chapter is to provide answers to the following three questions:

1. What are the important characteristics of woody plants?
2. What functions do they perform in the landscape?
3. What are the main problems and opportunities which they present to the Amenity Manager?

CHARACTERISTICS

Woody plants are tall, bulky and long-lived compared to other living landscape elements. They add a third (vertical) dimension to the flat two dimensions which elements such as grass and water contribute (Hoyle and Ruff, 1977). Because of their longevity, woody plants often provide long-term structure in the landscape. Their impact on the environment can be considerable (Bernatzky, 1978).

Table 11.1 lists both the main and lesser landscape features contributed by trees, shrubs and climbing plants.

FUNCTIONS

Trees and shrubs, because of the many functions which they perform, are valued and increasingly used in modern landscapes (Patterson, 1977). The main environmental functions performed by woody plants are summarized in Table 11.2 and are amplified by the descriptions which follow.

Table 11.1   The main landscape features provided by woody plants*

Landscape features	Plant locations	
Forests and woodlands	R	
Copses and spinneys	R	
Shelterbelts	R	
Avenues	R	U
Hedges	R	U
Scrub	R	
Mass or structure plantings		U
Shrub beds		U
Ground cover		U
Curtilage or foundation plantings		U
Plants on walls, fences, pergolas		U
Herbaceous borders and bedding displays		U
Container and roof garden plantings		U
'Specimen' and individual plants	R	U

Key: R = Mainly rural features, though many also occur in urban areas.
    U = Mainly urban components, but some are also found in rural areas, especially in
        privately owned amenity areas.

Note: * Trees, shrubs, wall plants and climbers.

CONTRIBUTION TO COST-EFFECTIVE LANDSCAPE
MAINTENANCE

Woody plantings are increasingly being used to replace other landscape
elements. Examples of this are:

- Low ground cover as a lower-maintenance substitute for mown swards;
- Native tree and shrub plantings to add interest and ecological value to
  'green deserts';
- Ornamental tree and shrub species to enrich hard surfaced areas, for
  example in urban environmental improvement schemes.

USE ON SITES REQUIRING REVEGETATION OR
RECLAMATION

Woody plants establish more successfully than any other vegetation on
certain difficult substrates (Bradshaw and Sheldon, 1976; Grubb, 1986) —
especially on sites which are low in nutrients and very freely drained.
They are therefore important in the revegetation of derelict and despoiled
landscapes, although even these need management support on very poor
sites. Many grow rapidly, for example birch, alder and willow, and are
important in the quick 'greening' of eyesores. They are thus major components of schemes designed to improve the appearance of interim as well
as long-term rehabilitation sites in urban, rural and fringe areas.

Table 11.2   The main functions performed by woody plants

Functions	Description
Visual	As structures of intrinsic beauty and interest, they: – provide, on both macro and micro scales, 'nature' and a variety of feelings associated with 'verdure'; – soften or contrast with other landscape elements; – define spaces; – direct the eyes and feet of users in accordance with the design intentions; – accommodate changes in level; – relate buildings to each other and to the site; – are the only type of vegetation that can absorb and encompass human activity or provide shade; – can provide a vertical scale that complements that of urban developments, particularly in the case of trees; – can be bought in at very large sizes from specialist nurseries to provide instant impact; – can provide a substantial mass of vegetation on a site at a very small cost in terms of lost groundspace.
Social	They provide: – screening; – privacy; – enclosure.
Physical	They: – demarcate boundaries, areas and features; – act as barriers to people, stock and vehicles; – direct pedestrian and vehicular circulation; – provide shelter from wind, rain and glare; – have a cooling effect directly by shading and indirectly through transpiration; – reduce air pollution through both filtration of carbon dioxide, dust etc, and enrichment with oxygen and moisture; – help to control erosion; – provide a low-maintenance landscape 'filler' for low-use, buffer areas.
Conservation and recreation	They provide: – habitats for wildlife and people; – both a backdrop and actual facilities for sport, play and recreation; – a wealth of teaching aids for environmental education;
Economic	They contribute directly through: – the production of crops: commercial, e.g. timber, semi-commercial e.g. country crafts, estate and local authority uses, non-commercial, e.g. kindling, pea and bean sticks, fruit leaf mould. They contribute indirectly through the habitats provided for: – game, fungi.

CONTROL OF EROSION AND THE STABILIZATION OF SOILS

Woody plants, because of their relatively deep rooted habit, together with the strength and longevity of their root systems, are important in certain types of erosion control. They are recognized by Water Authorities as being essential in preventing erosion in some waterside situations. In locations where the horizons of a soil profile are liable to slippage, woody plant roots can help to bond them together. This can be important whether the profiles are either natural or man-made (Foister, 1977).

AMELIORATION OF DEVELOPMENT

Woody plants are used extensively to soften the impact of both new developments and existing eyesores upon the environment. Tree and shrub planting is now frequently a major condition associated with planning permission granted for new developments.

In addition the ameliorative effects of woody plants, especially trees, upon the micro-climates of cities and industrial areas are well recognized (Bernatzky, 1978).

CREATION OF NEW HABITATS

Woody plantings are increasingly regarded as important habitats for people as well as for wildlife. They are acknowledged to be valuable features of informal recreation areas. The friendly and 'parental' stature of much woody vegetation is associated with the shelter and sense of enclosure provided. The three dimensional richness of many wooded areas provides a stimulating setting for children's play and a hospitable environment for many species of flora and fauna (Emery, 1987).

PROVISION OF SPORTING AND RECREATION HABITATS

The role of rural features, such as woods, copses, and hedges in countryside sports has been one of the major reasons why landowners and managers have been keen to conserve them in the landscape. Many landscapes depend in part upon sporting interests for the retention of significant features which might otherwise have been destroyed. As a source of revenue, game management can be an important feature on many estates and farms (Anon, 1976; Fraser, 1982; CRC Countryside Sports, 1983).

Woody vegetation often provides an essential backdrop for recreation areas such as caravan sites and country parks.

11.2 Problems and opportunities

The particular characteristics of woody plants – size, bulk and longevity – can create both problems and opportunities for an Amenity Manager. These are briefly reviewed in the following paragraphs.

SIZE AND BULK

Part of the charm of woody plants is that they can be as big as or bigger than people. Users of the landscape can therefore, be 'among' or 'under' the vegetation rather than just 'on' it. However, this can bring problems too.

SAFETY

The sheer size of trees as structures can spell danger if they become mechanically weak (Bridgeman, 1976).

The fact that people can hide in or among trees and shrubs is a problem, particularly in urban areas. The protection which woody vegetation provides for muggers and other potential attackers, or rather the perception of such protection in the eyes of the public, can discourage the use of these features near to areas which the public frequent. Some local authorities feel very strongly about these dangers.

DAMAGE TO PROPERTY

Trees, above and below ground, the capable of damaging services and structures. They are dynamic elements which grow and can exert great force, can block drains, can interfere with overhead lines and can disrupt the foundation of buildings (Brennan *et al.*, 1981; Biddle, 1987). The siting and management of trees needs to take account of this. Real care and thought in choosing and locating trees is essential and there is an abundance of information available on this. Taking the care to use this information can save a great deal of trouble subsequently.

Large trees produce quantities of leaf and other litter, which can create a significant amount of work for the Amenity Manager (Broadbent, 1985). Slippery organic matter such as berries can be a particular hazard when there are elderly people around, and on slopes.

AGE AND LIFE CYCLES

Woody plants have a rather prolonged period of 'childhood', during which they need careful nuturing. Their 'senility' is also often prolonged. At that stage they may also need a significant amount of management care. However, with good planning and early management the 'adult' tree may be quite maintenance-free.

Many woody species can be regenerated or rejuvenated by cutting. In this they are similar to grassland; for example, a woodland coppice cycle is similar to a greatly extended mowing cycle of growth – cut – recovery, rejuvenation and regrowth – cut –, and so on. This characteristic can be used to advantage by managers. For example, some ground cover shrubs can have their useful life span extended several times by cutting or 'coppicing' at say 15-yearly intervals (Thoday, 1982).

The main structure of trees and shrubs is perennial. This 'body' is influenced by early experiences, just as a human body is affected by childhood nurturing. If a plant is checked in youth it may never recover to fulfil its allotted role in the landscape. Trees can be permanently checked or traumatized by difficult conditions, such as drought when they are young. This is one reason why it is so important to carry out the correct establishment practices (Thoday, 1983). Checks affect growth rates, which can make management difficult. For example, the thinning of amenity plantings is difficult if the growth rates of the component plants cannot be predicted. Again it is very difficult to fuse ground cover plants satisfactorily if the individuals do not develop at either the expected or compatible rates.

SEASONAL MANPOWER REQUIREMENTS

Whereas much of the maintenance work associated with grasslands is specific to the summer, most woody plant maintenance can or should be done in the winter. Planting, most pruning and the application of residual herbicides, for example, are best done in the November to February period.

Areas of trees and shrubs can, therefore, be used by the Amenity Manager to balance out seasonal work loads. They will only do this, however, if they do not add unduly to the summer work load. Plantings which require much summer weed control, dead heading, and so on, will not help the manager.

The capital costs of establishing woody plants can be very much higher than that of establishing grassland, even when high quality turves are used. Experience shows that more careful management is clearly required if costly failures are to be avoided.

References

Anon (1976) *Management and Administration of Woodland Estates*. Forestry Commission Research and Development Paper 115.

Bernatzky, A. (1978) *Tree Ecology and Preservation*. Developments in agricultural and managed forest ecology, 2. Elsevier. Netherlands.

Biddle, P.G. (1987) Trees and buildings. In *Advances in Practical Arboriculture*. Bulletin 65. Forestry Commission. Edinburgh.

Bradshaw, A.D. and Sheldon, J.C. (1976) The reclamation of slate waste tips by tree planting. *Landscape Design*, **113**, 31–3.

Brennan, G., Patch, D. and Stevens, F.R.W. (1981) *Tree Roots and Underground Pipes*. DOE Arboricultural Advisory Note 36/81/TRL.

Bridgeman, P.H. (1976) *Tree Surgery*. David and Charles, London.

Broadbent, T. (1985) City Limits. *GC & HTJ*, 4th January.

Buckley G.P. (1978) Tree planting options on industrial wasteland. *Arboricultural Journal*, **3**, 263–72.

Cobham Resource Consultants (1983) *Countryside Sports*.

Emery, M. (1987) *Promoting Nature in Towns and Cities*: A practical guide. Croom Helm, London.

Foister, J. (1977) Planting to·stabilise steep slopes. In *Landscape Design with Plants*. (ed. B. Clouston) Heinemann, London.

Fraser, A.I. (1982) The role of deciduous woodlands in the economy of rural communities *Arboricultural Journal*, **6**(1), 37–47.

Grubb, P.J. (1986) The ecology of establishment. In *Ecology and Design in Landscape*. The 24th symposium of the British Ecological Society (eds A.D. Bradshaw, D.A. Goode and E. Thorp). Blackwells, Oxford.

Hoyle, D. and Ruff, A. (1977) The use of mature plants in urban areas. In *Landscape Design with Plants*, (ed. B. Clouston) Heinemann, London, pp. 99–126.

Patterson, G. (1977) Trees in urban areas. In *Landscape Design with Plants* (ed. B. Clouston). Heinemann, London.

Thoday, P.R. (1982) Ground cover – factors determining its success. In *Cost Effective Amenity Landscape Management* (eds P.R. Thoday and C.H. Addison). HEA Conference Proceedings. HEA, Bridgewater.

Thoday, P.R. (1983) Tree establishment in amenity sites. In *Tree Establishment* (ed. P.R. Thoday). Bath University.

Further reading   Allison, H. and Peterken, G.F. (1985) Changes in the number of non-woodland trees in Britain since 1945. *Arboricultural Journal* **9**(4), 259–270.

Anon (1983) *The Management of Semi-natural Woodland*. Hampshire County Council, Winchester.

Anon (1984) *Community Woodland Resource Pack*. The Woodland Trust, Lincoln.

Christensen, P.A. (1983) Management of natural vegetation on farms. In *Management of Vegetation*. British Crop Protection Council Monograph No. 26 (ed. J. M. Way). BCPC, Croyden.

Cobham, R.O. (1985) Blenheim: art and management of landscape restoration. *Arboricultural Journal*, **9**(2), 81–100.

Dartington Amenity Research Trust (1983) *Small Woods on Farms*. CCP, 143.

Foot, D.L. (1985) *Environmental Influences on Forestry Investment in the British Uplands*. Forestry Commission Research and Development Paper 143.

Harris, R.W. (1983) *Care of Trees, Shrubs, and Vines in the Landscape*. Prentice Hall, New Jersey.

James, N.D.G. (1981) *A History of English Forestry*. Blackwells, Oxford.

Last, F.T. and Gardiner, A.S. (eds) (1981) *Forest and Woodland Ecology*. *ITE*, Cambridge.

Malcolm, D.C., Evans, J. and Edwards, P.N. (eds) (1982) *Broadleaves in Britain*. University of Edinburgh Press, Edinburgh.

McCullen, J. and Webb, R. (1982) *A Manual on Urban Trees*. An Foras Forbartha. Dublin.

Osborne, L. and Krebs, J. (1981) Replanting after Dutch Elm Disease. *New Scientist*, April 23rd.

Patch, D. and Lines, R. (1981) *Winter Shelter for Agricultural Stock*. DOE Arboricultural Advisory Note 35/81/SILN.

Peterken, G.F. (1977) General management principles for conservation in British Woodlands. *Forestry*, **L**(1), 27–48.

Peterken, G.F. (1981) *Woodland Conservation and Management*. Chapman and Hall, London.

Pryor, S.N. (1982) *An Economic Analysis of Silvicultural Options for Broadleaved Woodlands*. Contract Research Report. NCC, London.

Rackham, O. (1976) *Trees and Woodland in the British Landscape*. Dent, London.

Small, D. (1983) Management of woodland and woodland vegetation for amenity and recreation with particular reference to the New Forest. In: *Management of Vegetation*. British Crop Protection Council Monograph No. 26 (ed. J.M. Way). BCPC, Croydon.

Steele, R.C. (1972) *Wildlife Conservation in Woodlands*. Forestry Commission Booklet No. 29. HMSO, London.

Steele, R.H. (1983) Management of woodland and woodland vegetation for wildlife conservation. In: *Management of Vegetation*, British Crop

Protection Council Monograph No. 26 (ed. J.M. Way). BCPC, Croydon.

Steer, C. (1981) Lowland small woods: past perfect, present indicative, future conditional? *Landscape Research*, **6**(3), 28–29.

Taylor, C. (1977) Street Tree Planning. *GC & HTJ*, 16th September.

Towler, R.W. (1986) Landscape Conservation in Norfolk 1. Trees in the landscape of Norfolk – past, present and future. *Arboricultural Journal*, **10**(1), 15–22.

Towler, M.N. (1986) Landscape Conservation in Norfolk 2. Management of small woodlands in Norfolk. *Arboricultural Journal*, **10**(1), 23–32.

Watkins, C. (1984) Woodland clearance in England and Wales – a case study of post-war changes in Nottinghamshire. *Arboricultural Journal*, **8**(4), 299–316.

Workman, J. (1982) Restoration of parks and subsequent management. *Landscape Research*, **7**(1), 29–30.

12 THE MANAGEMENT OF WOODY PLANTS: GENERAL AMENITY TREE AND SHRUB COMMUNITIES

12.1 Introduction

This chapter deals with all those plantings established at fairly close spacings, 2m centres or less, which are intended to form a closed canopy or mass of vegetation. These include all of the landscape features in Table 11.1 displayed earlier, whose component plants eventually interact and mingle as a community.

The establishment period of 'community' plantings can be said to have ended when the primary stresses on individual plants arise from their companion plants rather than from other factors in the environment. Thus typically, stresses induced by plant competition for water, nutrients, and light tend to predominate over those imposed by site conditions such as substrate compaction and exposure. At that stage management to promote transplant regeneration and growth usually starts to be replaced by management to control and manipulate growth involving pruning, thinning and so on.

Once mass plantings are established, their biological requirements for the original regime of maintenance inputs decreases. It then becomes necessary to decide which husbandry inputs are required both for the biological health of the plantings and for the fulfilment of other objectives.

For example, prestigious low ground cover plantings can biologically perform perfectly well in the presence of low numbers of emergent 'weeds'. The aesthetic function of the planting demands, however, that these be removed because they spoil the appearance. Nearly perfect weed control is therefore required in such situations. However, in 'out of sight, out of mind' locations, an informal mass planting of, say, native shrubs and trees could tolerate, in landscape terms, a fairly high population of weeds without impairing either its biological or its aesthetic performance; the requirements of the latter being fairly undemanding in such locations. This is not to say that weed control at the base of the plants can be relaxed in the establishment phase.

Another example is provided by an adventure play area surrounded by informal screen planting, which may be required to act both as a physical barrier to people and as a home for wildlife. In such a situation it may be acceptable, and even desirable, to leave a proportion of nettles and thistles to deter human access through the developing planting, and to leave thorny debris from thinnings or pruning to act as a further deterrent. The emphasis is on people management as much as on the maintenance of the woody plants themselves. Such action may not be acceptable in situations such as screen planting around a housing estate, where physical pressures on the landscape are likely to be less severe and the standard of weed control required to be high.

Management action, therefore, depends on the functional requirements. As mentioned in chapters dealing with other landscape components, action should be geared to accomplishing the specified objectives and no more. To do this successfully, the Amenity Manager needs to be absolutely clear about the intended roles of a planting.

This clarity of purpose is not always accompanied by clarity of action as the objectives may be multi-rather than single-purpose and, in some cases, conflicting. For example, rapidly growing plants, intended to provide quick impact, screening in a community, may be incompatible with slower growing species, intended to serve as the climax or long-term components. In such a case the short-term role of the planting as a rapid screen is, therefore, at variance with its longer-term function. Only with sensitive management can both objectives be fulfilled.

The same applies in the case of amenity mass plantings which are intended to become cost-effective features. Management action such as severe early non-commercial thinning may be required. This can be relatively quick and easy compared with later thinning, when the planting is denser and plants are larger. Yet it may be incompatible both with the biological needs of the planting for early mutual shelter and with its aesthetic function, as well as with its social roles as a screen and barrier. A compromise between the different requirements of a planting may therefore be necessary.

The sections which follow describe the main management operations involved in the care of tree and shrub communities. A distinction is made between the mature and senile phases on the one hand and the reestablishment phase on the other. Finally special attention is devoted to species and stock selection, to weed control, and to the roles of growth regulators.

12.2
The main management operations

The following is a list of the main management operations, some or all of which may be required in maintaining woody plantings, so as to fulfil their intended functions, during the period after their establishment:

- Weed control
- Growth regulation
- Fertilizer application
- Mulching

- Irrigation
- Pruning, clearing, brashing
- Thinning, coppicing, laying, layering, pollarding
- Under-or inter-planting

The extent to which these various operations need to be undertaken depends primarily upon the functions which the particular amenity tree and shrub plantings under consideration are required to fulfil. The appropriateness of both the planting design and the species selection in relation to the site constraints is another important factor. These operations are reviewed individually in the paragraphs which follow, with regard to both the specific functions and the operations mentioned earlier in the chapter.

AESTHETIC RELATED OPERATIONS

Most formal, intensive plantings, particularly those associated with the built environment, are intended to have a strong aesthetic function. Usually high levels of maintenance are required involving regular, though not necessarily expensive, maintenance inputs.

For such plantings, weed control operations are likely to be amongst the most important. Ideally there should be no weed cover. Certainly it should never be more than say 2 per cent, and then only for short periods of time. The methods used should be geared to prevent unsightliness, thereby preventing weeds at source. They entail the use of appropriate residual herbicides. This is preferable to the chemical treatment of emerged weeds which can look ugly. Contact systemic herbicides may also be required to control persistent perennials, such as bindweed and creeping thistle.

Periodic irrigation is likely to be required throughout the lives of woody plantings, grown in containers or beds isolated from the surrounding soil systems. It will also be required in dry locations, such as foundation plantings at the foot of walls on many other sites during very dry periods. However, if plants have been appropriately selected, irrigation is more likely to be needed for aesthetic than for biological reasons. Many common landscape plants are physiologically tolerant of moisture stress, *Cotoneaster*, *Pyracantha* and *Berberis spp.*, for example. They are able to recover readily from temporary checks caused by drought but they may look relatively unattractive during such periods of drought-induced dormancy. Irrigation may therefore be thought necessary, as it is in the case of good quality 'look-upon' turf, to keep plants green, turgid and actively growing.

PRIVACY AND COMFORT-RELATED OPERATIONS

Plantings which provide screening and enclosure are becoming increasingly important in modern landscapes. Many of them are of a semi-formal or informal nature. Thus, once the establishment phase is passed, the levels of weed control can be relaxed, since the presence of weeds, particularly in out-of-the-way locations, is tolerable.

Once the plants have been established, fertilizing, mulching and irrigation are unlikely to be necessary. Chipped or flailed prunings can be recycled as a mulch; fallen leaves are best left in situ as a natural mulch.

Pruning to accommodate passers-by may be required. In addition trimming, coppicing, laying and layering may be desirable in order to thicken the screen.

PHYSICAL BARRIER-RELATED OPERATIONS

Since many of the plantings are likely to be located in semi-natural or natural areas, the levels of management can be relaxed compared with those appropriate for highly manicured, formal landscapes.

Pruning and Under- or Inter-Planting techniques may be required to maintain or improve the barriers. Rural techniques, such as flailing or laying, may be appropriate and cost-effective.

Growth regulation by use of chemical retardants may also be an extremely effective way of ensuring that a woody barrier does not grow beyond bounds.

CONSERVATION-RELATED OPERATIONS

Most woody plantings except those in very formal, urban locations, are likely to have some wildlife function, and many purpose-built and managed landscapes are orientated very strongly towards the interests of nature conservation (Moffatt, undated). It is, therefore, likely that Amenity Managers will be required increasingly to consider wildlife when deciding on management and maintenance techniques for their sites.

Whilst the use of herbicides, particularly those which are persistent in the ecosystem, may not be compatible with the requirements of conservation, chemical weed control is likely to be essential to ensure the success of a planting scheme during the establishment phase. In very sensitive locations, such as either nature reserves or where children or volunteers are the main labour force in use, weed control will have to be undertaken by either manual or mechanical means.

Chemicals such as glyphosate and paraquat, which are extremely short-lived, especially when applied as spot or selective treatments, are likely to be most appropriate in areas managed for wild life. Applicators allowing precise placement of the herbicide, such as the hand-held rope or inch type, or the herbicide glove may be useful on a small scale. These are discussed more fully later.

Since many of these natural and semi-natural plantings are remote or isolated, low-volume applications such as the CDA or granule applicators may be appropriate to lessen the need for transporting bulky liquids over a distance. However, it has to be noted that such techniques tend to be relatively expensive compared with high volume methods.

Landscape Designers and Amenity Managers may wish to re-introduce a ground flora layer into established woody plantings, either deliberately through introduction of propagules or by creating conditions conducive to colonization. Chemical residues in the soil may militate against this. However, this is a subject on which there is relatively little applied knowledge. Consequently research would be welcomed.

Management for particular wildlife species usually requires a fairly detailed understanding of their ecology. However, the operations of thinning, coppicing, clearing, underplanting and layering are highly relevant in managing naturalistic tree and shrub areas, where the general aim is to increase ecological richness. The tasks involved include:

- The artificial creation of rides, clearings, glades and gaps;
- The regeneration of new plants through coppicing, planting and seeding.

The maintenance and perpetuation of a varied woody planting structure can be achieved through continued use of such operations. The resultant dynamic, uneven aged and structured woodlands provide a wide range of niches for wildlife. Such woodlands are also enjoyable places where adults and children alike can play, learn and enjoy their leisure.

Although the management of woody vegetation for timber production is well understood, the same is not yet true where the plantings are primarily intended to fulfil amenity and conservation objectives. The effects, for example, of species grouping and early spacings and thinning on later vegetation structure are still largely a matter of intelligent guesswork (Pryce, 1984). Much work remains to be done before detailed guidelines will be available to help managers interested in achieving certain effects under particular site conditions. For example, if it is desired to achieve a natural effect there are many planting options to take into account. Ideally species should be selected that are adapted to local conditions of drainage, fertility and pH rather than adapting the site to suit the plants. Ideally, indigenous local species should be chosen at all times. Seed grown stock should be used rather than vegetatively propagated clones.

Small feathered stock should be selected so that it grows to produce a natural form. Pruning to give clear stems, whether performed in the nursery or on site, is undesirable. If stock is planted close to give a rapid cover, thinning may be necessary so that mutual shading does not result in a similar clear stem habit.

Selective thinning, coppicing and delayed planting can be desirable to give a wide diversity of age and structure. Overly invasive non-native species such as sycamore should be gradually eliminated except from situations where it is particularly well adapted to site conditions, as in exposed northern coastlines. Selective felling will minimize disturbance and is sometimes preferable to clear felling. However, this can present considerable logistic difficulties and may reduce the financial viability of the woodland.

As well as its potential importance for timber production, rotational coppicing of appropriate species can be very beneficial to wildlife and ground flora. The shelter and shade of the growing coppice ensure that the site remains colonized by woodland herb species. By allowing more light and rainfall to reach the forest floor rotational felling greatly encourages the productivity of these plants.

The produce of pollarding typically has different uses from coppicing but in management terms the technique is in some ways similar. The major difference is the retention of a clear stem to keep new shoots out of the way of grazing animals. It can be particularly valuable for wildlife because the trunk acts as an undisturbed habitat for lichens, beetles, etc.

COMMERCIALLY-RELATED OPERATIONS

The distinctions between commercial and non-commercial woodlands, and between rural and urban woody landscape elements and techniques, are becoming increasingly blurred. Even where the primary function of a woodland is commercial, it is increasingly likely that the requirements of recreation and conservation need to be considered in management plans. At the other end of the spectrum there is growing interest in obtaining economic products and revenue from primarily amenity features.

The ability to obtain revenue from previously derelict or unmanaged woodland has helped to save many such features from neglect or destruction, particularly in rural areas.

Management for purely commercial timber production is a well documented subject and will not be dealt with here. Largely through the influence of the Arboricultural Advisory and Information Service of the Forestry Commission, it has been demonstrated that certain forestry concepts and techniques are appropriate to amenity plantings.

It appears that there may be a genuine commercial future for firewood, both as a primary economic product and as a by-product of woodland management. Initially this was largely associated with an increase in wood-burning stove ownership following the plague of Dutch Elm Disease. This is an important development in the survival of small woodlands and has a number of implications (Crowther and Patch, 1980). In appropriate circumstances it may in future be financially viable to:

- Thin a planting when, although silviculturally desirable, it was hitherto commercially unjustifiable.
- Manage woodlands by coppicing, with the sale of coppice products more than defraying the costs of coppicing. The old coppice-with-standards system may once again become common, resulting in pulpwood, fuelwood and timber being produced from the same area of woodland.

The benefits of such operations are well known to those interested in the conservation of woodland for visual, historic, wildlife and associated reasons.

If commercial aims are feasible and fit in with other management objectives, then post-establishment operations may entail:

- Pruning: it has been suggested that trees in parks and amenity open spaces could well be managed for timber on a rotational basis. 'Free-grown' trees in such situations would usually need regular pruning to maintain clean stems and knot-free timber.
- Thinning: This is required to produce timber quality trees. It is a very different operation from that required to produce ecologically rich and varied woodland. Thinning usually results in young woodlands which are more uniform and of less recreational value than those intended to be naturalistic. Nevertheless, the possibility of producing timber as part of the package of woodland benefits is one that merits consideration, particularly if such factors as access and local markets are favourable. If thinnings can be sold, for firewood or other purposes, or used 'in-house', this may be further justification for managing amenity plantings with an eye for timber production. Where thinning is performed solely for aesthetic or biological reasons there may be no market for the produce. Thus the disposal of thinnings may in fact represent an additional cost. Many authorities have invested in portable chipping machines which chop up the thinnings into a form that can either be left on site as a mulch or used elsewhere, in some cases as central heating fuel.

HE MUST HAVE BEEN THE BLOKE WHO MISSED PRUNING CLASSES.

**12.3
The mature and senile
phase**

The problems presented by mature and senile trees and shrub communities are usually more demanding in urban areas than in rural. In rural areas the plantings are often managed, even if casually, to exploit timber or wood products. Trees in particular are seldom allowed to become over-mature and if they have they more often become an asset to wildlife rather than a threat to the public.

MAIN ISSUES AND OPERATIONS

Occasionally woodlands contain areas of coppice that were abandoned over 50 years before and have become overmature. These large multi-stemmed plants may be unstable and will usually produce such deep shade that they inhibit the growth of the ground flora. They can either be raised to high forest by selecting out the strongest trunk and removing the rest or a new coppice cycle can be instated by felling the trees in blocks. A rota-tional system is desirable to promote age and structural diversity in the woodland and to allow wildlife to migrate from undisturbed areas.

If wildlife conservation is regarded as one of the land use objectives, structural diversity is increased by allowing a certain percentage of dead wood to be retained thereby extending the range of habitats available. It is also desirable that a few trees should be left unfelled and allowed to grow very large. These provide a valuable habitat for certain com-ponents of the woodland ecosystem, notably epiphytes.

Natural regeneration of the woodlands from seed is also easier if there is a diversity of structure, in particular if large mature trees are surrounded by open glades which new plants can colonize.

Away from roadsides it is also often the case that if a rural tree and shrub community does become overmature there is usually little risk to the public. Consequently there is less incentive to worry about the safety of ageing specimens. Many elms that died over the last decade have been left to stand, being felled for firewood as and when required.

Finally, the extensive nature of rural woodlands usually means that there is little concern over the fate of individual specimens of groups and few attempts will be made to extend their lifespan by treating problems.

In towns and cities there is an overwhelming need to consider the safety aspects of mature trees and it is also likely that the contribution they make to the environment will be regarded as so important that attempts will be made to conserve them.

It is worth noting that urban environments can impose constraints on tree and shrub growth that make them essentially 'overmature' for their chosen roles at a growth stage which in other circumstances would be regarded as 'young' or 'middle age'. This is particularly so if they have been poorly chosen for the site, have grown too large, begun to over-hang roads, damaged pavements and so on (Aldhous, 1979).

Given these extra problems it is therefore particularly disappointing that many urban woodlands are often left largely unmanaged, presumably because of financial constraints, until they reach a crisis stage that cannot be ignored any longer.

TREE INVENTORIES, SURVEYS AND INSPECTIONS

Management should, therefore, be based on a thorough inventory of all the individual trees under the care of a manager. This is particularly important in urban areas with large numbers of street trees. At present very few local authorities, for example, know the numbers, ages and conditions of the trees for which they are responsible. Without such information planned programmes of tree inspection, felling and replacement are not really possible.

Effective management of woody plantings, particularly trees, during the post-establishment phase is dependent upon accurate data. This applies especially during the period of senility. Indeed during any phase it is not really possible to manage trees rationally unless the 'nature of the resource' is known.

Amenity Managers should aim to prepare a proper 'data base' for tree management by:

- Carrying out a thorough tree inventory. A suggested check-list of information which should be sought in makng the inventories is given in Table 12.1; the data, collected from the field, include comments about the known history of the tree, the application of Tree Preservation Orders or local conservation restraints, and details of complaints from the public;
- Preferably putting the information on computer. Meaningful and representative costs of the equipment needed to computerize tree inventories cannot be provided here because hardware costs typically halve every three years and increasing power is constantly becoming available at a pace which outstrips progress in any other grounds management equipment.

The rapid growth in use of microcomputers in recent years is also likely to have implications for the costs and quality of associated tree inventory and management software. Feature articles which regularly appear in magazines, such as *Horticulture Week*, are likely to be the best source of information.

Despite the resistance and the worry that the installation of computer equipment can sometimes provoke, this is unlikely to be the greatest difficulty facing most authorities. The collection and compilation of the survey data represent the most significant problem for a busy workforce. Typically they involve a commitment over and above the existing work tasks (Buckley, 1983).

There are several points to bear in mind that will help to limit the work that is required to compile the information, namely:

Table 12.1   The management of woody plants: inventory checklist

Item
Precise location of tree
Species and variety of tree
Size of tree; height (m), crown spread (m), diameter at breast height (cm)
Presence of services
General condition of tree
Condition of stakes, ties, etc.
Work required to remove any hazard, nuisance or danger
Work desirable for cosmetic reasons
Frequency of future maintenance
Useful life expectancy of each tree
Number and location of planting positions not occupied
Number and location of trees which cannot be replaced
Ideal species and rotation for the next generation
Rating for aesthetic value

Source: Based on Lever (1982).

[1] Some local authorities, for example Bath City Council and the owners of private estates, have already taken the lead in rationalizing their tree management in this way.
Once a basic inventory has been made, a schedule of further inspections can be based on the information acquired. For example, trees which have been identified as potentially hazardous, because they are over-mature, diseased and so on, need to be checked more frequently than young and sound trees.

- Data such as tree height should be collected by categorizing the tree into one of several broad ranges rather than by attempting to measure too precisely;
- Data should not be collected, which will be of no real value to the management operation or which cannot be realistically acted upon within the resources of the department;
- Data should not be over-categorized when it could be summarized by just one heading, such as ratings for urgent work needed and explanatory comments.

Computerizing tree data can make it extremely simple to produce very valuable summaries of the requirement for work.

All trees prone to a particular disease, such as Dutch Elm disease, can be listed and a proper sanitation plan devised. If there are losses, an appropriate assessment of the damage can be determined and a replacement plan determined.

Yearly maintenance operations, such as the check on tree ties, or an inspection of senile trees, can be planned on a routine basis (Bridgeman, 1983).

A tree inventory is even more important in situations, such as Arboreta or plant collections, where individual specimens can have a historical and eductional importance that far exceeds their environmental impact.

Where collection of the data is beyond the resources or expertise of the managing authorities, private consultants can often provide a complete service from surveying to installation of the records system.

- In the case of potentially dangerous trees, a sensible frequency for inspections by local authorities and other bodies is likely to be bi-annual (once every six months);
- Local Authorities usually have a greater obligation to inspect trees capable of falling on public highways. DOE circulars specify these obligations;
- Once every 5 years is a minimum frequency for other trees which were healthy at the last inspection;
- Casual, visual inspections by experienced staff going about their daily business may also help to bring in additional information.

INSPECTIONS AND COSTS

Inspections may be made by an experienced arboriculturist on the ground using binoculars or by the aboriculturist working with an experienced arborist, who climbs the trees to inspect them. The time taken to inspect trees varies tremendously with size and condition. A large beech for example, could take two days to inspect; a young ash less than an hour. However, it is reasonable to assume that a row of 100 street trees can take 2 men 3 days to inspect, i.e. approximately 2.5 man hours per tree if the trees are to be climbed. Ground inspections can be achieved at much higher rates (up to 20/hour) as long as it is accepted that there may be physical faults and decay that cannot be identified.

Both ease of access to trees and their condition affect inventory costs. For example, working in streets where operators and their equipment must be coned off from traffic may take longer, by say 15–20 per cent.

FURTHER ACTION: RESOURCE REQUIREMENTS

The need to carry out further work on a tree may be revealed by a tree inspection or by events on site, such as storm damage. Programmed work, involving crown lifting or pollarding operations, for example, may also be needed.

Inevitably the question of cost arises. Costs depend on the nature of the tree itself, size, shape, health, etc., as well as on surrounding constraints such as access, proximity to buildings, frequency of traffic on adjacent roads and the presence of services above and below ground. In wet weather work will be delayed, because it can be unsafe to climb the tree.

To take a example, felling and removing a large tree from a back garden with only a side path for access could cost up to six times that of felling the same tree in the open grounds of a park. Felling deciduous trees in the winter is not always practical and adjustments to the time anticipated must take account of the greater danger as well as the greater volume and weight of material involved.

Costs, however, should not be allowed to influence the decision of whether or not to undertake work where public safety is at risk.

Table 12.2 The management of amenity trees: inspections post-establishment operations, and estimated resource requirements

Source	Operation	Resource input	Unit
TH	Inspections, surveys	6 days[1]	100 no
CRC[2]	Crown lifting	0.4 day	1 tree
CRC[2]	Crown thinning	1 day	1 tree
		SMV	
Sh	Feather trees over 12″ diam	5.00	1 no
Sa	Fell tree (6″ diam c 30′) trim off branches and dispose	78.00	tree
Sa	Cut up & dispose of tree bough (10″–12″ diam) J broken off	113.00	bough
D	Pollard plane trees (5 yrs growth)	245.00	tree
Sa	Tree lopping: include move ladder and dispose		
	up to 2″ diam	1.29	bough
	2″–4″ diam	2.16	bough
	above 4″ diam	3.90	bough
D	Cut branches off standing tree with handsaw, cut up and load to trailer: 0″–3″	3.40	bough
	3″–7″	7.90	bough
	7″–12″	20.50	bough
Sa	Grub out roots of tree (6″ diam × 30′) and dispose	68.50	tree
Sh	Paint wound with compound	0.80–2.30	tree
TH	Large stump removal (e.g. 0.6–1.0m diam elm), using a large chipper	15.00[3]	stump

Note: [1] This input involved 1 officer, 1 arborist
[2] These are average estimates for trees of up to 3m girth with good access. The task requires 2 operators.
[3] This represented a cost of c.£30 per stump (1983)

See Table 2.2 on p. 37 for details of sources.

Tables 12.2 and 12.3 provide indications of the physical and financial resources associated with the range of operations, which both may be and will need to be undertaken during the post-establishment stage. These guidelines have particular relevance for Amenity Managers involved in the care of trees which are approaching senility and finally die.

The majority of tree work will usually be performed by specialist operators, often on a contract basis. It should be recognized that even they cannot always predict accurately how long a given project will take.

Advice should be taken on the necessary frequency of inspection and treatment.

It should be possible in urban situations to dispense with the cost of operations such as pollarding, bracing and crown thinning by proper planning and maintenance early in the life of a tree. The following guidelines should be observed:

- Choose trees which are the right size for their location;
- Avoid the choice of tree species which will need pollarding;
- Prune the crowns of trees which have narrow forks while they are young. If this is done at planting time when the tree is laid on the ground, it is likely to take no more than between 5 and 10 minutes. This can save hours of subsequent work and expense associated with the need to check and brace trees with weak forks.

Unfortunately the existing legacy of large trees still represents a management problem that good intentions cannot solve (Clouston and Stansfield, 1981). It is also a fact of life that trees are often planted by well meaning but unqualified individuals and groups who are unaware of the future implications of their choices.

Other problems can of course occur at any time. For example, disease or snow can damage limbs and make a tree unsafe, requiring immediate treatment. Pruning will not necessarily prolong the life of a tree, but it can easily extend its safe life.

Pollarding, in particular, should be avoided wherever possible. The resulting branch re-growth is usually physically unstable and the maintenance commitment to this task becomes necessarily permanent.

Often a less drastic and less damaging treatment for trees that have grown too large is to lift or thin the crown. These options are said to improve the safety and appearance of the tree, reduce weight and lessen wind resistance, and admit more light and air to the ground (Bridgeman, 1976).

Before dramatic operations are performed on trees the Amenity Manager must usually ensure that no legal protections are involved, notably Tree Preservation Orders. However, if a tree is regarded as unsafe there is justification for commencing remedial work, or even felling, immediately.

FELLING AND REPLACING AVENUES

Avenues rely for their effect on a designed unity of spacing and tree age. Heated debates often rage over the best system to adopt to replace over-mature and senile avenues. Usually, replacement of individual specimens as they die is likely to produce a result that completely fails to meet the design objectives. If space permits a new avenue may be established outside or parallel to an existing one. Alternatively complete felling and re-planting, or felling in a few large sections, will probably represent the most appropriate options (Wright, 1982).

WOUND AND CAVITY TREATMENTS

The latest opinion from arboricultural experts is that special treatment of wounds or cavities in trees is unnecessary or even harmful (Clifford and

Table 12.3   The management of woody plants: tree felling and stump removal

---

Tree felling and stump removal
Prices are exclusive of any credit for the sale of the resulting timber

Tree felling up to 1.50 m girth
(Note: Trees of similar girth can differ considerably in height or spread depending on the species: the prices below are for average shape trees)

Cutting down tree to ground level and burning on site

	Relative Price Index*
Girth up to 600 mm:	10
extra for grubbing up roots	8.5
extra for carting tree and roots to tip from site not exceeding 13 km	13.7
Girth 600–900 mm:	14.0
extra for grubbing up roots	13.5
extra for carting tree and roots to tip from site not exceeding 13 km	24.0
Girth 900 mm-1.20 m:	16.1
Extra for grubbing up roots	14.9
extra for carting tree and roots to tip from site not exceeding 13 km	28.8
Girth 1.20–1.50 m	23.2
extra for grubbing up roots	22.9
extra for carting tree and roots to tip from site not exceeding 13 km	28.7

Tree felling over 1.50 m girth

Cutting down tree to ground level, stacking saleable timber and burning remainder on site (no credit allowed for saleable timber)

Girth 1.50–1.80	29.6
extra for grubbing up roots	28.2
extra for carting unsaleable timber and roots to tip from site not exceeding 13 km	34.7
Girth 1.80–2.10	44.9
extra for grubbing up roots	48.2
extra for carting unsaleable timber and roots to tip from site not exceeding 13 km	36.3
Girth 2.10–2.40 m	84.7
extra for grubbing up roots	80.6

Table 12.3 (cont'd)

extra for carting unsaleable timber and roots to tip from site not exceeding 13 km	51.5
Girth 2.40–2.70	110.2
extra for grubbing up roots	107.2
extra for carting unsaleable timber and roots to tip from site not exceeding 13 km	59.0
Girth 2.70–3.00 m	133.4
extra for grubbing up roots	139.9
extra for carting unsaleable timber and roots to tip from site not exceeding 13 km	69.6

* This is based upon taking a girth of up to 600 mm as a value of 10. The actual price in 1983 was £12.00.

Note: Above this size trees become so large that average pricing could be misleading; each one needs special individual pricing.

Gendle, 1987), although the placement of pruning cuts is critical to good healing (Lonsdale, 1983).

Recent research into the use of beneficient fungi inroculants looks promising as a means of reducing the likelihood of infection and of speedy wound healing (Lonsdale, 1987). A summary of the latest research in this very active field can be obtained from the Arboricultural Advisory Service of the Forestry Commission.

In some cases it may be worthwhile to paint new pruning wounds with a dark paint, in order to make them less conspicuous, either for aesthetic reasons or to avoid the attention of vandals. Apart from this, however, it seems that the most cost-effective treatment is to allow nature to follow its own course.

STUMP REMOVAL

Small stumps can be dug out by hand or pulled out using a winch and tractor. Large roots should first be severed.

Stumps are often left in the ground following treatment by stump killer. Such chemicals are best applied in the growing season. Addition of a nitrogenous salt, for example ammonium sulphamate, can also speed up the natural breakdown. Sometimes the stump can be partly burnt out. In rural areas explosives have sometimes been used.

The most cost-effective way to remove larger stumps is by chipping. The larger the chipping machine that can be used, and the more stumps that are chipped at one time, the cheaper, usually, will be the job. Smaller, slower machines may take up to 5 times as long (Wilson, 1981).

FERTILIZING MATURE TREES

Unless timber production is a major objective there will usually be no need to fertilize mature trees to promote growth. The only exception is when the health of the tree is declining because of some deficiency which threatens to shorten its lifespan (Smith, 1978).

Before commencing any such fertilizing operation it is sensible to consult specialist consultant advice to ensure that the cause of poor health is not in fact a disease or physical problem (Webster, 1978).

Soil fertilizer placement in many urban situations will require specialist powered soil augers or trunk injection systems.

An alternative approach is to add fertilizer to the soil surface or a mulch, but there should be no surface rooting vegetation present, particularly grass, or very little of the application will reach the tree roots. Application rates are about 1–1.5 kg per 30 mm of girth.

Forking around the trunk to incorporate the fertilizer can do more harm than good to an ailing tree and should be avoided.

Many alternative options exist, such as injected pellets that release nutrients slowly into the sap, liquid feeds similarly injected under pressure or foliar sprays.

Because the task is so infrequently necessary, and only rarely carried out, work values are not available. In many cases specialist equipment will be needed and specialist operators will be contracted to perform the work.

PEST AND DISEASE CONTROL ON MATURE TREES

For the most part suspected disease or pest attack on mature trees cannot be forecast in advance. The appropriate response may have to be determined as and when such a problem becomes apparent.

The very nature of mature trees can mean that any form of disease treatment is very difficult to implement. Spraying can require large and expensive operations. Trunk injection or soil drenching may be cheaper and more successful.

The diverse nature of amenity plantings means that epidemics are much rarer than in commercial monoculture plantations. Diseases that produce a decrease in yield rather than killing or badly disfiguring the plants are not usually considered important. If problems do arise and if local expertise cannot diagnose them, specialist advice is available from the Pathology Department of the Forestry Commission. However, there are certain tree diseases which are sufficiently common to warrant further comment. It must be emphasized that the following is not intended as an exhaustive list.

Tar spot is a common leaf disfiguring disease of sycamore in areas relatively free from air pollution. It is not serious and does not require treatment.

Aphids can be a problem in the case of particular tree species. It is often quoted that native trees and shrubs support many times the number of insect species than those carried by introductions such as sycamore. However, the few insects that do feed on these trees may be very successful and the sheer biomass of aphids in particular can become a major nuisance in urban areas. Sycamore and lime are the worst culprits and care should be taken with the siting of these species. Aphid-resistant limes species can be chosen.

Dutch Elm disease needs no introduction. Until recently the only hope of defence was through rigid sanitation control, but for a variety of reasons this has been unsuccessful in the vast majority of areas. Alone in the Southern Counties, Sussex shows what could perhaps have been achieved with greater diligence. Recently, however, there have been some research advances that offer hope of a cure for infected trees (Brasier and Webber, 1987; Grieg, 1984, 1986). Enquiries should be directed to the Arboricultural Advisory Service.

Fireblight is a severe bacterial disease of many members of the Rosaceae. *Crateagus*, *Pyracantha*, *Sorbus* and some cotoneasters are very susceptible. Work on selecting resistant types in underway, but there is no chemical treatment available. Careful sanitation is essential and diseased plants must be felled and burnt (Braham and Moffatt, 1987).

Canker is another bacterial pathogen that tends to attack the Rosaceae family, particularly *Malus* and *Prunus*. Infected plants should have the diseased portions cut out, but they are rarely noticed until the infestation is severe and death of the tree is possible.

Phytophthera is a soil-borne fungal disease that can attack and kill young and mature trees of a wide range of species. Once it is known to be present, soil sterilization or the replanting of resistant plants will be necessary.

Honey fungus is a soil-borne pathogen that spreads by long black underground runners from infected plants or stumps to nearby specimens. It is particularly common on land that has been cleared from woodland. Soil sterilization may be necessary if the planting cannot be restricted to resistant species – a guide to susceptibility can be found in Rishbeth (1987) and Grieg and Stroutts (1983). Careful sanitation of both infected stumps and sources of re-infection is important. Armillatox or other soil fungicides are sometimes effective. Particularly important trees can be protected by sinking a physical barrier in the soil around them which prevents the spread of the fungus.

Anthracnoses are a group of fungal diseases that attack many tree species. Some species of willow are very susceptible to an anthracnose attack including the common weeping willow. Resistant alternatives are available.

Plane tree anthracnose can be a major problem in cities during certain climatic conditions. The effects can range from browning and curling of leaves to defoliation, branch dieback or death. There is some debate about the scale of the problem, because some authorities believe that salt damage is often mistaken for anthracnose, but the disease can be devastating even away from the roadsides. Resistant clones have been identified and pressure should be placed on suppliers to make these available.

Larvae and caterpillar attacks can be so severe that complete defoliation of trees and shrubs results. With the exception of certain areas of the country and certain plant species, the attacks can be very hard to forecast or even to spot until they are far advanced. Unless the plant is already weak the defoliation will not prove fatal, but can be disturbing to the public. Some species of caterpillar can produce severe skin reactions if touched.

Animal pests may present difficulties. In various situations bullfinches, deer and squirrels can all be major pests. Control by trapping or shooting is not pleasant or popular. Repellants or forms of tree protection should be adopted where possible.

UTILIZATION OF TIMBER AND OTHER WOOD PRODUCTS

In theory it should be possible to sell timber from amenity trees which have been felled for non-commercial reasons. The land used for roadside tree planting in the new town of Milton Keynes, for example, could ultimately produce timber worth more than £100,000 a year, at a conservative estimate. However, unless sales are to unusual markets, such as local craft groups, it is likely that the form of many amenity trees will reduce their timber value. A plant with many branches that start from low on the trunk may be aesthetically desirable. Conversely a tree pruned to provide the maximum clear stem of timber can look very out of place. A notable exception is Scots Pine which often takes that form in a landscape setting, even when it is growing in isolation from other trees.

It should also be feasible to grow 'joint use' – amenity and timber – specimen trees in parks. Some species such as cherry and ash may be particularly suitable for this purpose.

In practice it is not always possible to sell good timber or even to give it away. If access is difficult or if there is only a small quantity of timber to take, a merchant may not be willing to buy it. Nevertheless, with the increased popularity of wood burning stoves it is possible to sell fuel wood in many areas. Organizations with waste timber products – thinnings, lop and top, and so on – may find it worthwhile trying to sell them either directly or to other outlets such as contractors and dealers.

At least one local authority saves good pieces of timber for use in the wood-working classes of local schools and colleges.

It is worth noting that in the United States some public authorities run recycling centres in which leaf mould, wood chips, fire wood, bean poles and other park products are either sold or given to local people. As legislation and finance make it more difficult and expensive to dispose of open space wastes in Britain, local authorities may also find the effort involved in promoting their re-use worthwhile.

It is important to recognize that for many reasons it is usually impossible to justify the presence of a tree in financial terms alone. Financial returns are a valuable way of recouping some or all of the planting, thinning and felling costs, but the quest for a profit should not interfere with the management of the tree to perform its primary objectives.

LEAF CLEARANCE

Adult trees shed large quantities of leaves, the clearance of which is a somewhat contentious issue. If leaves need to be removed it means that the presence of trees is, indirectly, creating work and therefore costing money. The Parks staff of some local authorities spend weeks in the autumn solely devoted to leaf clearance (Broadbent, 1985).

In some circumstances it is undoubtedly necessary to remove leaves. For example, heavy leaf fall on grass kills the foliage beneath. Leaves on roads and footways block drains, can make surfaces unsafe and rot down to produce unwanted organic matter, as they do in ponds. However, leaves should not be removed without a definite and rational objective in mind. A light scattering of leaves on medium to long grass is usually not harmful. Leaf fall on soil is positively beneficial, since it protects the surface and acts as a long-lasting source of organic matter. Therefore, unless leaves on shrub or flower beds are a definite nuisance, for example, making bedding-out difficult, or act as a source of blown leaves on paths, they are best left to lie where they fall.

Several methods and different types of machinery are available to assist clearance: leaves can be swept or raked by hand, swept, vacuumed or blown into heaps by machinery. Blowing leaves into windrows or piles for collection can be a cost-effective method for large areas.

Vacuum machinery ranges in size from the small 'billy goat' type to large articulated lorries designed for clearing roads. For small areas collection with a rake is as 'cost-effective' as any method.

The greatest cost can be transport and dumping of the leaves. A series of composting areas at short intervals often proves valuable.

Table 12.4 provides some work values for clearing up leaves using a variety of methods. In the case of hard surfaces (see chapter 23) Table 23.4 provides resource guidelines for other sweeping methods.

LEAF DISPOSAL

Associated with clearance is the problem of leaf disposal. Whilst several methods exist, the key management task inevitably involves identifying the method which is most cost-effective.

For legal and husbandry reasons the manager may be unable or unwilling to burn leaves. Disposal by tipping is expensive. There is at least some incentive to recycle leaves by converting them to leaf mould, which can then be used as a mulch or soil ameliorant. If possible the most cost effective solution is to place the leaves into nearby shrub beds

Table 12.4   The management of amenity landscapes requiring leaf clearance: estimated resource requirements

Source	Operation	SMV	Unit
Sh	Sweep leaves with Allen leaf sweeper	4.30	100 m^2
H	Sweep up leaves using Allen Pedestrian propelled sweeper heavy coverage	3.20	machine load
Sa	Rake up leaves, load to barrow, burn to dispose	59.20	100 m^2
D	Rake leaves from shrubbery and load to barrow	90.00	100 m^2
D	Rake leaves from flower bed and load to barrow	210.00	100 m^2
Sa	Rake up leaves and load to trailer	133.64	1.5 m^3 trailer load
H	Rake up leaves, load to barrow and dispose	15.70	Barrow
H	Rake up leaves, load to Geest Truck and dispose	48.00	Load
K	Sweep grass areas: Allen sweeper	4.68	100 m^2
Sa	Sweep grass using besom	25.94	100 m^2
D	Rake leaves from chipping pathway	10.00	100 m^2
L	Sweep leaves from chipped/gravel areas	13.14	100 m^2
D	Rake leaves from grass	10.00	100 m^2
L	Rake leaves from grass area	11.35	100 m^2

See Table 2.2 on p. 37 for details of sources.

as a mulch. They must be moist or sheltered, so that they do not blow away.

In the USA both the composting of leaves and the reuse of the leaf compost are common practices, particularly in golf clubs.

Kew Gardens in Britain accept some 7000m^3 of leaves annually from the Royal Parks, stack them and use the resulting leaf mould in the botanic gardens. Modern precedents therefore exist, and since recycling can save the expense both of disposal by other means and buying in mulching and soil conditioner materials, it may be a cost-effective option worth consideration by an Amenity Manager.

12.4
The re-establishment phase

In considering the re-establishment of an amenity tree community, there are certain key questions which need addressing. Trees age and eventually die. Should they be replaced? If so, why? Do people want them? How do they fit into the total landscape and its life cycle? What is the best way to establish them? How fast should they grow? These are some of the questions which the Amenity Manager may need to ask before taking further action.

WHY PLANT TREES AT ALL? DO PEOPLE WANT TREES?

Before planting new trees the manager needs to ask why he is planting trees at all. Trees should not be planted without specific objectives in mind, since they cannot be managed rationally unless their purpose is known. Not everyone wants trees or even likes them. Moreover trees, directly and indirectly, incur cost and need positive management, particularly at the beginnings and ends of their lives. The saying that 'if a job is worth doing it is worth doing well' is particularly apt in the case of trees. Trees cannot be put in the ground like an item of street furniture and left to their own devices. The decision to plant a tree implies a long term commitment to look after it (Insley, 1982). If this commitment cannot be fulfilled, it is normally best not to plant. Neglected trees in amenity situations can be worse than no trees at all (Gilbertson and Bradshaw, 1985).

HOW DOES PLANTING FIT INTO THE LANDSCAPE LIFE CYCLE?

Woody plants have a fairly long, but finite lifespan. Much amenity planting has occurred in bursts so that large numbers of plants are approximately even-aged. This can make management difficult, since trees are most expensive to maintain early and late in their life-spans. In particular, large numbers of even-aged trees are liable to become a very heavy maintenance burden in their declining years. Wherever possible, therefore, it should be management policy to phase new planting, in order to form a multi-aged population. This helps to distribute the work load over the years and to prevent 'peaks'. It also helps to ensure visual continuity.

HOW FAST DO WE WANT TREES TO GROW?

When attempting to programme management inputs into a planting scheme it is important to define the intended growth rates of the trees and shrubs.

In amenity plantings there are usually two immediate growth objectives. First, the plants should grow sufficiently to emerge quickly from the phase when they are vulnerable to weeds, surface drought, vandalism or other stresses. Secondly, the plants must grow to meet their design objectives such as providing shelter. Once these requirements have been achieved, further growth may be unnecessary and is often an embarrassment.

HOW DO DECISIONS AT PLANTING TIME AFFECT LONG-TERM PERFORMANCE?

Cost-effective management of trees entails thinking about them in the long term. Action taken early in the life of a tree may seriously affect

Table 12.5 Deaths associated with new tree plantings

Year	Percentage loss
76/77	36%
78/79	36%
79/80	39%
80/81	34%

Source: The Department of Transport

subsequent management requirements. For example, siting a large tree in a constricted location may cause much trouble and expense in later life when roots interfere with drains, branches obscure windows, etc.

In the long term, therefore, it must be cost-effective to take whatever care is necessary to ensure that trees are well selected, well located, well planted and well looked after until they have established. Good planning and good husbandry in the first five years may only take a few hours per tree longer than inadequate planning and care. They should result in a plant that will do its job and be relatively trouble-free for decades.

In contrast, the results of bad early management may result in hundreds of thousands of pounds worth of expense later on, damage to people or property, and cripped or ugly trees. A present-day manager should consider the Amenity Manager of tomorrow when he thinks about planting a tree.

Unfortunately, good practice in tree planting today is the exception rather than the rule. Too many trees are planted with too little thought and aftercare. A great deal of money, estimated at £50 million on trees alone in 1982 and perhaps £100 million on trees and shrubs together, is spent annually on amenity planting (Thoday, 1983). As Table 12.5 shows, official estimates put typical losses at over 30 per cent per year. In the case of dry years of difficult sites, losses may be more than double these levels; furthermore survivors are often severely checked. Why should such a waste of money, effort and materials be tolerated when it could be avoided? Bad practice creates unnecessary costs for the Amenity Manager in both the long and short term.

12.5
The key
re-establishment
operations

This section covers all the management and technical operations involved in ensuring effective establishment of trees and shrubs. There are exceptions, namely stock selection and weed control, which are considered to merit separate sections later in this chapter.

Planting and establishment performance is strongly influenced by the 'lowest common denominator' operation. All operations are critical and therefore limiting. Thus the level of success achieved will be determined by the extent to which all of the operations are properly carried out (Stoneham and Thoday, 1985; Insley, 1986).

INTRODUCTION

The temptations to take short cuts when planting trees and shrubs are sometimes very hard to ignore. However, both casual observation and research suggest that deaths regularly reach an average level of about 30 per cent, meaning not only a loss in terms of capital investment and a waste of time in site preparation, but also costly replacement and maintenance demands.

Table 12.6 shows that, at the prices current when the data was prepared, up to 6 waterings of standard trees in the first year of establishment were cheaper than the replacement of 30 per cent of failures. Whilst some trees may die anyway, despite watering, there may only be a need for one or two waterings to ensure greatly improved establishment (Cobham and Gill, 1976).

One-year replacement agreements with contractors are not necessarily adequate in ensuring establishment success. Many poorly planted trees, particularly large standards, can survive and produce small rosettes of leaves in the first season yet are internally damaged and unable to grow, requiring only a moderate drought in subsequent years to kill them off (Gilbertson, Kendle and Bradshaw, 1987). Many researchers have suggested a move towards a system of specification which requires performance to be assessed by growth rather than survival (Davison, 1983).

Another major cause of tree failure is insufficient attention to stake and tie maintenance which may not become critical until some years after planting (Patch, 1987).

Only a tree that has been on site for 3–5 years, is growing well, is self-supporting and has had the stake removed, can be regarded as an establishment success.

SELECTING PLANTS

Species should be chosen which suit objectives of planting site conditions. Stock should be used which is as young as other constraints allow and which is vigorous. Other techniques, such as the insertion of unrooted cuttings or direct seeding should be considered, if they are likely to succeed and meet the objectives; they may be cheaper. The most important management factors which need to be considered when choosing plants are discussed more fully later.

PREPARING THE SITE

A planted tree has modest needs: light, carbon dioxide, water and air at the roots and about a dozen mineral nutrients.

Table 12.6 Calculations to determine the cost of watering trees during the re-establishment phase of a landscape scheme, and the break-even point for bowser purchase

1. Assumptions	Each standard tree would need 10 litres of water on each occasion per year, (whips 2.5 litres each).
	On average there are between one and two waterings each year which are critical for the survival of a tree. Up to possibly 10 waterings may be desirable in the interests of plant growth.
	It takes about 1 minute per tree to discharge 10 litres from a bowser. Allowing for on-site transport and coupling to hydrants the average discharge time may well be nearer to 2 minutes per tree.
	In a 35 hour week, with two men per bowser it should be possible to water between 2,000 and 4,000 standard trees or four times those numbers of whips.
	Plant and planting costs per tree are £0.50 for whips and £6.50 for standards.
	Average losses in the first year after planting range between 10% and 40%, depending on the nature of the environment.
2. Costings	Labour, bowser depreciation, interest at 15% and maintenance at 5%, plus tractor costs per week are likely to amount to between £250 and £300.
	Cost of water is ignored.
	Thus depending on the rate of watering, the costs per tree per watering are:
	standard tree: 5.0–13.0 pence.
	whip: 1.25–3.3 pence.

3. Cost comparisons

Size of Tree	Average rate of replacement required	Cost of replacement	Cost of watering			
			Number of critical waterings required per year		Number of desirable waterings required per year	
Whips	10%	5p	2.5–*6.6*p	5–*13.2*p	7.5–*19.8*p	*12.5–33*p
	20%	10p	2.5–*6.6*p	5–*13.2*p	7.5–*19.8*p	*12.5–33*p
	40%	20p	2.5–6.6p	5–13.2p	7.5–19.8p	12.5–*33*p
Standards	10%	65p	10–26p	20–52p	30–78p	50–*130*p
	20%	130p	10–26p	20–52p	30–78p	50–*130*p
	40%	260p	10–26p	20–52p	30–78p	50–130p

The figures which are in italics indicate the stage at which watering becomes more expensive than replacement.

Source: Cobham and Gill (1976).

The list of items which it should not have is more extensive: erosion, high salt levels or toxic elements, vandalism, fire, trampling, grazing, barriers to roof penetration, severe exposure and management neglect.

Of all the qualities of the planting substrate, that which most affects the establishment and subsequent growth of woody plants is undoubtedly physical structure. The substrate must be easily penetrated by roots, should have reasonable moisture-holding properties, and should be free-draining (Binns, 1983). Cosmetic activities, such as the binding of compacted subsoils with poor quality top soil, should be avoided (Hackett, 1978). Instead existing substrates should be improved where feasible by deep digging and by incorporating soil ameliorants, such as organic matter if necessary.

If possible, compaction should be prevented from occurring at all by good construction and site discipline (Pryce, 1983).

Ideally, ground preparation should be undertaken in summer. The ground should then be left fallow, so that weeds are allowed to emerge prior to eradicating them with systemic herbicide.

In an ideal world the whole soil profile to which the plant roots will have access should be 'hospitable'. Luxurious compost-filled pots in a hostile substrate can often only provide short-term 'comfort', although the feasibility and necessity of long-term works depends on the precise nature of the substrate in question (Sheldon, 1979). There are distinct advantages to be gained from preparing the whole substrate so that it can be penetrated by the growing root system. If necessary, the transplant should be acclimatized by treating the immediate root zone with slow-release fertilizer and compost.

DELIVERING STOCK

It is essential to make absolutely sure that the transfer of stock from nursery to site keeps the plants alive and well. Roots can dry out and die in a few minutes. Real care and vigilance is needed. Although costly, it is undoubtedly cost-effective (Insley, 1979).

PLANTING DENSITY

In some tree planting schemes spacings as close as 0.8–1.0m are used (Moffatt, undated). There is consequently a need for heavy thinning as the individuals gain in size. Planting a mixture of shrubs and trees will possibly prove preferable as the shrub canopy should become shaded out as the trees grow in height. When growing large trees in exposed areas thinning cannot be delayed or ignored. Otherwise the individuals will develop a tall thin growth habit which is prone to windthrow. This risk is greater in poorly-drained soils.

PLANTING

Bare rooted stock should only be planted in the proper season: October to March. Often it is tempting to stretch the planting season. This should be resisted unless fully adequate irrigation can be guaranteed.

Planting should be completed before Christmas if possible. Whilst this may seem an early deadline, it can be justified on the grounds that the weather is typically very much worse during January and February and planting may then be delayed until March. Planting this early is not easy to organize, particularly as some trees do not drop their leaves until

November. However, trial results have shown that by the time of leafing out the new root extension of a December-planted tree can be ten times that of one planted in March (Gilbertson, Kendle and Bradshaw, 1987).

Conifers or evergreens should be planted in spring to avoid freezing winds, or provided with some form of protection.

If possible, pits should be watered before planting. The tree should be watered in immediately afterwards to remove air pockets (Baines, 1982). Containerized or root balled plants must have their soil watered before planting.

Trees should be planted to the same depth at which they were growing at the nursery.

STAKING

Details of the correct systems for staking and guying of standard trees will be found in *Spon Landscape Design Handbook* or BS3998. Although not yet in widespread use, the short staking systems detailed by Patch (1982) seem to offer some advantages.

The maintenance of tree support is important. A study of trees in Liverpool showed that twice as much damage was caused by tie strangulation and girdling of the bark, resulting from abrasion against wire guards and stakes, as by vandals (Gilbertson and Bradshaw, 1985).

Ties and stakes need checking every year. Broken ties leading to abrasion occur most often in windy weather. Tie strangulation becomes a problem if the trees are growing well.

A well grown tree should become self-supporting within three years and the stake can be removed.

FERTILIZING

The application of fertilizers is a relatively cheap 'fail-safe' practice as long as excessive dose rates are avoided and the practice is coupled with effective weed control. The use of a slow release fertilizer at planting time, followed by annual top dressing until the plants establish, is recommended (Harris, 1983). An inexpensive NPK fertilizer is usually adequate for top dressing purposes; low nitrogen, slow-release compounds stimulate less weeds, but are more expensive.

Fertilizer application is essential on poor sites, such as industrial reclamation areas, and must usually be continued for several years (Bradshaw, 1981). On such sites nitrogen is the most difficult nutrient to manage. It is very easily leached and can only be stored in the long term as organic matter. This can be added in the form of an overall treatment or in pockets prior to planting the trees. On inaccessible sites this task may involve a considerable extra labour requirement.

In some sites, for example peat bogs, there is organic matter present but it has a very high carbon content and can act as a temporary absorber

WE'D HANG HIM IF WE
HAD A TREE LEFT.

of nitrogen rather than as a contributor. Where this occurs lime and
phosphate need to be added to increase microbial activity and often
inorganic nitrogen will also be required to lower the C:N ratio (Russell,
1973).

The most cost-effective approach is to use nitrogen-fixing species such
as alder as part of the planting mix as these will upgrade the whole site
(Buckley, 1978).

Aside from nitrogen the most likely nutrient to be deficient is phosphorus. This is much less soluble. Thus an initial application of fertilizer
followed by occasional further treatments should suffice.

LIMING

Trees can tolerate a surprising range of pH levels, particularly when
transplanted, rather than having to establish themselves by seed. Liming
is therefore much less frequently practised in forestry than in agriculture.

However, in some of the more challenging soils found in amenity
situations or derelict wasteland, liming may prove valuable to control the
release of other nutrients. In design terms it can be used to encourage
a ground flora that matches the local woodland.

MULCHING

Mulching is expensive, but is often worth doing particularly on the smaller scale, intensively planted, prestigious sites (Litzow and Pellet, 1983). Mulches which are nutrient rich, for example FYM and sewage sludge, or are liable to contain weed seeds, such as some peats, should not be used unless good weed control can be guaranteed. The most cost-effective mulches have certain key characteristics:

- Chemically stable (i.e. will not rob the site of nitrogen);
- Long lasting;
- Not easily blown about;
- Nutrient-poor;
- Visually attractive;
- Fire proof;
- Provide a physical barrier to wind blown weed seed.

They also tend to keep the soil temperature higher during winter.

The site should be cleared of large perennial weeds before mulching, because these are as likely to benefit from the mulch as much as the trees and shrubs.

Some types make a very attractive finish to a planted bed which is often preferred to that of a herbicided bare soil. Coarse bark, grits, and shingle are three such materials. As well as providing a barrier to weed growth, these coarse mulches allow penetration of rain to the soil. However, capillary movement upwards is limited so that the soil water is conserved.

SHEET MULCHING

Various commercially available 'pre-made mulches' can be fitted to the base of a newly planted tree. These 'tree-spats' are usually made from bitumenized felt or similar substances.

Plastic sheeting used as a combined mulch and weed suppressant can be a cost-effective aid to plant establishment and has been used successfully in commercial horticulture since the 1960s (Parfitt *et al.*, 1980). Plants often show better growth with a plastic mulch than in bare ground. Appearances can be improved by covering with a decorative mulch, for example of shingle.

Black polythene can form part of a trouble-free establishment package, when used for mulching bare-rooted cuttings of easy-to-root species, such as poplar and willow.

CONTROLLING WATER SUPPLIES

Proper ground preparation should ensure that drainage and moisture retention are both adequate. The addition of planting composts and mulches can also help to ensure water retention. Good weed control is essential to prevent competition for water. Water capture can be improved by dishing ground around a tree (Bradshaw, 1981).

Small, vigorous stock planted into good ground conditions during the proper season can usually establish without watering. However, larger stock, such as standard trees and container plants, are likely to need irrigation, particularly if their planting is delayed until the growing season (Hebblethwaite, 1977). The same applies in the case of stock planted into harsh ground or in dry parts of the country.

Irrigation is only cost-effective, if coupled with good weed control.

New water holding polymers show some promise in ameliorating moderately severe droughts by improving water retention.

FENCING

Damage to trees by grazing and trampling can decimate years of work and capital investment on a site. Tree transplants and sheep are mutually incompatible. Consequently fencing or other protection is essential on may rural sites (Pepper *et al.*, 1985; Walshe and Westlake, 1977). Rural trees also need protection from hay burning, from poaching of the soil by animals looking for shade and from ploughing.

In urban areas fencing may be regarded as visually unacceptable. Careful design is therefore particularly important to ensure that desire lines do not cross the planting beds.

GUARDING AGAINST RABBITS

Rabbits can destroy thousands of pounds worth of stock in a very short time. Spiral plastic rabbit guards or tree shelters are an essential investment in rural areas.

At planting time most shrubs benefit from hard pruning back to between 15–30cm (Baines, 1982). Regrowth is vigorous, balanced and wind-firm. Bare rooted stock can be pruned back en-masse in bundles, quickly and easily.

SUPERVISING OPERATIONS

All critical aspects of the work, such as ground preparation, the care of stock, pre-planting, planting, weed control, should be supervised very closely and consistently. It is essential to ensure that all such operations are done properly or the whole 'package' may fail.

Success should be assessed on the basis of the extension growth made by the plants rather than by whether they are dead or alive.

TRAINING STAFF

The technical training of both contract and direct works staff should be improved. This involves making sure that they understand the reason for the critical operations and can carry them out properly on site. Every effort should be made to engender a sense of pride in the work carried out and to foster a long-term view. The results of poor workmanship, should, if appropriate, be shown and explained to them.

TRAINING CLIENTS

Clients should be informed of the advantages of good husbandry. The cost-effectiveness of such techniques as good ground preparation, the use of young stock, and the adoption of good irrigation and weed control practices should be stressed. Inadequate specifications should be altered. The need for a good husbandry approach should be explained. Financial, contractual and political pressures to carry out quick impact work should be resisted, whenever this is likely to endanger the long-term success of planting. Economies are rarely if ever cost-effective.

12.6 Choice of species, stock size and stock type

There are many factors that an Amenity Manager has to bear in mind when choosing stock. Careless plant selection can mean the failure of an entire planting scheme or worse (Biddle, 1985).

CHOICE OF SPECIES

Choosing the right species for the site is one of the most fundamental keys to success in planting schemes.

Plant species should meet the design intentions with regard to size, habit and form, leaf retention, seasons of special interest, longevity, and safety (Bridgeman, 1979). Growth rates and timber quality can be important commercially. Their ability to support wildlife can be important in ecological and rural style plantings (Bos and Mol, 1979).

A policy of using only native trees in rural areas may be superficially popular with local naturalist groups, but it is not always practical. Introduced trees include conifers valuable for softwood timber production, sycamore which is exceptionally wind tolerant and supports a very high insect population although of limited diversity, and also many of the most effective nitrogen-fixing trees which are particularly valuable for use on derelict land (Buckley, 1978). Where there are no special site constraints only native species should be used in rural or natural plantings (Beckett and Beckett, 1979).

The plants chosen should be biologically capable of withstanding the particular stresses of a given planting site.

Reclamation sites illustrate some of the most difficult planting conditions. Here the trees and shrubs available for selection fall into two categories, nitrogen fixers and the rest. Nitrogen-fixing plants can remain independent of nitrogen levels in the substrate and are able to grow

WE'RE ACTUALLY SAVING
THEN A LOT OF MONEY IN
WEEDING, THINNING, PRUNING
AND FERTILISING.

despite deficiencies that would stunt other plants. As they grow they can contribute nitrogen to surrounding plants from dying leaves and roots.

For companion species it is best to avoid plants which are adapted to high nutrient levels, for example sycamore. Even after many years of successful revegetation, many wastes will never be classified as fertile soils. Selection should be confined to those species which are adapted to colonizing newly disturbed ground where typically the organic matter levels are extremely low. Willow and birch are prime candidates.

Many conifers are very tolerant of low fertility which partly explains why they are so successful in upland plantations. They obtain this advantage by having an efficient internal system for cycling what few nutrients are available.

There is considerable scientific debate about the damage, if any, that conifers can do to a soil. However, it seems beyond doubt that by their very nature that they do not leak nutrients. They are therefore of less value on derelict land in helping with the progressive build up of a reasonably normal soil profile (Miles, 1981). However, conifers may have a valuable role to play in providing winter screening and protection of an area and can be included in a mixture for this reason.

An alternative stressful situation commonly encountered is in heavily exposed coastal areas. The tree species best adapted to these conditions include sycamore and white poplar. A frontal screen of tolerant shrubs such as *Eleagnus* may be beneficial to give the trees initial shelter.

CHOICE OF STOCK SIZE

It is not only easier and cheaper to plant small stock but young trees grow with more vigour and establish more successfully than large standards (Countryside Commission for Scotland, 1983).

Following undercuttings and lifting at the nursery, large trees have a greatly truncated root system. Not only will this be very much smaller than that of an undisturbed tree of similar age and size but it will probably also be barely adequate to support the amount of top growth that a large tree carries.

After five to ten years a well grown small transplant will almost certainly exceed the height of a standard planted at the same time. Stock of 1 + 1 or 2 + 1 age and certainly no more than 1 metre high should be chosen for all rural, natural or reclamation planting.

Conversely a standard tree is harder to kill than a small transplant. It has a greater internal supply of nutrients when planted and its roots extend down deeper, making it less prone to fatal damage during drought. Even if it never grows it may survive for several years.

Using small trees therefore calls for a commitment to ensure that no root drying occurs before planting and requires that both weed control and fertilizer application are undertaken properly for the first few years.

Large trees should be used for instant effect in relatively benign sites that are exposed to considerable public attention. Even so if a vigorous tree canopy is desired, it may prove valuable to interplant the large trees with small stock.

Containerized large trees can suffer from an even greater imbalance. Their roots grow in a very limited volume, which is smaller than that exploited by an equivalent bare root plant.

CHOICE OF STOCK TYPE

Introduction
The Amenity Manager essentially has four types of stock upon which to call when re-establishing tree and shrub plantings: containerized, bare-rooted, root-balled and seed. Each of these is reviewed in the paragraphs which follow.

Containerized stock
Many nurseries find a container production system preferable, with the result that many of the less usual plants are now very hard to find in anything other than a containerized form.

Containerized stock is more difficult to transport to, and around a site.

Although containerized trees undergo less root disturbance and hence desiccation than the equivalent bare root plant (Insley, 1982), this should not be used as an excuse to entend the planting season without additional irrigation. Early planting allows roots to exploit large volumes of soil moisuture before summer drought, whereas a typcial container can only last two or three days without watering. Japanese paper pots or other such very small containers can provide almost no buffering capacity against drought (Gilbertson *et al.*, 1987).

The container compost may, however, prove valuable as a localized temporary nutrient source.

Stock that has been grown too long in containers inevitably suffers from some form of nutrient deficiency. It will have lost much of its capacity for vigorous growth, and may develop root spiralling. The latter in the long term results in the death of the tree, even if it looks healthy on site initially.

Conversely, care should be taken to avoid using stock that has recently been lifted from the field and containerized.

Containers should be free of persistent weed species.

Some soil types, notably heavy clays, can form an impenetrable barrier to roots outside the planting pit. This effectively condemns the tree to a containerized existence for the whole of its, probably short, life. On poorly-drained soils the container can collect water like a sink. Death of the tree, in effect by drowning, follows. This problems is aggravated by the rich organic material that constitutes most container composts which can hold water like a sponge.

When planting stock on heavy soils it is important to avoid smearing the sides of the pit. Sometimes some form of drainage may have to be installed.

Bare rooted stock

A bare rooted tree transplant is prone to internal desiccation through water loss from roots. It is vital therefore that roots are protected at all stages in the period between lifting and planting out.

Transplants are likely to be cheaper and easier to transport. If healthy and well packaged, they are likely to establish better than containerized plants.

Root-balled stock

Root-balled trees can be labour-intensive to lift and handle but, if carefully produced, they can offer an ideal transplanting option. There are no dangers of root spiralling and roots are not exposed to desiccation. New nursery systems have been developed whereby trees are grown in wire baskets so that they can take up nutrients from the whole of the soil. At lifting they in effect become instantly rootballed.

Propagation material

It is important to ensure that the plant material delivered actually meets the specifications. Seemingly innocent substitutions of plant varieties can lead to dramatic differences in the ultimate size and form of growth achieved.

Where possible, grafted material should be avoided as problems of incompatibility and suckering may result. In the worst circumstances the mature trees may in fact be extremely unsafe with weak graft unions.

Growth habit

The growth habits of plants need to be considered carefully at the time of selection. Normally plants which are true to form should be chosen. There are, however, exceptions.

Trees pruned in the nursery to produce the traditional image of a 'lollipop' standard will tend to look artificial wherever they are planted. Nonetheless such trees are necessary in many public areas to allow unrestricted movement around them.

In rural and ecological plantings, or where a complete screen is desired, feathered trees should be chosen that have branches all the way down the trunk.

STOCK QUALITY

Experiments first conducted by the Forestry Commission demonstrated that something like 30 per cent of trees could be dead by the time they were delivered to site, because of desiccation of the roots (Insley, 1986).

By planting trees in a holding nursery for a season before putting them on site there is a good opportunity to assess the quality of suppliers. However, this adds several steps to the handling process which can be costly. It is also essential that the stock is handled well by the holding nursery staff. Otherwise good quality material can be spoiled.

It may prove beneficial if visits to the supplier can be made particularly during the lifting season, to assess quality and methods of handling.

Both the internal carbohydrate levels and the nutrient reserves of trees will be influenced by how well they have been grown in the nursery (Atkinson and Ofori-Asmoah, 1987). Both these in turn influence how quickly a tree becomes dependent on the planting site to provide all its needs and how quickly the roots can regrow to replace those which have been lost.

Stock of a good form should be chosen, for example standards must be free of competing or forked leaders. The stock should have been regularly transplanted and undercut.

STOCK HANDLING

Consignments must be deeply heeled in immediately after arrival and watered to remove air pockets. Any stock that is being taken for planting should be wrapped in AIRTIGHT plastic packaging. If trees are to be left for long periods, it may be preferable to line them out rather than leave them in large bundles. Otherwise small air pockets, which can be damaging, will inevitably be caught in the root mass. Large bundles tend to rock in the wind and areas of root can become exposed. Stock must not be heeled into frozen or waterlogged ground.

Certain species, such as birch, are more susceptible to root drying than others. Small stock is more susceptible than large. However, small stock can be kept wrapped up throughout the planting operation: several forestry companies sell special pouches fitted to shoulder harnesses which protect transplants whilst being carried immediately prior to planting.

TREE SEEDING

Trees grown from seed can, in some circumstances, greatly outperform transplants (La Dell, 1982; Luke and McPherson, 1983).

The root system of trees and shrubs grown from seed can develop to balance the top growth. Unlike transplants there is no root loss through lifting or undercutting. Often this allows the formation of a deep tap root that is particularly valuable for water gathering. The root system can also develop its depth and spread to match precisely the site conditions superimposed on an existing structure.

The technique is particularly appropriate where site topography makes normal tree planting techniques difficult.

Conversely, seeding onto a thick grass sward may not be successful because of the competition that the seeds undergo. This is particularly true of species with small light demanding seeds such as birch or salix. Physically, a slightly nutrient deficient, open sward is most suited for direct seeding unless a weed control regime is to be introduced as well.

As a general rule large seeds establish quickly, are more able to compete with herbage but are more prone to losses from vermin and birds (Luke, 1982).

The resulting seedings are obviously less resistant to fire or to occasional accidental mowing than are larger stock.

Trees grown from seed obviously do not provide the option of fine control over density, layout and the final composition of the species mix. The technique is best suited to formal or natural areas, but even then some thinning, selection and beating-up may be necessary.

Work has shown that the most damaging time for weed competition is in the period following leafing out of the tree: May to June. Weed control at this stage should be regarded as essential even if it is relaxed for the rest of the season (Insley and Buckley, 1980).

12.7
Weed control in the
establishment of
amenity plantings

INTRODUCTION

Weeds compete with woody plants for the essential growth requirements, namely for light, for nutrients and, most importantly, for water.

Uncontrolled weed competition can kill new transplants and is one of the main causes of the death or poor growth of new plantings (Davies, 1987). If an Amenity Manager wants to establish trees and shrubs as quickly and successfully as possible, adequate weed control is therefore essential. This is true even when the ultimate objective of the planting is to establish a natural and species-rich planting. Use of other inputs such as fertilizers, some mulches and irrigation are also likely to depend for their success on good weed control. Without it, the weeds benefit and the crop plants go without some or all of their growth requirements.

Some weeds are so noxious or rampant that there is a statutory obligation to control them near farmland. Apart from biological reasons, weeds are also unacceptable because they usually look unsightly. Thus they are particularly unacceptable in urban or prestigious plantings. Weed infested plantings can infect nearby relatively weed-free landscapes or gardens and therefore will be especially unpopular with the virtuous owners or managers.

It is for these reasons that weed control is so important and is given a special section to itself in the book.

Woody plants grow best in bare ground, without competition from other plants (Insley and Buckley, 1980). Research in orchards proved this point many years ago. Today most fruit and plantation crops are grown in weed- and grass-free soil. This demonstrates that commercial growers of woody plants find it cost-effective to control vegetation efficiently. More recent research by the Forestry Commission (Insley, 1983) has also shown that more moisture can be lost from mown than from unmown grass. Planting trees and shrubs in mown grass, a very common practice, is therefore clearly the worst possible option.

HOW MUCH WEED CONTROL?

Not all amenity plantings justify very intensive weed control beyond the establishment phase. The inputs needed depend on the result required and on its value. These depend in turn on the objectives of the planting. For example, weed control in commercial forestry is usually fairly relaxed relative to the standards that would be imposed in many urban parks, because appearance is not important.

In most amenity plantings it is worth keeping a weed-free area of at least 1 metre diameter around the base of establishing plants; typically for the first 3–5 years. Mass or ground cover plantings, which are at one metre centres or less, should therefore be maintained in overall bare ground if possible. This is best achieved by using chemical weed control methods. These, together with a range of the other inputs, making up the total establishment package, have proved to be cost-effective in a range of situations.

In less intensive amenity areas, for example in the establishment of rural roadside or field corner plantings, transplants are normally spaced at wider centres. Overall weed control is not usually necessary or even desirable in such locations. It can look ugly and out of place. Further-more, it can contribute to erosion problems, particularly on banks. In such situations some kind of spot treatment is therfore best. This involves using herbicide as well as some type of mulch or spat, to treat about a metre around each plant.

TIMING

The value of the weed control in terms of increased growth can be prolonged for as long as it takes for the natural canopy to become weed suppressing. This can be important if timber production is a primary objective. Usually, however, once the tree grows out of its vulnerable establishment phase, weed control can be relaxed and a reduction in growth rates accepted. Research suggests that this process takes on average 3–5 years, if the transplant is healthy and there are no other limiting site problems (Buckley *et al.*, 1981).

Manufacturer's recommendations for use of most residual herbicides paradoxically suggest that they should not be used in the first year after planting. Common practice by landscapers and nurserymen shows that on the heavier soil types there is little risk of damage. Even if some marginal damage does appear, it may be less harmful to the plants than the effect of rampant weed growth.

12.8
Weed control methods

The three main types of weed control are reviewed in the sections which follow.

PHYSICAL METHODS

Hand methods, such as hoeing and forking over, are very slow. They are also liable to damage plant roots and stems. While they may be the only feasible method of weed control in non-woody plantings, such as herbaceous borders, bedding schemes or rockeries, they should be avoided in woody plantings if possible. However, removal of occasional emergent annuals, such as *Chenopodium* (fat hen) in, say, a low ground cover planting, may be the most cost-effective and least harmful method if weed populations are not high. Table 12.7 gives some resource require-ment guidelines covering manual and chemical methods. It has to be recognized that such methods cannot always be regarded as alternatives. Some weeds are almost impossible to control by physical means and may even be encouraged by hoeing.

Cruder methods, such as using a sickle, may be needed in neglected plantings where spraying would be likely to damage the crop plants. However, they are usually very slow, as shown in Table 12.7 and should be replaced by chemical weed control wherever possible.

Mulches can act as physical barriers to weeds (Wittering, 1974). They

Table 12.7   Weed control in shrub areas (mass plantings): estimated resource requirements

Source	Method/Operation	SMV	Unit
	Manual: Hand Weed		
	(Does not include cleaning up and disposal)		
W	Pull or fork out weeds in shrub beds	92.00	100 m^2
K	Hand weed	61.60	100 m^2
Sh	Fork and weed shrubberies to the minimum depth required	119.60	100 m^2
D	Fork shrub bed	40.00	100 m^2
	Manual Hoe		
W	Hoe shrub beds densely planted	32.00	100 m^2
K	Hand hoe: 0–25% cover	84.92	100 m^2
K	Hand hoe: 25–75% cover	62.55	100 m^2
Sh	Hoe and weed	83.72	100 m^2
H	Hoe : light–medium weed coverage	60.00–225.00	100 m^2
	Chemical: Knapsack Spray		
W	Spray total ground area among shrubs, etc.	32.50	100 m^2
K	Weed spray over 25% cover	11.37	100 m^2
W	Spray around forestry transplants, and whips in grass	65.00	100 m^2
K	Spray weeds: 0–25% cover	18.72	100 m^2
FMH	Sprayer and guard	2.40	100 m^2
Sa	Apply herbicide with watering can and dribble bar	11.00	100 m^2
	Chemical: Granular Herbicides		
W	Apply by hand around small plants in grass	30.00	100 plants
W	Apply by chest mounted applicator — sparsley planted area	0.92	100 m^2
Sa	Apply powder (Prefix)	73.20	100 m^2
Sa	Apply herbicide with watering can and dribble bar	11.00	100 m^2

See Table 2.2 on p. 37 for details of sources.

provide more benefits than just weed control and these have been discussed earlier.

MECHANICAL METHODS

Flails, shrub cutters, brush cutters, mowers, rollers and other mechanical means are used in commercial forestry to help with weed control (Cloy, 1984). This is possible where spacings are wide enough to allow machinery between plants and where only a crude level of weed control is required. In the case of amenity plantings in grass, mowing may be used as a form of weed control. The weed eater type of strimmer can also be useful. However, the risk of harming the crop plants is high and these tools should be avoided whenever this is likely.

In the light of recent research (Insley, 1983), it seems that, if trees and shrubs are not completely physically smothered by weeds, they will be less damaged if the weeds remain uncut rather than if they are cut. Mechanical methods are therefore unlikely to be suitable in most amenity areas.

CHEMICAL METHODS

In the United Kingdom use of chemicals in landscape management is controlled under the Food and Environmental Protection Act 1985. The Control of Pesticide Regulations came into operation on 6 October 1986 under the 1985 Act, replacing existing control schemes. The word *pesticide* is used in its broadest sense in the Act and encompasses products such as herbicides and fungicides.

The regulations require that from 1 January 1989 users of pesticides comply with the new legislation by holding a recognized Certificate of Competence. Certificates can be obtained by passing a practical test. Certificates issued by the National Proficiency Tests Council and the Scottish Associates of Young Farmers Clubs are recognized. The new legislation also makes the approval of products a legal requirement: it is an offence to sell, supply, store, advertise or use unapproved pesticides. All users must comply with the conditions of approval. The MAFF/ Health and Safety Executive publication *Pesticides 1986* lists those products approved under the Control of Pesticides Regulations. *The UK Pesticide Guide 1989* produced by CAB International and the British Crop Protection Council gives valuable information on the use of approved products.

There is a whole range of approved chemicals which can be useful in managing amenity landscapes as shown in Table 12.8. Herbicides, properly used, can be effective, quick and safe in woody plantings. Indeed chemical weed control is usually by far the most cost-effective type of weed control in amenity areas (Davison, 1982).

Whilst some chemicals can be used to control weeds very quickly and simply, many of the clever control 'tricks' of chemicals only work if the application is undertaken really carefully and skilfully. For example, one annual application of dichlobenil (Casoron G) in established plantings can successfully control all weeds for a year without significant damage to the woody plants. However, application must be even, at the correct rate, and performed during the correct time of year. If not, the amenity plants can be killed.

The alternative to dichlobenil involves using a range of chemicals applied at different times and in different ways. This is clearly more time-consuming. Chemicals, such as simazine and alloxydim sodium (Clout), which can be applied with little risk of damaging crop plants, are particularly useful in amenity planting for this reason. These chemicals are described more fully in the following section.

Many other herbicides have 'windows of use' similar to that for Dichlobenil. Their use outside these periods may mean that they are less effective, or that there is increased risk of damage to the crop plant. This period of safe use is related to soil temperature and moisture conditions and as such can differ across the country. Guidance on such application times is given in Table 12.8.

Another obstacle to the rational use of herbicides in direct works

Table 12.8 The range of chemicals available for use in managing amenity landscapes

Plant establishment period	Chemical	Product	Distributer/ manufacturer	Formulation	Forestry	Specimen trees	Shrubs and roses	Herbaceous	Bedding
USABLE FROM PLANTING DATE	Alloxydim sodium	Clout 40 G	May & Baker	SG,SP		✓	✓		
		Clout	Hortichem	SG,SP		✓	✓		
	Atrazine+Dalapon–sodium	Herbon Lignum Granules	Atlas Agrochemicals	GR		✓	*	✓	✓
	Chloramben	Granular Naptol	Synchemicals	GR		✓	✓	✓	
	Oxadiazon	Ronstar	Hortichem	GR,EC		✓	✓	✓	✓
10–14 DAYS FROM PLANTING	Diquat+Paraquat+Simazine	Soltair	ICI Professional	SG		✓			
	Propachlor	Ramrod Granular	Monsanto	GR	✓	✓		✓	
4–8 WEEKS FROM PLANTING	Lenacil	Venzar	Du Pont	WP		✓			
1 GROWING SEASON	Propyzamide	Kerb	PBI	GR,WP	✓	✓			
1 YEAR	Atrazine	Ashlade 4% At Gran	Ashlade Formulations	GR	✓	✓			
		Ashlade Atrazine 50 FL	Ashlade Formulations	SC	✓	✓			
	Diuron+Paraquat	Dexuron	Chipman	SC	✓	✓			
	Hexazinone	Valpar Liquid	Selectokil	SL	✓	✓			
	Simazine	Syngran	Synchemicals	GR	✓	✓	✓		
		Gesatop	Ciba-Geigy	SC,WP	✓	✓	✓		
2 YEARS	Dichlobenil +	Fydulan	Chipman	GR	✓	✓	✓		

	Product	Manufacturer				
Dalapon	Casoron G & Casoron G4	ICI Professional	GR		/	/
Dichlobenil	Prefix D	Shell	GR		/	/
SPOT TREATMENTS **Throughout growth cycle**						
Ammonium sulphamate	Amcide	Albright & Wilson	SG	/		
Asulam	Asulox	May & Baker	SL	/		
Asulam	Asulox	Embetec	SL	/		
2,4-D	BASF 2,4-D Ester 480	BASF	EC	/		
2,4-D	BH 2,4-D Ester 50	Burts & Harvey	EC	/		
Glyphosate	Roundup	Monsanto	SL	/	/	/
Paraquat	Dextrone X	Chipman	SL	/	/	/
	Speedway	ICI Professional	WG		/	/
Triclopyr	Timbrel	Dow Chemical Co.	EC	/		/
	Garlon 4	Chipman	EC	/		/

KEY: EC; Emulsifiable concentrate
GR; Granules
SC; Suspension concentrate
SG; Water soluble granules
SL; Soluble concentrate
SP; Water soluble powder
SU; Ultra low-volume suspension
WP; Wettable powder
WG; Water dispersible granules
* Recommendations very limited

organizations is Union opposition. In some local authorities the use of all herbicides has been banned by the workforce and many have specific-ally banned paraquat. Weed control in these organizations cannot be as cost-effective as it would be if the complete 'armoury' of herbicides were available for use.

Apart from these problems there are also situations where it may be inappropriate to use herbicides: in some, but not all, nature conservation areas, for example (Marrs, 1984).

CHOICE OF CHEMICAL

Chemical weed control in the majority of amenity woody plantings is based on a very small number of herbicides. These can cope with most weed problems if they are used in an intelligent way. The purpose of this section is to explain why these chemicals are useful and how they can be used to deal with the main weed problems which occur in amenity tree and shrub areas.

It is assumed that readers are reasonably familiar with the main types of herbicides and their mode of action, i.e. residual contact and systemic (although some, such as Dichlobenil, can be described in more than one category) and with basic information on application methods, safety precautions, etc. References which provide more detail on these are given at the end of the section.

For completeness, readers are referred to the section on Chemical Weed Control in Chapter 19.

RESIDUAL HERBICIDES

The main characteristics of the most common residual herbicides in use today are described in the paragraphs which follow. New developments will doubtless appear in future years (Sale and Mason, 1986) and the following review is not to be regarded as definitive.

Simazine

Simazine is a root-acting residual herbicide which is effective against many germinating weeds. It forms the basis of most chemical weed con-trol programmes in woody plantings, and is the single most important herbicide in the maintenance of established beds. Its main characteristics are that it is:

- relatively cheap;
- effective against a wide range of germinating weeds;
- very safe to humans;
- not harmful to a very wide range of woody plants;
- relatively safe and easy to apply, since at normal rates it can be applied over woody plants without harming them at all. Spray drift does not normally harm grass;

- strongly fixed, i.e. neutralized in the soil and tends not to move or run, unlike propyzamide and dichlobenil;
- capable of being used on most established and some newly-planted woody plants at a rate strong enough to last an entire season.
- applied in the winter season and so helps to transfer part of the weed control task from the summer peak to winter.

Most weed control programmes use simazine as the basic herbicide, and make use of other chemicals to control those weeds with which it cannot deal. The most important of these weeds are:

- Established broadleaved perennials, such as docks, nettles and creeping thistle;
- Emergent annual weeds, which were present before the application of simazine or are not controlled by it;
- Perennial grass weeds, such as couch.

These weeds can be controlled by other herbicides discussed in the following chapters.

Propyzamide

Propyzamide is another residual herbicide which, like simazine, is applied in the winter, but at an earlier period. It has a limited contact action against small emergent annual weeds and hence helps to control those which would otherwise overwinter. It is also active against a number of species resistant to simazine. Its chief virtue is its ability to control and eventually eradicate established grass weeds, if applied annually over a period of 1–3 years, hence it can be used to eradicate established couch grass from infested plantings. This is an invaluable quality.

It is less toxic to plants than simazine, and is therefore sometimes used at low rates in new plantings as a basic residual herbicide. Propyzamide can be used safely with simazine at normal rates. Each residual complements the action of the other. Care needs to be taken when spraying propyzamide near to grass areas, since spray drift will damage them. It is also liable to run, and if applied to beds on banks above grass areas it can move down and damage the grass beneath.

Propyzamide is also available in granular form which can be applied with much greater ease especially on inaccessible sites where there is no local water source.

Dichlobenil

This is a highly persistent, root-absorbed, broad-spectrum residual herbicide, usually applied in granular form in early spring. It is active against most weeds, including deep rooted perennials. However, its use in planted areas is limited by the fact that it is:

- essential to ensure that the application is undertaken by a skilled operator so as to ensure that it is applied evenly at the correct rate;
- relatively expensive;

- a very potent chemical not suitable for use on young plants and on certain species;
- very persistent and its use may be undesirable in areas where, for example, herbicide residues are ecologically undesirable, or where ground flora regeneration or establishment is desired.

Where its use is feasible, however, it can do the work of many of the chemicals referred to in this chapter in one easy application. It can therefore provide an extremely cost-effective method of weed control.

Away from trees and shrubs, it is by far the best and most cost-effective chemical to use for the control of vegetation around obstacles in grass, along fence lines and so on.

CONTACT HERBICIDES

For many years these were the only type of herbicide generally available. Several of these herbicides unfortunately require very careful application in that surface run-off causes great harm (sodium chlorate is very prone to this problem).

Today the main contact herbicide is Paraquat. It is a non-translocated contact herbicide which has the following virtues: it is

- cheap;
- extremely quick acting;
- non-persistent and does not leave harmful residues;
- effective on areas largely confined to those touched by spray. Spray drift damage is likely to be more localized and less insidiously damaging than drift from systemics, such as glyphosate.

Paraquat is highly toxic to humans if not correctly handled. However, it is an excellent chemical if properly applied. Its main uses are in burning off emergent annual weeds and those perennials which do not have creeping root systems.

It is often easiest to remove large annual weeds by hand, and to use contact chemicals such as paraquat on low weed growth or newly emergent weeds only. This makes it easier to control spray drift because lances can be held low. Paraquat and hand weeding can often be usefully combined as summer treatments to cope with those weeds which have escaped residuals.

Systemics

Broad-leaved perennial weeds with perennial underground roots, such as dock and creeping thistle, are not controlled by either of the basic residuals, simazine and propyzamide, or by superficial treatments such as hand pulling, hoeing, forking or burning off with paraquat. They therefore need to be controlled by other methods. The only quick, reliable and cost-effective way of eradicating broad-leaved perennial weeds is through the use of systemic (translocated) chemicals. These are applied

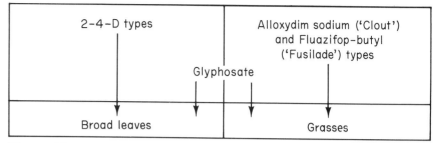

Figure 12.1   Chemical weed control in amenity plantings.

to actively growing foliage and are then translocated within the plants thereby destroying their root systems. Some of these herbicides, notably glyphosate, are also effective against perennial grass weeds, such as couch, if these have not been controlled by other means, for example by propyzamide.

These are also the principle chemical type systemics used to control 'woody weeds' such as heather, rhododendron, and regrowth from cut stumps.

Figure 12.1 displays the three types of systemic herbicide which are commonly used in amenity plantings:

1. The 2,4-D type of herbicides (for example 2,4-D, MCPA, Mecoprop), effective against broad-leaved plants only:
2. Glyphosate which is effective against nearly all plants;
3. The alloxydim-sodium types of herbicides, which are effective against couch and most other grass weeds.

2,4-D-type systemics
These are the type of chemicals used to kill broad-leaves in grassland. They are as active against broad-leaved woody plants as they are against herbaceous weeds. They can cause severe damage or death to trees and shrubs, especially to small or young plants, if herbicide spray touches the leaves. Extreme care is therefore necessary when applying these chemicals to weeds among woody plants. However, these qualities can also be exploited to control 'woody weeds' such as bramble.

These chemicals are not very weather-proof and need a few hours of dry weather after application in which to be absorbed by the weeds. Their application is therefore weather-dependent with regard to both wind, which will cause drift, and rain, which will wash off the herbicide. Where trees and shrub plants are well spaced out, it is possible to apply these chemicals by knapsack sprayer. Spray hoods should always be used and kept well down to the ground; spraying should only be done in windless weather; and the greatest care should be taken to prevent drift onto woody plant foliage. The skill of the operator and the care taken in application are therefore absolutely crucial. Treatment is safer if weeds are small or low, or if crop plants have sections of foliage-free stem which are clear of the weeds; as in standard trees, for example.

Glyphosate

This chemical is valued by Amenity Managers for its strong herbicide properties, its lack of persistence in the environment and its very low toxicity to people. Glyphosate is extremely toxic to plants and is not selective: it can kill broad-leaved weeds and grasses, herbaceous and woody plants. Even very low doses can cause long-term damage to woody plants. For this reason, it is best not to spray glyphosate among trees and shrubs except in absolutely windless weather, and with the utmost care by skilled operators. On the other hand, glyphosate is the chemical which is recommended for use in most of the spot type applicators such as the weedwiper or the herbicide glove (application techniques are discussed in more detail later). Used in this way it is excellent. However, great care should always be taken not to allow any drips to fall accidentally onto foliage of trees or shrubs.

Glyphosate is also by far the best herbicide for spraying out ground before planting, since it will kill out all the plants which are present. It is also ideal for spraying out turf around young trees in grass.

Alloxydim-sodium ('Clout') and Fluazifop-Butyl ('Fusilade')

These systemic herbicides are fairly new and very useful additions to the armoury of Amenity Managers. They are the opposite of the 2,4-D type of chemicals, since they are selective against grasses, leaving broad-leaved plants unharmed. They can therefore be sprayed through grass-infested trees, shrubs and broad-leaved herbaceous plants in full leaf without harm to the broad-leaves. These herbicides have a foliar systemic action: they enter the grass through the leaves and are carried down to the roots which they destroy. It seems that fluazifop-butyl is more active than alloxydim sodium.

These chemicals can be particularly useful in attacking grass weed problems on sites where propyzamide cannot be used, for example on slopes above grass; or in assisting the action of propyzamide on beds which are badly infested with grass.

However, it should be noted that these herbicides do not kill *all* grasses.

Care must be taken in spraying them near lawns since they will, of course, damage the grass.

Control of other woody weeds

Several other chemicals, notably Dicambra and ammonium sulphamate, can be used to control woody weeds. Their use is relatively uncommon in amenity areas as a result of the increasing recognition of the efficacy of glyphosate. Even so, they are still valuable in many situations. Ammonium sulphamate is often applied to the bark rather than to the foliage of woody weeds and is particularly useful as a stump killer.

There is currently great interest in the development of new formulations and chemicals designed to kill woody weeds in an attempt to fill the gap created by the loss of confidence in 2, 4, 5-T formulations. Appropriate advisory services, such as MAFF, The Forestry Commission or the Arboricultural Advisory Service, are able to give up-to-date information on the latest chemicals.

MATERIALS COSTS

Some guidelines on the comparative materials costs for the main herbicides used in controlling weeds within amenity tree and shrub plantings are provided in Table 19.5.

HERBICIDE APPLICATORS

Sprayers range widely in size. They include lightweight hand-held devices, often useful for small isolated areas, plastic knapsack sprayers with hand or occasionally mechanical pumps and tractor-mounted tankers with mechanical pumping. The latter may not be cost-effective on amenity sites unless the tanker can double for irrigation. Spray guards are important where selective application of wide spectrum herbicides is intended.

Ultra Low Volume and electrostatic sprayers are new developments which have become very important in Forestry areas. ULV sprayers are small hand-held devices which produce very fine droplets, often propelled in an air jet, which means that large areas can be covered without having to refill the tank repeatedly with water. By their very nature, they are often more useful in widescale herbicide treatments, such as scrub clearance, rather than for spot application. Electrostatically charged sprays have been developed to control drift of very small droplets, so that they adhere to nearby vegetation and do not spread to neighbouring fields. They have a drawback in that it is hard for the operator to see that the treatment has been applied. Consequently there is a tendency to overdose.

Granule applicators vary in size. The main types are small hand-held 'pepper-pot' applicators, chest-or back-mounted 'hoppers' and large tractor-mounted machines. Granules may be thrown out by some form of distributor or dropped straight to the ground. Tractor-mounted devices can often relate the distribution rate to the forward speed of the machine and to the need for turning circles. The machines can also be used for distribution of seed or fertilizer. It is rare on amenity sites that a need exists for very large-scale tractor devices. Small hand-held granule applicators can be invaluable for small, inaccessible sites or for working amongst large shrubs. Their convenience far outweighs the high cost of the chemicals.

For small-scale work a watering can with a rose or dribble bar may be adequate. It has the advantage that there is no danger of drift.

Because of the wide range of plant types grown in close proximity, selectivity in amenity plantings often depends on careful physical placement of systemic herbicides. Many methods are available which attempt to achieve this effect. These include spot applicators, such as small herbicide wicks and dabbers, weed gloves which have a sponge in the palm fed by a reservoir and which allows the operator just to wipe gel onto an identified weed, and tractor-mounted horizontal rope wicks which can be used to control tall weeds in a low crop, for example thistles in ground cover. These applicators are used in conjunction with gel formulations of systemic herbicides, usually glyphosate.

Many of these newer techniques have yet to be adopted by the amenity industry and there is a lack of relevant time data.

SAFETY CONSIDERATIONS

Herbicides in their concentrated form should be treated with care at all times. It is essential that appropriate safety and storage equipment is provided. Operators must be trained in safe handling (Shildrick, 1988). The need for careful cleaning of equipment should be explained.

Sprayers and application equipment should be washed after use, and adequately maintained and calibrated.

Many amenity sites provide awkward problems for ensuring that correct dose rates are applied. Beds are uneven and full of obstacles. As a general

Table 12.9 The management of general amenity plantings: the removal and lifting of trees and shrubs – estimated resource requirements

Source	Operation	SMV	Unit
	Removal		
L	Dig out tree	27.00	1 no
Sh	Dig out broken or dead tree	2.60	1 no
W	Dig up (small) tree	7.40	1 no
D	Dig out shrub manually	3.00	1 no
Sh	Dig out recently planted shrub prior to replacement	0.80	1 no
H	Dig out suckers round suckering shrub — 5′ area	10.00	1 no
Sa	Grub hedge and burn to dispose (inc roots)	13.12	1 no
Sh	Dig out old privet hedge up to 5′ high	12.27	1 m
	Lifting		
W	Lift tree (large) with JCB for replanting	7.00	1 no
W	Lift tree (20 cm min.diam) with JCB for replanting	26.00	1 no
W	Lift whip with shrub lifter	0.84	1 no
W	Lift heavy and extra heavy standard trees	37.52	1 no
Sh	Lift semi-mature tree and wrap in sacking	31.00	1 no
W	Lift standard trees	17.22	1 no
W	Lift feathered trees and whips	5.54	1 no
D	Lift small shrubs for replanting	3.00	1 no
H	Dig out hedge plants for replanting	15.00	1 no

See Table 2.2 on p. 37 for details of sources.

Table 12.10   The management of general amenity plantings: planting a range of nursery stock sizes – estimated resource requirements

Source	Forest transplants	Whips 60–180 cm tall	Shrubs		Standard trees	
	Notch planted		Bare-rooted	Container	Standard up to 270 cm	Heavy standard
			SMVs per Plant			
Wa	3.70	11.10	5.00	7.00	33.00	75.00
D	NA	11.00	4.00	NA	25.00	NA
Sh	NA	NA	3.40	NA	42.00	56.00

See Table 2.2 on p. 37 for details of sources.

rule always apply too little rather than risk severe damage to ornamentals. High volume low concentration sprays are preferable as localized over-dosing is likely to be less severe.

ESTIMATED RESOURCE REQUIREMENTS

Guidelines on the resources required to re-establish amenity plantings are provided by Tables 12.9 to 12.11 inclusive. These guidelines cover the

Table 12.11   The management of general amenity plantings: effects of plant size and site conditions: relative establishment costs per tree

Site condition	Good site		Difficult site	
Type of stock	Bare-rooted stock	Container-grown stock	Bare-rooted stock	Container-grown stock
Size of plant	Establishment	cost indices		
1. Transplants 10–20 cm	18	50	25	65
2. Transplants 20–45 cm	20	70	30	90
3. Hedge plants 45–90 cm	70	110	150	140
4. Whips 90–150 cm	100*	220	200	260
5. Standards 2–3 m	450	20	850	220
6. Heavy standards 3–4 m	700	NA	1,300	NA
7. Semi-mature 5 m	3,500	NA	5,000	NA

Notes: *   The costs involved in establishing bare-rooted whips in good site conditions was taken as 100.
   1. The costs of establishment include plant purchase, planting and first year maintenance, but exclude fencing and tree guards.
   2. The costs of plants are based on scale purchases of:
         1,000 rate for sizes 1–3
         100   rate for sizes 4–5
         10   rate for sizes 6–7
   3. A difficult site is one suffering from compaction, nutrient and/or moisture deficiency, weed infestation, etc.

most important operations and issues, with which managers need to be most concerned when re-establishing amenity plantings:

- The removal of broken or dead plants;
- The lifting of replacement stock for planting out;
- The comparison of times taken in planting out stock of varying types and sizes;
- The effects of plant size and site conditions upon establishment costs;
- The relationship between planting plot sizes and shapes and the costs of establishing rural field corner plantings.

References

Aldhous, J.R. (1979) *Trees and buildings: complement or conflict*. Tree Council/RIBA conference papers. RIBA Publications, London.

Atkinson D. and Ofori-Asamoah, T.E. (1987) The growth of the nursery root system and its influence on tree performance after transplanting. In *Advances in Practical Arboriculture. Bulletin 65*. Forestry Commission. Edinburgh.

Baines, J.C. (1982) Shrub planting – techniques for successful establishment. In *Cost Effective Amenity Landscape Management*. (eds. P.R. Thoday and C.H. Addison) HEA Conference Proceedings. Cannington College, Somerset.

Beckett, J. and Beckett, G. (1979) *Planting Native Trees and Shrubs*. Jarrold, Norwich.

Biddle, P.G. (1985) Arboricultural implications of revision of National House Building Practice Note 3 Building Near Trees *Arboricultural Journal* , **9** (4), 243–50.

Binns, W.O. (1983) Establishing trees on damaged soils. In *Tree Establishment*. (ed. P.R. Thoday) University of Bath.

Bos, H.J. and Mol, J.L (1979) The Dutch Example: native planting in Holland. In *Nature in Cities* (ed. I.C. Laurie). John Wiley and Sons, London.

Bradshaw, A.D. (1981) *Growing Trees in Difficult Environments Research for Practical Arboriculture* 93–108. Forestry Commission Occasional Paper 10.

Braham M. and Moffat, D. (1987) Fireblight, a cause for concern. *Landscape Design* **167**, 59–60.

Brasier, C.M. and Webber, J.F. (1987) Recent advances in Dutch elm disease research: host, pathogen and vector. In *Advances in Practical Arboriculture. Bulletin 65*. Forestry Commission. Edinburgh.

Bridgeman, P.H. (1976) *Tree Surgery*. David and Charles, London.

Bridgeman P.H. (1979) *Trees for Town and Country*. David and Charles, Newton Abbot.

Bridgeman, P. (1983) Computerised street tree management in the United Kingdom. In *Computerisation of Tree Inventories* (eds. C. Bickmore and T.H.R. Hall), Academic Publishers, Berkhamstead.

Broadbent, T. (1985) The Square Deal, *GC & HTJ*, 25th January.

Buckley, G.P (1978) Tree planting options on industrial wasteland. *Arboricultural Journal*, **3**, 263–72.

Buckley, G.P. (1983) Tree surveys: Objectives, constraints and computers. In *Computerisation of Tree Inventories* (ed C. Bickmore and T.A. and B. Hall), Academic Publishers.

Buckley, G.P., Chilton, K.G. and Devonald, V.G. (1981) The influence of sward control on the establishment and early growth of Ash (*Fraxinus excelsior*) and Norway maple (*Acer platanoides*). *Journal of Environmental Management*, **13**, 223–40.

Clifford, D.R. and Gendle P. (1987) Treatment of fresh wound parasites and of cankers. In *Advances in Practical Arboriculture. Bulletin 65*. Forestry Commission. Edinburgh.

Clouston, B. and Stansfield, K. (1981) *Trees in Towns – Maintenance and Management*. Architectural Press. London.

Cloy, C.J. (1984) *Mechanical Weed Control. Aspects of Applied Biology 5. Weed control and vegetation management in forests and amenity areas*. Assc. of Applied Biologists, Warwick.

Cobham, R.O. and Gill, C.J. (1976) Management and maintenance. *Gardener's Chronicle*, **179**(26) 39–43; **180**(2) 16–19; **180**(3) 16–18.

Countryside Commission for Scotland (1983) Information sheet 3.2.10 Planting small stock. In: *Plants and Planting Methods for the Country-side*. Countryside Commission for Scotland, Battleby.

Crowther, R.E. and Patch, D. (1980) How much wood for the stove? *Arboricultural Research Note. 23/80*.

Davies J. (1987) Weed competition and broadleaved tree establishment. In *Advances in Practical Arboriculture. Bulletin 65*. Forestry Commission. Edinburgh.

Davison, J.G. (1982) Effective weed control in amenity plantings. In *Cost Effective Amenity Landscape Management* (eds. P.R. Thoday and C.H. Addison). HEA Conference Proceedings. HEA, Bridgewater.

Davison, J.G. (1983) Weed control in newly planted amenity trees. In: *Tree Establishment* (ed. P.R. Thoday). University of Bath.

Gilbertson, P. and Bradshaw, A.D. (1985) Tree survival in cities: the extent and nature of the problem. *Arboricultural Journal*. **9**(2), 131–42.

Gilbertson, P., Kendle, A.D. and Bradshaw, A.D. (1987) Rootgrowth and the problems of growing trees in urban and industrial areas. In *Advances in Practical Arboriculture. Bulletin 65*. Forestry Commission. Edinburgh.

Grieg, B.J.W. (1984) *English Elm Regeneration*. DOE Arboricultural Advisory Note 13/84/PATH.

Grieg, B.J.W. (1986) Further experiments with thiabendazole for control of Dutch elm disease. *Arboricultural Journal*, **10**(3), 191–202.

Grieg, B.J.W. and Stroutts R.G. (1983) *Honey Fungus*. Arboricultural leaflet 2. HMSO, London.

Hackett, B. (1978) *Landscape Reclamation Practice*. IPC Science and Technology Press.

Harris, R.W. (1983) *Care of Trees, Shrubs, and Vines in the Landscape.* Prentice Hall, New York.

Hebblethwaite, R.L. (1977) Transplanting semi-mature trees. In: *Landscape Design with Plants* (ed. B. Clouston). Heinemann. London.

Insley, H. (1979) *Damage to Broadleaved Seedlings by Desiccation.* DOE/ Arboricultural Advisory and Information Service, Arboricultural Research Note 8.

Insley, H. (1982) The influence of post planting maintenance on the growth of newly planted broadleaved trees. In *Cost Effective Amenity Land Management*, (eds. C.H. Addison and P.R. Thoday) University of Bath, Bath.

Insley, H. (1982) The use of container-grown broadleaved trees. *Landscape Design*, **137**, 38–40.

Insley, H. (1986) Causes and prevention of establishment failure in amenity trees. In *Ecology and Design in Landscape.* The 24th Symposium of the British Ecological Society (eds. A.D. Bradshaw, D.A. Goode and E. Thorp) Blackwells, Oxford.

Insley, H. and Buckley, G.P. (1980) Some aspects of weed control for amenity trees on man made sites. *Arboricultural Journal*, **4**(2) 128–36.

Insley, H. and Buckley, G. (1980) *Some Aspects of Weed Control for Amenity Trees on Man Made Sites.* Proceedings of Weed Control in Forestry Conference 189–200. Wye College, University of London.

La Dell T. (1982) The practical application of direct tree and shrub seeding. In *Cost Effective Amenity Land Management* (eds C. Addison and P.R. Thoday). University of Bath, Bath.

Lever, K.G. (1982) Cost effective management of amenity trees. In *Cost Effective Amenity Landscape Management.* (eds P.R. Thoday and C.H. Addison) HEA Conference Proceedings. HEA, Bridgewater.

Litzow, M. and Pellett, H. (1983) The influence of mulch materials on growth of green ash. *Journal of Arboriculture.* **9**(1), 7–11.

Lonsdale, D. (1983) *A definition of the best pruning position.* DOE Arboricultural Advisory Note 48/83/PATH.

Lonsdale D. (1987) Prospects for longterm protection against decay in trees. In *Advances in Practical Arboriculture. Bulletin 65.* Forestry Commission. Edinburgh.

Luke, A.G.R. (1982) Know your tree seed. *GC & HTJ*, 8th January.

Luke A.G.R. and McPherson T.K. (1983) Direct tree seeding; a potential aid to land reclamation in Central Soctland. *Arboricultural Journal*, **7**, 287–99.

Marrs R.H. (1984) *The Use of Herbicides for Nature Conservation. Aspects of Applied Biology 5. Weed control and vegetation management in forests and amenity areas.* Assc. of Applied Biologists, Warwick.

Miles, J. (1981) The effects of trees on soils. In *Forest and Woodland Ecology* (ed. F.T Last) Institute of Terrestrial Ecology Symposium No. 8. ITE, Cumbria.

Moffatt, D (undated) *The 'Natural Approach' to Structural Open Space at Warrington New Town.* Warrington and Runcorn Development

Corporation

Parfitt, R.I., Stinchcomb. G.R. and Stott, K.G. (1980) The establishment and growth of windbreak trees in polythene mulch, straw mulch and herbicide maintained bare soil. Proceedings 1980 BCPC Conference – *Weeds*, 739–46.

Patch, D. (1982) *Tree Staking*. DOE Arboricultural Advisory Note 40/82/ARB

Patch D. (1987) Trouble at the stake. In *Advances in Practical Arboriculture. Bulletin 65*. Forestry Commission. Edinburgh.

Pepper, H.W., Rowe, J.J. and Tee, L.A. (1985) *Individual Tree Protection*. DOE Arboricultural Leaflet 10. HMSO.

Pryce, S. (1983) Tree planting. In *Tree Establishment* (ed. P. Thoday) University of Bath.

Pryce, S. (1984) Management problems of one to ten year old woody mass plantings. Techniques No. 45, *Landscape Design*, **2**(84), 29–41.

Rishbeth J. (1987) Honey fungus. In *Advances in Practical Arboriculture. Bulletin 65*. Forestry Commission. Edinburgh.

Russell, E.W. (1973) *Soil Conditions and Plant Growth*. 10th edn. Longman, London.

Sale, J.S.P. and Mason, W.L. (1986) *Alternatives to Simazine for Weed Control in Transplant Lines and Shrubberies at the Time of Planting*. DOE Arboricultural Advisory Note 65/86/SILS.

Sheldon, J.C. (1979) The growth of amenity trees in difficult conditions. In: *Tree Growth and the Landscape* (ed S.E. Wright, and G.P. Buckley) Wye College, London University.

Shildrick, J.P. (1988) *Code of practice for the use of approved pesticides in amenity areas. National Association of Agricultural Contractors / National Turfgrass Council*, Birgley, West Yorkshire.

Smith, E.M. (1978) Fertilising trees and shrubs in the landscape. Journal of Arboriculture, **4**(7), 157–61.

The establishment and growth of wind break trees in polythese mulch, straw mulch and herbicide-maintained base soil. *Proceedings 1980 BCPC Conference – Weeds*, pp. 739–46.

Stoneham, J. and Thoday, P. (1985) Some physiological stresses associated with tree transplanting. *Scientific Horticulture*. **36**, 83–91.

Thoday, P.R. (1983) Tree establishment in amenity sites. In *Tree Establishment*. (ed. P.R. Thoday) Bath University.

Walshe, P. and Westlake, C. (1977) *Tree Guards. Management and Design Notes. 6*. Countryside Commission. Cheltenham.

Webster, B.L. (1978) Guide to judging the condition of a shade tree. *Journal of Arboriculture*, **4**(11), 247–9.

Wilson, R.W. (1981) *Removal of Tree Stumps*. DOE Arboriculture leaflet 7. HMSO.

Wittering, W.O. (1974) *The Use of Black Polythene as a Weed Suppressor*. Forestry Commission Bulletin. 48. HMSO, London.

Wright, T.W.J. (1982) Large Gardens and Parks: Maintenance, management and design. Granada, London.

Further reading　WOODY PLANT COMMUNITIES – THE MATURE AND
SENILE PHASE

ADAS (1979) *Plum Aphids*. MAFF Leaflet 641. HMSO, London.

Anon (1976) *The Care of Trees on Development Sites*. Arboricultural
Association Advisory Leaflet. 3.

Anon (1981) *Phytophera Diseases of Trees and Shrubs*. Arboricultural
Leaflet, Vol. 198(11), 25, HMSO, London.

Anon (1984) *External Signs of Decay in Trees*. Arboricultural Leaflet 1.
HMSO, London.

Anon (1985) Injection protection, *Horticulture Week*, 13th September.
DED.

Anon (1989) A shot in the arm for tree care *Horticulture Week*, **205**, 33–5.

Bannister, A. (1987) Control of pesticides regulation. *Landscape Design*
169, 53–4.

Bassuk, N. and Whitlow, T. (1987) Environmental stress in street trees. In
The Scientific Management of Vegetation in the Urban Environment
(eds. P.R Thoday and D.W. Robinson) *Acta Horticulturae*, 195.

Berry, J.G. (1986) Is your tree really safe? *The Garden*, **111**(4), 158–64.

Billing, E. (1983) Fireblight, *The Garden*, **108**, 206–10.

Black, M.E. (1978) Tree vandalism: some solutions. *Journal of Arboriculture*, **4**(3).

Blatchford, O.N. (1979) *The Use of Chemicals in the Forestry Commission*.
Forestry Commission, Edinburgh.

Boddy, F.A. (1980) *Highway Trees*. Clarke & Hunter, Guildford.

Brook, A. (1974) *The Power Chain Saw*. BTCV, Oxford.

Brown, G.E. (1972) *The Pruning of Trees, Shrubs and Conifers*. Faber and
Faber, London.

Brown, R.M. (1973) *Cold Storage of Forest Plants*. Forestry Commission
Forest Record 88. HMSO, London.

Buckley G.P. and Insley H. *Sward Control Strategies for Young Amenity
Trees. Aspects of Applied Biology 5. Weed Control and Vegetation
Management in Forests and Amenity Areas*. Assc. of Applied Bio-
logists, Warwick.

Burnig, E.F. (1976) Tree forms in relation to environmental conditions;
an ecological view point. In *Tree Physiology and Yield Improvement*
(ed. N.G.R. Cannell and F.T. Last). Academic Press. New York, pp.
139–56.

Caborn, J.M. (1965) *Shelter Belts and Wind Breaks*. Faber and Faber,
London.

Caborn, J. (1975) *Shelter Belts and Microclimate*. Forestry Commission
Booklet 29.

Carter C., Cobham R.O. and Lloyd R. (1979) In *After The Elm* (eds. B.
Clouston and K. Stansfield) Heinemann, London.

Carruthers, S., Philpott, N. and Canneaux, P. (1986) Plane crash. *Horticulture Week*, September 5th.

Carruthers, S. and Stanfield, G. (1986) Timber from towns. *Horticulture
Week*, 5th December.

Chadwick, L.C. and Tilford, P.E. (1949) A study of some methods of fertilising shade trees. In *Proceedings of the American Hort. Sci. Soc.*, **55**, 319–26.

Chambers, K. (1986) Ten thousand pound bid to spruce up the inner city view. *Horticulture Week*, 25th July.

Cobham, R.O. and Hutton, P. (1983) Brown in memoriam: Blenheim Park in perpetuity. *Landscape Design*, **146**, 11–12.

De La Chevallerie, H. (1986) The ecology and preservation of street trees. In *Ecology and Design in Landscape* (eds. A.D. Bradshaw, D.A. Goode and E. Thoday). The 24th Symposium of the British Ecological Society. Blackwells, Oxford.

Decker, P. (1974) *Pests of Ornamental Plants* MAFF Bulletin 97. HMSO, London.

Domir, S.C. (1978) Chemical control of tree height. *Journal of Arboriculture*, **4**(7), 145–52.

Domir, S.C. and Roberts, B.R. (1983) Tree growth retardation by injection of chemicals. *Journal of Arboriculture*, **9**(8), 217–24.

Evans H,F. (1987) Insects and trees: present knowledge and future prospects. In *Advances in Practical Arboriculture. Bulletin 65*. Forestry Commission. Edinburgh.

Evans J. (1987) Tree shelters. In *Advances in Practical Arboriculture. Bulletin 65*. Forestry Commission. Edinburgh.

Gibbs, J.N. and Burdekin, D.A. (1983) De-icing salt and crown damage to London Plane. *Arboricultural Journal*, **7**, 227–37.

Good, J.E.G. and Steele, M.J. (1981) A survey of roadside trees in N. Wales – implications for conservation. *Arboricultural Journal*, **5**, 1–13.

Grace, J. (1987) Water relations and irrigation methods for trees. In *Advances in Practical Arboriculture. Bulletin 65*. Forestry Commission. Edinburgh.

Grainge, R.D. and Thompson, P. (1983) Computer assisted street tree management. *Arboricultural Journal*, **7**, 301–8.

Griffen, N. and Watkins, C. (1986) Liability for dangerous trees. *Quarterly Journal of Forestry*, **LXXX**, 23–26.

Harris, R.W. (1983) *Arboriculture: the care of trees, shrubs, and vines in the landscape*. Prentice Hall, New Jersey.

International Soceity for Horticultural Science (1984) Second international symposium on soil disinfestation. *Acta Horticulturae*, 152.

International Society for Horticultural Science (1984) Third international workshop on fire blight. *Acta Horticulturae* 151.

Ivens, G.W. (ed.) (1989) *The UK Pesticide Guide*, CAB International/ BCPC Publications, Wallingford/Bracknell.

James, N.D.G. (1972) *The Arboriculturists Companion*. Blackwells, Oxford.

Kenney, W.A. (1986) An inexpensive accurate and efficient method for estimating crown width of open grown trees. *Arboricultural Journal*, **10**(3), 203–10.

Lonsdale, D. (1987) Prospects for long term protection against decay in trees. In *The Scientific Management of Vegetation in the Urban Environ-*

ment (eds P.R. Thoday and D.W. Robinson) *Acta Horticulturae* 195.

Mackintosh, H. (1987) Tree preservation orders. The differing needs of urban and rural areas. *Quarterly Journal of Forestry*, **LXXXI**, 158–69.

MAFF/Health and Safety Executive (1986) *Pesticides 1986. Pesticides approved under the Control of Pesticides Regulation 1986.* HMSO, London.

Marrs R.H. (1984) *The Use of Herbicides for Nature Conservation. Aspects of Applied Biology 5. Weed Control and Vegetation Management in Forests and Amenity Areas.* Assc. of Applied Biologists, Warwick.

McP Dick, J. and Longman, K.A. (1985) Techniques for injecting chemicals into trees. *Arboricultural Journal*, **9**(3), 211–14.

Mercer, P.C. (1980) *Treatment of Tree Wounds.* Arboricultural research note. 28/81. Forestry Commission.

Newman, R. (1986) Keep your head. *Horticulture Week*, 18th July. Tree work safety.

Ogilvie J.F. (1984) *Control of Unwanted Conifers – Chemical Thinning and Replacement. Aspects of Applied Biology 5. Weed Control and Vegetation Management in Forests and Amenity Areas.* Assc. of Applied Biologists, Warwick.

Parker, E.J. (1974) *Beech Bark Disease.* Forestry Commission Forest Record 96. HMSO, London.

Patch, D, Coutts, M.P. and Evans, J. (1984) *Control of Epicormic Shoots on Amenity Trees.* Arboricultural research note. 54/84. Forestry Commission.

Pawsey, R.G. (1973) Honey fungus: recognition, biology and control. *Arboricultural Journal*, **2**, 116–26.

Pearce, R. (1986) Inner city blight. *Horticulture Week*, 18th July. Plane tree anthracnose.

Pepper, H.W. (1978) *Chemical Repellants.* Forestry Commission Leaflet 67.

Pepper, H.W. (1983) *Plastic Net Tree Guards.* DOE Arboricultural Advisory Note 5/83/WIL.

Pepper H.W. and Rowe, J.J. (1987) Wildlife research for arboriculture. In *Advances in Practical Arboriculture. Bulletin 65.* Forestry Commission. Edinburgh.

Pirone, P.P. (1959) *Tree Maintenance.* Oxford University Press, New York.

Pirone, P.P. (1974) Advances in general tree maintenance. In *Proceedings of the 39th National Shade Tree Conference*, **39**, 339–45.

Porter, J. (1986) Tree talks. *Horticulture Week*, September 26th.

Rackham, O. (1977) Hedgerow trees – their history, conservation and renewal. *Arboricultural Journal*, **3**, 169–81.

Rishbeth, J. (1983) The importance of honey fungus (Armillaria) in urban forestry. *Arboricultural Journal*, **7**, 217–225.

Robertson G. (1984) *Chemical Weed Control – Training in Application Techniques. Aspects of Applied Biology 5. Weed Control and Vegetation Management in Forests and Amenity Areas.* Assc. of Applied Biologists, Warwick.

Rudd, A. (1976) Trees in towns and their evaluation. *Arboricultural Journal*, **3**, 2–16.

Scott, S. (1985) Regeneration of hedgerow elms *Arboricultural Journal*, **9**(4), 285–92.

Shanks C.W. (1987) *Treeshelters – a Guide to their Use and Information on Suppliers*. Arboriculture Advisory and Information Service.

Shigo, A.L. (1977) A new look at tree care. *Arboricultural Journal*, **3**, 157–64.

Shigo, A.L. (1986) Wounded forests; starving trees. *Arboricultural Journal*, **10**, 299–308.

Smith, E.M. (1978) Fertilising trees and shrubs in the landscape, *Journal of Arboriculture*, **4**(7), 157–61.

Stott, K.G. (1977) *Living Windbreaks – Their Establishment, Maintenance and Effectiveness*. Long Ashton Research Station, University of Bristol.

Strouts, R.G. (1986) Phytophthera – plant destroyer. *The Garden*, **111**(7), 333–7.

Tate, R.L. (1984) Municipal tree management. *Journal of Arboriculture*, **10**(8), 229–33.

Tattar, T.A. (1981) Non-infectious diseases of trees. *Arboricultural Journal*, **5**, 111–16.

Thompson, M. (1982) Identification and control of honey fungus. *Landscape Design*, **138**, 37–8.

Thornton, P.P. (1971) Managing urban and suburban trees and woodlands for timber products. In: *Trees and Forests in an Urbanizing Environment*. University of Mass, pp. 129–32.

Thurman, P.W. (1983) The management of urban street trees using computerised inventory systems. *Arboricultural journal*, **7**, 101–17.

Tregay, R. (1986) Design and ecology in the management of nature-like plantations. In *Ecology and Design in Landscape*, (eds A.D. Bradshaw, D.A. Goode, and E. Thorp). The 24th Symposium of the British Ecological Society. Blackwells, Oxford.

Valentine, F.A., Westfall, R.D. and Marion, P.D. (1978) Street tree assessment by a survey sampling procedure *Journal of Arboriculture*, **4**(3), 49–57.

Ward, L.K. (1979) Scrub dynamics and management. In *Ecology and Design in Amenity Land Management*, (eds. S.E. Wright and G.P. Buckley) Wye College, University of London, London, pp. 109–27.

Welch, D. (1979) *Planting in the Streets*. 19th Askham Bryan Technical Course Report. Askham Bryan. York.

Young, C.W.T. (1977) *External Signs of Decay in Trees*. Arboricultural Leaflet 1. HMSO, London.

RE-ESTABLISHMENT PHASE

Baldwin, I and Stanley, J. (1982) Caning trees. *GC & HTJ*, **191**(24).

Binns, W.O. (1980) *Trees and Water*. Arboricultural Leaflet No. 8. HMSO.

Bloomfield, H.E., Handley, J.F. and Bradshaw, A.D. (1982) Nutrient deficiencies and the aftercare of reclaimed derelict land. *Journal of Applied Ecology*, **19**, 151–8.

Bradshaw, A.D. and Humphries, R.N. (1977) The establishment of woody plants on derelict land. *Scientific Horticulture*, pp. 23–33.

Broad, K.F. (1979) *Tree Planting in Man Made Sites in Wales*. Forestry Commission.

Browell, M. and Mead, H. (1987) Tree shelters. *Landscape Design*, April, pp. 51–60.

Brown I.R. (1987) Suffering at the stake. In *Advances in Practical Arboriculture*. Bulletin 65. Forestry Commission. Edinburgh.

Brown, M. (1976) Design against vandalism. In *Design for Pedestrian Areas Conference Proceedings*, Design Council, London.

Cambell-Lloyd, R. (1986) Mulching – doing it right. *Landscape Design*, October, p. 75.

Clarke, R.V.G., Gladstone, F.J., Sturman, A. and Wilson, S. (1978) The nature of vandalism. In *Tackling Vandalism*, (ed. R.V.G. Clarke) HMSO London, pp. 67–74.

Davies, R.J. (1983) Transplant stress. In *Tree Establishment*, (ed. P.R. Thoday) University of Bath.

Davies J. (1987) Tree establishment; soil amelioration, plant handling and shoot pruning. In *Advances in Practical Arboriculture. Bulletin 65*. Forestry Commission. Edinburgh.

Drury, S. (1987) Know your sprayer. *Horticulture Week*, 10th April.

Gunn, S. (1986) Water with care. *Horticulture Week*, 14th March. Tree irrigation.

Ingram, D.L. and Van de Werken, H. (1978) Effect of container media and backfill composition on the establishment of container grown plants in the landscape. *Horticultural Science*, **13**(5), 583–584.

Insley, H. and Buckley, G. (1980) *Some Aspects of Weed Control for Amenity Trees on Man Made Sites*. Proceedings of Weed Control in Forestry Conference 189–200. Wye College, University of London.

Kendle, A.D. and Gilbertson, P. (1985) Prune for prudence *GC & HTJ*, 13th December.

Kozlowski, T.T. (ed) (1968) *Water Deficits and Plant Growth*. I. Academic Press.

Kozlowski, T.T. (1985) Soil aeration, flooding and tree growth. *Journal of Arboriculture*, **11**(3), 85–96.

La Dell, T. (1987) Tree and shrub seeding. *Landscape Design*, **168**, 53–6.

Macpherson, R. (1979) The control of weeds in young trees. *Arboricultural Journal*, **3**, 466–9.

Marrs, R.H.; Owen, L.D.C.; Roberts, R.D. and Bradshaw, A.D. (1982) Tree Lupin: an ideal nurse crop for land restoration and amenity plantings. *Arboricultural Journal*, **6**(3), 161–70.

Matthews, W.E. (1979) New advances in tree planting and after care. In *Tree Growth in the Landscape* (ed. S.E. Wright and G.P. Buckley) Wye College. London.

Megginson J.R. (1984) *Successful Establishment of Farmland Amenity Tree Planting Schemes – the Case for Increased Levels of Maintenance. Aspects of Applied Biology 5. Weed Control and Vegetation Management in Forests and Amenity Areas.* Assc. of Applied Biologists, Warwick.

Mitchell, A.F. (1973) *Replacing Elm in the Countryside.* Forestry Commission Leaflet 57. HMSO, London.

Newman, R. (1984) Selective Lifting. *GC & HTJ Spt*, **7**, 18–19.

Partyka, R.E. (1982) The ways we kill a plant. *Journal of Arboriculture*, **8**(3), 57–66.

Pepper, H.W. (1982) *Rabbit Control – Phostoxin.* DOE Arboricultural Advisory Note 43/82/WILD.

Pepper, H.W. and Williams, R.V. (1982) Plastic mesh for urban trees. *Arboricultural Journal*, **6**(3), 211–16.

Roberts, B.P. (1977) The response of urban trees to abiotic stress. *Journal of Arboriculture*, **3**(4), 75–8.

Robinson, D.W. (1981) Chemical weed control in ornamental horticulture. In *Horticulture for the People*, *Acta Horticulturae* 105, pp. 35–9.

Robinson, D.W. (1987) Weed control in amenity plantings. In *The Scientific Management of Vegetation in the Urban Environment* (eds P.R. Thoday and D.W. Robinson) *Acta Horticulturae* 195.

Vaecenak, A.J. and Herrington, L.P. (1974) Estimation of water use in landscape trees. *Journal of Arboriculture*, **10**(12), 313–19.

Weatherell, J. (1957) The use of nurse species in the afforestation of upland heaths. *Quarterly Journal of Forestry*, **51**, 298–304.

Wright, T. (1982) Mulches and weed control. *Landscape Design*, **140**, 27–9.

CHOICE OF SPECIES, STOCK SIZE AND STOCK TYPE

Anderson, M.L. (1961) *The Selection of Tree Species.* Oliver and Boyd.

Gerhold, H.D. and Sacksteder, C.J. (1982) Better ways of selecting trees for urban plantings. *Journal of Arboriculture*, **8**(6), 145–53.

Gordon, A.G. and Rowe, D.C.F. (1982) *Seed Manual for Ornamental Trees and Shrubs.* Forestry Commission Research and Development Paper 59.

Gosling, P.G. (1984) *Dormant tree seed and their pre-sowing treatment.* DOE Arboricultural Advisory Note 56/84/SEED.

Goodall, R.A. and Gundry, C.S. (1982) The Long Ashton Clonal Selection Scheme for Trees and Shrubs. *Arboricultural Journal*, **6**(1), 9–12.

Kendle, A.D. and Gilbertson, P. (1986) Too much variety. *GC & HTJ*, **199** (20).

McVean D.N. (1966) Establishment of native trees and shrubs on Scottish nature reserves by direct seed sowing. *Scottish Forestry*, **20**, 26–36.

Mitchell, A. (1985) Trees for towns and cities. *Arboricultural Journal*, **9**(4), 271–8.

Reynolds, E.R.C.(1980) *Tree Roots and Foundations.* Arboricultural research note. 24/80. Forestry Commission.

Spencer, H.A. (1985) Container grown tree seedlings – a forestry technique for arboriculture. *Arboricultural Journal*, **9**(1), 57–60.

Taylor, C. (1977) Street tree planning. *GC & HTJ*, 16th September.

Thoday, P.R. (1982) Amenity trees for the future *Arboricultural Journal*, **6**(3), 175–82.

Winter, H. (1981) Cheaper trees. *GC & HTJ*, 8th May.

WEED CONTROL METHODS

Association of Applied Biologists (1984) *Aspects of Applied Biology 5. Weed Control and Vegetation Management in Forests and Amenity Areas.* Assc. of Applied Biologists, Warwick.

Bulmer, P.G. (1983) Maintenance of tree and shrub areas by local authorities with particular reference to weed control. MSc thesis (unpublished). Wye College. University of London.

Davies R.J. (1884) *Weed Control for Amenity Trees on Man Made Sites. Aspects of Applied Biology 5. Weed Control and Vegetation Management in Forests and Amenity Areas.* Assc. of Applied Biologists, Warwick.

Davison, J.G. (1983) Weed control in newly planted amenity trees. In *Tree Establishment*. (ed. P.R. Thoday) University of Bath.

Lane, P.B. (1984) *Chemical Weeding – Hand Held Direct Applicators.* DOE Arboricultural Advisory Note 53/84/WS.

Lane P.B. (1984) *Direct Herbicide Application by Weedwiper. Aspects of Applied Biology 5. Weed Control and Vegetation Management in Forests and Amenity Areas.* Assc. of Applied Biologists, Warwick.

MacKenzie, J.M., Thomson, J.H. and Wallen, K.E. (1976) *Control of Heather by 2,4-D.* Forestry Commission leaflet 64.

Marrs R.H. (1984) *Control of Some Woody Weeds in Nature Reserves. Aspects of Applied Biology 5. Weed Control and Vegetation Management in Forests and Amenity Areas.* Assc. of Applied Biologists, Warwick.

McCavish, W.J. and Insley, H. (1981) *Herbicides for Use with Broadleaved Trees.* DOE/Arboricultural Advisory and Information Service, Arboricultural Research Note 27.

NPTC (1987) *Pesticides Application.* National Proficiency Tests Council, National Agricultural Centre, Stoneleigh.

Palmer, C. (1983) *Weed Strategies for Hardwoods.* Forestry and British Timber, April.

Palmer, C.G. and Reid, D.F. (1984) *Control of Woody and Herbaceous Weeds in Forestry with Dicambra Formulations and Mixtures. Aspects of Applied Biology 5. Weed Control and Vegetation Management in Forests and Amenity Areas.* Assc. of Applied Biologists, Warwick.

Roberts, H.A. (Ed) (1982) *Weed Control Handbook: Principles.* Blackwell Scientific Publications, Oxford.

Scott, R. and Marrs, R.H. (1984) *Impact of Japanese Knotweed and*

Methods of Control. Aspects of Applied Biology 5. Weed Control and Vegetation Management in Forests and Amenity Areas. Assc. of Applied Biologists, Warwick.

Shaw M.W. (1984) Rhododendron ponticum – *Ecological Reasons for the Success of an Alien Species in Britain and Features that may Assist in its Control. Aspects of Applied Biology 5. Weed Control and Vegetation Management in Forests and Amenity Areas.* Assc. of Applied Biologists, Warwick.

Simcox, J.M. (1984) *Use of Controlled Droplet Application Systems for Herbicide Applications. Aspects of Applied Biology 5. Weed Control and Vegetation Management in Forests and Amenity Areas.* Assc. of Applied Biologists, Warwick.

Tabbush, P.M. (1984) *Experiments on Heather Control. Aspects of Applied Biology 5. Weed Control and Vegetation Management in Forests and Amenity Areas.* Assc. of Applied Biologists, Warwick.

Tabbush, P.M. and Sale, J.S.P. (1984) *Experiments on the Chemical Control of* Rhododendron ponticum. *Aspects of Applied Biology 5. Weed Control and Vegetation Management in Forests and Amenity Areas.* Assc. of Applied Biologists, Warwick.

Thoday, P.R. (Ed) (1980) *Weed Control in Amenity Plantings.* Conference Proceedings, University of Bath.

Tuley, G. (1984) *Trees in Shelters Do Need to be Weeded. Aspects of Applied Biology 5. Weed control and vegetation management in forests and amenity areas.* Assc. of Applied Biologists, Warwick.

Wild, C.J.C. (1984) *Control of Couch Grass in Ornamanetal Plantings with Alloxydim Sodium. Aspects of Applied Biology 5. Weed Control and Vegetation Management in Forests and Amenity Areas.* Assc. of Applied Biologists, Warwick.

13 THE MANAGEMENT OF WOODY PLANTS: INDIVIDUAL AND SPECIMEN PLANTS

13.1 Introduction

This chapter is devoted to describing the management and resource requirements of trees and shrubs grown as individual or specimen plants. They are an important and identifiable component of many contemporary landscapes, both urban and rural. Wide-spaced standard trees in grass or hard surfaces and street-side trees are the most common examples.

Justification for separate discussion of this particular landscape component goes beyond the fact that it has its own recognizable identity. The very isolation of these individual elements makes them vulnerable to physiological and other stresses which apply less forcefully to plants located in groups or communities. This vulnerability is especially marked during the establishment phase. It is these aspects in particular that are reviewed here, but inevitably the vast majority of the appropriate detail has been covered in earlier chapters. Chapter 12 in particular will be found to contain all of the appropriate references.

Precise definition of some landscape components presents problems. This particular component is no exception. For practical reasons, it has been decided to include individual plants, which, although not strictly isolated because they are widely spaced in 'groves' or groups, are nevertheless remote from their neighbours. This independence is such that they do not appear to interact with or benefit from their nearest neighbours during the post-establishment or early adult phases of the life cycle. For example, they cannot benefit from the mutual shelter effects which develop in mass plantings. However, isolation works both ways, since widely-spaced invidual woody plants, once established, are free from the stresses caused by competing neighbours.

13.2 Other stresses

There are three other important stresses to which reference should be made. These are reviewed in the paragraphs which follow.

HERBACEOUS COMPETITION

Because of their solitary nature, specimen and widely-spaced plants are commonly located in swards rather than in either beds or substantial areas of bare ground. They are, therefore, particularly vulnerable to inadequate weed control. The bulk of failures in modern standard tree plantings occur where the trees and shrubs are located in mown or unmown swards. If planted at wide spacings into swards, smaller trees, such as whips, suffer from both checked growth and an extremely high failure rate. They are also highly vulnerable to damage from maintenance activities.

DAMAGE FROM MAINTENANCE OPERATIONS

Individual plants in grass are obstacles, as far as mowing is concerned, and are therefore liable to damage by mowing machinery. Whilst larger plants are subject to accidental knocks and 'barking', smaller plants, particularly those in rough grass, may be mown by inattentive operators.

Spraying to control vegetation around small or low-branched individuals can easily cause damage, particularly if competing growth is tall.

Control measures, such as sickling or strimming around the base of standards, readily damages young bark.

Grazing animals are the chief hazard to woody plants in grassland which is controlled by stock.

VANDALISM

Isolated plants are often the normal targets of those whose aim is to do deliberate damage. Experience has shown that isolated individuals or groups of standard trees suffer from far more vandalism than similar plants grouped in beds or grown as part of mass plantings. Street trees are notoriously vulnerable to vandalism.

Research has shown that much of the damage attributed to vandalism is often really the result of a combination of wind and poor management. In particular damage to the trunk though tie strangulation and stake or guard abrasion forms a weak point where breakage can easily happen.

The Aboricultural Advisory Service advocates a system of low staking to make vandalism less damaging. This is said to spread the forces of any pulling action so that the tree bends rather than snaps at the pivotal point of the top tie.

Where vandalism of trees does occur, it is often as a result of children's play. There is some justification for the claim that it is one of the functions of modern landscapes to support and allow such play. At Thamesdown in Swindon planting around children's playgrounds consists of vigorous species, such as willow and popular, which can be legitimately 'vandalized' in the course of play.

POST-ESTABLISHMENT OPERATIONS AND RESOURCE
REQUIREMENTS

Once established, well sited individual or specimen woody plants are likely
to be relatively maintenance free for much of their adult lives.

Treatment of the over-mature and senile specimen plants has already
been mentioned in the section devoted to the chief operations involved in
managing group plantings of amenity trees and shrubs during the post-
establishment phase. Tree work to preserve often mature specimens can be
particularly important for specimen trees.

The intensive post-establishment inputs of thinning, which close-spaced
plantings require, are not normally needed. For example, a street tree or
specimen tree in grass, which has established after, say, five years, may
need no further attention at all for the next hundred years or more.
However, even the best specimens do incur a maintenance cost indirectly,
although the actual plant husbandry requirements may be negligible. This
is mainly due to the need to:

- Ensure that these large plants are safe;
- Deal with the leaf litter that they produce; and
- Attend to areas where grass has been shaded out.

SAFETY

Trees are large, tall 'structures' which, sooner or later, are bound to
become mechanically weak and therefore dangerous. The mechanical
strength of a tree deteriorates in old age and also through other factors
which affect its health, such as the entry of decay organisms, damage to the
tree, local ground disturbance, poor soil conditions, etc. Amenity Managers who are responsible for mature trees, particularly in urban areas,
therefore, need to ensure that trees will not damage adjacent property or
passers-by. The best and usual way of making sure that trees are safe, and
of identifying work that needs to be done to them, is through regular and
systematic tree inspections. In this respect the management of trees is
similar to the care of children's play equipment. Managers have the same
legal and moral responsibility to carry out regular inspections and immediate repairs in both cases. The subject is considered in greater depth in
the section on tree communities.

**13.3
Post-establishment
resource requirements**

It is difficult to generalize about the cost of any kind of tree work, because
trees vary so much in size, condition, ease of access, and so on. Although
some reasonably representative figures are given later in this chapter,
readers should be aware that in their own particular cases resource requirements and therefore costs may be quite different.

13.4
The challenge of the
re-establishment phase

From the stresses described earlier it is clear that isolated woody plants usually suffer more from biotic and man-made stresses during the establishment period than do close-planted trees and shrubs. Successful establishment and development is therefore more difficult in these situations. What can a manager do to improve the chances of success? The response to this question is reviewed in the following paragraphs.

13.5
Improvement options

GENERAL REVIEW

In many situations it may be cost-effective to establish plants in groups or masses rather than individually.

Wherever possible trees should not be isolated in mown grass, but – for their own biological well being and for the sake of easy mowing – should be positioned in beds with or without ornamental or non-competitive ground cover or understorey layers. It appears that it may be feasible and cost-effective in some cases to establish what are intended to be specimen trees by:

● Planting in beds initially;
● Then thinning out or removing unwanted plants once establishment of the trees is satisfactory, and
● Finally undersowing back to grass if a 'trees in grass' effect is required.

Far better establishment and less vandalism, and hence lower replacement costs, are likely to result from such a strategy. If smaller tree-planting stock is used, more shapely and naturally formed specimens are likely to result than from standards inserted into grass, although it is important to get the spacing and thinning regimes correct.

Plants usually do relatively well in paved areas if the substrate beneath is root penetrable and provides adequate moisture and nutrients, since the hard surface can help in preventing compaction of the root zone. Siting individuals in hard-surfaced areas is therefore often biologically preferable to siting them in grass or in beds, if maintenance of the latter is likely to be neglected.

Where fencing of transplants is necessary to exclude animal pests or grazing animals, larger areas of regular shapes are cheaper to fence. This is another reason for massing or concentrating woody plantings where feasible.

Other specific improvement considerations are reviewed in the paragraphs which follow.

CHOICE OF PLANTING STOCK

Wherever possible, physiologically juvenile transplants should be used, since these will establish faster and more vigorously than older, larger and less physiologically adaptive stock. Such plants are well known to outgrow more rapidly the early period of intense vulnerability to stress. They are also likely to produce a more natural and wind-adapted form.

CHOICE OF SPECIES; SPECIAL CARE

Individuals planted in difficult sites should be treated with special care, because of the extra stresses to which they are usually subjected. For example, more severe damage due to exposure is likely to be experienced by an isolated specimen than by group plantings. Where large specimens are to be planted to achieve impact and to avoid vandalism, species which are known to transplant badly as mature specimens should be avoided. An example of the latter is birch.

PROTECTION

The use of tree shelters is cost-effective in most cases where isolated trees or shrubs are to be established. Shelters protect plants from exposure,

Table 13.1   The management of individual and specimen plants: standard tree establishment – estimated resource requirements

Source	Operation	SMV	Unit
W	Plant standard tree	33.00	1 no
	heavy standard tree	75.00	1 no
	extra heavy standard tree, double staked	83.00	1 no
Sh	Plant standard tree	41.50	1 no
	heavy standard tree	56.00	1 no
	1.8 m high tree	11.00	1 no
	2.7 m high tree	25.00	1 no
FMH	Fertilizer Application (Top Dress)	2.40	1 no
W	Fertilizer Application (Top Dress)	0.12[1]	1 no
	Weed control		
W	Knapsack spray around standard trees in grass	1.36	1 no
K	Spray round 'obstruction'	0.19	1 no
FMH	Weed around trees (Knapsack Sprayer and guard)	0.30	1 no
	Stakes and Ties		
W	Check and replace if necessary	1.43	1 no
W	Restake	10.50	1 no
FMH	Check stakes and trees (blocks of trees)	0.60	1 no
L	Stake tree	4.60	1 no
L	Tie tree	2.00	1 no
D	Remove stake	7.00	1 no
L	Survey trees	1.60	1 no
D	Erect tree guard and stapling	4.00	1 no

Note: [1] This standard relates to a labour requirement of 6 minutes in the case of a planting density of 50 trees per 100 m^2.

See Table 2.2 on p. 37 for details of sources.

Table 13.2 The management of individual and specimen plants: standard tree establishment, and a comparison of ideal and normal practice resource requirements

Operation	Timing	Year	Comments	Time inputs				Normal practice
				'Ideal' or cost-effective practice minutes per tree				Minutes per tree/10 yrs
				Years 1–3	Years 4–7	Years 8–10	Total	Total
Prepare ground well, including ripping	Dry months if at all possible	1	X	30.0	–	–	30.0	15.0
Prepare tree pit with planting compost and fertilizer	At planting time	1	X if ground conditions are difficult	included in time for planting	–	–	–	–
Prune damaged root and shoots	At planting	1	[]	5.0	–	–	5.0	–
Formative crown pruning	At planting	1	O	5.0	–	–	5.0	–
Plant, stake and tie	Oct-Mar	1		33.0	–	–	33.0	33.0
Mulch	After planting	1	O	3.0	–	–	3.0	–
Control weeds	–	1–10	X	8.4	11.2	8.4	28.0	–
Water	As necessary Apr-Sept	1–3	X if there is any risk of drought	120.0	–	–	120.0	–
Top dress with NPK fertilizer	Apr-June	1–7	O especially if ground is poor	3.0	4.0	–	7.0	–

282

Table 13.2 (cont'd)

Operation	Timing	Year	Comments	'Ideal' or cost-effective practice minutes per tree				Normal practice	
				Years 1–3	Years 4–7	Years 8–10	Total	Minutes per tree/10 yrs	Total
Check stake and ties	At least 4 x/year	Until stake removed		4.2	5.6	–	9.8		–
Remove stake and ties	As soon as tree is wind firm	–		7.0	–	–	7.0		–
Prune out dead or damaged wood	As soon as possible	1–10	O Dead or damaged branches look unsightly and may encourage vandalism	15.0	20.0	15.0	50.0		–
Remove unwanted wood, e.g. 'feathers'	Nov-Feb	1–10	[ ]	15.0	20.0	15.0	50.0		–
							347.8 min		45 min
							(5.8 hrs)		

KEY: X = Essential operation: tree may be severely damaged or die without it.
O = Highly beneficial operation: plant may suffer significant check or loss of growth without it.
[ ] = Worthwhile operation: cost-effective in terms of time taken and benefits produced.

some mechanical damage, herbicide spray and many animals. Small, short shelters can be used for shrubs. The lighter coloured more visible shelters may be useful in acting as markers for plants in isolated or slightly over-grown situations. However, in some situations they are often regarded as likely to attract and encourage vandalism.

13.6 Re-establishment resource requirements

Tables 13.1 and 13.2 indicate the estimated levels of manpower inputs required for the various operations entailed in the effective re-establishment of specimen trees. The cost comparison between ideal and normal practice is revealing, but then so too is the effect!

14 THE MANAGEMENT OF WOODY PLANTS: SHRUB PLANTINGS AND BEDS

14.1
Introduction

To some extent the operations and resource requirements involved in the management of shrubs were covered in Chapter 13. However, since guideline figures are available for operations specific to the maintenance of shrub areas, it is clearly appropriate that they should be collated and presented.

One particular class of shrubs which requires separate coverage is roses. Guidelines concerning both the key maintenance operations and the associated resource requirements follow later in this chapter.

14.2
General operations

Unlike trees, which involve relatively few maintenance operations during the mature phase of their lives, amenity shrub plantings are likely to benefit from regular annual care and attention. However, although not to the same degree as trees, they too can experience a reduction in the levels of maintenance during maturity usually without harm.

The principal operations of importance during both the establishment and post-establishment phases are irrigation, pruning, rejuvenation, replacement, pest and disease control, the application of mulches, weed control, fertilizer dressing and litter picking (Baines, 1982). During the mature phase pruning, clipping and coppicing also become important.

Irrigation of established shrub beds is seldom necessary, although it may be valuable during the first year of planting.

PRUNING OF SHRUBS

The traditional practice with many shrub beds has been to clip each individual plant into uniform balls and columns. Not only is this treatment largely unnecessary, but it destroys the natural aesthetic formation of a closed weed-suppressing canopy.

Most shrubs need very little pruning, with the exception of the removal of diseased or damaged wood. Some specimens will give a better floral, foliage or stem colour display if they are cut back yearly or bi-annually. The time of year that this pruning should be performed will depend on variables such as the flowering time and whether the best display occurs on first year or older stems (Brown, 1972). As a general rule vigorous species are better coppiced to just above ground level rather than being simply trimmed.

Formative pruning should not be necessary as long as the bed is well designed for the site. If the plants have to be limited in terms of shape and size this should be done with sympathy for the habit of the plant. Summer pruning can serve to reduce the vigour of the regrowth whereas winter pruning usually makes the regrowth vigorous.

REJUVENATION

Shrubs that have become over-mature and senile can often be rejuvenated by a once-over complete coppice treatment. On poor soils, fertilizing and irrigation will aid the regrowth, but on most sites this will be unnecessary (Thoday, 1982).

REPLACEMENT

If possible shrub beds should be designed to contain plants that have similar lifespans and respond equally well to coppicing. Some species, notably many of the small Genistas and Cytisuses, can be relatively short-lived and will die out before the rest.

Losses also occur in severe winters when plants, regarded as hardy, are exposed to temperatures below their limit. Many broad-leaved evergreens, such as *Hebe*, are particularly susceptible. If the surrounding shrubs are not cramped, replacements may be necessary.

Shrub beds are often planted at high densities to give a good initial impact and cover. The use of short-lived plants in such scheme can be useful to remove the need for thinning.

PESTS AND DISEASE CONTROL

Most popular modern shrubs are relatively trouble-free and the mixed nature of the plantings usually means that any disease attacks are rarely severe or even noticeable. Certain broad spectrum pathogens, such as Honey Fungus and Phytophthera, can be a problem as they can attack most of the plants in a bed.

Mulches may need to be renewed if they decay or blow away and if their continued presence is biologically and aesthetically desirable. This is most likely in more open plantings or those which are periodically opened up for seasonal or functional reasons, for example deciduous shrub beds, beds of shrubs stooled for winter bark effects and formal rose beds.

WEED CONTROL

Hoeing, mulching and other physical methods of weed control are often employed in shrub beds. Certain weeds can be major problems, particularly those that cannot be controlled by mechanical means such as Ground Elder and couch. Careful spot applications of glyphosate will eradicate these. Bindweed can be a problem because it is difficult to separate from the foliage of the shrubs. Placing canes amongst the plants often encourages the bindweed to grow up above the shrubs where a dose of herbicide can be applied quite easily.

Regular spray applications of residual weed killer can be dificult to undertake amongst established shrubs, because walking at a steady pace to ensure an even dosing is difficult. Granular residuals, although more expensive, are easier to apply.

Sometimes the shrubs themselves can become awkward weeds, if they sucker invasively. Spot treatments of herbicide or sometimes flail mowing can be used to control the spread of suckers.

FERTILIZER DRESSING

Usually this practice is most valuable when the plants are growing. When mature it can be desirable to limit growth and often the best display of flowers or leaf colours occurs on slightly nutrient deficient soils.

**14.3
Estimated resource
requirements**

Tables 14.1 and 14.2 display a range of guideline figures covering the fertilizer application, mulching and pruning operations.

An assessment of the average annual labour inputs required to sustain shrub plantings over 20 years indicates that the five most important operations are rejuvenation, pruning, litter picking, replanting and handweeding. Table 14.3 displays the estimates in full. The overall resource requirements can certainly be reduced by the use of herbicides.

**14.4
Bedding roses**

Traditional rose beds look bare and, to some people, ugly for some five months of the year. Furthermore, if properly cared for, they are relatively labour intensive. since there is still a demand for such landscape features it is important that they should be managed as cost-effectively as possible.

OPERATIONS AND RESOURCE REQUIREMENTS

Table 14.4 provides guidelines concerning the type and frequency of operations and the associated labour requirements.

Planting up bare soil beneath formal rosebeds with a low evergreen groundcover, such as *Stachys*, is an approach used by the Natioinal Trust

Table 14.1   The management of wood plants: applying fertilizers and mulches to planted areas – estimated resource requirements

Source	Operation	SMV	Unit
	Fertilizer Application		
W	Application to total ground area in densely planted shrub by hand		
	a) Housing sites (Complex, small beds)	12.00	100 m^2
	b) Other	6.00	100 m^2
Sh	Application of fertilizer to garden areas	23.92	100 m^2
K	Application of fertilizer by hand	5.09	100 m^2
FMH	Application of fertilizer to shrub blocks	2.40	100 m^2
D	Application of fertilizer pellets	12.00	100 m^2
	Mulch Application		
W	Application to total ground area in densely planted shrub beds	90.00	100 m^2
Sh	Spread mulch (includes barrowing up to 50 yd)	233.20	100 m^2
K	Apply mulch	96.30	100 m^2
D	Mulch	120.00	100 m^2

See Table 2.2 on p. 37 for details of sources.

Table 14.2   The management of woody plants: pruning operations – estimated resource requirements

Source	Operation	SMV	Unit
Sa	Shrubs: prune, clear and dispose of cuttings	530.00	100 no
W	Shrubs: shape and cut out dead wood	380.00	100 no
Sh	Shrubs: prune and 'thin out': from 1′ – >8′	150.00 – 1,400.00	100 no
D	Shrubs: prune: secateurs	200.00	100 no
D	Lavender bush: clip	240.00	100 m^2
D	Shaped holly: clip from – ground	13.00	10 m^2
	– ladder	93.00	10 m^2
D	Laurels: prune	11.00	1 no
D	Rhododendrons: prune and paint cuts	43.00	1 no
Sa	Young tree: prune, clear and dispose of cuttings	7.90	1 no
W	Whips: cut out dead wood	400.00	100 no
FMH	Newly planted willows: coppice and chainsaws	12.00 min	100 m^2

See Table 2.2 on p. 37 for details of sources.

and others to retain a traditional feel, whilst at the same time reducing many of the maintenance demands.

Traditional hybrid roses usually need many inputs to maintain their long season of floral display. Feeding is required on a yearly basis at least. These

Table 14.3 The management of woody plant communities: estimated resource requirements[1]

Operation	Annual frequency	SMV per m²	% of area treated annually	In 100 m² bed area treated annually per m²	Total SMV per 100 m² annually
Spray residual herbicide	1	0.45	10%	10	4.50
Spot treat with applicator	1	0.15	15%	15	2.20
Spot treat with knapsack	1	0.45	15%	15	6.80
Handweed	1	0.80	15%	15	12.00
Fertilize 1/10 years + 10%/year	1	0.07	10%	10	0.70
Prune	1	5.00	7%	7	35.00
Remove dead plants	1	2.00	1%	1	2.00
Replant 1–3 plants/m²	1	15.00	1%	1	15.00
Rejuvenate[2] 1/20 yrs	1	10.00	5%	5	50.00
Apply mulch	1	1.00	7%	7	7.00
Scavenge	6	0.05	100%	100	30.00
					165.20

= or 2.75 hrs[3]

@ £7/hour=19.25/100 m²/yr

or £1.925/ha/yr

NB. No allowances factor included in these totals.

Notes: [1] The data source for the operation, frequencies and SMV's is Skelmersdale New Town.
[2] 'Rejuvenation' involves pruning hard or coppicing to ground level.
[3] An annual labour requirement of 2.75 hours per 100 m² represents a cost of approximately £19.25, i.e. £1925 per hectare. (1985 prices)

Table 14.4 The management of amenity planting: bedding roses and estimated resource requirements

Source	Operation	Typical annual frequency of operation: no of occasions	SMV	Unit	Typical annual labour inputs: minutes per 100 m² (based on 400 plants per 100 m²)/Yr
Sa	Deadhead	2 × per year	36.0	100 no	288
D	Deadhead	2 × per year	110.0	100 no	880
Sh	Summer prune	1 × per year	90.0	100 no	360
D	Annual prune	1 × per year	114.00–278.0	100 no	450–1100
Sh	Annual prune	1 × per year	130.0	100 no	520
Sa	Prune	1 × per year	143.0	100 no	570
W	Trim bed edges	12 (every other mowing)	23.0	100 m	110–550*
W	Half moon bed edges	2 × per year	80.0	100 m	64–320
W	Fertilize beds by hand	1 × per year	12.0	100 m²	12
W	Mulch	1 × per year	90.0	100 m²	90
M	Spray for pests or diseases	2 × per year	30.0	100 no	240
W	Knapsack spray weeds	2 × per year	32.5	100 m²	65
W	Handweed	1 × per year	92.0	100 m²	92
H	Hoe light weed	2 × per year	60.0	100 m²	120
Sh	Bedding roses: prune (HT, FLB)		130.0	100 no	
D	Bedding roses: prune (HT, FLB)		114.00–278.0	100 no	

* Depends upon shape of bed

TYPICAL ANNUAL TOTAL IN THE ORDER OF = 1800

See Table 2.2 on p. 37 for details of sources.

AN EXAMPLE : MODERN APPROACH TO THE MAINTENANCE OF ROSE BEDS
Shrub roses at 0.5 m to 1 m centres in 100 m² (10 m × 10 m) bed in grass
The Features to be maintained are:

– 100 m² of rose bed
– 40 metres of bed: grass edge

The estimated annual labour requirements are:
– Maintenance of rose bed which is the same as maintenance
  of a normal shrub bed, say   213 min per 100 m²
– Maintenance of edges (2 sprays, half moon 1–2 × per year)
  @ 0.75 min per metre   30 min per 40 m

ANNUAL TOTAL   243 min for whole bed
                                                              i.e. = 4 hours per rose bed per year

plants typically have low resistances to certain fungal diseases, particularly mildew and black spot. Consequently spraying may be necessary more than once a year. When establishing a new bed it is wise to obtain advice on the latest and most disease-resistant cultivars which can be used.

One of the most demanding maintenance inputs of traditional rosebeds is pruning. In the winter the beds receive an important overall structural pruning, cutting the main stems back to selected strong buds. Omitting to do this can result in large, woody and poorly flowering plants. Additional pruning is often given in the summer to remove dead flower heads and to prolong the display.

The formal spacing and design of traditional rosebeds can mean that a careful policy of replacement of dead or failing stock is necessary to preserve the design.

ALTERNATIVES

Compared with traditional bedding roses there are many highly attractive shrub roses and modern ground cover plants (Thomas, 1970) which are quite undemanding in that they do not require regular pruning, dead heading and so on. Shrub roses can be more than satisfactory substitutes for formal bedding roses in some situations.

References   Baines, J.C. (1982) Success with plants in housing rehabilitation. *Landscape Design*, **137**, 18–19.

Brown, G.E. (1972) *The Pruning of Trees, Shrubs and Conifers*. Faber and Faber. London.

Thoday, P.R. (1982) Ground cover – factors determining its success. In *Cost Effective Amenity Landscape Management*, (eds P.R. Thoday and C.H. Addison) HEA Conference Proceedings. HEA, Bridgewater.

Thomas, G.S. (1970) *Plants for Ground Cover*. Dent, London.

Further reading   GENERAL

Baines, J.C. (1982) Shrub planting – techniques for successful establishment. In *Cost Effective Amenity Landscape Management*. HEA Conference Proceedings, (eds P.R. Thoday and C.H. Addison) Cannington College, Somerset.

Boddy, F. (1986) The low-down on ground cover. *Horticulture Week*, 28th February.

Hyde, N. and Quinn, A.C.M. (1970) Trees, shrubs, groundcover plants and climbers for informal landscaping in areas of natural beauty or amenity. *Planning for Amenity, Recreation and Tourism*, **2**(3). An Foras Forbartha. Dublin. 1.

Nielsen, P.A. and Wakefield, R.C. (1978) Competitive effects of turf grass on the growth of ornamental shrubs. *Agronomy Journal*, **1**, 39–42.

ROSES

Allen, E.F. (1979) Fungicide and insecticides for roses. *The Rose Annual*, RNRS, St Albans, pp. 20–24.

Allen, E.F. (1980) Practical experience with pulverized bark mulch. *The Rose Annual*, RNRS, St Albans, pp. 13–15.

Brooke, H. (1976) Roses and ground cover. *The Garden, the Journal of the Royal Horticultural Society*, **101**(6), 310–15.

Coles, S. (1982) The garden at Mottisfont Abbey. *The Garden, the Journal of the Royal Horticultural Society*, **107**(8), 303–7.

Garelick, P. (1987) Tomorrow's roses. *Horticulture Week*, 3rd July.

Gibsen, M. (1979) Pruning roses. *The Rose Annual*, RNRS, St Albans, pp. 31–4.

Lucas-Phillips, C.E. (1979) Roses in difficult places. *The Rose Annual*, RNRS, St Albans, pp. 29–30.

Roberts, L. (1980) Chemical weed control in roses. *The Rose Annual*, RNRS, St Albans, pp. 26–7.

Toogood, A. (1978) A fresh look at ground cover. *The Rose Annual*, RNRS, St Albans, pp. 93–4.

Welsh, D. (1980) City roses. *The Garden, the Journal of the Royal Horticultural Society*, **105**(10), 278–80.

15 THE MANAGEMENT OF WOODY PLANTS: HEDGES

**15.1
Introduction**

The levels of maintenance of hedges are primarily determined by functional and locational considerations; those of rural hedges usually being lower than for more formal hedges in prestigious settings.

**15.2
Maintenance
operations**

The chief maintenance operations consist of:

1. Various methods and frequencies of cutting, including laying and coppicing (Brooks, 1975);
2. Spraying with growth retardants in certain urban or formal areas as a partial or complete substitute for cutting (Einert, 1973);
3. Gapping-up (Brooks, 1975).

**15.3
Hedge cutting:
methods, frequencies
and resource
requirements**

The methods and frequencies of hedge cutting are many and vary according to the type, age, length or area and function of the hedge. Several specialist advisory publications exist covering both manual and mechanical cutting techniques. The chief techniques are:

1. Annual trimming by hand, using a billhook, 'slasher', shears or secateurs;
2. Annual or even more frequent mechanical trimming, for example in the case of privet hedges. A tractor mounted flail or preferably a reciprocating cutter is appropriate for rural and large-scale projects. Lighter duty hand-operated machine cutters are more appropriate for smaller scale urban sites.
3. Periodic facing back of older and taller hedges either manually or mechanically. Where the vegetation to be cut is 3 years or more old, a shape saw is to be preferred.
4. Rotational coppicing of species which freely regenerate from the 'stools', using a mechanically-powered shape saw;

5.   Rotational laying and layering.

The system best adopted for pruning a particular species of hedge plant depends not just on its growth rate but also upon the formality, or otherwise, of the plant and of the desired hedge, and the lateral spread of the plant. The timing and frequency of cut depend on aspects such as whether the hedge is to flower and how it tolerates occasional hard cutting back. Foliage type is also important: deciduous species are usually cut in winter, evergreens in spring so that new growth can rapidly cover the cuts. Large-leaved plants can appear lacerated if cut mechanically and may have to be pruned back to leaf nodes using secateurs. Growth habit and frequency of cut can also affect the ease of maintenance, and hence the time inputs required.

Rural hedges composed of native species are typically cut much less frequently because the finished appearance is less important. The most common method of rural hedge cutting now involves using a tractor-mounted flail arm. The appearance immediately following such treatment can be startling, particularly if the hedge has long been neglected and is cut back hard.

Traditional methods of hedge laying are making a comeback in some parts of the country. Specialist craftsmen are increasingly available to undertake this work, as well as members of volunteer conservation groups.

Tables 15.1 to 15.3 inclusive, which follow, provide useful guidelines on the resources required to maintain both urban and rural hedges according to the frequency of cut specified. Table 15.4 indicates the extent to which economies of scale exist in maintaining long, as distinct from short, lengths of hedge. Such economies do not apply where the vertical height of a hedge is increased.

Table 15.1   The management of rural hedges: estimated resource requirements

Source	Operation	Time	Unit
FMH	Trim to A-shape (6 cuts i.e. 3 each side/length of	36 min	100 linear m
MH	hedge)	1 hr	100 linear m
CRC	Cut to ground level	15–36 hr	100 linear m
D	Lay	91 min	$100 \, m^2$
FMH	Pare with hook and fork into piles	2 hr	100 linear m
VC	Clear brashings	21–42 days	100 linear m
	Hedging – old hedge		
			Relative Cost Index
1983 CRC Flail cut both sides			1
1983 CRC Lay			5–12
1983 CRC Plant new hedge : fenced both sides			9300
: unfenced			3100

See Table 2.2 on p. 37 for details of sources.

Table 15.2   The management of urban hedges: estimated resource requirements

Source	Operation	SMV	Unit
W	Flail (long reach)	7.20	100 m^2
D	Tractor mounted mechanical cutter	14.50	100 m^2
W	Hand shears	249.00	100 m^2
Sh	Hand shears, depending on species	175.00–290.50	100 m^2
D	Secateurs	860.00	100 m^2
W	Tarpen	116.00	100 m^2
K	Tarpen up to @ 1.5 m height	94.00–101.00	100 m^2
	over 1.5 m height	81.18–116.01	100 m^2
D	Trim by hand from steps	700.00	100 m^2

See Table 2.2 on p. 37 for details of sources.

Table 15.5 provides guidelines on the frequency and season of hedge cutting involved for the main hedging species.

15.4 Chemical control of hedges

BENEFITS

Certain growth retardant chemicals have proved to be extremely effective in reducing the need for hedge cutting in urban areas. Dikegulak (as

Table 15.3   The management of hedges: relationship between hedge type, cutting frequency and average annual labour inputs, and estimated resource requirements

Type of hedge and maintenance	No of cuts per 10 Years		Man hrs per 100 m per year (average of 10 years)
	Man hrs per cut per 100 m	No of cuts per 10 yrs	
1. *Thorn or mixed native species*			
a. *Farm sites*			
1 m high – Laid	8.0	1	0.8
– Machine cut (flail)	0.6	5	0.3
b. *Urban locations*			
1 m high – Hand tools (shears)	10.8	30	32.4
– Machine (Tarpen)	4.3	30	12.9
2. *Beech, holly, yew, hornbeam, etc.*			
1 m high – Tarpen, etc.	4.3	20	8.6
2 m high – Tarpen	8.3	20	16.6
3. *Box*			
0.3 m – Hand (shears)	0.7	40	2.8
4. *Leyland cypress, thuja., etc.*			
2 m – Hand (secateurs)	71.7	10	71.7
2 m – Machine (Tarpen)	8.3	10	8.3
3 m – Hand, from steps	93.3	10	93.3

Table 15.4 The cutting of hedges: economies of scale and estimated resource requirements

Operation	Hours per year	Unit
Formal hedge 1.5 m high: cut 4 × per year (e.g. privet)	8	10 m
	50	100 m
Formal hedge 2.5 m high: cut 4 × per year	13	10 m
	95	100 m
Hedge 1.5 m high: cut 1 × per year, e.g. beech	2	10 m
	18	100 m
Hedge 2.5 m high: cut 1 × per year	4	10 m
	30	100 m

Source: Kent County Council.

Atrinal) is the chemical which is normally applied as a foliar spray. Dosage rates and the numbers of applications per year depend on species: normally one or two applications annually are sufficient to reduce the annual need for hedge cutting by up to 50%, depending on the previous cutting frequency. The chemical itself is relatively expensive (@ £38 per litre, 1983), but its use can be readily justified by reductions in labour requirements.

Table 15.5 The frequency and season of hedge cutting according to species selection

Species	Cutting frequency	Season of cut	Growth rate	Comment
Acer campestra	1	Winter	medium	
Buxus sempervirens	3	June-Sept	slow	very formal use
Carpinus betulus	1	Winter	medium	
Chaenomeles japonica	2	May-Winter	med to fast	preserve flowering wood
Cretaegus sp.	2	July-Winter	med to fast	
Cupresso-cyparis leylandii	1/2	July-Apr	very fast	
Euonymus sp.	1	June-Sep	medium	
Fagus sylvatica	1	Late winter	slow to med	retains dead leaves
Forsythia hybrid	2	May-Winter	med to fast	preserve flowering wood
Ilex equifolium	1	July/Aug	slow	
Ligustrum ovalifolium	4	May-Sep	fast	frequent cuts to maintain shape
Lonicera nitida	4/5	May-Sep	fast	
Prunus laurocerasus	1	May-June	slow	careful cutting with secateurs
Thuya plicata	1	March	moderate	
Taxus baccata	1	Winter	moderate	

Source: Wright, (1982).

A QUESTION OF CHOICES. ?

TIMING

Dikegulak is apparently absorbed very rapidly by foliage and this renders it comparatively 'weatherproof'. The timing of applications is, therefore, less critical in regard to weather conditions than is the case with retardants such as maleic hydrazide. Dikegulak is normally applied a few days or weeks after the hedge has been cut, so that sufficient new foliage has developed to absorb the chemical effectively.

Physiologically, one beneficial effect of the chemical is to stimulate the breaking of dormant buds and hence to increase the 'bushiness' of hedges.

In some situations, hedges treated with growth retardant can be left uncut until winter. However, the annual growth is then tougher than it would have been in summer and may require the use of different tools and equipment to cut it. Nonetheless the extra inputs required to deal with this are usually justified by the transfer of a peak summer task to winter, when labour resources are under less pressure.

Table 15.6   The management of hedges: savings gained by using growth retardants – estimated resource requirements

Operation	SMV	Unit	Frequency	Total mins 100 m^2 per year
A) *Cut hedge with Tarpen*	90	100 m^2	4	360
				Total 360
B) *Cut hedge with Tarpen*	90	100 m^2	1	90
Spray with growth regulant	40[1]	100 m^2	1	40
				Total 130
Technique B) takes only 36% the time of technique A)				
A) *Cut hedge with shears*	250	100 m^2	3	750
				Total 750
B) *Cut hedge with shears*	250	100 m^2	1	250
Spray with growth retardent	40	100 m^2	1	40
				Total 290
Technique B) takes 39% of technique A)				

Note: [1] Estimate based on Warrington Development Corporation figure of 32.5 min per 100 m^2 for ground spraying.

Table 15.6 indicates the levels of reductions in resource requirements, which can be achieved where hedges are maintained by a combination of growth retardants and trimming as distinct from solely trimming.

GAPPING UP

The operations of under – or inter-planting may be required to maintain or improve the physical and aesthetic qualities of a hedge. The key to success lies in effective site preparation, especially weed control. This is also the single most important post-planting operation.

References   Brooks, A. (1975) *Hedging – a practical conservation handbook*. British Trust for Conservation Volunteers, Reading.

Einert, A.E. (1973) Evaluating Chemical Pruning for Hedges *Grounds Maintenance*, **8**(1).

Wright, T.W.J. (1982) *Large Gardens and Parks: Maintenance, Management and Design*. Granada, St. Albans

Further reading   Beddall, J.C. (1950) *Hedges for Farm and Garden*. Faber and Faber.

Cameron, A.D. (1984) The biology and history of hedges, *Biologist*, **31**(4), 203–8.

Carter, E.S. (1983) Management of hedgerows and scrub. In *Management of Vegetation*. (ed. J.M. Way) British Crop Protection Council Monograph No. 26. BCPC, Croydon.

Cobham, R.O. (1983) The economics of vegetation management In

Management of Vegetation, (ed. J.M. Way) British Crop Protection Council Monograph No. 26. BCPC, Croydon.

Hall, J. (1978) Management of hedges and hedgerows. *Big Farm Management*, **2**, 29–32.

Hart, J. (1987) Hedges for colour, *Horticulture Week*, 22nd May.

Hooper, M.D. and Holdgate, M.W. (eds) (1986) *Hedges and Hedgerow Trees*. Symposium Proceedings Monks Wood Experimental Station.

Le Lievre, A. (1987) Hedge adventures, *Horticulture Week*, 22nd May.

MAFF (1980) *Managing Farm Hedges*, MAFF leaflet 762. HMSO, London.

Pollard, E., Hooper, M.D. and Moore, N.W. (1974) *Hedges*, New Naturalist series no. 58. Collins, London.

Part Four

The Management of
Other Plants and Plantings

This part deals specifically with four types of plantings, which were not covered in Part Three, namely: climbing and wall plants; herbaceous plants and seasonal bedding plants; container-grown plantings; and ground cover plantings. Each type of planting is described in a separate chapter. Their characteristics, maintenance operations and comparative resource requirements are presented. Both exterior and interior container-grown plantings are covered.

The uses of growth regulants and herbicides in maintaining ground cover plantings are extensively described. Inevitably the close relationship between these maintenance methods and plant selection receives attention.

16

THE MANAGEMENT OF OTHER PLANTS AND PLANTINGS: CLIMBING AND WALL PLANTS

**16.1
Introduction**

Climbing and wall plants specifically exploit the vertical dimension. Many do so extremely effectively, particularly those which are rapid growers. Perhaps because climbing and wall plants fall slightly outside the normal run of planting and maintenance specifications, their potential has tended to be under-exploited, particularly in the public sector. However, a relatively small input of management effort into plant selection, siting, and, most particularly, into the training and support of climbers, can reap large visual rewards, in terms of impact, screening and softening. Thus these plants can be highly cost-effective, in covering features such as walls, fences, screens, trellises, pergolas, etc.

Where the small but essential management inputs required during the life of these plants cannot be guaranteed, climbers are often best replaced by simpler landscape elements.

**16.2
Characteristics**

Most notable amongst the exceptional qualities of some species are:

- Their extreme rapidity of growth, for example *Polygonum baldschuanicum* (Russian Vine), *Clematis montana*, which makes them valuable in quick screening;
- Their self-clinging properties, for example *Parthenocissus* and *Hedera* species, which enable the plants to clothe vertical surfaces in 'two dimensional green', rapidly and with very little trouble;
- The fact that they occupy very little ground space for the impact achieved.

The primary uses made of climbing and wall plants are, of course, based upon their characteristics (Prokter, 1973). They are listed in Table 16.1.

Table 16.1   The management of climbing and wall plants: their uses

- To decorate vertical structures and surface (walls, fences, pergolas, live and dead trees);

- To 'green up' or screen dull, unattractive or ugly objects;

- To provide 'foundation planting' with the object of blending vertical and horizontal surfaces;

- To grow amongst and enliven dull plantings, e.g. hedges;

- To serve as low maintenance ground covers, e.g. *Hedera* spp. (ivys), *Lonicera* spp. (honeysuckles) and *Lathyrus latifolius* (everlasting pea).

**16.3
Cost-effective
operations and
requirements**

If climbing and wall plants are to be used cost-effectively, the considerations and operations described in the following paragraphs need to be borne in mind.

NURTURE

Planting and growing conditions at the foot of walls are notoriously difficult due to the presence of footings, builders' rubble, etc., and because walls tend to deflect rain. Planting pits therefore need to be well prepared and young transplants require special attention in the first few years, particularly irrigation.

PROTECTION

Young climbers are often planted as diminutive slender transplants fastened to a light cane, and as such are very vulnerable to accidental or intentional damage. Among other plants or weeds they are easily overlooked by maintenance staff. If sited at the foot of a wall in hard surfacing, climbers are vulnerable to passing foot traffic. Adequate protection during vulnerable stages of life is, therefore, essential.

SUPPORT AND TRAINING

If climbers or wall plants are intended to clothe or screen a surface, the necessary support to make this possible must be provided. Essential support includes both the physical structure (wires, wall, nails) and skilled manpower to carry out whatever training, tying-in and pruning is required. Some shrubs such as *Pyracantha* can be managed to clothe a surface with only a little pruning and some ad hoc tying in. However, the 'twiners', such as *Lonicera* species, and 'scramblers', such as *Forsythia suspensa*, cannot be expected to do other than sprawl along the ground if not properly

Table 16.2   The management of climbers and wall plants: key operations required by principal species

Species	Vigour rating	Training support, e.g. wire	Needed tying in	Skilled pruning	Comments and cost-effectiveness rating
Self Clingers					
Euonymus fortunei	1	–	–	–	Slow and small but can be attractive
Hedera (Ivy) *spp.*	3	–	–	–	Easy, useful
Hydrangea petriolaris	2	–	–	–	Slow but attractive
Parthenocissus	4	–	–	–	Easy and useful
Twiners & Scramblers					
Clematis jackmanii cvs	3	/	*	/	
montana cvs	4	/	*	–	
Clematis mattopetala, alpina, etc.	2	/	*	–	Can be grown up other climbers to increase their effectiveness
Lonicera spp. (Honeysuckle)	3	/	*	–	
Polygonum (Russian Vine)	5	/	–	–	Best over a large stout structure
Rosa albertine	4	/	/	/	
R. filipes Kiftsgate	5	/	–	–	Best in a large tree
Vitis coignetiae	4	/	*	–	
Vitis vinifera	3	/	*	–	
Wisteria spp.	5	/	*	/	Needs considerable attention on walls etc, but is extremely attractive
Wall Shrubs					
Ceanothus spp.	3	/	/	/	
Cotoneaster horizontalis	1	–	–	–	Very easy and attractive
Forsythia suspensa	2	/	/	–	Useful in shady locations
Garrya elliptica	3	–	–	–	
Jasminum nudiflorum	2	/	/	–	
Magnolia grandiflora	4	–	–	–	Highly attractive
Pyracantha spp.	2–3	/	/	/	
Herbaceous					
Humulus spp. (Hops)	3	/	*	–	Fast growing but can senesce early
Lathyrus Latifolia (everlasting pea)	2	/	*	–	

Key: Plants have been rated on a 1–5 scale for vigour, the most vigorous being 5.
    / Signifies that a particular type of training is needed.
    – Signifies that a particular type of training is not normally needed.
    * Signifies that a particular type of training is not essential, if an informal effect is acceptable or if a plant has plenty of room.

Table 16.3 The management of climbing and wall plants: estimated resource requirements

Source	Operation	SMV	Unit
Sh	Prune and tie back climbing or rambler rose	11.30	1 no
D	Prune wall shrubs and tie in where necessary	74.00	10 m^2
L	Prune climbers and ramblers	22.68	10 m^2
H	Prune rambling rose	9.60	1 no
H	String up rambling rose	2.00	1 no
H	Cut old ties and re-tie remaining shoots to stake, wire or rustic frame work	2.60	1 no

See Table 2.2 on p. 37 for details of sources.

supported and tied in. An eye for the support and training of most species is required. Lack of skill may again be a factor limiting effective use of climbing and wall plants.

Some climbers are extraordinarily vigorous and can produce several metres of extension growth each season – *Polygonum baldschuanicum* and *Rosa filipes*, for example. Many of the well known and much grown species, such as *Clematis montana*, *Lonicera* spp, and *Rosa* 'Albertine', are also relatively vigorous. It is essential, therefore, to grow these plants on structures which are capable of supporting their weight, and in spaces with adequate room to contain them. In contrast they should not be used on small garden fences, or near to other plants which are liable to be smothered, or where climbers can penetrate and damage gutters, roof tiles, etc.

Table 16.4 The management of climbing and wall plants: estimated average life-time resource requirements

Operation	Frequency of operation	Rate in min labour inputs per 10 m² or 1.5 plants	Total resource requirement over 50 years min per 10 m²	Average annual labour requirement
Wiring of wall (wire eyes and wires at 0.5 m spacings)	1 × per 25 yrs	120.00	240.00	4.8
– Planting of new container-grown plant, including pit: 1.5 plants per 10 m² of wall	1 × per 50 yrs	14.60	14.60	3.0
– Mulching	1 × per yr	3.00	150.00	3.0
– Irrigation: for years 1 to 5 inclusive	8 × per yr	7.50	300.00	6.0
– Fertilizing: for years 1 to 5 inclusive	1 × per yr	1.50	7.50	0.2
– Pruning	1 × per yr	7.50	375.00	7.5
– Tying in	1 × per yr	7.50	375.00	7.5
Removal of senile plant	1 × per 50 yrs	90.00	90.00	1.8
		TOTAL	1552.10*	

* This represents, on average, an annual labour input of approximately 31 minutes per 10 m².

Table 16.5   The management of climbing and wall plants: estimated average annual resource requirements for covering different surfaces

Example species	Type of surface covered	Expected average life span years	Average annual labour inputs required per unit area of surface over life span Minutes per 10 m^2
Parthenocissus spp.	Wall covered by a self-clinger (no extra support needed)	50	19.8
Wistaria spp.	Wired wall covered by a 'twiner'	50	31.0
Pyracantha spp.	Wired wall covered by shrub	50	31.0
Lonicera spp.	Chain link fence covered by a 'twiner' (no extra support needed)	50	26.0

N.B. Costs of maintenance, such as pruning and tying up, increase with height above ground and the need to use steps, ladders, etc.

A more cost-effective method, although not always suitable, is to plant the climbers so that they can grow into existing trees, whether dead or alive.

Table 16.2 indicates the main management operations required by a selection of the most popular climbers and wall plants.

PEST AND DISEASE CONTROL

Most climbers are relatively disease-free, although clematis wilt can be a problem. Unfortunately the warm and sheltered microclimate between the plant and the wall often provides a perfect habitat for the build-up of pests such as aphids and red spider mite. Occasional inspections are necessary.

RESOURCE REQUIREMENTS

Tables 16.3 and 16.4 indicate the approximate inputs typically required for the chief maintenance operations. Table 16.5 summarizes the inputs required to manage a range of climbing and wall plants over typical surfaces and to maintain an effective vegetation cover over a wall for 50 years.

References   Prokter, N.J. (1973) *Climbing and Screening Plants*. Faber & Faber, London.

17

THE MANAGEMENT OF OTHER PLANTS AND PLANTINGS: HERBACEOUS PLANTS AND SEASONAL BEDDING DISPLAYS

**17.1
Introduction**

Traditionally, herbaceous plants have been important components of park and garden plantings, notably in features such as borders and bedding schemes. Largely because of their susceptibility to the more persistent residual herbicides, herbaceous plantings can be relatively labour intensive to maintain, and this has tended to discourage their use in modern landscapes (Wright, 1982). Nevertheless, herbaceous plants can and do contribute significantly to landscapes today, chiefly as:

- Providers of colour and seasonal, 'bedding' plant displays;
- Permanent ground cover plantings.

**17.2
Seasonal bedding
displays**

HIGH COST CHARACTERISTICS

Traditionally colour has been brought into private and public landscapes through temporary plantings of flowering and foliage plants: typically the 'annual bedding' of parks departments. However, mass planting of close-spaced, throwaway 'annuals' (actually they are frequently biennials and perennials) to form a floral carpet is expensive for three reasons.

1. The plantings are changed frequently: at least bi-annually and on occasions three times per year. They are therefore expensive in terms of raw materials. The costs of either producing or purchasing plants for frequent replantings is a significant proportion of total bedding costs.
2. The plants are normally massed at very close spacings, in order to form a carpet effect quickly. This entails the use of a lot of plant material per unit area. Planting time is extended because of precise spacings and geometric designs which require marking out.

3. In order to be effective, bedding needs a high level of both husbandry and management. Traditionally these are characteristic of the 'gardenesque' era, involving preparation of a fertile, well-structured planting bed, thorough weed control and effective irrigation, in order to obtain maximum performance from the plants in a short time. The formal planting designs mean that a very small weed cover looks out of place and is intolerable.

EVALUATION

In the search for greater cost-effectiveness it is appropriate to ask two questions:

1. What are the rewards for carrying out this relatively expensive and demanding exercise, especially in the current economic climate? Why have bedding plants at all?
2. If they are to be provided, can the cost of the display be reduced?

There appear to be a number of valid reasons why this traditional, and to some minds anachronistic component should be retained and used in modern landscapes.

1. There is no doubt that the majority of the public still greatly enjoys bedding in its various forms: formal beds, tubs, window boxes, hanging baskets. Since it provides intense 'user satisfaction', it can probably be regarded as providing good value for money, at least on a relatively modest scale.
2. 'A little goes a long way'. Good quality is essential in temporary plantings, but a very small amount can produce a relatively large effect. Small sections of strategically sited bedding can be quite as effective as extensive 'carpets of colour'. They can be used to enliven less exciting plantings, just as a dash of colour can enliven the façade of a building.
3. Bedding helps to give many towns and villages, streets and buildings the essential character for which they are known. It can help to 'sell' them to tourists, visitors and customers, and therefore has an undeniable role to play determining the prosperity of the local inhabitants. Bath, a frequent winner of the 'Britain in Bloom' competition, is an obvious example. There the efforts of both public (parks department) and private (traders and property owners) interests combine in beautifying the city, using street planters, hanging baskets, window boxes and high quality bedding displays. Brighton and Aberdeen are but two other similar examples.

In the private sector numerous pubs, hotels, guest houses and restaurants are adorned with bedding plants, confirming that like other forms of cosmetics customers find them appealing.

There does appear to be scope for using 'instant colour' and throwaway plantings in new and perhaps more cost-effective ways. For example, established evergreen plantings can be 'cheered up' by the introduction of quite small, say 0.5m², areas of colourful annuals, if weed control regimes allow. Such inputs can be very important in institutional landscapes, particularly hospitals with long-stay immobile patients. Temporary plantings can either be conventionally planted into the soil or be introduced in containers as 'wheel in, wheel out' plantings, which may be 'plunged' or used as features in themselves.

It is possible that hardy and half-hardy herbaceous perennials could also be used in this way: grown in containers, brought 'on stage' for the duration of their flowering period and then removed. Gertrude Jekyll employed this technique to fill flowerless gaps in her borders, using such plants as hydrangeas and dahlias.

Just as there is a move amongst those involved in the commercial production of flowering pot-plants to research the use of less heat-demanding species which are cheaper to grow, so the managers may find more cost-effective displays among the hardier and less demanding members of the plant kingdom. Some new hybrid pansies flower for eight months of the year and are winter hardy, needing fewer rotations.

Use of cheap and cheerful hardy annuals, such as poppies, nasturtiums and English marigolds, to produce an annual bloom from seed on underdeveloped or temporarily vacant parts of a landscape may be a possibility. They are known to have particular attractions for children and voluntary groups. Rotovation to produce a bare sward each spring may be the only maintenance required in these informal beds.

17.3
Herbaceous borders
and rockeries

HIGH COST CHARACTERISTICS

Traditionally herbaceous borders and rockeries have been abandoned by many organizations as being too expensive to maintain. However, they are very popular with the public; certainly in many historic and prestige landscapes they will need to be preserved.

PRINCIPAL MAINTENANCE OPERATIONS

Careful design of the features can reduce the maintenance requirements. The principal maintenance operations are weeding, staking, dead heading and pruning, lifting and dividing the plants.

WEED AND PEST CONTROL

Weed control need no longer be one of the most time-consuming tasks in any herbaceous border, thanks to modern chemical control methods. However, most herbaceous plants are not very tolerant of residual herbicides. Lenacil-tolerant species can be selected to produce a herbaceous bed that can be treated by this herbicide, but this may prove too restrictive to the design.

In most cases germinating weed seeds still need to be controlled by mechanical means. Mulches aid in suppressing the germination and make it easier to remove the weeds. Limiting the amount of digging performed, through chemical control of perennial weeds and selection of species that do not need lifting, reduces the germination of soil-borne seed.

Perennial weeds, particularly those which spread rapidly by underground organs, such as couch or ground elder, could devastate herbaceous plantings, requiring almost complete removal of the vegetation, careful soil cleaning, and replanting from fresh. Today systemic herbicides could be used to solve this major problem with ease.

Perennial grasses, such as couch, are easily controlled with alloxydim sodium or other grass killers. Bindweed and other perennial weeds can be controlled by careful spot applications of glyphosate.

Pest and disease attacks on most common herbaceous plants are usually infrequent and not serious. However, some plants are prone to attacks from viruses and eelworms which necessitate removal and burning of the plants and often replacement with resistant species.

STAKING

Staking of herbaceous plants is one of the most labour-intensive operations to be performed in early spring. Many new compact and self-supporting varieties of herbaceous border plants have become available over the last few decades. These should be chosen wherever possible. Sometimes staking is unavoidable. In many historic gardens old, tall varieties may be chosen either because of the desired authenticity of effect, or because they are in keeping with the scale of the whole design. The tradition of backing borders by large evergreen hedges also tends to 'draw up' the plants through lack of light.

LIFTING AND DIVIDING

Lifting and dividing is necessary to keep certain species and varieties growing healthily and flowering well. Otherwise they will tend to lose vigour in the centre of the clump. Lifting the plants, digging and fertilizing the soil, and replanting healthy juvenile offshoots improves the display. These maintenance requirements should not be performed rigidly as a three-year ritual, but rather as and when certain plants seem to require it. Careful choice of species may limit the need for this treatment. As long as the plants are carefully labelled any necessary division can usually be performed in autumn or early winter when there is less need for grass cutting.

DEAD HEADING AND PRUNING

More of a problem is dead heading and pruning to improve the appearance of plants that have finished their floral display. In the case of some early flowering types, senescent flowers are evident as early as July. If they remain untouched, they can to an extent limit the aesthetic impact of the late flowering species.

This maintenance requirement can best be limited by careful design. Plants grouped in large clumps according to their flowering season often give a better effect and can be cut back en masse as required, using shears, a strimmer or even a flail or rotary mower. Many species will quickly regenerate a new hummock of fresh vegetative growth which is visually acceptable. Some may even flower again at the end of the season.

The alternative approach is to select those species which remain attractive even when the flowers have faded, such as many herbaceous geraniums. Late flowering types such as *Anemone japonica*, *Sedum spectabile*, *Schizostylus* and *Scabious* are also good choices.

COST-EFFECTIVENESS OF HERBACEOUS PLANTINGS

The preceeding brief discourse indicates that annual bedding areas and their allies involve high inputs: they are expensive both to produce and to maintain effectively. The achievement of high standards is usually essential if product quality is to be acceptable. Such areas also generate high outputs, in terms of user satisfaction. Thus such features can be justified on the basis that 'a little of what you fancy does you good', even if it is expensive.

It should be noted that Landscape Maintenance Staff usually enjoy working with herbaceous plants, particularly annuals. If their jobs mainly involve the maintenance of grass and woody plants, staff often appreciate the chance to work with different, more popular and colourful plants. Introduction of variety in this way can have a stimulating effect both on staff morale and on the interest and pride taken in tasks as a whole. Furthermore it adds, of course, a new element to on-the-job training. Therefore in many situations, such as the Dudley Hospital and the National Exhibition Centre, even a small amount of work with colourful herbaceous plants seems to be well justified.

LOCATION

The Amenity Manager also needs to ensure that herbaceous plantings are displayed in the most cost-effective way, thereby generating maximum enjoyment at the least cost. Temporary plantings (seasonal bedding displays) are particularly vulnerable to both accidental and deliberate damage and to theft. They therefore need to be sited where risks of losses are minimized and exposure to user appreciation is maximized. Inner urban roundabouts, prestigious city parks and curtilage areas are typical of normally sensible locations for such displays. Often settings of either high quality turf or hard surfacing provide an effective foil.

Because these plantings are largely intolerant of the residual herbicides, such as simazine and Dichlobenil, commonly used in amenity areas, they cannot be incorporated into other plantings unless protective measures have been taken. These measures may include leaving areas untreated, which can be time consuming to organize and supervise; removing areas of treated soil and replacing with untreated, which is suitable for very small areas only; and plunging plants in containers.

17.4
Comparative resource
requirements

SEASONAL BEDDING DISPLAYS

Top quality husbandry throughout the production process is essential to reap adequate benefits from seasonal bedding displays. The visually intense and often formal nature of such plantings often means that very low visible weed populations cannot be tolerated. Thus the Amenity Manager needs to be sure that the necessary resources are available for the proper care of these components before embarking on their establishment.

It has already been noted that traditional temporary plantings are expensive, particularly in terms of plant material and also in the manpower needed to plant, tend and renew them. Establishment of summer bedding produces a labour demand in the late spring to early summer period, conflicting with the initial seasonal requirements for grass mowing and weed control. With the exception of *Pelargonium* and *Helichrysum*, the species used in temporary plantings are not usually tolerant of substantial moisture stress and will not perform satisfactorily in substrates which have developed significant moisture deficits. Irrigation facilities are therefore often essential and must be operated as soon as, and whenever, necessary. This again can entail a significant maintenance burden, particularly, of course, in dry seasons, when containerized plantings prone to drying out have to be tended promptly.

Weed control is not usually a great problem if plantings are on a modest scale, say 1% or less of the total hard and soft landscaped areas. Thorough preparation of planting beds, pre-planting, close spacing of plants, rapid canopy closure and the quick turn-around of plantings usually preclude the need for much weed control. That which is required is normally done by hand, because the crop plants used in these types of display are not tolerant of residual herbicides. Perennial weeds should have been controlled by pre-planting treatments. Most emergent weeds are therefore annuals and are relatively easy to control by hand.

Table 17.1 provides guidelines on the labour inputs required for a range of operations involved in presenting seasonal bedding displays.

HERBACEOUS BORDERS, BEDS AND ROCKERIES

The labour inputs for some of the main operations involved in providing effective herbaceous borders, beds and rockeries are presented in Table 17.2. Comparative estimates of total labour inputs are given in Table 17.3.

17.5
Herbaceous ground
cover

CHARACTERISTICS

Hardly perennial herbaceous plants can provide effective and attractive ground cover in a range of situations. Many are tolerant of low light levels

Table 17.1   The management of herbaceous plants: seasonal bedding displays: estimated resource requirements

Source	Operation	SMV	Unit
Bedding Plants in Open Beds			
Sh	Shape/mound bed after cultivation: pre-planting	149.50	100 m^2
D	Plant from boxes (average size)	35.00	100 no
Sh	Plant from boxes (average size)	42.00	100 no
D	Plant from pots (e.g. geraniums)	53.50	100 no
Sh	Plant from pots (e.g. geraniums)	52.00	100 no
D	Plant bulbs between bedding plants	28.00	100 no
Sh	Plant bulbs between bedding plants	23.60	100 no
Sh	Dead head dahlias	21.00	100 no
Sh	Lifting for re-use, e.g. Geraniums, 'dot plants' (Fuchsia, Abutilon)	299.00	100 m^2
D	Lifting for re-use, e.g. Geraniums, 'dot plants' (Fuchsia, Abutilon)	27.00–70.00	100 no
Sh	Removal of annuals or bulbs	155.50	100 m^2
D	Raking leaves from flower beds, and load	210.00	100 m^2
Sh	Rake and shape beds after removal of bedding plants	101.60	100 m^2
Bedding Plants in Containers			
D	Liquid feeding single standard plants	140.00	100 plants
D	Liquid feeding tub plants	2.00	tub
D	Liquid feeding mixed bedding plants	26.00	100 plants

See Table 2.2 on p. 37 for details of sources.

Table 17.2   The management of herbaceous plants: herbaceous border and beds: estimated resource requirements

Source	Operation	Labour requirement	Unit
RB	Flower beds and borders	18 hours	100 m^2 per yr
RB	Flower beds and borders including production of bedding plants	33 hours	100 m^2 per yr
		SMV	
W	Lift feathered whips by hand	308.00	100 no
D	Lift for storage: *Abutilon*, *Fuchsias*, etc.	70.00	100 no
Sh	Dig out recently planted shrubs prior to replacement	80.00	100 no
Sh	Plant dahlias, geraniums from pots	52.00	100 no
Sh	Plant rock plants from boxes	50.00	100 no
Sh	Plant small shrubs, container grown	200.00	100 no
Sh	Dead head Dahlias, Begonias	21.00	100 no
Sh	Cut back Nepeta	16.84	10 linear m
L	Cut and remove herbaceous	17.50	100 plants
M	Herbaceous border: cut down	465.00	100 m^2
	hoe and weed	194.00	100 m^2
	fork and weed	159.00	100 m^2
Sh	Cultivate flower beds with 3 pronged cultivator	101.60	100 m^2
M	Rockery: hand fork and weed (@ 7/yr)	155.00	100 m^2

See Table 2.2 on p. 37 for details of sources.

Table 17.3 Comparison of annual labour requirements involved in maintaining herbaceous borders, beds and rockeries

Source	Landscape component	Operation	SMV	Unit	Frequency	Total annual labour requirement per 100 m^2
CRC	Herbaceous border					1470 min[1]
						TOTAL = 24.5 hrs[2]
JE	Rockery	weeding and tidying	155	100 m^2	7	1085 min
						TOTAL = 18 hrs
JE	Herbaceous bed	dig over, manure, shape, tidy	681	100 m^2	1	681
		hoe and weed	138	100 m^2	6	828 1509 min
						TOTAL = 25.2 hrs[2]

Source: Based on: Epstein, J. (1978) *Landscape in Housing and the Urban Environment* Institute of Advanced Architectural Studies.

Note:

[1] *Herbaceous Border: Estimated Annual Labour Requirements*
Basic assumption: Plants spaced at 3/m^2 i.e. 300/100 m^2

Season	Operation	Minutes per 100 m^2
Winter	– Lift and split up 0.25 = 25 m^2 = 75 plants @ 150 min/100 no	112
	– Replant 75 @ 100 min/100	75
	– Mulch @ 90 min/100 m^2	90
Spring	– Fertilize @ 10/100 m^2	10
	– Stake say 60/100 m^2	60
Summer	– Hoe and weed × 3 @ 194/100 m^2	582
	– Dead head × 4, 20% = 66 no @ 21 min/100 no	56
Autumn/ Winter	– Cut down @ 465	465
Winter	– Spot treat with paraquat @ 30% but with great care and slowly	20
		Total 1470 min

[2] These estimates compare with a total for a mixture of herbaceous beds and borders of *18 hours*

and drought. They are therefore particularly suitable for certain uses, such as providing low cover under shrubs or in woodland, or in dense shade. Grass is, of course, a form of evergreen herbaceous ground cover.

Unfortunately, few herbaceous plants are evergreen. Furthermore, the appearance of many deciduous herbaceous plants can leave a lot to be desired in winter, since they lack the framework of even deciduous shrubs. The careful design and siting of these elements is therefore important.

The fact that a number of species are tolerant of short-term residual herbicides, such as Lenacil, means that much of the burden of weed control is removed if plantings are established initially in clean ground, free from perennial weeds, and are then kept clean of annuals through the use of a residual.

Herbaceous ground cover is discussed in greater detail in the chapter on Ground Cover and the same management principles apply to small feature plantings of hardy herbaceous perennials. However, the provisos relating to herbicides noted elsewhere in this chapter apply wherever these plants are mixed into other plantings subject to a chemical weed control regime.

17.6
Other uses of
herbaceous plants

It is possible to create and maintain attractive landscapes through the use of native flowering herbaceous plants and bulbs in a variety of situations other than those already described. Two examples follow.

WILD FLOWER MEADOWS

The use of native flowering plants to create wild flower meadows, lawns and even whole gardens has become increasingly popular over the past ten or so years. Some Amenity Managers may look upon such 'flowery meads' as herbaceous plantings contaminated with grass, or as grassland contaminated by weeds! However, the essence of such plantings is that a range of attractive or interesting mono- and dicotyledons are managed as a long-term, self-renewing community. This is achieved through the use of low nutrient substrates and a low-input management regime.

If correctly established, such features have essentially low-maintenance requirements. They can be cost-effective if suitably sited and used. The creation and management of these features has already been discussed.

NATURALIZED BULBS

There are two main uses for naturalized bulbs, in grass and in beds.

Naturalized bulbs in grass can be very attractive and relatively trouble-free to manage, if they are sited with discrimination. Problems can arise if they are located in fertile soils, where grass growth is vigorous. The need to leave their foliage uncut for several weeks in the early growing season can entail mowing problems later on. Where possible, therefore, they are better sited in shady areas of open swards beneath trees (woodland bulbous plants, of course, do particularly well in such locations) or beds, where mowing is not a problem.

The establishment of naturalized bulbs in beds removes the problems of grass mowing mentioned above, but problems of herbicide incompatibility may then be encountered. Propyzamide and alloxydim-sodium are both

Table 17.4   The management of naturalized bulbs: estimated resource requirements

Landscape component	Operation	Time of year	Frequency	Labour input hours	Unit	Comments
Bulbs in Grass						
	Planting: Large (Daffodils) Small (Snowdrops)	Oct–Nov	Once only	45 min	100 no	Popular with children and volunteer groups
	Tidying up of grass after flowering: rotary mower × 2 raking × 2	Late June– Early July	Twice	40 min	100 m²	
Bulbs in Beds						
	Planting: Large	Oct–Nov	Once	17 min	100 no	
	Small			8 min	100 no	
	Lifting	May	Once	4 min	100 no	Easy before foliage dies down

active against non-grass monocotyledons and can damage bulbous plants, which therefore cannot be used in conjunction with these chemicals.

RESOURCE REQUIREMENTS

If residual herbicide is being used to ensure successful establishment, bulb planting amongst trees and shrubs may need to be delayed for three or more years.

Temporary bulb plantings for seasonal effect have more in common with bedding plants.

Bulb sales and bulb planting are both extremely seasonal, more so even than bare-rooted woody plant establishment. It is important to schedule labour for this task at the right time. Ideally it is a task for volunteers: the work is simple, the plants are robust and there is an obvious achievement upon completion.

Table 17.4 provides labour requirement guidelines for some of the operations associated with the use of naturalized bulbs.

**17.7
Overall
cost-effectiveness
appraisal**

Table 17.5 provides a comparison of the labour input requirements for the herbaceous features described and for a variety of alternative landscape components.

The table shows that, if well designed and managed, herbaceous plantings compare quite well with the more usual woody schemes in terms of labour

316

Table 17.5 Comparison of alternative ground cover treatments: cost-effectiveness guidelines

Landscape treatment	Annual labour requirements man hours per 100 m²	Approximate duration of flowering weeks		Appearance when not flowering
		Typical	Possible	
Annual bedding (excluding cost of plants)	800.00	16–30	36	nil-poor
Naturalized bulbs in grass	0.70	4–6	50	medium-poor
in beds	0.70	4–6	50	medium-poor
Herbaceous border (traditional)	43.50–54.80	24–28	12–30	medium-poor
Herbaceous ground cover	10.00–25.00	N/A		good
Rose bed: traditional	34.50–169.00	20	25	good
shrub roses	3.40	5	3–20	good-medium
Woody ground cover	3.40–8.00	N/A		good-medium
Shrub Bed : non-native, flowering	3.40–33.00	2–16	52	good-medium
native	3.40–33.00	8–10	8–10	good-medium — foliage, fruits, bark, form, etc., may be attractive
Grass mown 1 × per 7 days	1.00–3.00	N/A		medium
mown 1 × per 7–14 days allowing 'weeds' such as daisies to flower	1.00–3.00	short bursts over 4 months		medium

input. As landscape components herbaceous ground cover plants have characteristics which make them particularly suitable for certain uses. On the whole they are 'softer' in appearance than woody plants, and display a greater variety of form and texture. They can therefore form plantings which are more attractive and visually interesting to the average user than the standard woody ground cover which is currently so widely employed. Similar to the seasonal bedding displays described previously, herbaceous ground cover plants can be used in small quantities to add interest to more bland landscape elements.

References   Pryce, S. (1988) Colourful and cheerful bedding displays. *Landscape Design*, **171**, 39–42.

18 THE MANAGEMENT OF OTHER PLANTS AND PLANTINGS: CONTAINER-GROWN PLANTINGS

**18.1
Introduction**

Plants in all 'container grown' situations have certain features in common.

They are totally reliant on the volume of substrate within their container for water, nutrients and mechanical support. If reserves are inadequate they are unable to forage further afield for more. Attention by management to feeding and more particularly to irrigation requirements is therefore absolutely essential. The plants are intrinsically pot grown. If the ratio of substrate to transpiring leaf area is low, substrates can dry out extremely rapidly in dry weather during the growing season (Costello and Paul, 1975; Spooner, 1980; Fitzpatrick, 1981).

Conversely, if there is an excess of water and containers are not properly drained, the enclosed plants can drown. This is a common problem where tree pits are sited in hard surfaced areas, particularly those in low spots which can act as water collecting 'sumps' for the surrounding surfaces. Pits dug into compacted or impermeable substrates such as subsoil clays can also suffer the same fate (Patch, 1983). Adequate drainage of containers is therefore also essential.

**18.2
Principles**

DESIGNED CONTAINERS

Designed containers include:

- Roof gardens;
- Raised beds whose foundations seal the bed from the substrate below;
- Tubs, pots, hanging baskets and window boxes;
- Plant boxes.

The problems inherent in using designed containers should be considered in the context of the associated costs and benefits. Two questions need to be answered, namely:

1. Why have container grown plantings?
2. What are their advantages and drawbacks?

Table 18.1   The functions of container plantings

- To bring vegetation into basically 'hard' areas, or into locations where no soil profile exists (roofs, building façades);

- To raise plantings to levels where they are better displayed and/or better protected from litter, damage by people, dogs, vehicles, etc.;

- To raise plants above soil levels where they can interfere with services;

- To act as 'wheel in, wheel out' temporary displays which can be moved as required;

- To provide raised gardening facilities for disabled or elderly;

- To provide a more architectural function than ground level plantings could do, for example by acting as barriers or enclosures.

The functions and advantages of containerized plantings are summarized in Table 18.1. The major disadvantages are all related to the need to provide, in a very limited volume, all of the plant requirements normally provided by a complete soil profile. This means that the containers can require frequent, and sometimes costly, maintenance attention which simply cannot be relaxed (Baker *et al.*, 1977).

**18.3
Growing media**

The choice of compost to use in container plantings is important. A small soil volume has to meet all of the plants' requirements for aeration, water supply, nutrition, and support. Even the best garden loams on their own are not suitable, as they can rapidly lose structure in the container. The type of artificial composts developed for production of potted plants, based on peat, bark, sand or perlite mixtures, should be used (*Horticulture Week*, annual review). Organic matter in such composts gradually disappears through oxidation and breakdown. Thus some form of 'topping up' or replacement may be necessary.

Temporary containerized displays are less demanding and often consist of plants that are simply plunged into a neutral medium, such as peat, which does little more than hold water.

Incorporation of water holding polymers shows promise as a technique for reducing the required frequency of watering.

Roof garden plantings have special requirements. Because of the limited load bearing capacity of many roofs, the containers are made as light as possible. Lightweight composts containing a mixture of peat and perlite must be used. The containers are often very shallow. Because of the limited resources they provide, and in the interests of limiting the need for people to walk on the roof, they should incorporate an automatic watering and liquid feed system.

**18.4
Plant selection**

It is worth noting that a great many different plant types can and could be used in containers, particularly as temporary displays. The idea of using hardy herbaceous perennials has already been noted. Cheap species of woody plants grown from feathered whips are used on a relatively short-term basis (a few years) in Scandinavian container plantings to provide 'cheap and cheerful' greenery. They are discarded when they become too large. A more catholic attitude by Amenity Managers towards the range of plant species which could be effective in containers and their development on site is likely to reap rewards in the future.

The planting material chosen should, of course, be able to survive in a shallow soil. The stock should also be wind resistant. Access for maintenance teams with equipment, and users, if required, should be borne in mind at the design stage.

18.5 Maintenance operations for exterior plantings

The main factors and operations involved in the upkeep of container plantings are reviewed in the paragraphs which follow. These relate specifically to exterior plantings. The requirements for interior plantings are covered in a separate section.

PROVIDING AND REPLACING PLANTS

As mentioned above, the choice of plant material for use in containers can be very wide, and indeed there are good grounds for suggesting that a wider range should be used than at present.

Where there is a large turnover of temporary plantings, some authorities find it cost-effective to produce their own material. A realistic assessment of the costs and benefits of such a system should be made at frequent intervals.

In permanent plantings it is often desirable to select plants that do not demand either high water or nutrient levels.

An assessment should be made at regular intervals of whether the plants in a container are becoming too big or too ungainly. A container that is visually unattractive is usually not fulfilling its main objective and does not justify the maintenance inputs. Regular replacement, even of woody plants, may be necessary.

If the containers are very small, some consideration should be given to the hardiness of the plants. Soil temperatures in the container can fall much lower than those in the open ground and many plants which are marginally tolerant of cold conditions will not survive.

WATERING

Apart from the capital investment involved, the most costly aspect of providing containerized plantings is often manual watering. The operation can take a long time, particularly if the rate of infiltration is limited. Consequently it will often need to be repeated at frequent intervals.

Some form of automatic or semi-automatic irrigation system should in many cases be the most reliable and cost-effective way of providing adequate moisture to containers. Large-scale, compact, containerized, layouts, such as those existing in roof gardens, will almost inevitably justify the cost of a fixed irrigation system, even though the capital costs are high. This can be operated on a time system or through an electronic test of soil moisture.

Where containers are scattered over a wide area, such as plantings in a shopping precinct, a fixed irrigation system is unlikely to be justified. This is also true for hanging baskets, wheel-in plantings and areas exposed to public pressure. Mobile teams have to be provided with some form of water truck. It is important not to skimp on this essential maintenance feature, as one dry week can completely destroy the entire investment.

An alternative approach, which is cost-effective in many situations, involves limiting the need for irrigation by improving the water storage capacity of the container. There are two main alternatives. On the one hand the moisture retention of the planting mixture can be improved by adding a proportion of one of the recently introduced water-holding polymers, such as Broadleaf P4. These polymers are capable of extending the time between watering by at least 30%, depending on the capacity of the container and the weather conditions. Alternatively, containers are available which employ a reservoir system. This enables the containers to be topped up infrequently: water from the reservoir is fed by one of a variety of capillary or wick systems to the container soil.

Both of the above systems add to the capital cost of the planters, but the investment is rapidly recouped by the reduced maintenance requirement.

FEEDING NUTRIENTS

Simple temporary annual plantings may be able to survive in a soil treated with slow release fertilizer. For more permanent plantings it is likely that fertility of the container substrate will be limiting. To achieve the desirable effect of healthy and successful growth, additional fertilizer will have to be added. This is normally included as a liquid feed during alternate waterings.

**18.6
Maintenance of
interior plantings**

The use of permanent or semi-permanent plantings inside buildings has increased in popularity over recent years. This has been on a scale to match the plantings outside, rather than just small containers of potted plants.

As far as the growing media are concerned, these plantings have similar requirements to containerized plants outside. Plants are, of course, completely reliant on irrigation water, but this is usually balanced by the fact that the evapo-transpiration water loss is much lower indoors.

Additional problems are encountered indoors (Scrivens, 1980). These are reviewed in the following paragraphs.

LIGHTING AND HEATING

The greatest limitation to interior plant growth is low light levels. The plants ecologically adapted to low light levels are usually those from the understorey of tropical forests where there is very deep shade. This obviously introduces the problem of necessary heating. Temperatures in areas containing such very low light tolerant plants cannot be allowed to fall below 8°C.

SELECTING SHADE TOLERANT PLANTS

It is important that the plants are not only selected from species that tolerate shade, but that they are also bought on site from an intermediate acclimatization house rather than imported directly from a tropical country. Whilst they can tolerate shade, many of these plants can adapt their leaves physiologically to take advantage of higher light levels. If they are moved suddenly into shade, the leaves are likely to drop.

Under extreme low light levels even these plants cannot be expected to grow and they enter a kind of temporary stasis with greatly reduced respiration and almost no photosynthesis. Excess watering and fertilizing in these conditions are likely to be harmful. When choosing plants for such situations it may be impossible to provide a permanent display, but those evergreens with individual leaf lifespans of several years may survive a long time before they begin to senesce and need replacing.

Flowering plants or those with coloured or variegated foliage will not succeed in deep shade.

If light levels are higher, temperate understorey evergreens, such as *Hedera*, *Viburnum* and *Rhododendron*, will survive even if they do not flower. Temperatures are not so critical. As the light levels rise a wider choice of plants becomes available and there is the potential for flowering displays.

CONTROLLING PEST AND DISEASE

Pest and disease control is important in these situations. Certain pathogens, especially red spider mite and whitefly, can find the dry warm conditions within buildings ideal and become a major problem. Spraying treatment is possible, but the presence of high quality interiors and people can make it undesirable. Strict plant hygiene when stocking a new scheme is essential. There may be scope for the use of biological control organisms in the future.

RESTOCKING

The alternative to semi-permanent plantings is a rapid turnover scheme whereby containers are restocked on a monthly or even bi-weekly basis, often using temporary but more showy plant material.

The most successful types for replacement planting are evergreens, possessing leaves with a long life. These are adapted to conserving the resources available and they do not waste the effort of producing temporary organs. Examples are *Monstera*, *Philodendron* and *Ficus*.

MANAGEMENT CONSIDERATIONS

Interior schemes are usually restricted to a few prestigious or intensively used sites because of their cost. With the exception of watering, the maintenance of an interior scheme using direct labour is therefore unlikely to be cost-effective unless the organization already has the appropriately experienced staff and existing glasshouses and equipment.

Many specialist contractors exist that will provide a complete service as required, ranging from the supply of the containers and the plant material to a complete maintenance and replacement contract.

References   Baker, R., Stanfield, K. and Sturdy, R. (1977) Planting in artificial conditions. In: *Landscape Design with Plants* (ed. B. Clouston). Heinemann, London.

Bennet, R. (1984) Park Carpets, *GC & HTJ*, **95**(2), 239.

Costello, L. and Paul, J.L. (1975) Moisture relations in container plants. *Hort. Sci.*, **10**(4), 371–372.

Epstein J. (1978) *Landscape of Housing and the Urban Environment*. Institute of Advanced Architectural Studies.

Fitzpatrick, G. (1981) Water budget determination for container grown plants. *Proceedings of the Florida State Horticultural Society*, **93**, 166–168.

Horticulture Week Yearly supplements. Fertilisers and Growing Media. Turfgrass machinery. Landscape machinery.

Patch (1983) Tree Roots. In *Tree Establishment* (ed. P.R. Thoday) University of Bath, Bath.

Scrivens, S. (1980) *Interior Planting in Large Buildings*. Architectural Press, London.

Spooner, L.A. (1980) Container soil water relations: production, maintenance and transplanting. *Journal of Arboriculture*, **6**(12), 315–20.

Further reading   Balfour, D. (1986) Ramble and Climb. *Horticulture Week*, 4th July.

Balfour R.C. (1979) Climbing Roses for Today. *The Garden, the Journal of the Royal Horticultural Society*, **104**, (11), 446–450.

International Society for Horiticultural Science. (1984) International symposium on substrates in horticulture other than soils in situ. *Acta Horticulturae*, 150.

Proctor, N.J. (1973) *Climbing and Screening Plants*. Faber and Faber, London.

Scrivens, S. and Cooper, P. (1980) Irrigation. Technical study: general principles. *Arch. Journal*, 12th March, 537–540.

Scrivens, S. and Cooper, P. (1980) Irrigation. Information sheet 1: drip emitters. *Arch. Journal*, 12th March, 541–543.

Scrivens, S. and Cooper, P. (1980) Irrigation. Information sheet 2: pop up sprinklers and spray heads. *Arch. Journal*, 19th March, 583–585.

Scrivens, S. and Cooper, P. (1980) Irrigation. Information sheet 3: Irrigation control. *Arch. Journal*, 19th March, 587–588.

Thomas G.S. (1981) The history of climbing roses. *The Garden, the Journal of the Royal Horticulturae Society*, **106**, (6), 241–247.

Verdonck O. (1985) Composts as horticultural substrates. *Acta Horticulturae*, 172.

Wright, T.W.J. (1982) *Large Gardens and Parks: Maintenance, Management and Design*. Granada, St. Albans.

19 THE MANAGEMENT OF OTHER PLANTS AND PLANTINGS: GROUND COVER PLANTINGS

19.1 Introduction

The term 'ground cover' has several meanings: it is used to signify a particular form or characteristic of plant growth, as well as to describe a particular function which a certain type of plant is required to perform in the landscape. Colloquially, as well as professionally, the term describes plants which provide a continuous leaf cover over the soil surface, preferably for twelve months of the year. In the case of amenity landscapes, 'ground cover' is usually associated with low growing plants (other than grass) of less than one metre in height and more often of not more than half a metre tall.

Graham Thomas, that doyen of plantsmen, draws attention to the wide range of growth habits which characterize this group of plants, namely: sprawling, carpet, spreading, tuberous, clumpy and hummocky (Thomas, 1970). The plants involved are usually not required to accommodate the levels of pedestrian pressures which grass swards are expected to withstand. Whilst ground cover plantings most commonly consist of woody plant (shrub) material, a wide range of other landscape components – climbers, herbaceous plants, conifers, as well as grasses, ferns and even rushes – is used (Balfour, 1982; Percy, 1985). Because ground cover plantings span so many different genera, play an increasingly important part in modern amenity landscapes and are less easy to establish and manage successfully than is sometimes assumed, they are separated here for discussion.

In practice, either a single ground cover species or, less frequently, an association of species can be used to colonize an amenity area by either nature or nurture, or frequently a combination of each. The resultant cover can be regarded in two ways:

1. As visual cover, which can be described as 'entire' when, from the intended viewpoints, the planting appears to be a simple, uniform mass of vegetation screening the soil surface;
2. As dominant cover when the canopy of plants and their debris is so dense that it prevents growth of all other plants. In the case of low

ground cover plantings, dominance is rarely complete. While such low cover may prevent the establishment of other plants, it will not eradicate established weeds if they are taller.

The design and management of ground cover plantings from initial selection through establishment to renewal operations are therefore not as simple as the concept might imply. Nevertheless there is ample evidence from North America and mainland Europe that ground cover can be both a practical and aesthetically satisfying landscape component. However, as with all 'cropping' systems, there are certain critical cultural practices which must be followed in order to achieve success. These are discussed in the sections which follow.

19.2
Plant selection

Considerable design skill, and an understanding of the biology of the plants involved is necessary to achieve visually pleasing, low-maintenance plantings. In order to obtain and to make maintenance reasonably easy, plant associations forming any ground cover planting should consist of species which, when placed in association, respond similarly to irrigation, fertilizer and, in particular, to herbicide treatment. There is also a need to ensure that the growth habits of the plants are complementary at their boundaries. Certain plant types will tend to grow into each other to form a visually confusing cover which blurs the edges of the design and destroys the aesthetic effect.

Groups should also have similar aesthetic life spans, i.e. post-establishment periods of 'adulthood', in which they are capable of fulfilling the aesthetic roles required of them. These are likely to be both different from, and usually considerably less than, the biological lifespans of the component plants (Thoday, 1982). At the end of their aesthetic life, ground cover planting groups should be capable of responding to renewal treatment (either replacement, or heavy 'rejuvenation' pruning) as a group so that uniformity of the visual effect is retained. In short, the members of a ground cover community should have compatible husbandry requirements throughout their effective lifespans. Table 19.1 provides a categorization of shrubs according to their expected longeivity, with which suitable selections can be made.

19.3
Planting husbandry

Some essential husbandry operations are required both before and immediately after planting. Two requirements of particular importance are:

1. Perennial weed eradication, and
2. Stimulation of vigorous growth at an early stage of plant establishment.

It is vital to provide optimum substrate conditions and to use either mechanical or chemical means to rid the site of perennial weeds.

Sites with chemically or physically poor substrates should be treated so as to achieve much vigorous initial growth of the desired species. This

Table 19.1   Categorization of shrubs according to their expected life-times or longevity

Long-lived (25–50 years) genera	Medium life (10–25 years) genera	Short life (5–10 years) genera
Arbutus	*Abelia*	*Buddleia*
Aucuba	*Berberis*	*Calluna*
Azalea	*Camellia*	*Caryopteris*
Magnolia	*Chaenomeles*	*Ceanothus*
Rhododendron	*Chimonanthus*	*Ceratostigma*
	Cotoneaster	*Choisya*
	Deutzia	*Cistus*
	Enkianthus	*Cotinus*
	Escallonia	*Cytisus*
	Forsythia	*Erica*
	Fothegilla	*Helichrysum*
	Fuchsia	*Lavandula*
	Hamamellis	*Olearia*
	Hibiscus	*Potentilla*
	Hydrangea	*Rosmarinus*
	Indigofera	*Santolina*
	Kalmia	*Senecio*
	Kolkwitzia	
	Mahonia	
	Osmanthius	
	Philadelphus	
	Prunus (laurocerasus)	
	Ribes	
	Salix	
	Skimmia	
	Spiraea	
	Styrax	
	Syringa	
	Viburnum	
	Weigelia	

Source: Based on Wright, T.W.J. (1982) *Large Gardens and Parks*. Granada.

Note: This table should only be used as an approximate guide. Actual lifetimes vary greatly due to differences in soil, climate, aspect, management, etc. For example, some of those genera listed in the medium and short life columns can in some circumstances enjoy longer lives.

involves the addition of nutrients and possibly of soil ameliorants, loams, grits or bulky organics, depending on the form and condition of the original substrate.

The plant material used to establish ground cover must be young and vigorous. Woody species must be in a juvenile condition, because starved or prematurely mature specimens will not produce the volume or form of growth necessary to create an entirely fused canopy.

Optimum planting density is that which rapidly achieves a stable, uniform, densely prosperous plant cover. Investigations suggest that the most desirable plantings arise from plant populations that take approximately two growing seasons to reach visual cover. Closer populations can cause damaging competition and reduce the aesthetic lifespan of a planting, particularly if it suffers from environmental stress. Indeed close planted old nursery stock may never produce a uniform canopy.

It has been found that, depending on their vigour, the majority of the low shrubs used as ground cover in public sites are best planted within the range of 1 to 2 plants per square metre.

This is primarily important for plants that retain their individual identity within the ground cover, such as *Hebe rakiensis*. Too wide a spacing will delay the formation of complete cover. Too close a spacing can ultimately damage the form and health of the individual plants: some may even be suppressed and die leading to a very patchy appearance. Many plants, through suckering, underground rhizomes or rooting of surface stems, essentially determine their own density and function as a community in equilibrium: *Hypericum calycinum* is a good example. Initial planting density can therefore only affect the time it takes to achieve this stability (Thoday, 1982).

19.4 Post-planting maintenance

The key operations required to ensure vigorous growth in the early years of a planting are weed control and, whenever feasible, irrigation and nutrition. Weed control is dealt with as a single topic later in this Chapter.

Irrigation is a valuable aid in most seasons when establishing transplants. If there is a drought in the early part of the first growing season, irrigation may prove vital. The prevention of moisture stress will optimize the form and quality of juvenile growth achieved over the initial two to three years involved in establishing a ground cover planting. Application should be in the order of 100,000 litres per hectare and be repeated at least fortnightly during periods of drought.

Nutrition deserves careful consideration. If the base fertility of the site has been raised before planting, potassium and phosphorus are unlikely to be limiting. Nitrogen should be applied annually, in spring, at a rate of 75 kilograms per hectare, preferably in granular form to prevent leaf scorch.

Coarse mulches are frequently used during the establishment phase. Although their nutrition and water conservation roles are somewhat in doubt, they probably assist in weed suppression and certainly give the planting a finished appearance prior to achieving visual cover. A frequently used mulch is coarse bark, applied at a rate of 300 cubic metres per hectare.

**19.5
Post-establishment
maintenance**

Once established, ground cover should prove to be minimal maintenance and low cost components of landscape schemes, as indicated by Table 19.2 and later by Table 19.9.

Nutrition and irrigation may be discontinued. On most sites, in the absence of vandalism, weed control should be continued until dominant cover is reached. The need to remove litter and autumn leaves will depend on specific site conditions, but it is usually necessary to programme for these operations. However, it should be noted that the ability of ground cover plantings to 'swallow' extraneous materials varies according to the types and species of plant involved.

Pruning is a crucial but infrequent husbandry activity required in the maintenance of established ground cover. Unfortunately it is not well understood as an operation. Ground cover is not a hedge: clipping-over or edging-up are inappropriate. Although these actions are sometimes forced upon a planting by inappropriate design and plant selection, annual pruning, if it is required at all, should generally be restricted to the removal of dead, obtrusive or unshapely branches.

Infrequent but programmed, heavy pruning is a very important operation which should certainly be undertaken when, or just before, a planting is coming to the end of its aesthetic lifespan. For many of the most commonly used ground cover plants, this is likely to be between 10 and 15 years. At this time a decision must be made either to scrap and replant the scheme, or else to prune heavily.

Many ground cover shrubs will respond to regeneration operations, such as stooling or coppicing at near ground level. Species which are known to

Table 19.2 Operations and suggested costs per 100 m^2 of *Lonicera pileata* ground cover in beds of 5 to 20 m^2

A	Treat with glyphosate prior to planting.	£ 11
B	Cultivation	£ 45
Ca	Plant 30–45 cm *Lonicera pileata* at 5 m^2	£ 400
Cb	Plant at 4 m^2	£ 320
Cc	Plant at 2.5 m^2	£ 200
D	Apply residual herbicides twice during first growing season	£ 22
Ea	Mulch with coarse chopped bark	£ 100
Eb	Mulch with spent mushroom compost	£ 48
Fa	Apply residual herbicides twice annually after first growing season	£ 22
Fb	Supplement Fa with one application of glyphosate per season	£ 11
Ga	Hoe cultivated soil during first season after planting	£ 165
Gb	Hoe handweed £ 110 per season and pro-rata	
Gc	Hoe untreated soil first season after planting	£ 200

Source: Percy, D (1982) Cover Design, *GC&HTJ*, **193**, 17.

respond successfully to this treatment are *Lonicera pileata*, *Senecio greyii*, *Viburnum davidii*, *Symphoricarpus 'Hancock'*, *Cornus alba*, *Salix purpurea 'Gracilis'*, *Mahonia aquifolium* and *Hypericum calycinum*. The work should be carried out in the dormant season with hand operated or pneumatic pruners.

The prunings can be passed through a chipper and returned to the site as a mulch. The remaining stumps must be encouraged to sprout rapidly and evenly in order to regenerate a new, young and full canopy. The most valuable contribution to achieving this is the application of nitrogen at a rate of 75 kilograms per hectare.

The opening of the canopy will necessitate a return to the herbicide programme recommended for use in the establishment phase. The period of extended lifespans achieved by regeneration operations varies from species to species. For example, it is well known that willows can survive

Table 19.3 The management of woody ground cover plantings: suggested herbicide programme

Time	Operation
Year 1 July-September	*Pre-planting* Apply glyphosate at 2.2 kilograms per hectare prior to cultivation to eradicate perennial weeds
October	Cultivate
October-March	Apply paraquat at 1.12 kilograms per hectare to control weed seedlings
	Post planting
March	Immediately apply simazine at appropriate rate Repeat every 8 weeks, if low rates have been used Applications beyond July are often unnecessary
December	Apply Propyzamide to control weeds and certain established annual and perennial weeds
Year 2 March	Apply simazine and/or propyzamide as above Integration of Lenacil into the programme will prevent the build up of Simazine-resistant weeds
A fused canopy should now exist	
Year 3 onwards (This may not be necessary) January-March	Apply dichlobenil at the appropriate rate Propyzamide may be used at 1.4 kilograms per hectare to control *Agropyron repens*, which is a major problem in much low ground cover

Notes: This table should be viewed in conjunction with Table 19.7 – for the specific herbicide tolerances of individual genera. Rates refer to the concentration of active ingredient applied per unit area.

many coppicing rotations. However, success with all species is dependent on winter weather and spring moisture levels.

There is some evidence to suggest that flail mowing may be successful with some subjects, for example *Calluna vulgaris*.

GROWTH REGULANTS

If ground cover is to persist as a component of designed and managed landscapes, it is likely that greater understanding and use of chemicals to manipulate and thus optimize the growth form of ground cover plants will develop. This applies particularly in the case of the density and durability of plant canopy. The use of chemical growth regulators appears to be a practical possibility. Current research, based on such materials as maleic hydrazide is worth following.

19.6
Chemical weed control

Two distinct weed control programmes need to be prepared, namely for pre- and post-planting. These are displayed in Tables 19.3 and 19.4 and are reviewed separately in the paragraphs which follow.

PRE-PLANTING HERBICIDE TREATMENTS

Most weed problems associated with establishing ground cover plantings are a result of the failure to eliminate perennial weeds from the planting

Table 19.4   The management of herbaceous ground cover plantings: suggested herbicide programme

Time	Operation
Year 1	*Pre-planting*
July-September	Apply Glyphosate at 2.2 kilograms per hectare prior to cultivation to eradicate perennial weeds
October	Cultivate
October-March	Apply paraquat at 1.12 kilograms per hectare to control weed seedlings
	Post planting
March	Immediately apply Lenacil at appropriate rate (see Tables 19.2, 19.6 and 19.8) Repeat every 8 weeks Applications beyond July and often unnecessary
December	Apply paraquat at 1.12 kilograms per hectare as an overall spray to deciduous herbaceous plants for controlling winter weeds and certain established annual and perennial weeds
A fused canopy should now exist	

Notes: This table should be viewed in conjunction with Table 19.8 for the specific herbicide tolerances of individual genera. Rates refer to the concentration of active ingredients applied per unit area.

site (Thoday, 1980). Pre-planting cultivations are normally effective in suppressing annual weeds. However, they usually do no more than delay the development of in situ perennial weeds which regenerate from perennating organs, as in the case of couch grass (*Agropyron repens*) and docks (*Rumex* spp).

Most of the traditional total herbicides, which are effective, have the disadvantage of possessing marked residual activity. This means that a lengthy delay between application and planting is inevitable. At the very least this period will be 6–8 weeks, as in the case of aminotriazole. Such inconveniences have discouraged the use of pre-planting herbicide treatments. However, if at all possible, a period of 'summer fallow' is recommended before the planting season. This stimulates growth of existing weed propagules so that their aerial parts can then be treated with a translocated, non-persistent herbicide such as glyphosate. Particularly persistent weeds such as bindweeds (*Calystegia*, *Convolvulus*) and horsetails (*Equisetum*) may need special treatment, but if this entails the use of more persistent chemicals the need to allow for residues in the soil must be borne in mind. Flushes of annual weeds before planting are best treated with paraquat.

SOIL STERILIZER TREATMENT

Particularly on relatively small areas of ground cover or in areas where it is estimated that weeds and soil pathogens may be a serious problem; or where the quality of post-planting weed control is in doubt, the soil can be fumigated to destroy weed seeds, perennating organs, and soil pathogens. The sterilizer, dazomet, is recommended for this. Although relatively expensive, it may be cost-effective in the types of situation noted above.

Dazomet can be applied to cultivated land any time between mid-April and December. It is applied in granular form and rotavated into the soil to a depth of 20 cm, so that the toxic gas, methyl isocyanate, is released. The optimum temperature for the release is 7°C, although the material is effective down to 2°C.

Table 19.5   The treatment of ground cover plantings: application rates for residual soil acting herbicides

Chemical	Rates of application	
	Light soils	Clay/organic soils
Dichlobenil	6.70 Kg/ha	8.4 Kg/ha
Lenacil	1.70 Kg/ha	3.4 Kg/ha
Propyzamide	0.80 Kg/ha	1.7 Kg/ha
Simazine	0.84 Kg/ha	2.2 Kg/ha

Note: Rates refer to the concentrations of active ingredient applied per unit area. With established, tolerant genera, application at higher rates may not necessarily result in damage. Conversely acceptable weed control may be achieved below the above rates.

Sealing the treated areas with polythene sheeting to retain gas is recommended, but on soils characterized by small particle size rolling the surface achieves equally good results.

A rate of 570 kilograms per hectare is recommended by the manufacturers for killing microorganisms. However, half that quantity seems sufficient to kill weed seeds and rhizome fragments. It should, therefore, be adequate for normal amenity plantings. Six to eight weeks should normally be allowed to elapse between application and planting, although this waiting period is dependent upon prevailing temperatures. The reduction in the number of viable weed propagules caused by dazomet greatly reduces the need for post-planting residual herbicide treatments in the first year, although air-borne seeds can still be a problem.

POST-PLANTING HERBICIDE TREATMENTS

The soil disturbance associated with planting inevitably results in a flush of weed seed germination. This can be controlled by applying a residual herbicide immediately following planting. The age and degree of establishment of woody plants greatly affects their ability to tolerate residual herbicides. Thus reduced rates are recommended for newly planted material, although this reduces the period of herbicide effectiveness and entails repeat applications. Most residuals are inactivated to some extent in organic and clay soils; higher rates are therefore needed on these soil types, as indicated by Table 19.5. It follows that there is inevitably a greater risk of damage on soils low in these constituents.

Most of the residual herbicides suitable for post-establishment use, such as simazine, are only effective on germinating weed seedlings, and must be applied to weed-free surfaces. They are best applied to ground cover as medium to high volume sprays at rates of between 225 litres per hectare and 1000 litres per hectare. The relative material costs of some of these herbicides are detailed in Table 19.5.

Table 19.6 The relative material costs of herbicides required to treat similar-sized areas

Herbicide/sterilant	Index figures
Dazomet	700–1400
Dichlobenil	182–240
Glyphosate	45
Lenacil	50–100
MCPA	6–7
Paraquat	10–18
Propyzamide	30–65
Simazine	6–13

Note: The figures are based on taking the cost of paraquat as an index of 10.

Table 19.7   Susceptibility of woody ground cover to residual herbicides applied during establishment period

Plant Genera	Simazine at up to 1.1 Kg/ha	Lenacil at up to 3.4 Kg/ha	Dichlobenil at 6.7 Kg/ha on plants established for 2 yrs
Berberis	T	T	T
Calluna	T	T	T
Caryopteris	T (0.56 Kg)	–	–
Cistus	T (0.56 Kg)	–	–
Cotoneaster	1-T	T	T
Deutzia	S	–	T
Erica	T	T	T
Euonymus	I	–	T
Forsythia	S	–	T
Genista	T	–	–
Hedera	T	–	–
Hypericum	T	T	T
Juniperus	T	T	–
Ligustrum	S	–	T
Lonicera	I	–	T
Mahonia	T	–	T
Pachysandra	T	–	–
Philadelphus	I	–	T
Potentilla	T	T	T
Prunus laurocerasus cvs.	I	T	T
Rhumnus	T	–	S
Rhododendron	T	T	T
Rosa	T	T	T
Rubus	T	T	–
Salix	T	T	–
Sambucus	T	–	S
Sarcococca	T	–	–
Senecio	I	T	S
Spiraea	I	T	T
Stephandra	T	–	–
Symphoricarpus	T	T	S
Viburnum	I	T	T
Vinca	T	T	–

Note: Rates refer to the concentrations of active ingredient applied per unit area.

Key: T = Tolerant
S = Susceptible
I = Intermediate
– = No Recommendation Available

Table 19.7 provides guidelines on the tolerances and susceptibilities of different plants to the main types of residual herbicide available for use during the establishment phase.

HERBICIDE TREATMENTS FOR ESTABLISHED WOODY GROUND COVER

The necessity to continue residual herbicide application once the foliage canopy has fused depends largely upon the form of the constituent plants.

Evergreen species maintain a leafy canopy all year, and as a result are relatively resistant to weed penetration. Overall applications of herbicides may therefore become unnecessary after canopy closure. In contrast deciduous material is more prone to weed colonization during the dormant season, although in established plantings winter weed development may be unimportant if the summer foliage canopy is of sufficient depth and density to suppress the weeds when growth recommences.

Most established plants taller than 600 mm exercise their own weed control.

Gradual weed invasion is likely in low-growing ground covers. An annual application of residual herbicide is thus advisable. Since established plantings are more resistant to residual herbicides, the use of chemicals such as dichlobenil, which kill both seedlings and many established weeds, may become possible.

Translocated herbicides, such as glyphosate, may be safely used to 'spot treat' weeds growing through an established ground cover canopy, if the selected chemical is first mixed with wallpaper paste. It can then be painted on to foliage, or applied via a herbicide glove, or with one of the patent spot applicators now available.

HERBICIDE TREATMENTS FOR HERBACEOUS GROUND COVER

Few herbaceous plants exhibit a tolerance to herbicides to the degree characteristic of woody plants. Recommendations in Table 19.8 are general; some species and cultivars may exhibit damage at these rates.

If perennial weeds are eliminated prior to planting the inherent susceptibility of herbaceous plants to many residual herbicides is no longer of crucial importance as annual weed seed germination can be controlled by a herbicide programme based on Lenacil.

In the case of deciduous ground cover species without green stems a contact herbicide, such as paraquat, can be used during the winter at 0.6–1.1 kilograms per hectare to eradicate annual and shallow-rooted perennials. Since selectivity is a function of dormant bud structure and the depth of dormancy, applications should take place before the end of February.

Table 19.8   Susceptibility of herbaceous ground cover to residual herbicides applied during the establishment period

Species	Tolerance
Acanthus spp.	M
Achillea	M
Aconitum	T
Agapanthus	M
Alchemilla mollis	T
Anaphalis triplinervis	T
Ancusa azurea	T
Anemone × hybrida	M
Anthemis spp.	T
Aquilegia	T
Asperula oderata	T
Aster spp.	T
Astilbe spp.	M
Aubretia	M
Bergenia	T
Campanula spp.	M
Centaurea	M
Chrysanthemum	T
Coreopsis	T
Delphinium	T
Dianthus	T
Dicentra spp.	T
Digitalis grandiflora	M
Erigeron	T
Eryngium spp.	T
Euphorbia spp.	T
Gaillardia	T
Geranium spp.	M
Geum	T
Gypsophila	T
Helenium	M
Helianthus	M
Helleborus spp.	T
Heuchera	T
X *Heucherella*	T
Hosta spp.	T
Hypericum spp.	T
Iris spp.	M
Kniphofia spp.	T
Liatris	T
Lupinus	M
Lythrum spp.	T
Nepeta spp.	T
Paeonia spp.	T
Polygonum spp.	T
Potentilla spp.	T

Table 19.8 (cont'd)

Species	Tolerance
Prunella	T
Ranunculus spp.	T
Reynoutria	T
Salvia spp.	T
Scabiosa	T
Sedum spp.	T
Sidalcea	T
Solidago	T
Stachys spp.	T
Tradescantia spp.	T
Trollius spp.	T
Veronica spp.	T
Vinca spp.	T
Viola spp.	T

Key: T = Tolerant
     M = Medium

Notes: This Table was compiled from the JCLI booklet on herbaceous plants.
     The information was supplied to them by the Weed Research Organization.
     Information on the suceptibility of herbaceous ground cover to residual herbicides, applied during the establishment period, is somewhat scanty. This is in part due to the effect of soil type.
     Comparative susceptibility guidelines have been given for the following few spp.

Plant Genera	Simazine at 0.6–1.1 Kg/ha	Lenacil at 1.8–2.2 Kg/ha	Chloroxuron at 3.4–4.5 Kg/ha
Alchemilla	S	T	T
Bergenia	T	T	T
Euphorbia	I	T	T
Geranium	I	T	–
Hemerocallis	T	–	–
Hosta	T	T	T
Polygonum	I	T	–
Stachys	S	T	T

Key: T = Tolerant
     S = Susceptible
     I = Intermediate
     – = No Recommendation Available

19.7 Conclusions

It will be appreciated that there are many factors which have to be considered when selecting either a single species or an association of plants to provide ground cover plantings which are cost-effective to manage.

There are also many alternative approaches to establishment and subsequent management, which influence not only the material and labour costs per operation, but also the subsequent growth rate and the speed at which a self maintaining cover is attained.

A comparison between many of these approaches is summarised in Table 19.9.

Table 19.9   Some suggested costs of various methods of establishing *Lonicera pileata* ground cover

Method/operations*	A	B	Ca	Cb	Cc	D	Ea	Eb	Fa	Fb	Ga	Gb	Gc	Years	£
Total herbicide Control	*	*			*	*			2	2				3	334
No cultivation Bark yr 1 Handweed yrs 2,3	*				*			*				2×1/6		3	384
Bark yr 1 Handweed yrs 2,3	*	*			*			*				2×1/6		3	392
Residual yr 1 Bark yr 2 Handweed yr 3	*	*			*	*		*				1/6		3	396
Total herbicide Control	*	*		*		*			*	*				2	430
No cultivation Hoe yr 1 Herbicide yrs 2,3,4	*				*				3	3		*		4	457
Bark yr 1	*	*		*				*						1	476
Residual yr 1	*	*	*		*									1	478
No cultivation Bark yr 1	*			*				*						1	491
Hoe yr 1 Herbicide yrs 2,3,4	*	*			*				3	3	*			4	520
Bark yr 1	*	*	*					*						1	556
Mushroom yr 1 Handweed yr 1	*	*	*					*				1/2		1	559
Mushroom yrs 1,2,3 Handweed yrs 1,2,3	*	*			*		3					3×1/2		3	565
Mushroom yrs 1,2 Handweed yrs 1,2	*	*		*			2					2×1/2		2	582
No herbicide preparation Hoe yr 1 Bark yr 2 Handweed yrs 3,4		*			*			*				2×1/6	*	4	582
No cultivation Bark yr 1	*		*					*						1	586
No cultivation Mushroom yrs 1,2 Handweed yrs 1,2	*			*			2					2×1/2		2	597
Hoe yr 1 Herbicide yrs 2, 3	*	*		*					2	2	*			3	607
Hoe yr 1 Herbicide yr 2	*	*	*						*	*	*			2	651
Hoe yr 1,2	*	*	*								*		*	2	731

Table 19.9 (cont'd)

Method/operations*	A	B	Ca	Cb	Cc	D	Ea	Eb	Fa	Fb	Ga	Gb	Gc	Years	£
Hoe yr 1 Mushroom yrs 2,3 Handweed yrs 2,3	*	*		*				2			*	2×1/2		3	741
No herbicide preparation Hoe yr 1 Mushroom yr 2		*	*					1				1/2	*	2	748
Hoe yrs 1,2,3,4	*	*			*						*	3		4	751
Hoe yrs 1,2,3	*	*		*							*	2		3	761
No herbicide preparation Hoe yr 1 Mushroom yrs 2,3 Handweed yrs 2,3		*		*				2				2×1/2	*	3	771
No herbicide preparation Hoe yrs 1,2		*	*								*		*	2	800
Hoe yrs 1,2,3	*	*		*							2	1		3	816
No herbicide preparation Hoe yrs 1,2,3,4		*			*						3		*	4	895

Source: Percy, D. (1982) Cover Design, *GC&HTJ*, **193**, 17.

Note: * The operations are defined in Table 19.2.

References   Balfour, D. (1982) Cover and Colour. *GC & HTJ*, **192**(1).
Percy, D. (1985) Cost Cutting Canopies. *GC & HTJ*, 25th January.
Thoday, P.R. (ed) (1980) *Weed Control in Amenity Plantings*. Conference Proceedings, University of Bath.
Thoday, P.R. (1982) Ground cover – factors determining its success. In: *Cost Effective Amenity Landscape Management* (eds P.R. Thoday and C.H. Addison) HEA Conference Proceedings, HEA, Bridgewater.
Thomas, G.S. (1970) *Plants for Ground Cover*. Dent, London.

Further reading   Ashberry, A. (1966) *Alpine Lawns*. Hodder and Stoughton, London.
Percy, D. (1982) Cover Design. *GC & HTJ*, **193**, 17, 31–37.
Wittering, W.O. (1974) *The Use of Black Polythene as a Weed Suppressor*. Forestry Commission Bulletin, 48. HMSO, London.

Part Five

The Management of Other Surfaces

This part covers the management of two other types of amenity surfaces: water bodies and hard surfaces. In addition, the operations and resources involved in providing the main structures and services required for effective recreation and leisure activities are described.

Chapter 20 outlines the diverse functions which water bodies are called upon to perform, before reviewing the principal maintenance operations. Inevitably, attention focuses on the implications of managing aquatic vegetation through physical, chemical and biological methods of control.

The second chapter in this part provides further guidelines on aquatic weed control, based on a case-study example concerning the management of amenity lakes at Milton Keynes.

Chapter 22 describes the operations and resource requirements for the maintenance of formal and informal water areas. Water displays and fountains in particular are covered; likewise ponds and ditches.

In Chapter 23 the maintenance requirements of hard surfaces, such as hoggin, tarmac, concrete slabs, concrete blocks and asphalt, are evaluated and compared in terms of cost-effectiveness. Maintenance operations, and in particular the uses of herbicides, are reviewed.

Chapter 24 covers the management of amenity landscape structures and services. These include fences, walls and gates; seats, litter bins and signs; play equipment; drainage; and lighting.

20 WATER BODIES: INTRODUCTION

20.1
Introduction

Water, apart from being one of the essential landscape management resources, is often present as a feature in its own right. In this chapter an attempt has been made to present information drawn from a variety of sources on the cost-effective management of water features.

Water bodies in the landscape can offer 'concentrated' value for money as they are usually very attractive both to users and wildlife.

They can be costly both to create and to manage however. Management therefore needs to be based on very clear objectives together with a good working knowledge of ecological principles, if the result is to be cost-effective.

Broadly two types of water body occur in the landscape. First, there are those which are primarily informal in character. Frequently they are of natural origin or are designed and managed to appear natural. They are usually located in rural or 'nature-like' settings and are managed with wildlife conservation interests to the fore. Secondly, in contrast, there are formal water bodies, such as ornamental lakes and ponds. These are normally purpose designed and built. They are frequently associated with hard landscaping and are situated in prestigious or high-use locations.

Both types are considered in this chapter. First, however, readers are presented with a short description of the most important features and management principles which need to be considered before preparing a management plan.

20.2
Critical features

CHARACTERISTICS

Water bodies are extremely vulnerable ecosystems whose functioning can be readily altered or even destroyed by quite small changes in their environment. Pollutants are rapidly dispersed within them, and fauna and flora may find it difficult or impossible to escape from adverse events occurring in their habitat.

Interference in the aquatic environment can therefore have results which are more far reaching, in both space and time, and potentially more damaging than similar action in terrestrial landscape features. For this reason great care is required, for example, in the aquatic use of herbicides.

THE CATCHMENT AREA

The natural boundary of a pond or lake may seem obvious, but for management purposes this must be extended to include the whole catchment area. The condition of a lake or pond depends on the quality of the water which feeds the water body. This water will have undergone a number of complex chemical reactions as it is filtered through the soil. It may have become contaminated by industrial or sewage effluents, fertilizers, herbicides or other chemical pollutants.

WATER QUALITY

Water quality maintenance is critical for some waterbodies, such as those used for drinking water extraction. In some others, however, such as those used for sailing and water sports, it is usually sufficient to maintain fairly clean, clear water. Water quality is usually rapidly reflected in the clarity of the water and in plant growth.

ALGAL GROWTH

In a natural or semi-natural waterbody the abundant growth of algae may cause the water to become green and turbid. Not only is this unattractive, but it may also have undesirable effects on the other plants. Dense algal growth can absorb nearly all of the incoming sunlight in the surface waters and effectively shade the submerged plants beneath. This may in turn have undesirable effects on fish, through diminishing shelter and breeding sites, and may destroy a valuable source of food for a variety of animals.

NUTRIENTS

All plants including algae require light, water and nutrients to grow. In natural systems one or more of the essential nutrients is likely to be in short supply and will therefore restrict algal growth, so that it does not become a problem. In some areas, however, the rivers are used as a means of disposal for sewage effluent which is extremely rich in nutrients, especially nitrates and phosphates. In East Anglia the water quality has altered rapidly. It was once renowned as 'gin clear' but is sadly now green and turbid and, as a result, has lost many of the decorative reed species that used to grow in the Broads and rivers. Overloading of nutrients is known as eutrophication.

FLUSHING

Algal populations and influxes of effluents and nutrients may not be a problem if the water is flushed out rapidly. This prevents a build-up of algae and can restrict the effects of toxic substances. If the flushing rate is low, however, a relatively small amount of nutrients can cause a prolonged and significant build-up of algae. The dilution and flushing effects should be given careful consideration when using chemicals in or near a water body.

EVAPORATION AND SILTATION

Slow moving or static water bodies are liable to dry out, particularly if they are shallow with significant emergent vegetation. This can use up a significant volume of water and also contribute to the silt layer on the bottom so further decreasing the water depth.

DISTURBANCE

When disturbing a water body, particularly if removing weed or adding chemicals, it is important, where possible, to carry out the procedures incrementally on 'a little at a time' basis. This allows animals to escape and to leave some areas undisturbed, so that there is a source of flora and fauna for recolonization of the site.

Care is also required to ensure that controlling the population of one plant or animal does not result in the runaway growth of another even more obnoxious species.

ASSESSMENT

Management of water bodies – particularly of natural or informal features with a significant wildlife component – needs to be cautious and sensitive to the delicate inter-relationships existing in the habitat. The selection of management methods is best preceded by a thorough survey of the particular water body so that the likely outcome of action can be forecast with reasonable accuracy. Information on water sources and destinations, flow rates and currents, rates of dilution, water quality, and so on, is usually required. The same applies to data on human and wildlife uses, their requirements and likely impacts upon the habitat.

FUNCTIONS AND USES

These will of course vary from site to site, but most water bodies are attractive to a variety of users whose needs may conflict. Active sports such as motor boating and water skiing conflict with quieter pastimes such as swimming and angling. These, in turn, may conflict, and may also be incompatible with interests such as nature conservation or visual appreciation.

AQUATIC VEGETATION – ECOLOGY AND CLASSIFICATION

It has been noted above that characteristics of the aquatic environment are expressed most immediately through the growth of aquatic vegetation. Important characteristics include the nutrient status of the water and

Table 20.1   Classification of aquatic vegetation

Emergent	usually erect, productive, high-biomass plants, which may have their roots submerged for part or all of the time, but normally carry at least half their height clear of the water surface, (for example, reeds, rushes).
Floating	may be free floating (for example duckweed) or root (for example water lilies) and tend to colonize the surface of the water in a horizontal layer.
Submerged	typical water weeds which may be rooted, or free-floating but submerged.
Algae	small free-floating non-vascular plants with great powers of reproduction.
Bankside	plants including trees may be included in classifications of aquatic vegetation, as they are important to the habitat and its management.

associated sediments, the bank profiles, the depth of water, the disturbance of water and the light levels.

Aquatic vegetation is normally classified as shown in Table 20.1.

**20.3
Management
principles**

INITIAL ASSESSMENT

Whatever the management objectives may be, the periodic control of vegetation usually plays a major role in their achievement. This applies in the case of both formal and informal water bodies. However, vegetational changes are not themselves causes but rather symptoms of the environmental factors present in the aquatic habitat. Unwanted vegetation is therefore most cost-effectively controlled by manipulating causes where this is possible rather than by treating symptoms which may continue to recur. In addition, dredging or cleaning to remove accumulations of silt is necessary for the maintenance of most water features.

MANAGEMENT METHODS: VEGETATION CONTROL

There are four main methods for controlling vegetation in both formal and informal water bodies: physical (manual and mechanical); chemical; biological, and environmental.

Physical control
Physical methods include various means of cutting or dragging off unwanted vegetation. Hand methods tend to be labour-intensive and slow. Furthermore the results of physical methods are likely to be relatively short-term. It may be impossible or prohibitively expensive to reach some areas by physical methods because of access problems. However, boats, pontoons,

Table 20.2 Chemicals approved for use in water

Chemical	Emergent and bankside	Floating	Submerged	Algae
Chlorthiamid		*	**	
Dalapon	**			
Dichlobenil 6.75%	**	*		
Dichlobenil 20%	*	**	***	
Diquat		*	**	*
Glyphosate	**	*		
Maleic hydrazide plus 2,4-D	*			
Paraquat	*			
Tebutryne		*	***	**
2,4-D	**	**		

Key: *** denotes the greatest suitability for use.

etc. can be used, and draglines can reach a considerable distance, many metres from the shore.

Where maintenance of a fragile ecosystem is the prime aim of management, physical methods may be the least ecologically destructive way of manipulating vegetation. Thus, despite their limitations, they may be the preferred option.

Chemical control

Chemical methods are based on a number of herbicides which are officially approved for use in water. These are referred to in Table 20.2. Chemicals can be extremely effective in controlling aquatic weeds and can produce long-term results at relatively low cost. It is well known that the potential for producing unwanted side-effects is high. Hence their use requires particular care and sometimes Water Authority approval. Table 20.3

Table 20.3 Susceptibility to herbicides of some commonly occurring aquatic weeds

		Dalapon	2,4-D amine	Diquat	Chlorthiamid	Dichlobenil	Glyphosate	Terbutryne	Cyanatryn	Asulam
Emergent Monocots										
Buttomus umbellatus	(Flowering rush)			MR		R		R	R	
Carex spp.	(Sedges)	MS		MR		R	S	R	R	R
Glyceria fluitans	(Floating sweet grass)	MR		MR	S	S		R	R	MS
Glyceria maxima	(Reed sweet grass)	MR		MR		MR	S	R	R	MS
Juncus spp.	(Rushes)	MR		MR		R	S	R	R	MR
Phalaris arundinacea	(Reed canary grass)	S		MR		R	S	R	R	MR
Phragmites communis	(Common reed)	S		MR		R	S	R	R	MR

Table 20.3 (cont'd)

		Dalapon	2,4-D amine	Diquat	Chlorthiamid	Dichlobenil	Glyphosate	Terbutryne	Cyanatryn	Asulam
Schoenoplectus lacustris	(Common chub rush)	MR		MR		R		R	R	
Sparganium erectum	(Branched but-reed)	MS		S		MR		R	R	
Typha latifolia	(Bulrush)	S		MR		R	S	R	R	MR
Emergent dicots										
Alisma plantago-aquatica	(Water plantain)		MS	MS	MS	S			R	
Equisetum fluviatile	(Water horsetail)		MR	MR	S	S			R	MR
Equisetum palustre	(Marsh horsetail)		MR	MR	MS	S			R	MR
Hippueris vulgaris	(Marestail)		R	MR	MS	S		MS	R	
Nasturtium officinale	(Watercress)		MS	MS	MS	MS	S	S	R	MR
Rumex hydrolapathum	(Water dock)		MR	MR	MS	MS			R	
Saggittaria safittifolia	(Arrow head)		R	MS	MS	S			R	
Floating SPP										
Callitriche stagnalis	(Common water starwort)	R	S	S	S			S	S	MR
Lemna minor	(Common duckweed)	R	MS			R	S	S	S	
Nuphar lutea	(Yellow water-lily)	MR	MR			MR	S	R	R	MS
Nympheae alba	(White water-lily)	MR	MR			MR	S	R	R	
Potamogeton natans	(Broadleaved pondweed)	R	MS	MS		MS		MR	MS	MS
Polygonum amphibium	(Amphibious bistort)	MR	MR			MR		R	MS	
Ranunculus spp.	(Water crowfoot)	R	S			S		S	S	MR
Submerged vascular										
Ceratophyllum demersum	(Rigid hornwort)			MR	S	S	R	S	S	
Elodea canadensis	(Canadian waterweed)			S	S	S	R	S	S	
Hottonia palustris	(Water violet)			MS	S	S	R	S	S	
Lemna trisulca	(Ivy leaved duckweed)			S			R	S	S	
Myriophyllum spp.	(Water milfoils)			S	S	S	R	S	S	MS
Potamogeton crispus	(Curled pondweed)			S	S	S	R	S	S	
Potamogeton pectinatus	(Fennel leaved pondweed)			S	S	S	R	S	S	
Zanichellia palustris	(Horned pondweed)					MS	R		S	
Algae										
Cladophora spp.	(Cott)			S	R	R	R	S	S	
Enteromorpha intestinalis	(Bladderweed)			R	R	R	R	S	S	
Rhizoclonium spp.				MR	R	R	R	S	S	
Spirogyra spp.	(Cott)			MR	R	R	R	S	S	
Vaucheria spp.				R	R	R	R	S	S	

Key:
S   Susceptible – complete or almost complete kill. Little or no regrowth during season of application.
MS   Moderately susceptible – Partial kill or effectively suppressed during season of application.
MR   Moderately resistant – Temporary suppression – Regrowth during year of treatment.
R   Resistant. No effect.

Source: British Agrochemicals Association.

displays the susceptibility of some commonly occurring aquatic weeds to herbicides.

Aquatic herbicides can be applied as:

- A foliar spray on to the plants to be controlled;
- A solution added to the water;
- Granules, which when added to the water, are dissolved for general dispersal and for absorption by bottom silt.

Foliar sprays can be selective in space, but the water-borne methods are selective only through the differing physiological sensitivities of plants in treated zones. Granules allow slow release and dispersal which is valuable in moving water bodies.

Whereas general principles of herbicide use apply in aquatic as in terrestrial vegetation, water bodies suffer from the fact that they are readily polluted by the decay of affected vegetation in situ. This problem can be ameliorated by:

- Applying herbicides early (April/May) when the biomass is relatively low. However, this may be particularly damaging to fauna living on treated plants.
- Treating vegetation in sections as described above.

Herbicides adsorbed on to bottom mud can have a residual action and hence prolong the period of control, but also of course the period of potential water contamination.

Biological control

Healthy aquatic habitats depend upon the maintenance of balanced food chains whereby population numbers of any one species are controlled and waste products consumed. Sufficient 'inoculum' for the development of such a system can often be obtained by transferring a few buckets of silt from an established water body to a new one. Specific species of fauna, such as water snails, or flora can also be transferred if desired.

Non-native species can be used for biological control, and can be very successful in targeting specific plants. However, they have considerable potential for harm if they are either too 'successful' or 'escape' to colonize other habitats. This has occurred abroad with water hyacinth and in Britain with the hybrid marram grass, *Spartina*. One example of a non-native species currently receiving attention is the Chinese Grass Carp (*Ctenopharyngodon idella*). This is a herbivorous fish which 'grazes' on a variety of submerged and floating plants including filamentous algae and duckweed. The results of experiments to assess its potential in the biological control of such weeds are quite promising.

Terrestrial grazers such as sheep, cattle, geese and ducks can be used to control bankside vegetation where this is appropriate. However, the poaching effect of larger stock at the water's edge may be unacceptable. Care should be taken that manure does not add to the fertility of the water.

Environmental control

1. **Control of light levels**

   Bankside plants, particularly trees, can be used to keep submerged and floating vegetation in check through the effects of shade on photosynthesis. However, where small enclosed bodies of water are concerned, the silting and eutrophication effects of fallen leaves and litter may produce more problems than are solved by shading.

2. **Control of water depth**

   Deepening channels and steepening banks reduce the scope for colonization by emergent vegetation. These operations, by increasing flow rates, can discourage the development of other forms of aquatic weeds. Increasing depth also reduces the volume of water which is well illuminated and thereby decreases the scope for photosynthesizing plants. However, it does significantly decrease the conservation and wildlife value of the water body.

3. **Control of nutrient status**

   A high nutrient status causes growth of biologically productive weeds in water, as it does on land, and reduces species diversity. Excess eutrophication can deoxygenate water to the extent that it becomes dead as a habitat.

   Techniques to immobilize an essential nutrient have been used to control macrophyte growth where it is not possible to control eutrophication of water. Ideally water quality needs to be controlled at source by reducing inputs, such as sewage, farm effluents, fertilizer leachates, products of decay and so on.

4. **Erosion control**

   Erosion of banks by precipitation, run-off, moving water and waves can be a serious problem in some water bodies, the Broads, for example. Motor boats can cause severe and destructive erosion of banks with resulting recession of shorelines, high levels of water turbidity and siltation. Bankside vegetation can be used to control erosion by the buffering effect of its foliage and the binding effect of its roots.

21 WATER BODIES: GUIDELINES ON WEED CONTROL IN AMENITY LAKES – AN EXAMPLE

**21.1
Introduction**
At this stage it may be helpful to refer to an example of weed control in amenity lakes. These guidelines were prepared by an ecologist as a result of experience gained whilst on the staff of the Milton Keynes Development Corporation. They emphasize the importance of understanding the biological and ecological characteristics of any situation where weeds are a problem, before choosing between mechanical and chemical control measures.

BIOLOGICAL CHARACTERISTICS

In the case of the amenity lakes at Milton Keynes, *Elodea candensis* was the particular weed causing concern. It was recognized, however, that other species could become the focus for attention in future.

The main features of *Elodea* are that it appears to have a growth rate that is erratic: sometimes it is slow and remains as a small spreading plant, whilst at others it 'blossoms'. The growth rate and form appear to change from year to year and from place to place. It seems to disappear from some places and to appear in others. *Elodea* only becomes a problem for boats if its growth is sufficiently extensive to reach or come close to the surface and it does not always do so.

Most important is the fact that *Elodea* is a weakly-rooted species. Consequently *Elodea* is likely to be largely resistant to any herbicide that relies upon being taken up through the roots.

LOCATIONAL CHARACTERISTICS

It is important to map the distribution of the offensive aquatic plants accurately before deciding upon a particular plan of control. Even relatively small patches of weed in a large area of water can severely affect sailing and other recreational activities.

Aquatic weed control that involves burning a hole in a sea of weed appears to be relatively easy. Removing patch(es) of weed in a sea of water is difficult and costly.

KNOCK-ON EFFECTS

It is well known that if cut weed is not removed it is likely to cause a deoxygenation problem. In addition it will float around the lake and seriously interfere with sailing and wind-surfing. Some or a lot of it may come to rest on banks, where it will rot down and produce a local environmental problem.

The breakdown of the plants will also release nutrients back into the system, whilst cropping results in their removal.

21.2
Selection of control method

After these important preliminaries have been concluded, consideration needs to be given to the basic characteristics of the two main management techniques:

1. Mechanical management
2. Chemical management

Each of these is reviewed in turn.

MECHANICAL MANAGEMENT

Mechanical management has advantages in the treatment of patches of weed. Specific areas can be dealt with; it does not involve the treatment of the whole lake.

Other factors considered by the ecologist included:

- There is a need for a boat or boats that will cut and harvest. Relatively cheap craft capable of achieving this do not seem to be available. There are one or two craft on the market, but none of these were suitable for the purposes concerned. This is a situation in which the involvement of an imaginative engineer is essential.
- Vehicles and elevators are needed. A site for disposal is also required; the further it is from the lake the greater the transport costs.
- The machinery is in use for a very short time. For most of the year it is in store.
- The hiring of contractors and plant has its difficulties. Contractors with expertise in aquatic weed control are difficult to find: only one was known to the ecologist. Equipment can be hired, either for between 6 and 8 weeks to cover all eventualities, or for the week it is needed. The latter is also usually the week when everyone wants to cut weed.
- The cost implications of these alternatives are also important.
- Skilled operators are needed, or need to be trained, to operate in boats.

CHEMICAL MANAGEMENT

Factors of basic importance are the modes of action, the times of application and the availabilities of the various herbicides under consideration.
Other factors considered by the ecologist included:

- The effects on other parts of the ecological system, for example fish
  spawning sites and emergent macrophytes. It is undesirable to kill plants
  that have been specifically planted.
- The form of chemical: whether granular or liquid. This has implications
  for both the quantity required and the method of handling. Concentrated granules are preferred because they reduce the bulk, the amount
  of handling and the number of return trips for re-loading.
- The method of application.
- The breakdown period.
- Any other effects, safety precautions, and so on.
- Costs.
- The scope for partial treatment. In the lake in question, it was only
  necessary to treat 25 hectares out of a total of 40 hectares, comprising a
  southern basin. Only a small percentage of the 25 hectares was actually
  affected, the individual banks of weed being spread throughout the
  sailing area. The remaining 15 hectares were outside the sailing area
  and they were required to provide spawning areas, shelter and food for
  fish and other animals. The objective of controlling a few hectares of
  weed by applying to 25 hectares a dose – calculated, in the interests of
  ensuring no dilution, on the basis of 40 hectares – is not really efficient.
- The purchase or hiring of appropriate equipment, including boats with
  adequate capacity for the operators, applicators and a reasonable
  amount of chemical.
- A suitable method of application needs to be devised to ensure an even
  distribution of the chemical. The position of the boat and its speed has
  to be related to the application operation.
- Skilled operators used to handling both boats and chemicals are
  required.
- The Anglian Water Authority (AWA) requires that the water level be
  dropped by 300 mm, from a usual water depth of 1.7 m to 1.4 m, and
  that no water is let out of the lake during the breakdown period of the
  chemical. This has considerable implications: the water level could be
  down for considerably longer than four weeks, depending upon the
  weather.
- One effect of chemical treatment could be an algal bloom, which could
  cause all manner of problems. For example, it might lead to an extensive growth of filamentous algae that might affect boating and angling
  interests. If the bloom were of blue-green algae, they might wash up on
  the shoreline in large numbers and rot down, causing another environmental problem, both to the nose and to paddlers.

ADMINISTRATIVE CONSIDERATIONS

Almost as important as the choice of technique are the supporting administrative arrangements. These required careful attention in order to ensure that the control measures were effective. The main items are listed below:

- Budgets had to be prepared in September/November. The implications of this are that budgeting and purchasing decisions have to be made before it is known whether there is going to be a weed problem.
- The availability of equipment and chemicals. If a decision is left until the last minute then neither the equipment for mechanical or chemical management nor the chemicals may be available.
- The availability of financial and manpower resources:
  (a) to keep growth under surveillance
  (b) to carry out the work.
- In general, the landscape maintenance departments of local authorities are not used to working close to or in water and lack the necessary expertise in both mechanical and chemical control. This can be overcome by training, but staff turn-over needs to be taken into account.
- The work is also relatively short-term and involves at the most five days per year.
- There is the need to comply with the Health and Safety at Work Act.
- In order to do this work, men have to be taken off other jobs at one or two days' notice. This has had its difficulties because of sudden sickness or coincidence with a Royal or Ministerial visit. Priorities have to be ordered.
- The lowering of the lake for chemical control needs to take into account recreational and other aspects. It may coincide with a Bank Holiday, a sailing or other competitive event or an official opening. A host of interested groups, engineers, planners, recreation managers, landscape maintenance superintendents, clubs, societies, etc., have to be informed.
- Planning of the work in relation to weather is essential. The work has to be done on relatively still, warm days, of which there can be few in early Spring.
- The purchase of equipment has to be assessed in terms of capital and maintenance and the related loan charges.
- The management options depend upon the recreational use of a lake. A lake with a single use, for example water ski-ing, can be managed simply as a tank of water, whereas a lake with multiple uses, for example sailing, angling, nature conservation and with people walking and sitting around it, is very much more difficult.

**21.3
Implementation**

Once the use of a herbicide has been agreed with the AWA in principle, the procedure is as follows:

1. The rate and extent of growth is kept under surveillance;

2. When it is about 150 mm, various interest groups within Milton Keynes Development Corporation are consulted about the need to drop the water level;
3. The AWA are requested to drop the water level, which takes several days;
4. The men and equipment are organized;
5. When the water has reached the required level, it is necessary to wait for suitable weather in which to apply the herbicide;
6. This process can result in the chemical being applied some 20 to 30 days after growth was noted, by which time it may have grown 1000 to 1500 mm. The shortest possible time, if all is running well, between the growth being first noted and the application, is about 14 days.

21.4
Conclusion

In reflecting on his experiences the ecologist suggested a number of improvements which he felt would help considerably, not least financially. These were the need for:

• A better understanding of the biology of aquatic weeds;
• The development of a relatively cheap cutting cum harvesting machine. Such a machine, if it were available, might be the answer to the problems encountered and to those of others where the need is to control small patches in a large area of water.
• A herbicide and a method of application, at an operational scale, that could be used for, and would be effective, in the spot treatment of weeds in lakes.
• A better understanding and control of nitrogen and phosphate cycling. Hitherto the effect, not the cause, has been treated. If weeds are treated by either mechanical or chemical methods and not removed, the end result is likely to be a series of circular problems.

Such improvements would greatly ease the task of the Amenity Manager.

22 WATER BODIES: MAINTENANCE OF FORMAL AND INFORMAL WATER AREAS

22.1
Formal water areas

It is difficult to present meaningful figures for the maintenance of formal water areas, since they differ greatly in area, depth, water flow characteristics, accessory aids such as cascades, rills, channels, fountains, and so on. However, some guidelines are available on the maintenance of formal pools featuring fountains. The latter are probably the most problematic and costly maintenance items, where formal water bodies are concerned. They are therefore given special attention in this chapter.

22.2
Capital costs

It is difficult to provide a general picture of fountain costs, because of the many variables involved. However, an indication of representative costs can be obtained from the four examples given in Table 22.1

22.3
Operational considerations

Fountain pools and the fountains themselves require both regular and sometimes costly maintenance to keep them in good operating condition. It is important to recognize this at the planning and design stages, and not after the pool and fountain have been installed.

The design of pools and fountains for cost-effective management requires considerable attention to detail.

WATER DEPTH

Pool depth is a particularly important consideration and is influenced by several factors:

- Underwater lights are designed to be water cooled and operate best with 10 mm of water over their covers;
- When fountain pools are cleaned the total volume of water may have to be replaced. However, if pool water is appropriately strained,

Table 22.1   Water displays: capital cost guidelines

Type of installation	Cost	
	From £	To £
A simple jet with no underwater lighting	100	1 000
A programmed multiple jet fountain with lighting	1 000	20 000
A floating fountain on a lake or river	5 000	25 000
A programmed water light sound organ	50 000	500 000

Notes: The figures provided relate to 1980.
         Cost depends on complexity and scale.

filtered, treated with chemicals and sited away from potential sources of debris, this should not be necessary too often. Local water authorities will charge for the refilling of pools and should be consulted regarding the scale of charges. For example, in 1980 a pool of 400 m³ water volume cost approx. £75 to refill.

- Shallower water is usually less dangerous. This is particularly relevant in the case of fountains that attract large numbers of people, some of whom may get into the water wilfully or by accident.
- The various components of a fountain should look unobtrusive when the pool is empty. Unsightly parts, if exposed in a jumble, are likely to attract rubbish dumping and vandalism;
- Maintenance work, if carried out when a pool is filled with water, can be dangerous, because of the need to step over and around submerged pipework, cables, lamps, jets and pumps. In purpose-designed pools the approach pipework can be built into the concrete.

In the light of all these considerations, a reasonable operating water depth is usually between 400 mm and 700 mm.

There are several other functional requirements which need to be considered at the design stage.

Water quality
Procurement of a reliable supply of good quality water is important. Whilst chlorine and copper sulphate in the form of liquid or crystals can be used to keep water clear, their use depends on the type and location of the fountain. If plants and fish are to share water with a fountain, a healthy ecological balance must be established and maintained for them; too high a concentration of copper sulphate can kill off water life, but too little can cause pump filters to block up with algae. About five parts per million is a typical concentration. Algae can become resistant to either chlorine or copper sulphate, but not to both if they are used in combination and

alternated every two weeks or so. Fairly large doses every 3 or 4 days are more effective than smaller doses every day. If a fountain is intended to attract people into its pool, the water should be treated as if for a swimming pool. It is usually cost-effective to install automatic purification equipment for a larger fountain pool.

Topping up facilities
To avoid the labour cost of topping up formal pools, losses from evaporation, spillage and water blown out of the pool by the wind can be made up by an automatic topping-up system.

Wind speed and direction
If it is necessary to prevent water jets being blown out of the fountain area, a wind speed sensor can be utilized to step down the jet height or to cut off all supply when a particular wind speed is recorded.

Maintenance of pipework
The repainting of pipework in situ is not desirable. Properly galvanized or pre-treated paintwork should be used and can last for many years. It can, if desired, be touched up for the sake of visual appearance when the pool is repainted.

Selection and siting of pumps
Good quality pumps can run for years, but strainers must be checked regularly. It is a good idea to install a cut-out device to protect blocked pumps from damage.

Generally, submersible pumps need less pipework, a simpler pool construction and less maintenance. They are usually more expensive to install, but more economic to run. However, non-submersible pumps are preferable when a high degree of control is required, as it is, for example, in water organs. They are easier to repair and maintain, because they are not under water, but they do require a pump room.

Treatment of nozzles
Very fine jets are liable to block unless the water is kept clean. If it is not practical to maintain clean water, they will probably need to be checked regularly, but if possible nozzles below 5 mm diameter should not be used.

Lights
The replacement of lamps normally takes place only once a year. Unless the lights are mounted below the pool basin, behind glass, it is best if they are designed to be lifted clear of the water for bulb replacement so that the need to drain the pool is avoided.

Light glasses require regular cleaning in natural lakes or rivers, because their warmth and light encourages the growth of algae and weeds.

Winter maintenance

It is advisable to drain fountain pools including pipework during the periods when ice is most likely to form. If it is not practical to bring a large floating fountain ashore in winter, pumps should be filled with an anti-freeze solution or be sufficiently far below the water surface to prevent freezing up.

22.4
Operating costs

Two main types of operating costs are involved:

1. The running costs, consisting primarily of the energy required to power the fountain pumps. Fountains can consume a considerable amount of energy, depending on size and the number of running hours. At the prices ruling in 1980 a fairly large fountain comprising two 15 kw pumps and twelve 500 watt lamps consumed in the order of £2-worth of electricity per hour. The question of running times needs to be considered carefully at the design stage, and related to the planned operating budget. Some allowances should be made for un-predictable demands such as longer night-time running on summer evenings or special occasions. The budget for electrical energy consumption is best estimated by assessing the load required and by consulting the local electricity board regarding the appropriate tariff.
2. The maintenance costs incurred in performing routine cleaning tasks and in replacing certain parts, such as lamps.

MAINTENANCE SCHEDULES

Tables 22.2 and 22.3 illustrate the operations that need to be considered when planning fountain maintenance.

In drawing up the tables, no account has been taken of vandalism.

Table 22.2   Maintenance operations: guideline frequencies

Operation	Frequency
Switch on/switch off/attend	daily
Chemically treat	
(a) manually	2 or 3 day intervals
(b) check automatic dosing system	weekly
Clean strainer/filter	weekly
Check topping up and overflow systems	weekly
Clean pool (varies depending on local conditions)	from weekly to 6-monthly
Check and clean lamp glasses	monthly
Replace lamp bulbs	annually
Repaint pool and touch up pipework	annually
Check contractors of control system	annually
Check and clean nozzles	annually
Take precautions against ice	annually

Table 22.3   Replacement of parts: guideline frequencies

Item	Frequency
Service or exchange pump	every 2 years
Repair pool	5–15 years
Replace nozzle	5–50 years
Replace electric cables	10 years
Replace control system	10–20 years

Note: Generally faults are more likely to develop in mechanical than electrical parts.

22.5
Maintenance
of informal water
bodies

RESOURCE REQUIREMENTS

Whilst the availability of reliable resource requirement data is limited in the case of formal water features, there are some published guidelines for the maintenance of water bodies such as ponds and ditches. These have been collated and are presented in Table 22.4.

Table 22.4   The management of ponds and ditches: estimated resource requirements

Source	Operation	Time	Unit
FMH	Cut: tractor and flail	1 hour	1000 m
FMH	Cut: by hand	1 hour	100 m
Sa	Clear silt from bottom of ditch to bank using shovel, and dispose	3.7 hour	100 m
FMH	Clean ditches	5 hour	100 m
FMH	Clean and spread (in meadows) + JCB	10 hour	100 m
VC	Village pond restoration with vegetation and silt clearance	24–30 days	small pond
VC	Pond creation/sluice building	150–180 days	small pond
CCH	Clean pond (20–30 m diam)		
	(a) mechanically	6–10 hours	every 7–10
	(b) by hand	16–24 hours	years
Sh	Feed the ducks	15 mins	occasionally

See Table 2.2 on p. 37 for details of sources.

Further reading   Anon (1969) *Wildfowl Management on Inland Waters*. Booklet No. 3. The Game Conservancy.

Anon (1973) *Manual of Wetland Management*. International Waterfowl Research Bureau.

Barrett, P.R.F. (1981) *Aquatic Herbicides in Great Britain, Recent*

Changes and Possible Future Development. Proc. Aquatic Weeds and their Control. Assoc. Appl. Biol., Oxford, pp. 95–103.

British Waterways Board (1981) *Vegetation Control Manual*. British Waterways Board, Director of Engineering, London.

Brooks, A. (1976) *Waterways and Wetlands*. BTCV, Oxford.

Cave, T.G. (1983) Management of vegetation in or near water. In *Management of Vegetation* (ed. J.M. Way) British Crop Protection Council Monograph No. 26. BCPC, Croydon.

Dawson, F.H. (1979) Ecological management of vegetation in flowing waters. In *Ecology and Design in Amenity Land Management* (eds S.E. Wright and G.P. Buckley) Wye College, University of London.

Dawson, F.H. and Haslam, S.M. (1983) The management of river vegetation with particular reference to shading effects of marginal vegetation. *Landscape Planning*, **10**, 147–69.

Eaton, J.W. (1986) Waterplant ecology in landscape design. In *Ecology and Design in Landscape*. (eds A.D. Bradshaw, D.A. Goode and E. Thorp). The 24th symposium of the British Ecological Society. Blackwells, Oxford.

Eaton, J.W., Murphy, K.J. and Hyde, T.M. (1981) *Comparative Trials of Herbicidal and Mechanical Control of Aquatic Weeds in Canals*. Proc. Aquatic Weeds and their Control. Assoc. Appl. Biol., Oxford, pp. 105–116.

Ellis G. (1986) Go with the flow. *Horticulture Week*, 11th April. Herbicides in water.

Granfield, E.F. (1971) *Design, Construction and Maintenance of Earth Dams and Excavated Ponds*. Forestry Commission Forest Record. 75. HMSO.

Haslam, S.M. (1973) The management of British Wetlands. I. Economic and amenity uses. *Journal of Env. Mgt.*, **3**, 303–320.

Haslam, S.M. (1974) The management of British wetlands. 2. Conservation. *Journal of Env. Mgt.*, **4**, 345–361.

Haslam, S.M. and Wolsely, P.A. (1981) *River Vegetation – its Identification, Assessment and Management*. Cambridge University Press.

Kabisch, K. (1984) *Ponds and Pools – Oases in the Landscape*. Croom Helm, London.

Kelcey, J.G. (1981) *Weed Control in Amenity Lakes*. Proc. Aquatic Weeds and their Control. Assoc. Appl. Biol., Oxford, pp. 15–31.

Lewis, G. and Williams, G. (1984) *Rivers and Wildlife Handbook: a Guide to Practices which Further the Conservation of Wildlife on Rivers*. Royal Society for the Protection of Birds/Royal Society for Nature Conservation.

Liddle, M.J. and Scorgi, H.R.A. (1980) The effects of recreation on freshwater plants and animals: a review. *Biological Conservation*, **17**, 183–206.

MAFF (1979) *Guidelines for the use of herbicides in or near watercourses and lakes*. MAFF Booklet 2078. HMSO, London.

Miles, W.D. (1976) *Land Drainage and Weed Control*. Proceedings of symposium on Aquatic herbicides. British Crop Protection Council Monograph No. 16, 7–13.

Murphy, K.J., Eaton, J.W. and Hyde, T.M. (1982) *The Management of Aquatic Plants in a Navigable Canal System for Amenity and Recreation*. Proc. EWRS 6th Symposium on Aquatic Weeds. Novi Sad, Jugoslavia, pp. 141–151.

Newbold, C. (1975) Herbicides in aquatic systems. *Biological Conservation*, **7**, 97–118.

Newbold, C., Purseglove, J. and Holmes, N. (1983) *Nature Conservation and River Engineering*, NCC.

Price, H. (1981) *A Review of Current Mechanical Methods*. Proceedings of Symposium on Aquatic Weeds and their Control. Association of Applied Biologists, 77–78.

Roberts, H.A. (ED.) (1982) *Weed Control Handbook: Principles*. 7th edn. Blackwell Scientific Publications, Oxford.

Robson, T.O. (1976) *Aquatic Plants in Britain – their Occurrence and Significance as Weeds*. Proceedings of symposium on Aquatic Herbicides. British Crop Protection Council Monograph No. 16, 1–6.

Thornley, D.G. (1979) Water. In *Landscape Techniques* (ed. A.E. Weddle) Heinemann, London.

Witton, B.A. (1979) *Rivers, Lakes and Marshes*. Hodder & Stoughton.

23

THE MANAGEMENT OF HARD AND SYNTHETIC SURFACES: INTRODUCTION

23.1
Introduction

Typically an Amenity Manager has significant areas of open space and hard landscapes to manage and maintain as part of the total area and facilities available to the public. These include play areas; paths of hoggin and tarmac; pavements of concrete slabs; hard standings of concrete blocks and asphalt. Such areas need to be kept clean and weed free, safe and in good repair. Inevitably these requirements prompt a number of questions:

- What functions are the hard materials required to perform?
- What materials are available?
- What operations, tasks and methods are involved in ensuring that the materials perform the intended functions?
- What is the schedule of operations which typically require to be undertaken over a year?
- What resources are required in maintaining the hard surfaces?
- How much do the resources cost?
- What criteria should be used when considering the selection of materials for renovating hard surfacing in amenity areas?

The answers to these questions depend on many factors, principally:

- The material of which the surface is made and the way in which it has been designed, constructed and previously maintained;
- The functions which the surface are required to perform;
- The types and levels of use which the surface receives;
- The levels of maintenance required.

A main purpose of this chapter is to respond to these questions by providing some answers and guideline figures. It begins appropriately with a review of the range of hard surfaces, their characteristics and functions. This is followed by a check-list of the typical maintenance operations which need to be considered in the course of preparing a Management Plan. Accordingly, an indicative maintenance schedule is shown.

Attention then turns to the important matter of resource requirements.

These, as in the case of the other landscape components, have been collated from several sources. They are intended to provide no more than initial guidelines. The maintenance costs of hard surfaces are particularly difficult to specify as the reader of this chapter will discover.

FUNCTIONS

There are seven essential functions, which materials used for the hard surfacing of amenity areas are expected to perform:

- Hard wearing, especially in the case of those subjected to intense human and vehicular uses;
- Easy to construct, maintain and repair;
- Cost-effective to construct, maintain and repair;
- Visually attractive;
- Durable i.e. have a naturally long life;
- Helpful, where necessary, in delineating different functional areas or codes of behaviour, especially where traffic management is concerned;
- Safe for the intended types and levels of use.

The sections which follow immediately elaborate on each of these functions in turn.

Wear

Providing a surface which can withstand intensive wear is the main function of hard-surfaced areas. Roads carry vehicles, paths carry foot traffic, school playgrounds bear the intensive pressure of children at play and pedestrian precincts accommodate constant streams of shoppers. Thus the basic characteristic of materials used in such areas is a capacity to withstand wear or loads.

Many sports require hard wearing surfaces. Some of these are described in the chapter covering 'Sports Turf' and surfaces. Materials described in this chapter, such as asphalt and concrete, are used both informally and formally for many games.

Low maintenance

Hard surfacing can be used specifically to create areas which will require little maintenance. For example, much post-war corporation housing was set in a landscape of tarmac and concrete slabs in an attempt to create a maintenance-free environment. On a smaller scale, householders often convert even diminutive front gardens to paving or concrete, in order to save themselves the trouble of maintaining areas of grass.

Hard surfacing may be the best way to treat areas such as very steep slopes or inaccessible corners, the maintenance of which would otherwise be difficult. Small features, for example mowing trims, can also be constructed using materials which are relatively maintenance-free. Brick and granite setts are two such examples.

Appearance

Hard materials are used to create surfaces, which are usually attractive particularly in prestigious areas such as city centres and near to important buildings.

Durability

Durability and longevity are particularly desirable characteristics of costly materials such as asphalt and setts, since the toughest and most resistant surfaces are often expensive to construct.

Traffic control

Hard-surfacing materials can be used in a number of ways to guide, warn or slow down vehicles and pedestrians. The demarcation of parking spaces, using lines of setts in tarmac, is one example. 'Uncomfortable' surfaces can be used to discourage traffic. For example, sleeping policemen on roads serve to reduce vehicle speeds, and rough cobbled surfaces discourage pedestrians.

Safety

A range of specially-designed safety surfaces is available for use in children's playgrounds. They help to absorb shock and to prevent abrasions when children fall.

Loose materials like sand, leca and bark can serve the same purpose.

Bark and chips can make a safe but informal and resilient surface for trim track stations on jogging tracks and bridle ways.

THE MAIN MATERIALS

There are many different types of materials used for the hard surfacing of amenity areas, the main ones being:

- Rigid materials   e.g., in situ concrete;
- Units   e.g., slabs and setts;
- Flexible (unbound) e.g., gravel and crushed rock;
- Self-binding   e.g., hoggin and Redgra;
- Flexible (bound)   e.g., tarmac and asphalt.

The typical uses of both these and certain special surfaces are described in Table 23.1, which also summarizes the main merits and demerits of the materials.

The special surfaces have been designed primarily either for sporting or rural activities in situations where both the intensity of use and appearance are important. 'Pseudo-grass' falls into this category; special units are available to create hard-bearing surfaces which look 'green'. Fire path pots and the grasscrete type of blocks are examples. When filled with soil and grit they can support both a cover of plants and use by vehicles. These blocks are used for some rural car parks, for fire roads across grass and similar purposes.

Table 23.1 Hard surfaces: comparative evaluation of management requirements: cost-effectiveness

Type of surface	Examples of material	Typical uses	Advantages	Disadvantages
Rigid	In-situ concrete: plain, reinforced or fibrous with special finishes e.g. cobbles, brushed and washed aggregates	Farm yards and roads; Forecourts; Industrial areas; Many landscape uses	• Few problems if properly laid • Salt treatment of snow and ice needs care • Relatively cheap? • Easy to clean and repair • Very Strong, if well laid • Resistant to chemicals, e.g. oil, diesel	• Spread finishes difficult to match at repair stage. • Problems mainly from poor construction and may cause cracking • Sub base or solid ground formation not thick or consolidated enough • Lack of or inconsistent re-inforcing mesh • Insufficient or incorrectly positioned expansion points • Cost of repair can be high and specialist contractors needed for some work
Unit	Paving slabs – concrete – stone Setts Cobbles, pebbles Tiles, mosaics, terrazzo Bricks, brick paviors Blocks Firepath posts, Grasscrete, etc.	Many uses Prestigious landscapes Trims, features, prestigious landscape Anti-pedestrian and ornamental surfaces Very prestigious sites Many uses including hard/heavy wear uses 'Green' hard standing	• Few problems if properly laid • Factory made surfaces ensures consistency • Laying does not require special equipment or skill • Can tolerate some subsidence without problems • Small units are aesthetically attractive	• Insufficient thickness of sub-base or solid ground formation can causes movement, subsidence tilting, cracking of larger slabs • Mortar pointing may break up; poor drainage may wash out bedding and mortar or clay joining can wash through; damaged or dirt filled joints promote weed growth; sunken joints and brick encourage

Type	Material	Uses	Advantages	Disadvantages
	Wood, e.g. sleepers, log sections	Board walks; Mainly in private gardens, Stepping stones in grass	• Most repairs do not need specialist contractors • Relatively long-lasting (say 15 years) if properly treated and if foundation well drained	growth of moss making surface slippery • Unsuitable bricks will spoil in frost. Smooth units are prone to icing. Leaves and litter tend to stick to them • Not very hard wearing • Expensive to lay – may be skilled job • Hard to cut
Flexible Unbound	Loose gravel, crushed rock, gravel, sand, Leca, Bark, wood chips	Play areas Informal paths; bridleways; trim track station surfaces	• Relatively cheap • Appropriate appearance informal settings • Self draining	• Unsuitable for heavy vehicular use (causes rutting, pot holing) • Unsuitable for steep slopes (surface may wash downhill) • Stable ground formation, well constructed sub-base, edging, surface water drainage essential • May be difficult to walk on; very loose surfaces can make passage of prams, wheelchairs, etc., impossible • Weed growth can be severe
Self-binding	Hoggin, Redgra, cinders	Low wear drives; paths; tracks; mainly rural Sports surfaces	• Repairs cheap and easy	• Clearance of snow and ice by machine is difficult without damage to surface • Loose surfaces cannot be kept by sweeping • Subject to abuse by children

cont'd

Table 23.1 (cont'd)

Type of surface	Examples of material	Typical uses	Advantages	Disadvantages
Flexible	Tarmac, Bitmac with or without special finish e.g. grit, pea shingle, or colours, or painted finishes	Playgrounds Kickabouts Hardwear paths Roads	• Easy to lay • Will last for many years if well constructed • Easy to keep clean • Economic on large areas • Readily available • Simple to repair – can reduce glare	• Relatively unattractive in appearance • Movement of sub base or soil. • Insufficient thickness of sub-base or surfacing, chippings inadequately bound together can cause cracking or break down of surface which is aggravated by use • Badly coated stone can be broken up by heavy rain • Use of too coarse chippings reduces • Poor drainage falls or puddling can aggravate break-up through nature permeating to formation causing soil movement • Too much tar/bitumen can melt in hot weather and cause patches which are slippery in wet or frosty weather. • Wet paper or leaves on surface can be very slippery • Lack of edgings can cause spreading, especially in warm weather

		• Resurfacing needs to be by specialist contractor • Difficult to lay on tortuous designs • Damaged by oil or diesel. • Expensive • Insufficiently thick or consolidated sub-bases • Inconsistent density of wearing layers can cause cracking, etc. as for tarmac • Badly damaged and constructed drainage falls • Poor falls and levels can cause hazards, as asphalt can be very slippery and even thin ice can be dangerous.
Asphalt	Very heavy wear areas, e.g. motorways	• Is lowest maintenance surfacing material, if properly laid • Hard tough heavy duty • Waterproof • Can be laid to fine tolerance, so ensuring good drainage
Other	Special surfaces, e.g. Tartan Track Synthetic Turf Safety surfaces, e.g. rubber tiles and mats e.g. Terrain Reinforcing meshes, e.g. Netlon	Good quality, hard wear sports areas Top quality, sports pitches Playgrounds Construction of temporary roads Reinforcing grass in rural car parks

23.2
The maintenance tasks

The principal maintenance operations entailed in the upkeep of the chief hard surfacing materials are displayed in Table 23.2. They fall into five main categories. A review of those items requiring special comment follows, including mention of appropriate methods.

CLEANSING OPERATIONS

The most important day-to-day maintenance operation on hard surfaces is cleansing. The bulk of this work usually consists of the removal of litter, including fallen leaves. From time to time it is likely that mud or snow will need to be cleared and ice will have to be removed. Prestigious hard surfaces need periodic washing down and stains may need special treatment or scrubbing.

EFFECTS OF USERS

The need for cleaning hard landscape depends very largely on both the activities and behaviour of people using an area. The amount of litter and rubbish which people drop differs between areas and parts of the country.

Landscapes near to shopping areas, take-away food shops or bus stops are liable to receive a lot of litter. Playgrounds in 'rough' areas are likely to receive more broken glass and rubbish than those in quieter neighbourhoods.

The way in which domestic and trade rubbish is collected and the location of litter bins affects the need for cleansing. For example, if plastic sacks used for refuse are left out on the pavement for the dustmen, they are likely to be torn open by dogs. Such collection systems can allow an inordinate amount of rubbish to escape into the landscape, leaving the Amenity Manager to contend with a by-product of the Cleansing Department.

METHODS

The methods which can be used to clean hard surfaces, and hence the time required, depends on the type of surface to be cleaned and the design of the hard area.

Materials which have a firm cohesive surface are relatively easy to clean. They can be swept; blown or vacuumed free of certain types of rubbish; be scraped free of mud or snow; and washed or scrubbed down to remove dirt or algae.

In contrast, those materials which have a loose or unbound surface are difficult to clean without taking part of the surfacing material away with the rubbish. Alternatively, self-binding materials like hoggin may start to break up if they have been badly laid, over used or badly maintained. The same may apply to tarmac, concrete, brick and other materials. Indeed all

Table 23.2 Management of hard surfaces: checklist of maintenance operations

Material Operation	Rigid	Slabs	Unit				Flexible		Tarmac	Asphalt
			Setts cobbles	Bricks paviors	Inter-lock	Tiles	Unbound	Self-binding		
Check and repair										
Subsidence	/	/	/	/	/	/	Roll regularly; fill and relevel ruts etc	/	/	/
Cracks	/	/	/	/	/	/	–	–	/	/
Joints	/	/	/	/	/	/	–	–	/	/
Spalling	/	–	–	/	/	/	–	–	–	–
Surfaces	/	/	Keep spare pavers for repairs			/	Rake roll and retap with stone as necessary		/	/
Sweep or Collect litter	/	/	/	/	/	/	Rake to clean litter and to enhance appearance		/	/
Check and Clean										
Drainage systems	/	/	/	/	/	/	/	/	/	/
Stains	/	/	/	/	/	/	–	–	/	/
Control Weeds	/	/	/	/	/	/	/	/	/	/
Moss, Algae	/	/	/	/	/	/	–	–	?	?
Snow and Ice Clear	/	/	/	/	/	/	Care needed to prevent damage to surface		/	/
Grit	/	/	Grit needed on smooth surfaces		/	/	/	/	Grit needed on smooth surfaces	
Salt	Beware salt on concrete	/	/	/	/	/	/	/	/	/

Key: / operation required
     – operation not required
     ? operation possibly required

materials, except the most durable, eventually present the same type of cleaning problems as unbound surfaces.

The easiest way of cleaning loose surfaces is by hand picking of rubbish and by raking. These methods are slow and not very satisfactory. Not all litter can be removed in this way and the loose material inevitably becomes contaminated with fine debris, such as soil, leaves and litter over time. It then starts to lose its 'hard' surface character, may become unsightly and can also be dangerous. For example, glass in children's sand pits is a serious hazard.

Design can help in preventing contamination. For example, play areas can be built with a raised rim to help prevent the entry of rubbish and to deter dogs.

ECONOMIES OF SCALE

Costs of hard-surface maintenance can be much reduced if operations such as sweeping or litter collection can be mechanized. Mechanization may be worthwhile if total areas of hard surface, layouts and access facilities are suitable. The scope for mechanizing maintenance operations is therefore partially dependent on good design.

Factors which favour use of machines include:

- Large unit areas in close proximity, so that machinery does not have to be transported far between sites. A large park or school grounds, for example, with paths, playgrounds and kickabouts, may justify a sweeper of its own;
- Large areas without obstructions, such as street furniture or trees;
- Continuous levels, uninterrupted by steps;
- Suitable widths of paths and entrances to, for example, playgrounds, enabling machinery to gain easy access for work.

TOOLS AND EQUIPMENT FOR CLEANING

Machines for sweeping and cleaning may be based on a rotating brush, a vacuum head, or a combination of both. Some come as accessories to powered units which a manager may already possess. Machines which blow are also available and are used mainly for accumulating autumn leaves into piles for easier collection.

Staff tend to prefer mechanical to manual litter collection methods and may positively enjoy using machines such as the 'Billy Goat'. This is a real benefit of mechanization.

It may be worthwhile to hire rather than buy sweepers for occasional use, such as the removal of autumn leaves or litter collection after a special event.

However, it should be noted that a brush and shovel supplemented by hand picking is still a cost-effective way to clean hard surfaces in many situations and are widely used. They are versatile, quickly loaded and unloaded and easy to transport.

REPAIRS AND OTHER NON-ROUTINE OPERATIONS

The need for these operations depends on some of the factors mentioned at the start of this chapter. It is possible to compare hard surfaces with cars in relation to repairs. It may be cheaper to keep an old car running, even though it needs frequent repairs, than to invest in a new, trouble-free model. However, there is a break-even point where cost and the nuisance value of having a faulty landscape (or car) out of use and of having to arrange for repair outweighs other factors. Bearing this in mind, a manager needs to decide how much repair is warranted and when the time is right to renew or replace the particular hard surface.

THE MAINTENANCE SCHEDULE

An Amenity Manager is likely to need a guideline schedule for the maintenance of hard surfaces, as part of the overall Management Plan for the particular amenities and landscape involved. Table 23.3 provides an example of such a schedule, covering the principal operations and the associated frequencies. The frequency with which maintenance operations are carried out during a week, month, season or year, depends very much on a combination of functional, aesthetic and financial factors. Frequencies may be hard to predict, with the result that a regular schedule of inspection is needed. Usually inspection is likely to entail no more than a quick glance from operatives as they carry out other work in the vicinity. Allocating time for inspection is therefore often unnecessary. However, an Amenity Manager is responsible for the safety of users, and has a duty to act accordingly. A cost-effective policy may be to inspect known potential trouble-spots frequently, such as tarmac which is starting to break up, so that remedial action can be taken when appropriate. This is less time-consuming than regular inspections of all surfaces.

23.3
The resource
requirements

These requirements fall into two categories: physical and financial. Each is reviewed separately in the paragraphs which follow.

ESTIMATES OF PHYSICAL RESOURCES

Some resource estimates for the chief maintenance operations entailed in the management of hard surfaces are given in Tables 23.4 to 23.8 inclusive. Specifically these tables cover litter collecting, sweeping, cleaning, and controlling weeds; managing all-weather surfaces; transporting materials; repairing a range of surfaces.

Table 23.3 Management of hard surfaces: suggested maintenance schedule

Intensity of use: Type of area:	Very intensive Ornamental Formal Prestigious		Heavy Urban		Heavy Rural		Medium Urban		Little Urban	
Operation	CHECK	ACTION	CHECK	ACTION	CHECK	ACTION	CHECK	ACTION	CHECK	ACTION
Sweep or rake	1/day	1/day	1/day	1/1–5 days	1/day	1/1–5 days	1/wk	1/2–4 days	1/mth	As nec
Clean drains and ditches	1/day	As nec ASAP	1/wk	As nec	1/wk	As nec	1/2 wks	As nec	1/mth	As nec
Clean gullies, Silt traps, etc.	1/wk	As nec ASAP more frequently at leaf fall	1/mth	As nec	1/wk	As nec	1/mth	As nec	1/mth	As nec
Clean Stains	1/day	As nec ASAP	1/day	As nec	–	–	1/mth	As nec	1/mth	As nec
Wash	1/day	1/wk or As nec	–	–	–	–	–	–	–	–
Control weeds	Apply persistent residual herbicide late in winter–early spring Spot treat with contact herbicide or hand weed as necessary									
Control algae Moss	Apply algicide									
Monitor nature and levels of usage										
Check and repair	1/day	As nec ASAP	1/wk	As nec ASAP	1/wk	As nec ASAP	1/2 wks	As nec	1/mth	As nec
Cracks	1/day	As nec ASAP	1/wk	As nec ASAP	1/wk	As nec ASAP	1/2 wks	As nec	1/mth	As nec
Joints	1/day	As nec ASAP	1/wk	As nec ASAP	1/wk	As nec ASAP	1/2 wks	As nec	1/mth	As nec
Spalling	1/day	As nec ASAP	1/wk	As nec ASAP	1/wk	As nec ASAP	1/2 wks	As nec	1/mth	As nec
Surfaces	1/day	As nec ASAP	1/wk	As nec ASAP	1/wk	As nec ASAP	1/2 wks	As nec	1/mth	As nec

Table 23.4 Management of hard surfaces: estimated resource requirements

Source	Operations	SMV	Unit
	Collecting litter, sweeping, cleaning		
T	Litter pick: hard surfaces	9.90	100 m^2
T	Litter pick: footpaths	1.26	100 m^2
Sh	Vac Air Vulture	3.00	100 m^2
D	Sweep paths with parkamatic	18.00	100 m^2
D	Sweep paths and dispose	10.00	100 m^2
T	Sweep footpaths	6.18	100 m^2
Sa	Sweep paths and dispose	69.97	100 m^2
Sh	Sweep paths and playgrounds (manually)	15.57	100 m^2
L	Sweep asphalt/slabbed area	9.93	100 m^2
Sa	Sweep tarmac/concrete areas and dispose	28.63	100 m^2
T	Sweep paved areas (covered/open)	12.40	100 m^2
W	Clean accumulated mud, etc., from porous surface, paths, cut back overhanging soil edges	474.00	100 m^2
L	Rake ash/gravel paths	9.96	100 m^2
D	Rake leaves from chipping pathway	10.00	100 m^2
Sa	Scrape mud off path or road, clean off and dispose	143.16	100 m^2
T	Wash down hard areas	37.00	100 m^2
	Weed control		
W	Spray total ground area: knapsack sprayer	32.50	100 m^2
W	Tractor-mounted sprayer and boom	1.76	100 m^2
W	Apply granular herbicide by hand along fence lines, etc.	2.70	100 lm
W	By chest-mounted applicator	0.92	100 m^2

Table 23.5 Management of all-weather surfaces: estimated resource requirements

Source	Surface/maintenance operation	Time input	Unit
H	Maintenance to Redgra tennis court (lute, brush, roll)	120.00	Tennis Court
Sa	Redgra: Rake (1 m rake × 2 ways)	2.34	100 m^2
Sa	Lute (1.3 m lute × 2 ways)	1.90	100 m^2
Sa	Brush (1 m brush × 2 ways)	1.71	100 m^2
Sa	Roll (1.3 m roller × 1 way)	1.12	100 m^2
Sh	Spread Ohsit	47.90	100 m^2
Sh	Spread Dri-pla	51.50	10 m^2
Sa	Brush and roll Redgra, combined operation	1.15	100 m^2
H	Roll tennis court in conjunction with Sweeping	22.50	Tennis Court
Sh	Roll Ohsit, Dri-Pla fast gear	4.31	100 m^2
	slow gear	5.99	100 m^2
Sa	Dig and rake sandpit (long jump)	30.00	Pit
H	Rake and level long jump sand	6.80	Pit

Table 23.6   Management of hard surface–transport and disposal
activities: estimated resource requirements
See also ground preparation

Source	Operation	Time input	Unit
Sh	Load dumper	12.00	dumper
Sh	Load wheelbarrow	1.60	barrow
L	Load materials by hand: sand, soil, ash, etc.	23.99	100 m^3
L	Load materials by hand: rubbish, weeds, leaves	19.26	100 m^3
Sh	Load broken masonry, etc., largely by hand	37.93	m^3
L	Unload materials by hand	72.30	m^3
L	Walk with barrow laden	2.34	100 m
Sh	Walk with barrow full and empty	2.19	100 m
L	Walk with barrow unladen	2.06	100 m
D	Wheel loaded barrow up to 25 m, tip and return	10.00	100 m
L	Attach trailer to tractor	1.00	occasion
Sh	Travel by tractor with tractor within park	7.44	1000 m
Sh	Drive tractor with trailer on public highways	3.27	1000 m
L	Unhitch trailer from tractor	4.30	occasion
D	Travel : under 1 kilometre	3.12	1000 m
	over 1 kilometre	7.28	
L	Tip load from trailer	3.52	occ
H	Tip to unload 0.57 m^3 vehicle	3.00	load

Table 23.8 provides an illustration of how the data can be used to compare the total annual maintenance requirements of two alternative surfaces. However, work rates for hard surface maintenance need to be treated with great caution, because so many variables are involved. The fact that only a few Authorities provide values for these activities indicates how hard they are to measure. In particular, the need for litter picking and cleaning depends almost entirely on the attitudes and habits of people in different locations.

As a general guide, it is sensible to allow an overall figure of, say, between 2.5 and 5.0% of staff time for the maintenance of hard surfaces in an organization where hard surfacing accounts for 10% of the total landscaped area.

FINANCIAL CONSIDERATIONS

The variability of site and other factors makes it impossible to provide any meaningful average cost figures for hard surfaces. In the absence of such data, Table 23.9 enumerates some of the main factors that influence costs.

Most hard surfaces are relatively expensive to construct compared to say grass or planted areas.

Maintenance costs depend mainly on the nature of the original ma-

Table 23.7 Management of hard surfaces – repairs: estimated resource requirements

Source	Operation	Time input	Unit
L	Spread ashes, chips, etc.	125.60 mins	100 m^2
Sh	Spread ash, chatter up to 7.6 cm – 15.2 cm	6.47 – 30.42 mins	10 m^2
	deep from heaps on or near site	or 19.02 – 28.90 mins	m^3
Sh	Spread (7.6 cm × 3.8 cm) hardcore up to 15.32 cm	17.49 – 38.92 mins	10 m^2
	from heaps on or near site	or 16.22 – 35.97 mins	m^3
Sh	Spread asphalt base coat	40.96 mins	10 m^2
Sh	Spread asphalt topping	34.49 mins	10 m^2
Sh	Roll hardcore: low gear	9.46 mins	100 m^2
Sh	high gear	14.97 mins	100 m^2
Sh	Roll asphalt: base and top coats depending	29.94 – 56.68 mins	100 m^2
	on size of area		
FMH	Tarmac repairs	4.00 hrs	100 m^2
Sa	Lay ready mixed concrete	40.81 mins	m^3
FMH	Hoggin repairs (roads)	10.00 hrs	100 m^2
FMH	Hoggin repairs (paths)	3.30 hrs	100 m
Sh	Lay edging – stone 91.4 × 15.2 × 5.1 cm	9.30 mins	1 lm
	Lay kerbstone 91.4 × 25.4 × 12.7 cm	20.01 mins	1 lm
Sa	Lay paving stone 61 × 61 × 61 cm with manual	18.26	1 no
	transport		
Sa	Lay paving stone 61 × 61 × 61 cm tractor	16.59	1 no
	assisted		
H	Lay paving slab	12.00	1 no
H	Lift, level and relay slab	5.20	1 no

terials, the quality of construction, the use to which the surface is put and the quality of previous maintenance and repair operations.

TOTAL LIFE-TIME COSTS

The selection of material should not be made on the basis of either capital or maintenance costs on their own. It is total costs, represented by the combination of both capital and maintenance expenditure over the lifespan of the surface, which should be the prime financial consideration.

The longevity of the hard-surface materials is an important consideration. Some materials, such as setts, are extremely durable: some cobbled roads have survived for centuries. Asphalt is also long-lived. Concrete block paving is highly durable and resistant to damage from loads, wear or chemicals.

The lifetime of most materials, depends very much on the amounts and types of use, as well as abuse, they receive. Well-laid and maintained self-binding porous surfaces can last for decades in locations of light occasional use such as private driveways. The same surface can break up in a few months, if subjected to heavy use from vehicles or horses. Poor

Table 23.8   Management of hard surfaces–cleansing: comparative estimates of resource requirements

Operation	SMV	Paviors: prestigious	Heavy use	Hoggin:	Light use
		Frequency Hrs/100 m²/yr	Total labour	Frequency Hrs/100 m²/yr	Total labour
Sweep or rake	10.00	1/day = 365/yr	60.80	1/mth = 12/yr	2.00
Clean drains and ditches	30.00	–	–	2/year	1.00
Clean gullies; silt traps, etc.	15.00	4/year	1.00	–	–
Clean stains	15.00	3/year	0.75	–	–
Wash	37.00	1/2 mth = 6/yr	3.70	–	–
Control weeds	32.50	1/yr	0.50	1/year	0.50
Control algae, moss	32.50	1/yr	0.50	–	–
Collect litter	10.00	–	–	1/wk = 52/yr	8.70
Check and repair subsidence	240.00	1/2 yr = 0.5/yr	2.00	–	–
Check and repair cracks	60.00	2/yr	2.00	–	–
Check and repair joints	60.00	2/yr	2.00	–	–
Check and repair surfaces	240.00	–	–	1/year	4.00
Total			75.20		16.20
Days/100 m²/year			9.40		2.03
Days/ha/year			940.00		203.00

Note: The table compares the total Annual Labour Requirements for two surfaces under different levels of use.

construction techniques shorten the lifetime of hard surfaces and in-adequate maintenance hastens deterioration.

**23.4
Renovation**

One of the chief problems associated with hard surfaces facing an Amenity Manager is the very high capital cost of most of these materials. A manager may be faced with crumbling tarmac or hoggin paths which are becoming increasingly expensive to maintain and repair. Grass in parks may be crossed by desire lines which are muddy and unattractive to look at and use. Access to sites may be by routes neither wide nor durable enough to take the vehicles which are needed in maintaining the landscape cost effectively.

The clients of such an Amenity Manager may consider that they are not being well served. His own staff will almost certainly find it difficult and unrewarding to carry out their work. Last, but not least, the maintenance

Table 23.9 Factors involved in estimating the maintenance costs of hard surfaces

a) Sweeping	i)	Size of area. Hand or machine, one man or two.
	ii)	Texture of surface. Smooth surfaces are quicker to clean. Gravel is difficult to sweep.
	iii)	Weather. Wet surfaces take longer, and dirt may become muddy and need washing.
	iv)	Severity of dirt. Food wrappings and waste and wet leaves take longer than light dust and dry leaves.
	v)	Amount of use. Well-used areas need more regular sweeping and dirt may be trampled.
b) Weeding	i)	Size of area. Small areas may need watering can or knapsack sprayer, large areas machine mounted sprayer.
	ii)	Texture of surface. Tarmac/asphalt only require edge treatment; paving, joints and edges; gravel, whole surface treatment.
	iii)	Weather. In windy weather spraying takes longer since more careful spraying or low drift nozzles will be used. In wet weather, spraying may be delayed.
	iv)	Severity of weed growth. In moist warm summers weed growth will be stronger and will require longer spraying times.
	v)	Type of growth. Type of chemical and mode of and time taken for spraying will depend on weed type.
	vi)	Amount of use. Heavily trafficked areas will have less weed growth but will require higher standards of removal. Chemicals may have to be restricted (for example, Play areas).
	vii)	Aspect. Shaded areas may have moss/lichen growth.
c) Repairs	i)	Size of area. Larger areas may need contract repairs, smaller areas may be done by hand, but may be difficult. Machine Hire may be necessary.
	ii)	Texture of surface. Tarmac/asphalt should require minimal treatment; paving and gravel more regular. Gravel is easy to work, tarmac more difficult.
	iii)	Weather. More repairs may be needed after frosty weather when sub-bases may have lifted or after wet weather when surfaces may have washed out or broken up. Wet weather work takes longer and may need protection.
	iv)	Severity of damage. As for i). Where many small areas of damage occur, contract repairs may be best.

cost graph is likely to be rising without commensurate benefits. What should be done?

The objectives are not hard to establish: to resurface ageing footpaths for pedestrians; to cater for users by providing them with new paths on appropriate desire lines; and to construct landscape maintenance tracks for staff use. The challenge is to achieve these objectives in the most cost-effective ways possible. The key questions which need to be faced are therefore:

- Which surfaces will perform and wear the best, need little maintenance and last a long time?
- Which surfaces should be selected?

In most cases the prime management decisions concerning hard surfaces cannot be divorced from design decisions.

CHOICE OF SURFACE

Where large capital sums are involved, an Amenity Manager simply may not be able to find enough money to carry out the job as desired. If at all possible, however, materials should be chosen that are fully capable of withstanding the types and levels of expected use. Failure to meet this basic requirement is likely to be counter-productive, resulting, within a few years, in a repetition of pot-holed hoggin, cracked concrete and rising repair and maintenance bills.

Some of the criteria which an Amenity Manager needs to consider in the selection process are:

Functional requirements
What materials can perform the required functions? Can merely restricted areas be treated with expensive materials without spoiling the desired effect?

For example, little-used rural farm roads are sometimes laid down as two wheel-tracks rather than as a complete road. Attractive ornamental effects can be produced even from cheap materials, perhaps with a proportion of higher quality units, such as setts, if design is good.

Pressure tolerance
Will the materials considered to be suitable stand up to all the pressures that are likely to be put upon them? Can pressures be restricted? For example can 'free range' motorcyclists be kept off hoggin paths by using barriers or other means? Is it certain that heavy lorries will not travel over the proposed brick-set pedestrian areas? Will the proposed tarmac hard-standing in reality be subjected to the erosive effects of diesel drips?

The surface chosen should be able to withstand all the stresses which the manager cannot be sure of controlling adequately.

Multi-purpose roles
Are the materials suitable for all the roles which they must play?

For example, brick is attractive but soon becomes messy and slippery in shaded locations. Most smooth surfaces also become slippery if they are wet, muddy, snowy or icy, or coated with damp leaves and litter. These points require particular attention if children or elderly and infirm people are to use the surfaces. Unbound surfaces, such as gravel, are relatively cheap to construct but present difficulties both for walkers with high-heeled shoes and for pram pushers.

It may be tempting to use hard surfacing to the exclusion of other landscape elements on sites where high wear or low maintenance is anticipated. The concrete and asphalt 'jungles' of many inner urban areas were built in this way, but they have provided a depressing and degrading environment for housing areas and schools. Money is now being spent on improving some of them by introducing planted areas and other internal landscape features. This is not to say that 'all-hard' landscapes cannot be attractive. However, they need to be sympathetically designed and may be more appropriate to city centre areas and building surrounds than to the main areas where people live and play.

Cost-effectiveness

How much will the surface cost to construct and will the result be cost-effective?

Poor standards of design or construction may lead to rapid deterioration of the surface, increased maintenance and higher repair costs, as well as a shortened lifespan. Badly built surfaces can also result in discomfort or danger to users. Movement or cracking of surfaces can cause accidents. Poor levels can lead to puddles and muddy patches, which become more hazardous in icy weather. Features such as ramps, steps and slopes, which are too steep or unexpected, can be dangerous.

A common design-cum-construction fault is an inadequate base, sub-base or sub-ground formation leading to the movement and cracking just described. Other design faults may cause problems indirectly. For example, path widths which are too narrow may make access for maintenance vehicles difficult or impossible. If vehicles do use the paths, wheels are likely to damage both path edges and the landscape beside them.

Hard surfacing may be more expensive on certain types of ground, such as very soft soils or sand. Some materials may be unsuitable for the topography of the site. Porous surfaces, for example, are unsuitable on steep slopes, since loose surface material is liable to move downhill under wear and weather.

The design of features adjacent to hard surfacing, such as beds and grass areas, is also important. For example, if soil levels are raised above hard areas, soil is liable to wash onto the surface. The resulting mud spoils appearances, may be hazardous and is difficult to clean off porous materials.

Loose surfacing materials, such as gravel or Leca, are liable to be thrown about by children. Pebbles on an artificial beach are likely to end up in the pond.

Base materials exposed through surface wear may also provide users with missiles.

Mechanization

Will layout and scale allow maintenance work to be mechanized and supply machine operators with machines which are easy to work?

Ease of access to and from the site, as well as internal access to all parts of the hard surfacing to allow effective operation, are important.

Mechanization can significantly reduce operating costs, but, as in the case of grass areas, scale is an important consideration. To some extent, though, this issue has dimininished in importance as a range of pedestrian and ride-on machinery has developed.

Cleaning

How easy is the surface to maintain and how frequently is cleaning required?

Despite fulfilling functional uses, such as that of sand in a play pit, it might be difficult to keep clean. All loose surfaces such as sand, gravel, bark and Leca are impossible to sweep. They are therefore difficult to keep free from leaves, litter and broken glass.

The amount of maintenance required by a surface depends on function as well as on the nature of the material. Children's play areas, for example, must be kept as safe and as hygienic as possible, free of glass and fouling by dogs. Prestigious or much frequented areas, such as shopping malls and precincts, also need frequent cleaning to maintain the standards required.

In contrast little-used paths may need only occasional attention.

Repair

Can the surface be repaired by direct labour or will specialist contractors need to be engaged? Are materials for repair easy to obtain? If work is to be done by unskilled or volunteer staff do the materials suit their capabilities?

Informal paths and walkways have been built quite satisfactorily by voluntary labour in rural areas. As the Riverside Walk by the Liverpool Garden Festival Site demonstrates unskilled, but well supervised, MSC teams have shown that they are capable of building prestigious hard areas to a high standard.

CONCLUSION

It is clear that the choice of surface should not depend only on construction or maintenance costs. Each manager will need to evaluate the many different factors involved, in order to make the most cost-effective selection.

Further reading   Anon (1987) Just like the real thing? *Horticulture Week*, 10th July.

Baker, S.W. and Bell, M.J. (1986) The playing characteristics of natural turf and synthetic turf surfaces for Association football. *Journal of the Sports Turf Research Institute*, **62**, 9–35.

Barnes, M. (1987) Concrete block paving. *Horticulture Week*, 19th June.

Percy, D. (1987) Paving all the way. *Horticulture Week*, 17th April.

Percy, D. (1987) Setting a style with stone. *Horticulture Week*, 21st April.

Percy, D. (1987) A new iron age. *Horticulture Week*, 1st May.

Shirley, D.E (1980) *An Introduction to Concrete*. Cement and Concrete Association.

Sports Turf Research Institute (1984) Artificial surfaces. *Sports Turf Bulletin*, **144**, 3–5.

Sports Turf Research Institute (1986) Artificial cricket wickets. *Sports Turf Bulletin*, **152**, 4–6.

24

THE MANAGEMENT OF STRUCTURES AND SERVICES: INTRODUCTION

24.1
Introduction

This chapter discusses the management of the structures and services which are likely to be under the care of an Amenity Manager. It covers such features as fences, seats, litter bins, play equipment, drainage and lighting, which form a part of landscaped areas. These features, as indicated in Table 24.1, perform a variety of functions. They tend to be dispersed throughout the landscape, and to be made of similar materials. In many ways maintenance and management of these features has more in common with the maintenance of buildings rather than of landscapes. Nevertheless Amenity Managers often find themselves responsible for their inspection, cleaning, repair and renewal.

   This chapter is intended to help Amenity Managers in planning and in carrying out their work in a cost-effective manner.

24.2
Characteristics

A brief account of the main characteristics of the structures follows, covering their composition, durability and longevity.

COMPOSITION

Most of these landscape structures are made of metal or wood, though concrete, stone and other materials may also be involved in their construction.

   Some of them, such as playground equipment, seats, gates, litter bins, are intended for active use. Others such as signs, bollards, walls and fences, lighting and drainage systems have a passive role.

DURABILITY

Metal
Whilst the capital costs of steel and wood are broadly similar, the former is more durable than the latter, if it is properly prepared and maintained. Galvanizing by zinc metal spray produces a very long lasting finish. Well-maintained galvanized steel items may last for 25 years or more, whereas wood is unlikely to last more than 10 years. Galvanized steel can be painted for cosmetic reasons, but painting is not necessary to prevent

Table 24.1   Main functions of structures and services

Structures and services	Functions
Playground equipment	Informal recreation
Playing field equipment	Formal sport and recreation
Fences and railings	Barriers and screens
Walls	Barriers and screens
Gates and stiles	Control of access
Seats	Rest and passive recreation
Litter bins	Collection of litter
Bollards	Restriction of access
Signs	Direction and information
Plant containers	Ornamental display
Tree grilles	Protection, whilst enabling irrigation, feeding and aeration
Pergolas, arbours and trellises	Ornamental display, shade and passive recreation
Drains and gulleys	Drainage
Lighting	Illumination

corrosion, as it is in the case of untreated steel. The maintenance requirements of galvanized metal are therefore far lower.

Wood

Timber is an attractive material, but it has a number of disadvantages. The quality of soft-wood may be variable and it needs treatment against decay. Round section soft-wood, for example as used in many play structures, tends to split along the grain. This can allow water to penetrate the untreated inner zone and provides easy access for knife damage, insertion of broken glass, etc. Even sleepers which are normally durable may vary in their capacity to withstand heavy use.

Timber shrinks for 2–3 years after installation. Bolts therefore need to be tightened up consistently over this time, especially in play equipment and where vandalism is likely.

All timber elements are vulnerable to vandalism by fire, knives, and so on. This may preclude the use of wood in areas which are very prone to damage.

LONGEVITY

Like hard surfaces, structures cannot develop; they only deteriorate. However, their life-times can be extended indefinitely in some cases by preventive maintenance such as rust proofing and painting.

24.3
Maintenance
operations and
schedules

For the most part maintenance involves cleaning and repairing the effects of use, of decay, and of accidental or deliberate damage.

Maintenance schedules are normally similar to those used for hard surfaces. They cover routine inspections, resulting in action when the need arises, and programmed operations such as periodic repainting or replacement of parts.

INSPECTIONS

A regular routine of inspection is needed for all those structures whose condition can affect the safety of users. Play equipment is the most important item in this respect. Specific guidelines follow later in the chapter (Figure 24.1 and Table 24.2).

Inspection of other items such as seats and litter bins can be less frequent but should nevertheless be part of a regular programme.

Log of equipment			Date of purchase		
Item			Date of installation		
Manufacturer			Warranty/		
Address			guarantee expires		
			Cost		
Tel No			Installation by		

Faults occurring	Date	Action taken	By whom	Cost	Signature

NPFA Playground Inspection Record

Date of inspection	Fault (if any)	Action taken	Date of repair	Signature

Figure 24.1   Sample record sheet for inspection of playgrounds and equipment

Table 24.2   The recommended 'fair play for children' safety checklist for inspections of playgrounds and equipment

---

Daily/Weekly Inspection. Site Inspection Record
Chipping parish council memorial field
Name of Inspector .... Date ....

1. *The site*
   - Is the access in good condition
   - Are all notices in good condition
   - Is the play area clean and tidy
   - Have litter bins been emptied
   - Is the surface under and around equipment in good condition
   - Are fencing and gates secure
   - Is seating in good repair
2. *Items of equipment – applicable to all*
   - Are all fittings in position and secure
   - Are there any protrusions or sharp edges
   - Are all moving parts working freely and quietly
   - Is the paintwork or other finishes in good repair
   - Are all safety measures in good repair
   - Is there any damaged woodwork
3. *Specific features*
   a) *Swings*
      - Are the seats damaged
      - Are shackles and chains in good condition
      - Is the main frame secure
   b) *Slides*
      - Is the sliding surface secure and free from obstructions
      - Is access to the slide entry complete and in good condition
      - Is the main frame secure
   c) *Rotating/rocking equipment*
      - Are pivoting and rotating bearings in good working order
      - Is the ground clearance correct
   d) *Other structures*
      - Are these complete and secure
      - Is the main frame secure
4. Have previously reported defects been rectified

Source: Playing Fields Association

REPAIR

It is usually good policy to repair damage to landscapes as soon as possible after it occurs. Neglect tends to encourage further damage; many Amenity Managers have found that speedy action is cost-effective because it significantly reduces further damage.

Landscape structures are particularly prone to vandalism. Smashed lamps, broken seats, torn netting, burnt stockades, cut bolts and surfaces covered in graffiti are everyday problems in inner city areas particularly.

It is therefore an important part of cost-effective management to ensure that the materials, design and construction used in these features can withstand deliberate damage as well as normal wear and tear. For example, fastenings should be hidden or sunken wherever possible. In some areas this may be impossible. Vandals today use efficient tools and may employ chainsaws, bolt cutters and other effective means to destroy landscape structures. In very badly affected areas it may not be cost-effective to repair or replace damaged features continually but much can be done through good establishment methods, such as community involvement in projects and good supervision after repairs are completed.

24.4 Organization considerations

Successful management of amenity structures involves coming to terms with four main considerations:

1. Access and therefore location of the features is important for easy and trouble-free maintenance.
2. The availability of spare parts is essential. A faulty or missing part may make a structure like a swing unsafe and therefore unusable even if the rest of it is quite sound. Features, such as play equipment, may therefore become obsolete if spare parts are unobtainable. Continuity of parts therefore affects the life expectancy of such structures. However, whilst standardization of structures and their spare parts can help to keep down costs, it may be desirable for other, design, reasons.
3. The features are usually fixtures, small and widely dispersed throughout the landscape.
4. The structures tend to fall outside the normal routine of landscape management since none of them relates exclusively to the landscape. Any or all of the amenity structures under the care of a local authority may be managed by a range of departments: Leisure and Recreation, Engineering, or Environmental Health.

Some organizations set up special teams to manage the structures and services for which they are responsible, because of the special requirements which these entail. Playground structures, in particular, need frequent inspections and maintenance to a very high standard for safety reasons. Playground maintenance alone may justify the establishment of a special unit to clean, inspect, paint, grease, repair and replace equipment to the standards required. Inspection and repair are usually carried out most cost-effectively from a vehicle and convenient access is therefore very important. Bromley Borough Council and Warrington New Town, for example, use mobile repair vans which can carry out work in situ. Bringing items back to a workshop for repair greatly increases the cost of maintenance.

24.5 Resource requirements and the management of specific structures

The cost of maintaining hard landscape structures and services depends on their function, their construction and the way they are used and maintained. Since each structure differs in these respects, the management of each feature needs to be considered separately.

The remainder of this chapter is devoted to outlining the management and maintenance requirements of the following specific structures: playgrounds and play equipment; fencing; gates, benches and seats; litter bins; pergolas, arbours and trellises; and lighting. These are the main structures and services which feature in open spaces provided for public enjoyment.

24.6
Playgrounds and play
equipment

The main emphasis in managing playgrounds and play equipment is on safety. Those who are responsible for play areas, and this includes many Amenity Managers, have a legal and moral duty to make sure that these elements are safe at all times. For this reason, play areas need extra care over and above the routine maintenance required to keep them sightly and in working order. The need for safety is best met by a system of routine inspections, a schedule of regular programmed servicing and repair, and if possible by call-out service to deal rapidly with emergencies.

The relevant British Standard (BS5696 Part 3 1979 Amendments AMO 3470) and the NPFA 'Playground Management for Local Councils' provide useful guidance on reasonable and practical schedules of inspection, maintenance and repair. Local authorities who are acknowledged experts in this field, such as Bromley Borough Council, may also be willing to give advice.

MAINTENANCE OPERATIONS

The maintenance of playgrounds involves several operations, the main ones being:

- Routine cleansing. This covers sweeping, washing, litter picking, etc. The normally advised frequency for these operations is daily, especially when the facilities are intensively used.
- Visual inspection. A check list, such as that shown in Table 24.2, can be used to cover all the necessary points. If inspection reveals that further work needs to be done, it should be followed by immediate repair in the case of minor defects. Where major faults are identified, a more detailed inspection is probably desirable prior to undertaking major repairs.
- Repair: minor jobs. It may be possible for maintenance staff on the site to carry these out as and when they occur. In any event, equipment which has become hazardous should be immobilized immediately, even if it cannot be repaired at the time.
- Major repairs. These should be carried out as quickly as possible, either by specialist operatives on site or by removing the faulty item to a workshop.
- Detailed inspection. At regular intervals suitably qualified staff, engineers, should carry out a detailed inspection of all equipment before undertaking any necessary services and repairs as recommended by the

manufacturers. As a general guideline the frequency of the detailed inspections of playgrounds and equipment should be at least annually, preferably twice yearly or even quarterly, depending on the intensity of use, incidence of vandalism, and so on.

Records of inspection and repairs need to be kept. These can serve both as management aids and as evidence in cases of legal action and other disputes. A sample record sheet is shown in Figure 24.1.

● Rolling programme of repairs, replacement, improvements. As parts reach the end of their lives they need to be replaced. Moving parts wear out particularly quickly, but even the main components may have a relatively short lifespan.

REPLACEMENT

The periodic need to replace play equipment presents an Amenity Manager with the opportunity to improve the cost-effectiveness of the services provided. Often the choice of available equipment is large, including updated versions of the existing designs; home designed and constructed items; and novelty items.

Frequently the view is taken that the risks associated with new types of equipment are substantial, on account of the possibility of design faults and high maintenance costs. Well-tried and tested, i.e. BSI approved equipment, is therefore usually regarded as the most cost-effective. Even then the range of available equipment is often large.

Tables 24.3 to 24.6 inclusive, which follow, present a generalized summary of the merits and demerits for each of the main items of commercially manufactured play equipment. The figures are based directly upon guidelines published by the National Playing Fields Association.

SURFACING UNDER EQUIPMENT

The surface on which play equipment stands is also important to the safety of children. At present experts still disagree about the most suitable type of surface. The NPFA booklet for example recommends special safety surfaces and does not recommend the use of tarmac. Other experts are of the opinion that the presence of safety surfaces encourages children to take risks that they would not normally hazard.

Other areas of disagreement are the impact absorption properties of sand, and the suitability of grass and soil as playground surfaces. Readers are advised to inspect a range of surfaces under intensive use before choosing the one most appropriate to their circumstances.

The advantages and disadvantages of different surfaces are summarized in Table 24.7. They are based on guidelines published by the NPFA.

Estimates of the resources required for cleaning, repairing and replacing the various surfaces are given in Chapter 23.

Table 24.3 Guidelines for play equipment replacement and selection: swings

Equipment type	Advantages	Disadvantages
1. One bay, single-seat swings[1]	By far the most popular item of equipment	Susceptible to vandalism (especially seats)
	Relatively cheap to purchase and install	Relatively high level of maintenance required
	Wide selection of sizes and types	Can be dangerous, but hazards can be reduced by impact absorbing seats and other safety measures, e.g. barriers
	Especially suitable for small children	
	Some designs visually attractive	
2. Multi-seat swings	Popular item of equipment	As above, but increased use entails greater risk because of proximity to users
	Relatively cheap to purchase, install and maintain	
	Wide selection of sizes and types	
	Suitable for older children	
3. Large tyre swings	Popular with groups of children	Weight of tyre and children can prove hazardous
	Relatively cheap to purchase and install	Usually timber frame with high level of wear and maintenance, especially to shackle components
		Subject to fire and other damage

[1] Frame: Tripod preferable for safety
2.45 m for toddlers and cradle seats
3.05 m for older kids and flat seats

Tyre seats are not advised, since they are often subject to burning or hacking. Constant replacement is therefore required.

Table 24.4 Guidelines for play equipment replacement and selection: slides

Equipment type	Advantages	Disadvantages
1. Free standing slides	Popular with children	Potentially hazardous due to heights. Should never exceed 2.5 m
	Wide selection of sizes	Expensive to purchase and install
	Modern stainless steel types require less maintenance	Older types difficult to repair and some subject to bimetal corrosion
2. Log cabin or mound slides[1]	Popular with children and and offering high play value	Expensive but can be cost-effective in long term
	Safer	
	Wide selection of sizes	
	Modern stainless steel types require less maintenance	
	Relatively easy to install	
[1] Log cabin	Provides shelter	Can serve as an unsalubrious nocturnal hang-out for teenagers;
Mound	The safest form	The mound is expensive to provide. Surfacing must be appropriate: soil/grass not suitable.

TYPES OF NEW EQUIPMENT

The risk that new types of equipment will reveal design faults, be hard to repair, need a lot of maintenance or be dangerous is high. Tried and tested, BSI approved equipment is therefore usually the most cost-effective.

DIY EQUIPMENT AND ADVENTURE PLAYGROUNDS

'Home-made', non-specialist designed items and adventure playground equipment is not suitable for unsupervised play. A human presence is needed to substitute for more capital intensive items in situations when such equipment is used.

THE MANAGEMENT OF PLAYGROUNDS AND EQUIPMENT: AN EXAMPLE

The Recreation Department of Bromley Borough Council is responsible for about 70 playgrounds and 500 individual items of play equipment. The

Table 24.5 Guidelines for play equipment replacement and selection: rocking horses

Equipment type	Advantages	Disadvantages
1. Rocking horses	Popular with younger children	Non-limiting motion types extremely hazardous
	Fairly cheap to purchase, install and maintain	
2. See-saws	Popular with younger children	Non-limiting motion types extremely hazardous
	Fairly cheap to purchase, install and maintain	
3. Roundabouts	Popular item for all age groups	Fairly expensive, particularly to maintain;
	Wide choice of types available	Hazardous without speed limiting motion or correct ground clearance
		Susceptible to vandalism
		Not-compatible for differing age groups if installed singly

following sections provide both a summary of the ways in which maintenance operations are organized and an indication of the resources required to undertake the principal maintenance tasks.

Routine cleansing is carried out by parks maintenance staff who visually inspect the playground. If anything is wrong, staff telephone the Development Division who aim to provide a 'same-day service'. If this proves impossible, then at least the faulty equipment is immobilized on the same day. This operates through a call-out service, which also handles other emergencies, such as fallen trees.

Repairs are carried out by a two-man team of engineers working full time and operation from a four-ton box lorry. Scheduled servicing is carried out quarterly by the same team. Each round of servicing takes about 2 weeks, therefore each playground takes about 2 hours to service.

This work is measured for bonus purposes as indicated in Table 24.8. About 20 minutes per item is allowed for each piece of equipment. Repairs which are likely to take longer than this are carried out separately on another visit or, if necessary, are taken back to the depot for attention.

Table 24.6 Guidelines for play equipment replacement and selection: climbing frames

Equipment type	Advantages	Disadvantages
1. Climbing frames	Fair cheap and easy to install	Limited play value
	Low maintenance	Potentially dangerous when wet or dirty, particularly those with high fall heights and with large diameter timber members rather than slender steel. (Hard for children to grip)
2. Timber multi-play	Very popular	Fairly expensive to purchase, install and maintain
	High play value, visually attractive	Some types susceptible to vandalism, especially fire
		May have a relatively short lifespan
		Older children tend to dominate and discourage smaller ones
3. Fibre-Glass/plastic	Popular with children.	Difficult to repair
	Relatively cheap and easy to install	Some types susceptible to vandalism or fire
4. Sand box and water play	Especially valuable for younger children	Requires protection against contamination by animals
	Relatively cheap to install and replenish	Frequent maintenance N.B. a sand pit will normally require daily maintenance

REPAIRS AND IMPROVEMENT

A rolling programme for the overhaul, renovation and replacement of timbers and bearings is carried out as time and labour permits. Other teams, for example those used in landscape construction, may help in this work.

Table 24.7   Guidelines for the choice of playground surfaces

Type of surface	Advantages	Disadvantages
1. Concrete	Very hard wearing	Fairly high cost
	Can be easily brushed clean	Serious injury can occur at extremely low fall heights
	Long life	Not recommended
	Virtually no maintenance	
2. Coated macadam hot-rolled asphalt	Hard wearing	Fairly high cost
	Can be brushed clean fairly easily	Serious injury can occur at extremely low fall heights
	Life expectancy 10 years	Can induce much higher rate of corrosion at ground level
	May be safer than some 'safety' surfaces, as children are less likely to take risks when playing on it.	
3. Synthetic rubber	Varying degree of impact absorption depending on type	Very high cost
		Subject to vandalism in some cases
	Little maintenance if not vandalised	Requires concrete or macadam foundation
	Durability questionable in some instances.	Not all have sufficient performance data available
		Some adhesion problems can be experienced
		May encourage children to take unwarranted risks

Acceptable if high cost can be justified particularly for up-grading existing concrete or coated macadam. In situ bonded granular materials may be most satisfactory.

cont'd

Table 24.7 (cont'd)

Type of surface	Advantages	Disadvantages
4. Rounded sand, fine shingle sand: min. 0.25 mm; max. 1.5 mm Shingle: min. 3 mm; max. 12 mm.	Fairly cheap to install (minimum depth 300 mm)	Impact absorption less good than commonly thought
		Needs to be contained within raised edging
		Requires high level of maintenance
		Easily contaminated by glass and animals and is difficult to clean
		Can become dirty
		Larger sizes can be thrown
		Can be dangerous if spilt onto adjacent hard surfaces – liable to penetrate bearings and increase wear on adjacent items of equipment
		Difficult to obtain in some areas
	Recommended if animal and maintenance problems can be overcome. Supervision may help prevent fouling, throwing, etc.	
5. Tree bark wood chips	Good level of impact absorption	Requires fairly high level of maintenance
	Fairly cheap to install (minimum depth 300 mm)	Can become contaminated by glass and animals, though indications are less than sand
	Reusable as a mulching material to planted areas when replaced	Can become dirty
	Pleasant to handle and use	
	Recommended when properly maintained	
6. Lightweight man-made aggregates	Good level of impact absorption	Can be fairly expensive to install
	Light in weight (minimum depth 300	Requires special attention to perimeter to

Table 24.7 (cont'd)

Type of surface	Advantages	Disadvantages
	mm)	retain material
		Is dangerous if spilt onto adjacent hard surfaces
		Breaks down and can become dirty with use
		Readily thrown
		Difficult to clean
	Acceptable if high cost can be justified	
7. Grass	Cheapest surface	Not particularly good level of impact absorption (can become very hard when baked dry)
	Better than concrete or macadam	Extremely dirty when wet
	Durability can be improved by better grass seed mixture or reinforcing	Wears out quickly
		Requires high level of maintenance and reinstatement so can transfer dirt to equipment when wet
		Dry soil contaminated with glass, stones, etc., is very hazardous
	Acceptable only if properly maintained and regularly re-instated	

Sources: 1. NPFA Playground Management For Local Councils. (see NPFA Booklet for more refs.)
2. BS5696.
3. Pers. comm. Bromley Borough Council.

RESOURCE REQUIREMENTS

Table 24.9 summarizes the estimated labour inputs which are used by the Recreation Department in planning the management of the play equipment for which the Borough is responsible.

**24.7
Fencing**   TYPES

The maintenance requirement of fencing are significantly influenced by the type of construction materials chosen. The latter differ in their longevities and thus frequency of replacement.

Table 24.8   Guidelines for calculation of staff bonuses: quarterly servicing of children's play equipment

London borough of Bromley – parks department
Children's play equipment – Quarterly service

Explanatory notes		Calculation of performance
Map No	Refers to 3″ to 1 mile Borough Map 1972 Edition.	*Site allowance and small repairs –* comprises 19.50 SMS for Site Allowance and 8% of net std hours for small repairs. More extensive repairs should only be undertaken after consultation with the Technical Officer, when extra time will be allowed.
Ref	Each item is given an identification number. In the case of swings and other duplicated items, this is stencilled onto the equipment itself.	
Time	The studied value for carrying out a full and thorough inspection and service.	*Mileage* Based on one man at 5 SMS per crow mile, calculated on the distance from the previous site. Hence, at the end of each day, the Engineer dates the Schedule at the last site and additional mileage is then allowed for his return journey to base. Extra mileage is then allowed next day for the journey from base to next site, less the incorporated mileage from the previous site.
S	Stability, checking all support legs and ground fixings.	*Additional allowances* Each day, the following standard allowances are included: –
C/D	Corosion or decay of metal, timber and fibre glass parts.	Load Vehicle 4 SMS Unload Vehicle 3 SMS Daily Site (Vehicle) 40 SMS 47 SMS
M/P	Moving parts, checking all bearings, shackles, chains, etc., for wear and tightness. Grease or lubricate.	Each week of the service the Engineer books his time on a standard bonus sheet, merely recording the sites visited. The Technical Officer will then total the net standard hours for each site, add the additional mileage, allowances and any approved extra work and thus calculate the performance.
P	Paintwork and Finish. Report on condition.	
B	Bases. Report on condition.	
G	Gates. Check for rusting, rotting, split welds, etc. Grease or lubricate.	
G.P.	Gate Posts. Check for corosion, decay and stability.	

* Indicates the inspections and services carried out.

When checked and serviced, if satisfactory, make oblique line into a tick. If still faulty, make a cross and write explanatory details in the Notes column (continuous overleaf if necessary).

All checking, adjustment and lubrication must be carried out to ensure the continued safe and efficient operation of each item.

Table 24.8 (cont'd)

Site and entrance	Ref	Equipment	Make	Time SMS	Time Hrs	S	C/D	MP	P	B	G	GP
22 Ethelbert Road Tennis Courts		Entrance LS		1.80							*	*
		Tennis Courts										
		6 × LS		20.80							*	*
		Walking		2.23								
		Records Book		6.44								
		Site Allowance		1.03								
		Mileage		3.00								
		Site Total		35.45	0.59							
23 Queens Gardens, Queens Road, Bromley.		Lownds Avenue 2 LS & LD		8.40							*	*
		Walking		2.60								
		Records Book		3.68								
		Site Allowance		1.03								
		Mileage		3.00								
		Site Total		15.56	0.32							
36 Widmore Recreation, Pembroke Road, Bromley.	1	Swings 2 Flat 10′	Wicks	10.45		*	*	*	*	*		
	2	Stressed Arch Swing 1 × 10′ – Cradle	SMP	1.89		*	*	*	*	*		
	3	Jungle Gym	Wicks	2.92		*	*		*	*		
	4	Whirling Platform 10′	Wicks	4.12		*	*	*	*	*		
	5	Rocking Horse	Wicks	7.06		*	*	*	*	*		
	6	See Saw	Hunt	3.24		*	*	*	*	*		
		Site Allowance and Small Repairs		23.60								
34 Mottingham Rec. Grd. Elmhurst Road.		Elmhurst Road LD		3.80							*	*
		Records Book		0.90								
		Site Allowance		1.03								
		Mileage		15.00								
		Site Total		74.01	1.24							
33 Mottingham Sports Grd. Grove Park Road.	1	Swings 8′ 3 flat	Wicks	23.74		*	*	*	*	*		
	2	Swings 10′ 3 cradles	Wicks			*	*	*	*	*		
	3	Log cabin	Gumitine	2.92		*	*	*	*	*		
	4	Merry Go Round 8′	Wicks	4.12		*	*	*	*	*		
	5	Rocking Horse	Wicks	7.06		*	*	*	*			

Table 24.9   Management of play equipment: estimated resource requirements

Item	Operation	SMV	Unit
Ocean Wave	Street lighting – Erect column into hole with hiab	63.00	per occasion
Roundabout	Assemble R/A and grease centre bearing	559.00	r/about
	Load or unload R/A from lorry	40.00	r/about
	Renew arms on R/A	41.00	r/about
	Tighten bolts	0.50	bolt
	Drill out bolts or holes in metal	3.70	blt/hole
	Renew damaged side board	64.00	board
	Dismantle old R/A	414.00	r/about
Rocking Horse	Remove and load to lorry	45.00	r/horse
	Renew plastic seat	21.00	seat
Swings	Uncouple and load swings (Bromley)	5.87	swing
	Job allowance (Bromley)	14.83	per item of playground furniture
	Renew swing seat	27.00	seat
	Renew tyre swing seat	63.00	seat
	Remove swing frame – Hacksaw legs, pullover with vehicle, hammer over legs. (2 bay 8 leg)	184.00	frame
	Assemble and erect Hunts frame	744.00	frame
	Assemble and erect Wicksteed frame	928.00	frame
	Drill and fit grease nipple	32.00	per occasion
	Renew top bar studs (provided old stud requires extracting and top bar has to be lifted off)	181.00	per occasion
	Cut and fit, or remove chains from frame	20.0E	chain
See-Saw	Remove and load to lorry	45.00	see-saw
	Remove and refit all bearings	456.00	see-saw
	Fit 4 steel safety plates at fulcrum	194.00	see-saw
	Drill and fit 2 new sides and 2 new ends	153.00	see-saw
	Renew plant and paint	227.00	see-saw
	Cut wood to expose grease nipple	41.00	see-saw
	Remove whirling platform,		

Table 24.9 (cont'd)

Item	Operation	SMV	Unit
	dismantle and load to lorry	414.00	per occasion
	Renew plank on see-saw	227.00	per occasion
	Undo swing shackles and remove swings	15.00	swing
	Remove nuts from top bar studs	17.00	nut
	Remove swing set top bar to check studs	240.00	per occasion
	Check studs (top bar not removed)	122.00	per occasion
Routine maintenance	Assemble roundabout	539.00	per occasion
	Load lorry with roundabout pieces	40.00	per occasion
	Load tools	18.00	per occasion
	Clear lorry	27.00	per occasion
	Test and load generator	11.00	per occasion
	Renew arms of whirling platform	326.00	all arms
	Erect metal framed park bench	109.00	per occasion
	Fit new swing to swing (inc. remove old)	27.00	per occasion
	Pull down 6 leg swing frame hacksaw through legs, pull over with vehicle, hammer over legs	184.00	per occasion
	Remove see-saw from base and load	47.00	per occasion
	Remove rocking horse from base and load	43.00	per occasion
	Paint swing top bar bracket bolts	3.00	per bolt
	Fit new seat to rocking horse	21.00	per occasion
	Fit malleable iron link to swing chains	5.00	per occasion
	Remove and replace tyre swing	63.00	per occasion
	Repace side panel in merry go round	64.00	per occasion
	Erect 'Hunts' 8 leg swing frame and position	156.00	per occasion
	Remove roundabout centre column	26.00	per occasion
Lubrication of	Boat lubrication	14.10	per occasion
playground	Ocean wave	5.06	per occasion
equipment	Plank swing	11.52	per occasion
	Rocking horse	7.06	per occasion

cont'd

Table 24.9 (cont'd)

Item	Operation	SMV	Unit
	Swings: (grease gun)	1.42	swing
	(grease pins)	15.40	swing
	check seats and legs	7.61	set
	See-saw lubricate	3.24	per occasion
	Roundabout lubricate	4.12	per occasion
	Tyre Swings (large and small)	12.32	per occasion
	(with nipples)	1.42	per occasion
	Check static pieces	2.92	per occasion
	Small repairs	8.32%	site
	Large repairs	21.50	day
	Equipment out and away	19.50	site
Painting playground	Prime 2″ dia. tube	0.85	run
furniture	Undercoat ditto	1.03	run
	Top coat ditto	0.81	run
	Scrape and sand ditto	1.55	run
	Wire brush and sand ditto	0.57	run

The main fencing types and their characteristics can be summarized as follows:

1. Wood – Provided the softwood is pressure-treated in accordance with BS Specifications, the fencing should last for between 15 and 20 years.
2. Chain-link – Galvanized heavy-duty chain-link (9.5 gauge) normally lasts 20–30 years under normal atmospheric (not salty or polluted) conditions. Plastic-coated chain-link may last even longer, but its lifespan is not yet tested in practice.
3. Railings – Older railings may often be worth retaining on account of costs: new materials are extremely expensive. In terms of appearance, they also have considerable merit. Careful maintenance may therefore be a cost-effective investment.

ESTIMATED RESOURCE REQUIREMENTS

The estimated labour inputs required both for the erection and repair of different types of fence are set out in Table 24.10.

24.8
Gates, benches and seats

The only maintenance-free seats are concrete, and even these are not vandal-free.

Where soft wood is used the best material for ease of maintenance is probably pressure-treated and oiled timber.

Oak, teak or mahogany are usually cheaper in the long term as they do not break, splinter or chafe and need no maintenance.

Where painting of these structures is required, the frequency of operation is likely to be approximately every three years.

Table 24.10   The establishment and maintenance of fencing: estimated resource requirements

Source	Operation	Inputs			Unit
VC	Post and wire and vegetation clearance	10 days			100 lm
Sh	Erect chestnut paling fencing (approx) (Sum of 3 separate activities)	400.00 mins			100 lm
Sa	Erect chestnut fencing	16.70 mins			3 m section
H	Erect posts for fencing (concreted in)	36.00 mins			post
H	Erect chain link fencing	19.30 mins			1 lm
Sa	Erect post and wire (2 strand) tence (temporary)	3.10 mins			3 m section
Sh	Erect barbed wire fence 4' high (approx) (Sum of 3 separate activities)	246.00 mins			100 yd
W	Repair chestnut paling	119.00 mins			100 lm
Sa	Take down chestnut fencing	19.00 mins			3 m section
W	Dismantle chestnut fencing	115.00 mins			100 lm
Sh	Remove chestnut fencing	100.61 mins			100 lm
Sh	Remove chain link fencing (6') from posts	317.15 mins			100 lm
	Chespale				
L	Remove existing	180.00 mins			100 lm
L	Set out posts and drive into ground	7.80 mins			post
L	Renew chespale with top and bottom rail	1096.00 mins			100 lm
	Wire				
L	Erect straining posts	98.00 mins			post
L	Stay straining post	11.00 mins			post
L	Renew 5 strand wire fence	1096.00 mins			100 lm
L	Renew post	9.00 mins			post
L	Repair wire	2466.00 mins			100 lm
L	Level post with saw	3.00 mins			100 lm
H	Erect post for fencing (corrected in)	36.00 mins			post
H	Erect chain link fencing	3660.00 mins			100 lm
	Erection of high tensile spring steel fencing	(Time in minutes)			
		All soil types	Clay with few stones	0.3 m of soil over shale	Peat
FC	Dig and fill post hole, fit and firm post	–	56.00	60.00	38.00
FC	Fix cross-member to post	9.00	–	–	–
FC	Fix one strut and thrust plate	23.00	–	–	–
FC	Bar one stake hole	–	1.10	1.20	–
FC	Drive one stake	–	1.60	1.60	1.30
FC	Fix tis-down (stake driven in wire stapled to stake and attached to fence)	7.00	–	–	–

cont'd

Table 24.10 (cont'd)

Source	Operation	Inputs		Unit
FC	Fix tie-down (Molex anchor)	9.00	– –	–
FC	Fix apron (per metre)	4.20	– –	–
FC	Place sods to fill gaps under netting (per metre)	2.80	– –	–

Block total times

i) Block total per metre

Carry tools
Fetch strainer and stakes
Roll out and join net
Staple wires   } – 2.50 minutes per metre
Clip net
Staple net
Walk and prepare
Take out wire

ii) Block total per strain length

Strain wire   } i) Using hot strainers for straining net:
Make off wire | 20.00 minutes per strain length.
Wrap guy links } ii) Using monkey strainers for straining net:
Strain net | 16.00 minutes per strain length.
Make off net   }

See Table 2.2 on p. 37 for details of sources.

Such data as have been collated on maintenance requirements are presented in Table 24.11.

24.9
Litter bins   EMPTYING

The need for emptying depends on the size of bin and the level of use. Emptying may be daily in busy shopping areas, weekly in urban parks, fortnightly or less in rural car parks. It is usually best combined with a normal cleansing or maintenance routine.

Speed of emptying depends on the design of the container as well as on the volume to be removed.

Unlined bins appear to be easier to manage than lined ones. 'Loose' linings are liable to be stolen or damaged. If they are locked in to place, locking and unlocking is a time-consuming process. Operative are then likely to leave the linings locked in and to empty them by hand, so by-passing the original purpose of lining.

MAINTENANCE

Galvanized steel is probably the most maintenance-free and damage-proof material for litter bins.

Wood needs maintenance, and wooden bins usually need to be very

Table 24.11   The maintenance of benches, seats and gates: estimated resource requirements

Source	Operation	SMV	Unit
a)	*Benches and seats*		
Sh	Wipe park benches	2.60	1 bench
H	Wash and clean park seats	29.00	1 seat
H	Oil teak park seat	26.50	1 seat (Once per year: c.f. painting once per three years)
b)	*Lubrication of gates*		
LB	Equipment out and away	1.03	1 site
LB	Walking between gates	0.01	1 l metre
LB	Oil and check large single gates	1.80	1 gate
LB	Oil and check small single gates (Bowling Greens, etc.)	0.86	1 gate
LB	Oil and check large double gates	3.80	1 pr gates
LB	Oil and check small double chainlink gate	1.42	1 pr gates
LB	Fill in records book and visually check	0.92	1 gate
LB	Oil/grease large double gates (over 10′ where ladder required)	8.48	1 pr gates

See Table 2.2 on p. 37 for details of sources.

sturdily built. Less robust designs, such as those with slatted sides, are very liable to damage.

The capacity must be appropriate both to the use received and the frequency of emptying. For example, large open planters are used as bins in Oxford Street to cope with the substantial volumes of rubbish generated.

24.10
Pergolas, arbours and trellises

It is important that structures intended to carry climbing plants are built to last, and to last without maintenance. Once covered by plants, particularly twiners such a clematis, they cannot be painted or treated without serious damage to the plants.

The main materials used for these structures, their maintenance characteristics and their labour requirements are similar to those described earlier in this chapter.

24.11
Lighting

The two main uses of lighting in the landscape are:

1. *Functional*: to help people to see at night and to promote safety.
2. *Decorative*: as features in their own right or to illuminate other points of interest such as building façades, fountains or trees.

The lighting facilities themselves must, of course, be safe. For instance, it is important that low-mounted fittings should be able to withstand some damage without exposing passers-by to the dangers of electric shock.

ROUTINE MAINTENANCE

Lighting needs a programme of regular checking and maintenance to change lamps, clean lamps, check installations for faults, and so on. Regular maintenance helps to keep the service working effectively, and also reduces costs since old or dirty lamps use electricity inefficiently. As in the case of play equipment and other structures, rapid repair of damage helps to reduce the chance of vandalism.

Maintenance schedules and methods vary according to the performance of the installation. Some maintenance of temporary or seasonal systems can be done under cover when they are brought in for storage. Permanent installations have to be serviced outside and require the establishment of a maintenance calendar.

The main operations required are cleaning, replacing bulbs and checking of fittings. These are described in the sections which follow and summarized in Table 24.12.

FIXED INSTALLATIONS

Bulb replacement and cleaning

The need to change lamps (i.e. bulbs, etc.) depends on the economic life of the lamp. Light output, and therefore efficiency, drops after a certain period of use, and the lamp then becomes increasingly less cost-effective to use.

For example, a 400w mercury discharge lamp consumes during its rated life more than ten times its purchase price in electricity. This figure is typical for many lamp types and indicates the fallacy in retaining lamps long after their light output has dropped below the economic change point. The light produced by an old lamp may be half that of a new one but the cost of energy remains the same.

The frequency needed for replacing lamp bulbs depends on the economic life of the lamp, which can be obtained from the manufacturer, and on the amount of use it receives. For example, if the lamp is switched on at sunset and switched off at 10 pm it will be in use for approximately 1200 hours per year. However, this will not be distributed evenly throughout the year, but will follow the pattern shown below. The incremental totals are shown in parentheses.

Month:	Jan	Feb	March	April	May	June
Hours:	174	135(309)	110(419)	62(481)	38(519)	23(542)

Month:	July	Aug	Sept	Oct	Nov	Dec
Hours:	28(570)	51(621)	82(703)	129(832)	173(1005)	197(1202)

Table 24.12   Maintenance of lighting fixtures: suggested schedule of operations

---

A   Fixed installations in use all the year round
    Fittings: Clean and check fittings for weather tightness and repair bi-annually in March and September
    Fitting body: clean and repaint if necessary
    Electrical Connections: check for corrosion
    Gaskets: ensure still resilient and effective
    Glass: clean
    Reflector: clean, and polish if material allows
    If possible check more frequently for damage for example as part of regular landscape maintenance in the area, so that repairs can be done as quickly as possible. This helps to discourage vandalism
B   Fixed installations: seasonal use
    At the end of the season ensure all circuits are isolated and check that fittings are weather tight
    Clean and check that the system is functioning properly before switch-on the following season
    Seasonal installations
    These can be taken indoors for seasonal maintenance before storage
    Carry out maintenance as for fixed installations

A lamp with a 7500 hour life under these conditions should last just over six years.

It is convenient if replacement of lamps can be arranged to coincide with cleaning, thereby avoiding two separate visits. However, in the example given above, cleaning will obviously need to be carried out more frequently than lamp replacement. A separate cleaning schedule therefore needs to be worked out.

Long-lived lamps should be dated, so that their time for changing is not forgotten.

In the case of a filament lamp with a 100 hour life the problem could be more complex. With a 1200 hour year, lamp replacements would, starting in January, occur at the end of November, the last week of October in the following year, mid-August in the next year, and so on. The intervals would not be regular due to the seasonal variation in day length. As filament lamps are relatively cheap, changing the lamp in January and August, and so using 600 hours of its life, would probably be justified economically.

Where a large number of lamps are used, such as in promenade festoons, it may be economical to wait until say 10% or 20% of the lamps have failed and then to change them all. In such situations a number of failed lamps would not be as conspicuous as they would in building floodlighting.

Where the actual amount of light is important, perhaps for security or work purposes, it is possible to calculate from data supplied by manufacturers the lamp life to the critical level. An alternative method is

Table 24.13 The relative cost performance of difference lamp types

The prices given in the table below are only indicative of the cost of average equipment and the beginning of 1980. Bulk purchase can reduce the prices shown just as high quality or unique performance may increase it. The range of prices given roughly equates to the range of wattages available in the lamp type.

Lamp type	Initial cost (Lamp and luminaire with any control gear)	Energy Consumption[7] (for equal light)	Annual operating costs (over 2000 hours/annum)	Ease of maintenance and relamping	Luminaire physical size	Colour rendering	Colour appearance	Beam control[4]	Projection range	Patch shape[6]	Cold weather operation
Incandescent reflector PAR	£13/55	£430	£5/12	Good	Small	Good	Natural	Good	Short	Circular	Very Good
Incandescent GLS and Class B	£100/200 long range £30/70 wideangle	£350	£15 £12	Very Good	Small to Large	Good	Natural	Fair	Short to Long	Circular	Very Good
Tungsten-halogen	£20/60	£240	£13	Good	Small to Medium	Good	Natural	Fair	Short to Medium	Elipse	Very Good
Mercury MB	£100/200	£130	£12	Fair	Medium to Large	Poor	Good	Good	Short to Medium	Circular or Elipse	Fair

Lamp type											
Mercury fluorescent MBF	£100/200	£130	£12	Poor	Small to Large	Av	Cool	Fair to Good	Short to Medium	Circular or Near Circular	Fair
Metal halide MBI	£150/220	£100	£12/40	Good	Medium to Large	Good	Cool	Good	Short to Medium	Circular or Elipse	Good
Metal halide Fluorescent MBIF	£150/220	£100	£12	Poor	Medium to Large	Good	Cool	Fair to Good	Short	Circular or Near Circular	Good
High pressure Sodium SON	£150/250	£65	£12	Good	Medium to Large	Poor	Very Warm	Good	Short to Medium	Circular or Elipse	Good
Low pressure Sodium SOX and SLI	£100/150	£40	£8	Poor	Medium to Large	N/A	Orange	Fair to Good	Short	Elipse	Fair
Tubular fluorescent MCF	£50/80	£90	£6	Poor	Usual. Long	Av to Good	Cold to Warm	Poor	Short	Elipse	Poor

Notes:
1. Does not include lamps below 250 W or above 2kW.
2. Does not include compact source iodide lamps CSI.
3. Includes relamping and maintenance costs but excluding energy costs. Where lamp life exceeds 2000 hours a proportion of the lamp cost is taken.
4. Beam control improves as the light source gets smaller relative to the reflector size.
5. Ease of maintenance will vary with ease of access to the luminaire and the difficulty of handling large lamps.
6. Patch shape assumes that projector is perpendicular to lit surface. Shape can be modified by optical system and in some cases depends on whether the lamp is at right angles or perpendicular to the beam.
7. Cost of providing 100,000 lumens for 2000 hours with electricity at 3p/unit. Due to differences in the optical performance of luminaries this does not imply equal illumination of the target.

periodically to measure the illumination level at specific points. This will indicate not only the ageing of the lamp but also the soiling of the luminaire and so help to determine the cleaning interval.

Cleaning schedule
The frequency of cleaning depends on the location and the orientation of lamps. For example, an upward pointing fitting in an industrial town needs cleaning much more frequently than a downward pointing one in a country town.

The need for cleaning can be established objectively by measuring the light of lamps in use at some convenient point and at, say, every two months until a certain fall-off, perhaps 30%, has occurred, remembering to allow for the lamp ageing. This will then establish the cleaning interval which should then be observed without further measurement.

Having decided upon a suitable cleaning interval, a regular schedule can be introduced and lamp replacement arranged to coincide with at least periodic cleaning in order to minimise costs.

FINANCIAL CONSIDERATIONS

Locational factors
Access to fittings affects the ease of, and hence the time needed for, changing lamps. If awkward or over-robust fittings have been used it may take 10 minutes or longer to unbolt them, to replace the bulb and to close them again. The problem is worse if the lamps are in awkward locations, for example high off the ground, and if vehicular access to them is difficult. Initial planning and design decisions can therefore seriously affect maintenance costs. Nevertheless, robustness is required and installations need to be designed to resist both deliberate and accidental damage.

Running and maintenance costs
These are influenced by the type of installation and by subsequent maintenance. Table 24.13 compares the cost and performance of a range of lamp types.

A range of tariffs is available from the Electricity Board and it is advisable to consult the Board about the most cost-effective type.

The effect of economic lamp life and of cleaning upon efficiency and running costs have already been discussed.

Further reading   Garelick, P. (1987) Setting a standard for play. *Horticulture Week*, 27th March.
Heseltine, P. (1987) Playing by the rules. *Horticulture Week*, 27th March.

Part Six

Synthesis and Practice

This final part demonstrates how the resource guidelines or 'building blocks', presented in the earlier parts can and should be combined in preparing maintenance work schedules.

Chapter 25 describes the five sets of skills required in order that realistic work programmes and budgets can be successfully prepared.

In Chapter 26, a few select examples of work programming are provided. These cover both manual and computer-based approaches.

Chapter 27 suggests various ways in which computerized information systems may develop. A variety of novel applications, including contingency planning activities, together with the implications of the Local Government Act (1988), are covered.

The book concludes with a general request to Amenity Managers to help with periodic updating.

25 SYNTHESIS AND OTHER SKILLS

25.1
Building blocks

The main function of Parts Two and Five of this book is to provide the reader with what, in effect, is a series of 'building blocks'. To be more specific, the building blocks are intended as a source for use by Amenity Managers and Landscape Contractors in estimating the time, resource and financial implications of undertaking individual elements of maintenance work.

25.2
The synthesis process

In order to gain an overall picture of all the maintenance operations covered by, say, either a Landscape Management Plan or Contract, the synthesis of several building blocks is involved. It will be appreciated that careful synthesis is required in order to identify and then finalize the most cost-effective maintenace work programme for an amenity site.

Complex maintenance operations are often based on several small elements of work. Skill is required on the part of the Amenity Manager to use the type of source information contained in this book. This applies particularly in preparing maintenance specifications, resource budgets and work programmes, whether they be for a year, a season or a month. It also applies regardless of whether the tasks refer just to the area, which is the responsibility of a particular work gang, or to the amenity management plan for a whole county, district or municipality. The synthesis process is central to the tasks of Amenity Managers and Landscape Architects, involved in preparing cost-effective work programmes, maintenance specifications and contract documents. Synthesis is similarly central to the job of contractors when preparing tenders for maintenance operations.

25.3
Other skills

Planning, to produce costed work programmes and realistic budgets, is but one of the skills possessed by successful Amenity Managers. This needs to be combined with other essential skills, if public amenities are to be managed cost-effectively. As mentioned in Part One, the application of horticultural, ecological, silvicultural, personnel and recreation management skills are fundamental to providing a successful amenity service. Seen in this overall context, the skill entailed in work planning and budgeting should never be regarded as more than part of the armoury of management.

In order that the synthesis tasks are viewed in proper perspective, the skills referred to above are described further:

First there are the horticultural and ecological skills, leading to sound technical practice. Despite tight budgets, physical standards need to be upheld.

Thus it is essential that there is full understanding of how each maintenance operation should be performed. A knowledge of both well-established, traditional techniques and of the application of modern technology is required, in order that operations are performed in the most cost-effective manner.

Secondly, there are the skills involved in timing maintenance operations. As in managing most living objects, timing is of the essence. Amenity landscapes are no exception. Many landscape operations are seasonal or have to be performed in a particular sequence. Some, on the other hand, are specific to a particular week or month. Others can be undertaken on a more flexible basis. Knowledge about the essential timing of operations greatly assists Amenity Managers when the need arises to spread the work load over the seasons. Such timing decisions not only enable resources to be used effectively but can also help in providing staff with permanent employment throughout a year. Often the work programme can be 'juggled' somewhat so as to iron out peaks and troughs. A more evenly distributed work profile can reduce the total number of workers required but at the same time provide work for longer periods. The same applies in relation to the preparation of usage programmes for the main items of machinery, such as tractors, trucks and sprayers.

Thirdly, there are the skills required to establish work priorities, in terms of both resources and operations. It is essential that Amenity Managers are able to distinguish between absolutely essential, 'core' operations and those which permit a degree of latitude and thus, if delayed, do not jeopardize results. Such knowledge is important in preparing contingency plans for the 'what if' scenarios. Managers generally need to be prepared for responses to such almost inevitable questions as:

(i)   What if either the budget is reduced or manpower is not available for the period?

(ii)   Which operations may be omitted or need to be re-scheduled?

Fourthly, there are the skills required for determining the availability of resources and their likely performances for a range of situations. For all manpower, machinery and material resources, knowledge about availabilities, productivities and costs is essential. The identification and provision of the appropriate persons, tools and materials for each operation are essential parts of an Amenity Manager's job.

Fifthly, there are the skills involved in knowing the 'assets' and constraints of the sites, which are to be maintained. For instance, it is essential for an Amenity Manager to know whether or not the use of machinery may be constrained by access problems, steep slopes or obstacles. Ground conditions can vary greatly and thus restrict the choice of maintenance methods which may be effectively used. Decisions have to be made about whether or not a particular maintenance operation can be undertaken and, if so, which of the range of estimated manpower requirement figures provided in Parts 2 to 5 of this book, should be adopted. For example, where a range of values, say 12 to 16 SMV per hectare, is quoted, a choice has to be made between either the two values or an intermediate figure.

25.4 Accurate data requirements

Successful work programming and budgeting depends on access to appropriately reliable data. For purposes of estimating, approximate data will suffice. However, if a detailed work programme and budget is required, then the accuracy of the data is of paramount importance. The production of such a programme depends in the first instance upon accurate data concerning the physical dimensions of the areas to be maintained. This data needs to be available in the appropriate units, for example: square metres of shrubbery; hectares of gang-mown grass; numbers of young trees and trees of different age groups/size; metres of fence-line gully. It is important from the outset to:

- Zone a site according to the different levels of maintenance (e.g. high level/well manicured; intermediate level; low/rural level);
- Distinguish on a site between areas of similar appearance which require different maintenance regimes (e.g. gang-mown and triple-mown areas).

The physical dimensions of such distinct areas need to be measured separately.

25.5 Data sources

The main sources of site data are as follows:

- site surveys, involving direct measurement on the ground;
- measurement from aerial photographs or maps, using a digitiser or planimeter and supported by ground verification;
- construction or 'as built' drawings and bills of quantity.

The choice of work measurement data (standard man values) for the appropriate operation, when related to the relevant areas of the site receiving that particular maintenance operation, provides the basis for preparing a work programme. If SMVs are not available for the operations required on the site, for which the programme is to be prepared, then the SMV for the same operation performed under similar conditions elsewhere can be used. Such data is presented in Parts 2 to 5 of this book. However, ideally a maintenance organization of reasonably large size should seek to establish its own SMVs, through on-the-job work measurement.

25.6
Work programming

Work Programmes can vary, both in terms of size and timescale. They range from an annual programme requiring, for example, just two man days per week for a small neighbourhood site to the maintenance schedule associated with large scale Master Plans for intensively used urban or country parks and even for whole cities, districts or countries. Usually the work programmes distinguish between the resource requirements for the different landscape components, such as climax tree species, shrubs, water, hard surface features and site furniture, play equipment, etc. Master plans generally describe the short and longer-term design objectives, covering as appropriate the functional, social, aesthetic, economic and financial aspects. They thereby provide the broad terms of reference for the preparation of detailed short-term maintenance programmes. Many such Master Plans and maintenance programmes have been published, including those for New Ash Green, Peterborough, Skelmersdale New Town and Stockley Park (Cobham, 1977, 1989).

The cyclical nature of plant growth, which is also seasonal, of employment and of financial activities means that the majority of work programmes cover at least one year. This provides a convenient time-scale for use in planning, undertaking, monitoring and reviewing work.

Work programming this lends itself to systematic operation. This enables the experience of the previous year's performance, gained through monitoring, to be used in preparing the forthcoming year's programme. The adoption of a continuous information feed-back, i.e. systems approach, helps the Amenity Manager to 'sharpen' the performance of the maintenance team and thus the service provided to the users (consumers). As Figure 25.1 indicates, such a system involves four principal components:

1. *Planning* the work lead, through establishing an annual work programme;
2. *Organizing* the manpower, machinery and material resources so as to ensure the operations are undertaken in the most cost-effective manner;
3. *Directing* i.e. scheduling and supervising the work as it is being carried out over a particular period, such as a week, month or season;

Figure 25.1 Principal components of the systems approach.

4.   *Controlling* the results through monitoring and analysing the outcome with the original plan.

References   Cobham, R.O. (1977, 1989) Landscape Management and the Fourth Design Dimension, in *Landscape Design with Plants*, (ed. J.B. Clouston) 1st and 2nd Edition, Heinemann.

26 APPROACHES AND APPLICATIONS IN PRACTICE

26.1 Introduction: work programming in practice

This chapter contains a few select examples of work programmes prepared in practice, using the type of data contained in Parts 2 to 5 of this book. Basically there are two broad approaches which can be adopted, namely Work Programmes, which can be prepared by hand and those which are largely computerized. The remainder of this chapter provides practical examples of both approaches.

26.2 The manual approach

Work Programmes, particularly those which are not too complex, can be prepared manually. Site information is required, together with knowledge of the operations to be performed and the resource requirements (labour productivity, materials, etc.). Based on this information, the total manpower input can be calculated relatively evenly.

The example, given in Table 26.1 displays the information used manually to calculate the manpower requirements for a high quality rose garden of almost 1 hectare at Wolseley Garden Park in Staffordshire. In order to calculate the total requirement, each maintenance operation needs to be considered individually in relation to the two main periods of the year: the dormant and growing seasons.

The estimated figure of 5227 hours per year can then be used to calculate the annual labour requirement. This figure needs to be adjusted to allow for non-scheduled work, such as stoppages due to weather, mechanical failure, sickness, personal needs, etc. In this example a figure of 20% has been added before drawing the following management conclusions:

- Either three people should be employed full time throughout the year, with the summer peak requirements being met either by employing casual labour or by working over-time;
- Or four people should be employed full time, extra work being found on other maintenance operations outside the rose garden.

Summer season work can be interrupted during the peak visiting months. Inevitably visitors like to question staff about various aspects of a garden.

Table 26.1 Work programme calculated manually for a rose garden open to the public

Operation	Feature	Inventory	Operations per year	SMV	Labour (Nov-Mar)	Hours (Apr-Oct)	Total
Roses							
Heavy prune	Roses	3500 no	1	1.8/plant	105	–	105
De-head	Roses	3500 no	16	1.3/plant	–	1213	1213
Light prune	Roses	3500 no	1	1.3/plant	75	–	75
Fertilize	Roses	3500 no	1	1.0/plant	58	–	58
Replacement planting	Roses	3500 no	2%	2.7/plant	4	4	4
Spray for pest/disease	Rose bed	875 m²	3	300/100 m²	–	13	–
Climbers							
Pruns and tie-in	Climber	150 no	1	25/plant	63	–	63
Tie-in new growth	Climber	150 no	2	20/plant	–	50	50
Hedges							
Trim hedge top	Hedge	116 m	3	2.4/metre	14	28	42
Trim hedge side	Hedge	116 m	3	0.9/metre	7	14	21
Herbaceous Areas							
Lift, replant, etc.	Herbaceous plants	4316 no	1	6.0/plant	431	–	431
Cut back in autumn	Herbaceous plants	4316 no	1	3.0/plant	216	–	216
Water Features							
Pool maintenance	Pool	1 no	1	960/year	16	–	16
Grass							
Mow grass 24" machine	Ornamental grass	1777 m²	52	200/1000 m²	–	308	308
Other maintenance	Ornamental grass	1777 m²	8	295/1000 m²	–	70	70
Half-moon edge	Grass edge	1184 m	2	1.2/metre	23	23	46
Long handle shear edge	Grass edge	1184 m	12	0.3/metre	–	71	71
Trees							
Prune fruit trees	Mature fruit trees	5 no	1	120/tree	120	–	120
Other maintenance	Mature fruit trees	5 no	1	60/tree	60	–	60
Tree maintenance	Young trees	10 no	1	60/tree	60	–	60

cont'd

Table 26.1 (cont'd)

Operation	Feature	Inventory	Operations per year	SMV	Labour (Nov–Mar)	Hours (Apr–Oct)	Total
Shrubs							
Replacement planting	Shrubs	4361 no	2%	2.7/shrub	4	–	4
Shrubs/Roses							
Spread mulch	Shrub/rose bed	2440 m²	1	900/1000 m²	36	–	36
Weed and dig in mulch	Shrub/rose bed	2440 m²	1	4700/1000 m²	191	–	191
Hand weed	Shrub/rose bed	2440 m²	24	800/1000 m²	–	780	780
Hard Surfaces							
Weedkill paths	Paths	778 m²	1	300/1000 m²	4	–	4
Spot-treat paths	Paths	778 m²	4	300/1000 m²	–	12	12
Sweep/rake paths	Paths	778 m²	104	100/1000 m²	67	67	134
Structures							
Structures maintenance	Structures	1 no	1	6000/year	100	–	100
General Maintenance							
Watering	Garden areas	6000 m²	12	500/1000 m²	–	600	600
Litter Collection	Rose garden	6778 m²	360	9/1000 m²	162	162	324
Total Hours required					1816	3411	5277
No Scheduled work: 20%					363	682	1045
Gross Total Hours required (A)					2179	4093	6272
Total Hours available per labour unit * (B)					665	1015	1680
Total number of labour units required (A) ÷ (B)					3.3	4.0	3.7

Note: * This is calculated on the assumption that 7 productive hours are worked per day for 5 days per week for 240 days per year. The latter are divided between the two seasons as follows:

108 working days in Nov – March less 13 days leave = 95 days

153 working days in April – Oct less 8 days leave = 145 days.

Indeed visitors derive particular pleasure from having their personal questions answered when visiting such a garden. Thus an important management decision needs to be made about how best to respond. There are a number of options. For example, visitors' enquiries can be handled by one or more of the garden staff, due allowance having been made in the work programme for this operation.

Alternatively a special garden guide can be employed; at least during the height of the visiting season. Either way, the work programme needs to cater for the vitally important job of looking after visitors. A third option is the somewhat more arm's length' approach, which seeks to minimize personal communication between visitors and the garden staff. Instead the aim is to satisfy enquiries through enabling visitors to purchase guide books and leaflets, and even in some cases, to hire the use of 'self-guiding' tapes and the use of Walkman cassettes.

26.3 Computerized approaches

More complex work programming can involve very detailed calculations. In a number of instances computer systems are used to assist both the development and implementation of annual work programmes.

The first of these systems to be developed in the UK was the Planned Maintenance Programme used by the London Borough of Bromley. (Long, 1982). The system was originally conceived as an aid to planning and as a method of administering the then new bonus system. Its development followed the amalgamation of London Boroughs resulting from the *Local Government Act* (1963). This Act led to Bromley inheriting a variety of landscape maintenance teams. Analysis of the work done by each maintenance team revealed that, although the work methods and infrastructures of the old and new boroughs differed, the basic horticultured work was, not surprisingly, very similar.

Establishment of this initial computer system involved several tasks, which included:

- undertaking site surveys;
- completing individual site record cards;
- agreeing which particular maintenance activities should be performed on a borough-wide basis by mobile teams as distinct from those which would be undertaken by the 'resident' maintenance teams assigned to specific sites;
- determining for each site the operations to be performed in the case of each of the measured features;
- combining the above information with knowledge of the time taken to complete each operation, together with the week/s in which it should be performed.

The results of these tasks enabled the computer to prepare a work programme, showing the total number of hours' work required on each site for each week of the year.

All of these tasks could, of course, have been done manually. However, the use of Bromley's mainframe computer allowed the systems approach to be taken one stage further. The Bromley bonus scheme, based on measured day-work, involved a considerable amount of reporting back on the work actually performed. This data was all handled by the computer. Had it been necessary to calculate the resultant bonus entitlements manually, more clerical and office staff would have been required than gardeners!

The computer-generated work programmes were based on data relating specifically to the areas requiring maintenance and to the expected labour productivities. Managers were, in effect, provided with a tool which enabled them to know in advance the range of resources required and to assess more easily the level of performance actually achieved. Through comparison of the actual and expected or planned productivities, rapid calculation of the bonus entitlements was made possible.

Productivity comparisons and other computer-produced information have enabled Bromley to manage their amenity budgets successfully. Essentially, computers have made the task of updating work programmes not only simple but quick. This is important to an organization such as the London Borough of Bromley, whose annual Landscape Management Division budget now exceeds £3.5 million.

Computer facilities can also be used to sort and classify data required for the production of special reports. Examples of the special management tasks which computers can assist include the calculation of:

- The amount of Casuron G which needs to be purchased, leading to identification of which maintenance teams should receive allocations for application;
- The cost savings, if any, which are to be made through applying such growth regulators as Mowchem.

26.4
Modern computer systems

Developments in computer technology have allowed movement away from mainframe systems, which rely on input cards and sheets of print-out. Modern systems operate using powerful microcomputers, which when located on the desk of the Amenity Manager provide virtually instant management information.

One such system has been developed in the USA by De Leuw, Cather and Co. Their Maintenance Management System has been extensively used throughout the world to assist managers in the planning and control of routine maintenance activities (De Leuw, Cather, 1984, 1986).

The main features of the De Leuw, Cather system involve the preparation and provision of a series of 'inputs' namely:

An *inventory of features*, listing by area each feature to be maintained together with a measurement of the feature (area, number, etc.).

A *resource list*, recording the labour, equipment and materials available within each area and, importantly, their cost.

AYE, IT LOOKED LIKE BILLY, HE MUST
BE DOING WORK STUDY OR BONUS SCHEME.

A *master activity sheet*, setting out for each operation the following details:

- the features to be maintained;
- the daily productivity expected;
- the frequency of operation each year;
- the resources required to undertake the operations;
- the priority of the operations;
- the percentage of the activity occurring in each month.

Activity sheets, applying the Master Activity Sheet to an individual area and, for each operation, giving detailed information on:

- the number of days' work involved each month for completion of the operations;
- the total cost allocated between labour, equipment and materials;
- the unit cost of the activity.

Table 26.2 provides an example of an Activity Sheet.

Based on these various 'inputs' described above, the computer provides the manager with a series of 'outputs'. These 'outputs' include:

A *work programme*, providing a line–item summary of all the activities, occurring in each area or group of areas. Table 26.3 provides an example.

'What if' statements, which assist a manager in planning for contingencies and in exploring the effects of changes to a whole number of variables.

Table 26.2 Example of an activity sheet

MAINTENANCE MANAGEMENT SYSTEM
DeLEUW, CATHER & COMPANY   PAGE: 1

ACTIVITIES PRINTOUT   DATE: 5/06/88
                                                  TIME: 11.00

PRINTOUT TYPE: ALL activities of PARK GROUNDS MAINTENANCE within the range 5280 to 5280

Activity: 5280 FERTILIZE FAIRWAYS
Management Unit: PARK GROUNDS MAINTENANCE
                   ACTIVITY SUMMARY

			Desired	Planned
Feature Inv:	20.0 FAIRWAYS			
Daily Prod:	3.4 FAIRWAYS			
Hours/Day:	7.8	Quantity Standard: (i.e. number of operations per year)	2.00	2.00
Cost/Crew Day:	398	Annual Work Quantity: (i.e. number of fairways)	40.80	40.80
Cost/Unit of Work:	117	Total Cost:	4770	4770
Standard Crew Size:	1	Labour:	562	562
Deviation in Level No.1: *1	5%	Equipment:	608	608
Deviation in Level No.2:	10%	Material:	3600	3600
Deviation in Level No.3:	15%	Total Crew Days:	12	12
Print Work Orders:	Yes	Total Man Days:	12	12
Priority:	1	Cost/Unit of Inv: (i.e. fairway)	293	293

APR	MAY	JUN	JUL	AUG	SEP	OCT	NOV	DEC	JAN	FEB	MAR	CREW DAYS
0	4	0	0	0	0	4	0	0	0	0	4	12

RESOURCE DETAIL

LABOUR (6/HR)	EQUIPMENT (7/HR)	MATERIAL (300/DAY)
2002-GARDENER 1.0	2020-TRACTOR 1.0	2050-FERTILIZER 50.0
	2012-FERT SPREADER 1.0	

FEATURE INVENTORY DETAIL

CODE	NAME	TOTAL*2	1	2	3	4	5
1060	FAIRWAYS		(NO)				
	INVY	20.00					
	QTYS	2.00					

TOTAL INVENTORY = 20.00 DES. EQUIV. QS. *3 = 2.00 AWQD *5 = 40.80
PLN. EQUIV. QS. *4 = 2.00 AWQP *6 = 40.80

*1 The system can be instructed to report only on activities which have deviated by Level No.1 i.e. 5%. Deviation levels can be set separately for each individual activity.
*2 The categories 1, 2...5 provide scope for distinguishing between five different conditions of the particular feature, e.g. fairways with high leaf fall: fairways with wet areas etc. These different conditions may require a different quantity standard, details of which are held in the Inventory of features.
*3 This is the desired equivalent quantity standard
*4 This is the planned equivalent quantity standard. If there were different conditions for the feature, each condition may have a different quantity standard. If this is the case, the DES EQIV QS and the PLN EQUIV QS would reflect the average quantity standard.
*5 This is the Annual work quantity desired.
*6 This is the Annual work quantity planned.

For example 'modelling' exercises can be undertaken based on different assumptions about productivities, unit costs, operation frequencies, the timing of operations, etc.

In each case, the effects of either different individual or combinations of assumptions upon both work programme and budget can be viewed almost instantly. Comparative budgets can also be prepared enabling the 'ideal' to be assessed against the 'affordable' maintenance levels.

Work schedules, using the microcomputer. As individual operations are scheduled, work order sheets are produced. As the example provided by Figure 26.1 indicates, these act as time sheets for use in reporting the completion of operations. They also serve as aids to an operator in planning the work and to the manager, when comparing the actual results with the original work programme established at the start of a financial year.

Work reports, summarizing as part of the work scheduling process, complaints and additional requests for work. These are collated and printed out by the computer, when required. A manager can call upon the system to provide full analysis of outstanding requests and details of their completions.

ACTY: 5280 FERTILISE FAIRWAYS	WORK ORDER AND REPORT	WO: 1	DATE: 06/01

MGMT: PARK PARK GROUNDS MAINTENANCE   CREW SIZE: 1
CREW LEADER: S. REDSELL   LOCATION: FAIRWAYS

2.00 GARDENER 8.0	2002 TRACTOR 7.8 2012 FERT SPREAD 7.8	2050 FERTILISER 52.00 25 KG

MIS. COST: 0   ACTY. HRS.: 8.0
WORK REQUESTS: –   –   –   –   –
FACILITIES: ALL   –   –   –   –
ACCOMPLMT.: 3.5   FAIRWAYS

ENTER A-ACCEPT C-CHANGE D-DELETE: [ ]

Figure 26.1 Example of a work schedule.

Table 26.3 Example of a work programme and budget

WORK PROGRAM AND BUDGET FOR FY 1988
MAINTENANCE MANAGEMENT SYSTEM
DeLEUW, CATHER & COMPANY

PAGE: 1
DATE: 5/06/88
TIME: 17:18

MGMT. UNIT: PARK GROUNDS MAINTENANCE
REPORT TYPE: SUMMARY

ACTIVITY	FEATURE INVENTORY	SERVICE LEVEL	AWQ	AVG PROD	CREW DAYS	CREW SIZE	MAN DAYS	COST DISTRIBUTION LABOUR	EQUIPMENT	MATERIAL	TOTAL COST
5010 SWISH GREENS	19 GREENS	132.00 GREENS	2508	38.3	65	1	65	3,042	5	0	3,047
5011 AERATE GREENS	19 GREENS	2.00 GREENS	38	1.2	32	1	32	1,498	1,126	0	2,623
5012 SLIT GREEN CUSHMAN	19 GREENS	30.00 GREENS	570	29.0	20	1	20	936	704	0	1,640
5013 SPRAY GREENS	19 GREENS	4.00 GREENS	76	29.0	3	1	3	140	110	90	340
5020 CUT GREENS	105 GREENS	200.00 100 M S	20900	253.8	82	1	82	3,838	1,599	0	5,437
5030 CUT GREEN SURROUNDS	475 GREEN APRONS	112.00 100 M S	53200	625.9	85	1	85	3,978	2,321	0	6,299
5040 CHANGE HOLES	19 GREENS	200.00 GREENS	3800	45.3	84	1	84	3,931	2,962	0	6,893
5050 WORM KILL GREENS	19 GREENS	1.00 GREENS	19	12.6	2	1	2	94	73	36	203
5060 FERTILISE GREENS	19 GREENS	7.00 GREENS	133	12.6	11	1	11	515	420	594	1,529
5070 ROTORAKE GREENS	19 GREENS	6.00 GREENS	114	5.2	22	1	22	1,030	669	0	1,699
5090 CHANGE FLAGS	19 GREENS	3.00 GREENS	57	96.7	1	1	1	47	35	45	127
5100 SWEEP GREENS	19 GREENS	10.00 GREENS	190	11.7	16	1	16	749	562	0	1,310
5110 RAKE BUNKERS	76 BUNKERS	134.00 BUNKERS	10184	91.8	111	1	111	5,195	3,905	0	9,100
5120 RENEW SAND	76 BUNKERS	1.00 BUNKERS	76	14.2	5	1	5	225	245	510	980
5140 EDGE BUNKER	76 BUNKERS	2.00 BUNKERS	152	12.1	13	1	13	608	57	0	665
5141 STRIM BUNKERS	76 BUNKERS	7.00 BUNKERS	532	45.9	12	1	12	562	187	0	749
5150 CUTTING TEES	140 TEES	200.00 100 M S	28000	241.6	116	1	116	5,429	2,262	0	7,691
5151 CUT TEE SURROUNDS	333 TEE APRONS	112.00 100 M S	37240	625.9	59	1	59	2,761	1,611	0	4,372
5152 CHANGE TEE MARKERS	19 TEES	200.00 MARKERS	3800	290.0	13	1	26	1,217	456	0	1,673
5153 WORM KILL TEES	19 TEES	1.00 TEES	19	12.6	2	1	2	94	73	72	239
5154 FERTILISE TEES	19 TEES	7.00 TEES	133	45.9	3	1	3	140	115	162	417
5155 ROTORAKE TEES	19 TEES	6.00 TEES	114	5.2	22	1	22	1,030	669	0	1,699

Item	Base	Unit									
5156 AERATE TEES	19 TEES	2.00 TEES	38	1.2	32	1	32	1,498	1,126	0	2,623
5157 SLIT TEES CUSHMAN	19 TEES	30.00 TEES	570	29.0	20	1	20	936	704	0	1,640
5158 SPRAY TEES	19 TEES	4.00 TEES	76	29.0	3	1	3	140	110	90	340
5160 REINSTATE PART TEE	19 TEES	10.00 TEES	190	29.0	7	1	7	328	248	455	1,030
5190 TOP DRESS	19 TEES	2.00 TEES	38	13.4	3	1	3	140	107	240	487
5200 REPLACE HOLE CUPS	19 GREENS	3.00 GREENS	57	131.8	0	1	0	0	0	0	0
5210 SPIKE TEES	19 TEES	1.00 TEES	19	36.6	1	1	1	47	35	0	82
5250 TRIM TEE MARKER	19 TEES	1.00 MARKERS	19	145.0	0	1	0	0	0	0	0
5260 CUT FAIRWAYS	1,730 FAIRWAYS	123.00 100 SQ	212790	1208.3	176	1	176	8,237	10,296	0	18,533
5270 SPIKE FAIRWAYS	20 FAIRWAYS	1.00 FAIRWAY	20	2.9	7	1	7	328	246	0	573
5271 HOLLOW TYNE FAIRWAY	20 FAIRWAYS	5.00 FAIRWAY	100	9.9	17	1	17	798	597	0	1,292
5280 FERTILISE FAIRWAYS	20 FAIRWAYS	2.00 FAIRWAY	40	3.4	12	1	12	562	608	3,600	4,770
5290 HARROW FAIRWAYS	20 FAIRWAYS	7.00 FAIRWAY	140	4.5	31	1	31	1,451	1,451	0	2,902
5300 WEEDKILL FAIRWAYS	20 FAIRWAYS	.33 FAIRWAY	7	7.3	1	1	1	47	51	225	323
5310 WORMKILL FAIRWAYS	20 FAIRWAYS	.33 FAIRWAY	7	7.3	1	1	-1	47	51	216	314
5320 HOOK AND ROD DITCHES	1,250 DITCHES	1.00 DITCHES	1250	96.7	13	1	13	608	662	0	1,271
5330 SCAVENGE DITCHES	1 DITCHES	4.00 DITCHES	4	1.8	2	1	2	94	0	1	95
5340 CLEAN DRESSINGROOMS	1 TOILETS	104.00 TOILETS	104	3.7	28	1	28	1,310	9	70	1,389
5350 SWEEP CAR PARK	35 HARD SURFACE	26.00 CARPARK	910	126.9	7	1	7	328	1	1	329
5360 CLEAN TROLLEY TANKS	1 TROLLEY TANK	52.00 TANKS	52	7.3	7	1	7	328	1	0	328
5370 CHANGE VALVES	71 WATER VALVES	104.00 VALVES	7384	435.0	17	1	17	796	597	0	1,392
5380 CLEAN SHED	1 SHED	2.00 SHED	2	14.5	0	1	0	0	0	0	0
5390 TEST IRRIG SYSTEM	1 IRRIG SYSTEM	1.00 SYSTEMS	1	1.6	1	1	1	47	0	0	47
5400 EMPTY BINS	1 BINS	200.00 ROUNDS	200	7.3	28	1	28	1,310	983	196	2,489

Table 26.3 (cont'd)

WORK PROGRAM AND BUDGET FOR FY 1988

MAINTENANCE MANAGEMENT SYSTEM
DeLEUW, CATHER & COMPANY

PAGE: 1

MGMT. UNIT: PARK GROUNDS MAINTENANCE
REPORT TYPE: SUMMARY

DATE: 5/06/88
TIME: 17:18

ACTIVITY	FEATURE INVENTORY	SERVICE LEVEL	AWQ	AVG PROD	CREW DAYS	CREW SIZE	MAN DAYS	COST DISTRIBUTION			TOTAL COST
								LABOUR	EQUIPMENT	MATERIAL	
5410 CUT ROUGH	1,014 ROUGH CUT	6.00 100 M S	6084	725.0	8	1	8	374	468	0	842
5420 CUT SEMI-ROUGH	590 SEMI-ROUGH	123.00 100 M S	72570	725.0	100	1	100	4,680	5,850	0	10,530
5430 CUT MEADOWS	1,096 LOW MAINTENA	2.00 100 M S	2192	483.3	5	1	5	234	410	0	664
5431 BALE MEADOWS	1,096 LOW MAINTENA	2.00 100 M S	2192	120.8	18	1	18	842	1,544	0	2,387
5440 FLAIL ROUGH AREAS	514 FLAIL CUT	3.00 100 M S	1542	61.3	25	1	25	1,170	1,463	0	2,633
5450 CUT AM. LAWNS	945 AMENITY LAWN	18.00 100 M S	17010	120.8	141	1	141	6,599	0	0	6,599
5460 SET OUT VIRGIN PITCH	4 SPORTS PITCH	1.00 PITCHES	4	0.7	6	1	6	281	9	3	293
5470 MARK ESTAB PITCH	4 SPORTS PITCH	39.00 PITCHES	156	11.4	14	1	14	655	22	98	775
5480 MARK PITCH	4 SPORTS PITCH	1.00 PITCHES	4	8.2	0	1	0	0	0	0	0
5490 CUT LINES	4 SPORTS PITCH	3.00 PITCHES	12	14.5	1	1	1	47	20	0	66
5500 SAND GOALMOUTHS	4 SPORTS PITCH	3.00 PITCHES	12	8.2	1	1	1	47	51	17	115
5510 PAINT GOALPOSTS	4 SPORTS PITCH	1.00 PITCHES	4	3.0	1	1	1	47	7	10	64
5520 RAKE WORN	4 SPORTS	4.00 PITCHES	16	14.5	1	1	1	47	1	6	53

AREAS	PITCH										
5530 SPREAD SEED	4 SPORTS PITCH	3.00 PITCHES	1	15.3	12	1	1	47	35	92	174
5540 TOP DRESS PITCH	4 SPORTS PITCH	1.00 PITCHES	0	14.5	4	0	0	0	0	0	0
5550 SPIKE GOAL AREAS	4 SPORTS PITCH	8.00 PITCHES	3	12.8	32	1	3	140	0	0	141
5570 ROLL PITCH	4 SPORTS PITCH	5.00 PITCHES	9	2.3	20	1	9	421	351	0	772
5580 MOW 5 UNIT GANG	345 SPORTS PITCH	14.00 100 M S	4	1208.3	4830	1	4	187	234	0	421
5590 CONTRAVATE PITCH	345 SPORTS PITCH	2.00 100 M S	6	120.8	690	1	6	281	913	3,450	4,643
5600 WOOD MAINTENANCE	2,380 PLANTATIONS	1.00 100 M S	64	37.4	2380	2	128	5,990	5,741	0	11,731
5610 MAINTAIN YOUNG TREE	5,000 TREES	2.00 TREES	83	120.8	10000	1	83	3,884	2,913	0	6,798
5620 TRIM PATH EDGE	1,229 FOOTPATH	4.00 10 METR	54	90.6	4916	1	54	2527	1,714	0	4,241
5630 TRIM CYCLEWAY EDGE	143 CYCLEWAYS	1.00 10 METR	2	90.6	143	1	2	94	63	0	157
5640 TRIM BRIDLEWAY EDGE	221 BRIDLEWAYS	1.00 10 METR	2	90.1	221	1	2	94	63	0	157

GRAND TOTALS FOR PARK GROUNDS MAINTENANCE

REGULAR TIME COST:	155,315	REGULAR TIME MAN DAYS:	1,819
OVERTIME COST:	0	AVERAGE NO. MEN NEEDED:	7.3
OVERHEAD 11.0% OF LABOR:	9,363		
OVERHEAD 23.0% OF TOTAL:	35,723	OVERTIME MAN HOURS:	0
TOTAL BUDGET:	200,401		

LABOR COST:	85,120 (54.8 PERCENT)
EQUIPMENT COST:	59,916 (38.6 PERCENT)
MATERIAL COST:	10,279 (6.6 PERCENT)
	(OVERHEAD NOT INCLUDED ABOVE)

*1 Annual work quantity
*2 Average productivity
*3 Physical activity = Slitting; Feature = Golf green; Machine = Cushman slitter
*4 Notional values

Performance reports, produced in a number of forms at a variety of levels and showing all activities or just those with exceptional deviation from the Work Programme. Table 26.4 provides an example of a Report, which highlights those activities which deviated from the plan by at least 20% (over or under).

Projected budgets, analysing expenditure throughout the year and projecting it into the future to ensure that it is 'on-target'.

Facilities files, which allocate work, when it is reported back, to a cost location. This allows both contract work and costs to be monitored for individual clients.

26.5
Wider applications

The example given using the De Leuw, Cather systems describes the maintenance of a high quality golf course with surrounding sports pitches and public areas. Maintenance Management Systems, however, can be used to plan and control a wide variety of routine maintenance work.

The De Leuw, Cather system was originally conceived for programming and scheduling highways maintenance. It has since been used in the USA for maintaining National Park Trails, roads and bridges, parks and recreation areas, sports fields and environmental infrastructure, e.g. drainage and flood control works. There is also the potential to use similar systems for other types of landscape management work. For example, this could include the management of coastlines rivers and heritage properties, as well as building maintenance and cleansing operations.

The management of all types of landscape, both man-made and natural in the UK and overseas, lends itself to the adoption of a computerized systems approach (Cobham Resource Consultants, 1986).

One such example is the development of a microcomputer system, using standard software, for maintaining outdoor work by Kirklees Metropolitan Council. It was estimated at the outset that this was saving the Council £50,000 a year (Horticulture Week, 1986). Another example is provided by Bath City Council which has invested in Infospec software to assist the management of its Parks Department. The system installed now provides an accurate record of every park site, helps with estimating, rescheduling, costing and horticultural stock control.

Table 26.4 Example of a performance report

STOCKLEY PARK AMENITY AREAS
PEFORMANCE REPORT
FOR THE PERIOD APRIL – MAY   MAINTENANCE MANAGEMENT SYSTEM
                               DeLEUW, CATHER & COMPANY

PAGE: 1

DATE: 5/06/88
TIME: 11:02

MGMT. UNIT: PARK GROUNDS MAINTENANCE
REPORT TYPE: SUMMARY
EXCEPTION THRESHOLD: 20%

CODE	ACTIVITY DESCRIPTION	TIME FRAME	CREW DAYS			ACCOMPLISHMENT			PRODUCTIVITY			UNIT COST		
			PLAN	ACTUAL	PCT	PLAN	ACTUAL	PCT	PLAN	ACTUAL	PCT	PLAN	ACTUAL	PCT
5050	WORM KILL GREENS	M.T.D.	.0	.0	100	.0	.0	100	.0	.0	100	.0	.0	100
	GREENS	Y.T.D.	1.0	.0	0*	12.6	.0	0*	12.6	.0	0*	8.1	.0	0*
5060	FERTILISE GREENS	M.T.D.	.0	.0	100	.0	.0	100	.0	.0	100	.0	.0	100
	GREENS	Y.T.D.	2.0	1.9	96	25.2	24.0	95	12.6	12.5	99	11.0	14.4	130*
5070	ROTORAKE GREENS	M.T.D.	4.0	4.5	112	20.8	24.0	115	5.2	5.3	103	14.9	13.7	92
	GREENS	Y.T.D.	9.0	9.6	107	46.8	48.0	103	5.2	5.0	96	14.9	18.1	122*
5090	CHANGE FLAGS	M.T.D.	.0	.0	100	.0	.0	100	.0	.0	100	.0	.0	100
	GREENS	Y.T.D.	1.0	.6	64*	96.7	56.0	58*	96.7	87.4	90	1.3	1.7	133*
5100	SWEEP GREENS	M.T.D.	1.0	.0	0*	11.7	.0	0*	11.7	.0	0*	7.0	.0	0*
	GREENS	Y.T.D.	2.0	.8	38*	23.4	9.0	38*	11.7	11.7	100	7.0	7.0	100
5151	CUT TEE SURROUNDS	M.T.D.	9.0	2.6	28*	5633.1	1600.0	28*	625.9	624.0	100	.1	.1	100
	100 M SQ	Y.T.D.	15.0	9.7	65*	9388.5	6600.0	70*	625.9	677.4	108	.1	.1	92

cont'd

Table 26.4 (cont'd)

CODE	ACTIVITY DESCRIPTION	TIME FRAME	CREW DAYS			ACCOMPLISHMENT			PRODUCTIVITY			UNIT COST		
			PLAN	ACTUAL	PCT	PLAN	ACTUAL	PCT	PLAN	ACTUAL	PCT	PLAN	ACTUAL	PCT
5152	CHANGE TEE MARKERS	M.T.D.	1.0	1.0	101	290.0	300.0	103	290.0	296.2	102	.4	.4	98
	MARKERS	Y.T.D.	2.0	1.0	51*	580.0	300.0	52*	290.0	296.2	102	.4	.4	98
5153	WORM KILL TEES	M.T.D.	2.0	.0	0*	25.2	.0	0*	12.6	.0	0*	9.5	.0	0*
	TEES	Y.T.D.	2.0	.0	0*	25.2	.0	0*	12.6	.0	0*	9.5	.0	0*
5154	FERTILISE TEES	M.T.D.	1.0	.0	0*	45.9	.0	0*	45.9	.0	0*	3.0	.0	0*
	TEES	Y.T.D.	1.0	.0	0*	45.9	.0	0*	45.9	.0	0*	3.0	.0	0*
5155	ROTORAKE TEES	M.T.D.	4.0	2.6	64*	20.8	17.0	82	5.2	6.6	128*	14.9	13.8	93
	TEES	Y.T.D.	8.0	6.4	80	41.6	41.0	99	5.2	6.4	123*	14.9	15.6	105
5156	AERATE TEES	M.T.D.	8.0	8.6	107	9.6	14.0	146*	1.2	1.6	136*	68.3	50.3	74*
	TEE	Y.T.D.	16.0	11.5	72*	19.2	18.0	94	1.2	1.6	131*	68.3	52.3	76*
5157	SLIT TEES CUSHMAN	M.T.D.	3.0	.0	0*	87.0	.0	0*	29.0	.0	0*	2.8	.0	0*
	TEES	Y.T.D.	6.0	5.0	83	174.0	150.0	86	29.0	30.0	103	2.8	2.7	97
5200	REPLACE HOLE CUPS	M.T.D.	.0	.4	*****	.0	100.0	*****	.0	260.0	*****	.0	.7	*****
	GREENS	Y.T.D.	1.0	.9	90	131.8	164.0	124*	131.8	182.7	139*	1.2	1.5	119
5271	HOLLOW TYNE FAIRWAYS	M.T.D.	4.0	.0	0*	24.0	.0	0*	6.0	.0	0*	13.7	.0	0*
	FAIRWAYS	Y.T.D.	4.0	.0	0*	24.0	.0	0*	6.0	.0	0*	13.7	.0	0*
5280	FERTILISE FAIRWAYS	M.T.D.	4.0	5.8	144*	13.6	20.0	147*	3.4	3.5	102	116.9	105.2	90
	FAIRWAYS	Y.T.D.	4.0	5.8	144*	13.6	20.0	147*	3.4	3.5	102	116.9	105.2	90

*1 PCT = Percentage of plan
*2 MTD = Month to date
*3 YTD = Year to date
*4 ACCOMPLISHMENT is measured in the units of the inventory as stated under the DESCRIPTION column
*5 PRODUCTIVITY is measured in units per day is ACCOMPLISHMENT divided by CREW DAYS
x   Indicates a Deviation from the Plan by more than +/− 20%
***** Indicates an activity which was performed even though it was not planned for that month

References   Cobham Resource Consultants, (1986) *Maintenance Management System Overview*, CRC.

De Leuw, Cather (1984) *A Park and Recreation Facility Presentation: Town of Brookline*, Department of Public Works, DLC & Co.

De Leuw, Cather (1986) *Maintenance Management Concepts*, DLC & Co.

De Leuw, Cather Engineering Management Services (1986) *The Role of Computers in Park Maintenance Management*, presentation for New Jersey Recreation and Park Association, DLC & Co.

De Leuw, Cather Engineering Management Services (1986) *Park Maintenance Management: concepts, applications and benefits*, presentation for New Jersey Recreation and Park Association, DLC & Co.

De Leuw, Cather Engineering Management Services (1986) *Implementing a Park Maintenance Management System*, DLC & Co.

Hood, P. (1987) Time of reckoning, *Horticulture Weekly*, 16th January.

Horticulture Week (1986) Monitor work by computer, 12th December.

Long. S.L. (1982) Mowing by microchip (An overview of a computer aided planned maintenance programme), Askham Bryan Technical Conference.

27 THE FUTURE

27.1
Developments in 'the
pipeline'

Computer systems are constantly developing and the existing De Leuw, Cather Maintenance Management System by no means represents the final stage in the relationship between the microchip and the landscape. Already there are significant developments in computer-aided landscape design. The development of a computer-based landscape management system, which accepts inputs in graphic form (maps, aerial photographs, etc.) and is capable of making direct measurements from such sources, is well advanced. This particular development is the result of close collaboration between Dr John Handley of the Ground Work Trust and Dr Colin Fairhurst of the University of Salford (Handley and Fairhurst, 1988). The outputs generated by their system are in the form of tables and diagrams which provide essential management information.

27.2
Future scenarios and
contingency planning

It is likely that future developments of computer systems will bring to the Amenity Management profession much greater investigative powers. At least three possible developments are already apparent:

1. For undertaking more sophisticated 'What-if' appraisals;
2. For evaluating the consequences of possible future scenarios;
3. For assessing risks as the basis for preparing contingency plans.

Amenity Managers generally would welcome the facility to investigate the outcomes and implications of many different physical and financial scenarios. It may never be possible to predict the occurrence of such events as the storm, which devastated the trees of S.E. England in October 1987. However, one day with access to powerful computer modelling facilities, the Amenity Manager may be able more readily:

1. to assess the vulnerability of the landscape to freak events, as well as other implications; and
2. to explore the long-term consequences and resources involved, in terms of both resources and aesthetics.

Thus in this way the Amenity Manager of tomorrow may, for instance, be better able to handle all the many variables which need to be considered when planning the remedial plantings after a particularly damaging storm. This stems from the opportunity to explore a number of options, in terms of the choice of species with differing life-spans and growth rates, according to visual requirements, historic precedents, etc., as well as the species, age and condition of the surviving tree cover in whatever form: individual specimens, copses, roundels, belts, avenues, etc. This is but one example of the many extensions of the 'What if' programmes and contingency planning aids, which await development.

**27.3
Competitive tendering
and the systems
approach**

Over a significant period, Local Authorities were prepared for the need to organize the management of parks and leisure facilities on a more competitive basis (CURS/ILAM/CLOA, 1986). Thus there were few surprises when the *Local Government Act* (1988) became law at the end of March 1988. It introduced to landscape management some very large changes. Traditionally Local Authorities had undertaken their own landscape maintenance work, using an 'in-house' direct labour force. The Act has in effect forced Local Authorities to bid competitively for their landscape work in the open market, thereby giving appropriately experienced landscape contractors an equal chance of undertaking the work.

As a consequence the landscape management activities of Local Authorities have had to be split into client and contractor roles, because there is no guarantee that the in-house team would win tenders. The section of the Authority, responsible for performing the client role, plans the work to be done and presents it in the form of a tender document. Naturally the contracting arm of the Authority hopes that it will be appointed as the successful tenderer. Having been appointed, the successful contractor is paid the contract rate for the job regardless of the resources actually used in undertaking the work.

The Act requires that every Local Authority will put out to tender at least 20% of their total landscape management work on or before 1st January 1990, followed by another 20% each year thereafter until eventually all public amenity work has in effect been privatized. It is expected that under the Act some direct labour forces may become quite small and that larger contractors will develop to take their place. The actual outcome remains to be seen, most probably it will result in the market being dominated by a mixture of both efficient private contractors and highly-motivated Local Authority 'contract' teams.

As a direct spin-off of the Act, it seems likely that, in a bid to become more competitive, both local government and contractors will start to adopt the systems approach. This will undoubtably involve a greater investment in computer maintenance systems. It is to be hoped that this will yield both a better knowledge and understanding of amenity maintenance operations, as well as the processes, resources and costs involved. In addition, it is to be expected that both the volume and quality of management information will improve. Through both better monitoring facilities and a greater sharing of data, the results achieved by the amenity management profession should, in general, become increasingly cost-effective. As a result, even in the face of inflationary forces, it should be possible not only to maintain but to improve standards.

It must be stated however, that considerable reservations and scepticism were expressed about both the measures contained in the Act and, more particularly, the reasons given for its introduction (Fulford, 1987). The alleged improved 'value for money' objective of the Act was questioned, in view of the strong possibility that certain of the previously enjoyed indirect benefits, associated with direct works employment, would be lost. Whilst the doubts and fears are justified, there are ample grounds for expecting that real benefits with result from improvements in competition. Already the many enlightened Authorities have demonstrated that they are well placed to compete with the 'traditional' private sector.

27.4
The way forward

Whilst the completion of this book marks the culmination of contributions from many committed Amenity Managers, it is hoped that in reality its publication represents the beginning of what will become a continuing process. That is the process of codifying successful practical experiences and of updating data, which can thereby be shared widely.

Amenity Managers in general are asked to make available any information, which is likely to render possible subsequent editions of the book more helpful to their professional colleagues. Through such co-operation in pursuit of cost-effectiveness, the Amenity Managers of tomorrow should be better able to do their jobs. That, in short, means helping to ensure that the green inheritance of both present and future generations is not only conserved but enhanced: for all to enjoy. 'Paradise' can surely never be regained, unless the green spaces of a country are managed and maintained cost-effectively?

References

CURS/ILAM/CLOA (1986) *Grounds Maintenance in a Competitive Climate*, Seminar Papers.

Fulford, M. (1987) Local Government Bill – myths and fact, *The Leisure Manager*, October.

Handley, J. and Fairhurst, C (1988) *Computers in Landscape Management*. The Groundwork Trust System.

Local Government Act (1988) HMSO.

Further reading

Cobham, R.O. (1985) Blenheim: The art and management of landscape restoration, *Arboricultured Journal*, **9** (2), 81–100.

Horner, H. (1984) *Computing in a Small Business*, Hutchinson Computer Studies Series.

Workman, J. (1982) Resoration of parks and subsequent management. *Landscape Research*, **7**, (1).

LIST OF FIGURES

LIST OF TABLES

INDEX

Page numbers in **bold** refer to tables, in *italics* to figures. Cited-only authors have not been indexed.